LEADERSHIP

REGIONAL AND GLOBAL PERSPECTIVES

Whether you are leading a small team or a multinational corporation, within the public or private sector, a thorough understanding of the theory and best practice of leadership is essential. *Leadership: Regional and Global Perspectives* provides a fresh approach to leading in contemporary business environments. The text's discussion of creativity, innovation, power, ethics and diversity provides students with strong foundational knowledge and skills, and supports them to become dynamic modern leaders.

A focus on strategic application complements the theory component. Each chapter features case studies highlighting the practical application of key concepts by organisational leaders in the Australasian region, while accompanying questions encourage students to think critically. Learning is further supported through the inclusion of learning objectives, key terms and review questions. An extensive bank of web resources is available to lecturers to support their teaching.

Written by an expert team of academics from across Australia, *Leadership* gives students the tools they need to navigate their leadership journey.

Nuttawuth Muenjohn is Senior Lecturer in the School of Management at RMIT University.

Adela McMurray is Professor in the School of Management at RMIT University.

Mario Fernando is Professor in the School of Management, Operations and Marketing at the University of Wollongong.

James Hunt is Lecturer in the Newcastle Business School at the University of Newcastle.

Martin Fitzgerald is Associate Professor in the Newcastle Business School at the University of Newcastle.

Bernard McKenna is Associate Professor in the UQ Business School at the University of Queensland.

Ali Intezari is Senior Lecturer in the School of Management at Massey University.

Sarah Bankins is Senior Lecturer in the Department of Management at Macquarie University.

Jennifer Waterhouse is Senior Lecturer in the Newcastle Business School at the University of Newcastle.

LEADERSHIP

REGIONAL AND GLOBAL PERSPECTIVES

Nuttawuth Muenjohn

Adela McMurray

Mario Fernando

James Hunt

Martin Fitzgerald

Bernard McKenna

Ali Intezari

Sarah Bankins

Jennifer Waterhouse

CAMBRIDGE
UNIVERSITY PRESS

CAMBRIDGE
UNIVERSITY PRESS

University Printing House, Cambridge CB2 8BS, United Kingdom

One Liberty Plaza, 20th Floor, New York, NY 10006, USA

477 Williamstown Road, Port Melbourne, VIC 3207, Australia

314–321, 3rd Floor, Plot 3, Splendor Forum, Jasola District Centre, New Delhi – 110025, India

79 Anson Road, #06–04/06, Singapore 079906

Cambridge University Press is part of the University of Cambridge.

It furthers the University's mission by disseminating knowledge in the pursuit of education, learning and research at the highest international levels of excellence.

www.cambridge.org
Information on this title: www.cambridge.org/9781108459297

© Cambridge University Press 2018

First published 2018

Cover designed by Anne-Marie Reeves
Typeset by Integra Software Services Pvt. Ltd
Printed in China by C & C Offset Printing Co. Ltd, July 2018

A catalogue record for this publication is available from the British Library

A catalogue record for this book is available from the National Library of Australia

ISBN 978-1-108-45929-7 Paperback

Additional resources for this publication at www.cambridge.edu.au/academic/leadership

To my parents Seangthong and Ladda,
my wife Napasorn, and my children Peamawat and
Bunnawat.

Nuttawuth Muenjohn

To my family, with love, for all of time.

Adela McMurray

To my wife Shamika, and our children Mario Jr.
and Andrea.

Mario Fernando

CONTENTS

FIGURES AND TABLES

Tables

CASE STUDIES

ABOUT THE AUTHORS

NUTTAWUTH MUENJOHN is Senior Lecturer in the School of Management, Royal Melbourne Institute of Technology University, Australia. His primary research focuses on the complexity of leadership in Asia and cross-cultural issues in management. Nuttawuth's research works have been undertaken through various collaborations in the Asia–Pacific region such as China, Japan, Singapore, Thailand, Vietnam, Malaysia, Hong Kong, India and Australia. Nuttawuth has written books and book chapters for top international publishers. He has also published numerous research articles in high-quality journals.

ADELA McMURRAY is Professor in the School of Management at RMIT University, Australia. She has extensive experience researching innovation and culture in public and private sectors and has published several books and more than 250 refereed publications. Her research is internationally recognised and she is the recipient of four Australian Research Council grants, two industry Collaborative Research Centre grants alongside other major grants. Adela has won teaching and leadership awards, chaired the USA Academy of Management's International Theme Committee, and is an Editorial Advisory Board member for several academic journals. Adela's high-impact research expertise addresses workplace innovation, organisational culture, change and development, risk management and sustainability.

MARIO FERNANDO is Professor of Management in the School of Management, Operations and Marketing at the University of Wollongong, Australia. His research, published in high-impact journals, explores how responsible executive action leads to positive individual, organisational and societal outcomes. His key research areas are responsible decision-making, business ethics and human resource management. He is a recipient of national grants and awards for research and teaching. The impact of his contribution to a range of teaching and learning activities has been acknowledged at national and international levels. He has authored two books and serves on three journal editorial boards. Before joining academia, Mario was a corporate Board Director and held senior executive roles in the business world for more than a decade.

JAMES HUNT is MBA Program Director at the University of Newcastle, Australia, where he lectures in leadership and organisations at postgraduate level. James has lived and worked in the UK, Spain, Bahrain, Malaysia, the Philippines, Indonesia, Singapore, Hong Kong and Australia. He has served as an academic for more than 27 years, and in 2003 was awarded the Centenary Medal of Australia by the Office of the Prime Minister for service to the university sector. James has authored more than 50 academic publications and remains an active researcher in areas such as emotional intelligence, leadership and personality. Throughout his career, James has received seven awards for excellence in university teaching.

MARTIN FITZGERALD is Associate Professor in Leadership and Organisational Studies in the Newcastle Business School at the University of Newcastle, Australia. He works with students and executives in the areas of leadership, decision making and leading organisational change and has been institutionally recognised for his exceptional contributions to teaching and the student learning experience. He has more than 20 years' experience as a senior and executive leader across public and private sectors, including as a corporate lawyer, university senior executive and CEO, and national president of a non-profit organisation. His research focuses on values-driven leadership, decision making and smart work, and he has created the Smart Work Research Group, in which he examines how information and communication technologies can improve employee engagement, revolutionise work design and stimulate new leadership styles. He has published more than 50 works in these areas, including academic papers, book chapters, books, commissioned research reports, position papers, international keynote speeches and other presentations.

BERNARD McKENNA is Associate Professor in the UQ Business School at the University of Queensland, Australia. He has also presented workshops internationally. Bernard has published extensively in such journals as *Leadership Quarterly, Public Administration Review, Management Communication Quarterly, Journal of Business Ethics* and *Journal of Vocational Behaviour*, and is on the editorial board of several journals. His co-authored book *Managing Wisdom in the Knowledge Economy* provides an important overview of wisdom in management. Bernard has won two nationally competitive Australian Research Council grants, and regularly provides consultancies to industry and government.

ALI INTEZARI is Senior Lecturer in the School of Management, Massey University, Auckland, New Zealand. His current research interests include the theory of organisational wisdom, organisational knowledge and culture, decision making and knowledge management. His work has appeared in such journals as *Decision Sciences, Journal of Knowledge Management, Communications of the Association for Information Systems, International Journal of Knowledge Management, Journal of Business Ethics, Journal of Business Ethics and Education*, and *Business Strategy and the Environment Journal*. He is the co-author and co-editor of the books *Wisdom, Analytics and Wicked Problems: Integral Decision Making in and Beyond the Information* and *Practical Wisdom in the Age of Technology: Insights, Issues and Questions for a New Millennium*.

SARAH BANKINS is Senior Lecturer in the Department of Management, Macquarie University, Australia. She completed her PhD at the Queensland University of Technology, Australia. Her primary research interests span two areas: the employee–employer relationship through the lens of the psychological contract, and the roles of individuals in innovation processes within organisational and regional contexts. She links these by focusing on the role of people in work processes, exploring how people navigate cultural, political and power dynamics to achieve innovative outcomes. She has published her work in leading journals such as the *Journal of Organisational Behavior, R&D Management* and the *Australian Journal of Public Administration*.

JENNIFER WATERHOUSE is Senior Lecturer in the Newcastle Business School at the University of Newcastle, Australia. She has researched, published and lectured in the areas of negotiation, human resource management and organisational change, with a particular focus on the public sector. Her research focuses on analysis of organisational networks across sectors. She is interested in how negotiation is used to forge and maintain inter-sectoral and inter-organisational collaborations to better address complex social issues.

INTRODUCTION

James Hunt and Martin Fitzgerald

LEARNING OUTCOMES

After reading this chapter, you should be able to:

1. define the terms *leader* and *leadership*, and explain how leadership differs from management

2. identify the positive and negative effects of leadership in organisations today

3. explain the meaning of the term *organisational climate*, and explain why leaders can be viewed as architects of climate in organisations

4. define the term *emotional intelligence*, and explain why this is relevant to leadership effectiveness

5. explain the importance of self-assessment for leaders today.

INTRODUCING LEADERSHIP

THIS CHAPTER INTRODUCES you to the concept of leadership in modern organisational life, and touches on leadership in broader society. The positive as well as the detrimental effects of leadership are discussed, to highlight the importance of leadership to all of us throughout our lives and our professional careers. Key differences in the activities and behaviours of leaders and managers are noted, and the central concern of leaders for harnessing and steering collective human effort is emphasised.

This chapter draws attention to the impact that leadership can have on organisational performance, and discusses the importance of leadership skills development. Concepts such as emotional intelligence and leadership competency profiling are introduced, and opportunities for leadership self-assessment are discussed. The chapter concludes by pointing to the profound and far-reaching effects that leadership can have on individuals and on organisations today.

DEFINING LEADERSHIP

> **Leader** – A person who guides, conducts or shows the way; one who exercises influence over others; one who enlists the cooperation of others to achieve specific outcomes; one who sets a vision for the future.

Etymologists – those who study the genesis and evolution of words in a language – have traced the word **leader** to its earliest origins in the Old English word *laedere*, which became *leder* or *ledere* by late medieval and early renaissance times. The word shared strong similarities with Dutch, German, Swedish, Danish and Icelandic words of the same period, and commonly conveyed two somewhat distinctive meanings. The first meaning referred to a person who guides, conducts or shows the way, and was used to designate an individual who would lead a touring party of soldiers or pilgrims through foreign lands, or someone who would lead a group of explorers through unfamiliar territory (Johnson, 1775; Fowler, 1926; Klein, 1971). This meaning captured the notion of a leader as an individual with special or expert knowledge, rather than someone with formal authority over the group being led. The second meaning of *leader* in this era was a ruler or chieftain; someone with widely recognised status and acknowledged authority over others.

> **Leadership** – A principal dynamic process that uses influence and persuasion to motivate and coordinate individual and collective effort; the process of enabling or guiding others to achieve goals; the process by which a person leads or shows the way.

The word **leadership** did not come into use in English until the early 1820s, when it was used to refer to the position of a leader as well as the manner and extent to which that leader exercised influence and authority. Accordingly, the word *leadership* was typically used to refer to a process, rather than just a single act. By the late nineteenth century, however, the meaning of the term leadership was extended to include the characteristics and capabilities considered necessary to be a leader (McSparran, 2006).

These origins help to explain the usage of the word *leadership* today, and serve to indicate the differing emphasis placed on the practice of leadership in modern organisations. Although the term has been defined in many ways by a variety of prominent contemporary writers, there is a broad consensus among current scholars that leadership is a principal dynamic process that uses influence and persuasion to motivate and coordinate individual and collective effort (Bass, 1985; Bennis, 2009). In the organisational arena, leaders are often seen as enablers or guides who have the capacity and the inclination to empower others to act and to achieve individual and organisational goals (Northouse, 2010). This perspective on leadership echoes the early notion of a leader as a person who shows the way. Others in contemporary organisations see leaders as individuals who exercise influence by using more formally designated power and authority, for example, as a nominated team leader or the appointed leader of a steering committee. This interpretation of leadership is closer to the concept of a leader as a ruler or chieftain – someone who has authority vested in them due to their position.

THE IMPORTANCE OF LEADERSHIP

Leadership is one of the most widely researched topics in the world today. It is an area that attracts considerable interest in societies and communities all around the globe. An internet search reveals that more than 35 million published articles on leadership have been written in English alone since 2000, including more than half a million fully refereed academic journal articles. The concept of leadership is highly relevant to our understanding of how our modern organisations operate, with institutional successes and failures increasingly attributed to leadership decisions and actions. Government entities, hospitals, schools, sporting teams, corporations, small businesses and not-for-profit organisations all require some form of leadership to function effectively.

The positive effects of leadership

One of the most important aspects of leadership today is its capacity to enhance the performance of individuals, groups and organisations and, in doing so, to motivate, energise and empower people in all walks of life to achieve their best. This magnifying effect can be seen in schools and corporations, in hospitals, universities and sports teams, and in small businesses. Behind these success stories there is often a distinctive leadership presence that helps to transform people and to elevate them to develop a sense of self-belief that enables them to perform beyond expectations. This approach to leadership is variously referred to as *authentic*, *inspirational* and *transformational*. **Transformational leadership** approaches have commanded a lion's share of attention in both the popular and academic literature over the past 15 years.

Transformational leadership – A leadership style consisting of the following four elements: idealised influence, inspirational motivation, intellectual stimulation and individual consideration.

In the corporate arena, names such as Richard Branson (Virgin), Janine Allis (BOOST Juice) and Naomi Simson (RedBalloon) have become synonymous with the concept of inspiring leadership that draws out the best in people. Simson's uniquely uplifting leadership approach has enabled her to create a successful organisation that has been recognised by BRW as one of Australia's best places to work (Smith, 2015). This form of leadership often enables the leader to command great loyalty from followers, and to also wield considerable influence over them. When this influence is used in the best interests of followers to assist them to achieve and to develop as people, it is referred to as transformational leadership (Bass, 1985, 1998).

The detrimental effects of leadership

When our organisations falter, we often see more frequent changes in the leadership of those institutions. For example, Australia had just four prime ministers in the 32-year period between 1975 and 2007. However, in the more volatile times that have followed the global economic crisis of 2008, the office of the Prime Minister of Australia has seen no fewer than five leadership changes, in less than a decade.

In extreme cases, when leadership becomes highly ineffective, it can trigger complete organisational collapse. We saw this in Australia with One.Tel, HIH Insurance and Borders. One.Tel became Australia's fourth largest telecommunications company before going bankrupt in 2001, and HIH Insurance remains our nation's largest corporate failure of all time: two of its most senior executives served jail sentences for their respective leadership roles in the insurance company's demise. Similarly, a succession of strategic leadership failures on the part of executives at the REDGroup led to the eventual closure of Borders Australia's 26 retail stores in July 2011, resulting in the loss of 1759 employees' jobs (Speedy, 2011). Internationally, one of the most spectacular leadership failures in recent organisational history came in September 2008 with the collapse of US investment banking firm Lehman Brothers. The company's chief executive officer, Richard S. Fuld Jr, was vilified by analysts for his reckless and cavalier approach to leadership, an approach that saw the 158-year-old firm drown in an unprecedented corporate debt of US$613 billion (Quinn, 2008).

Leadership in both the public and private sectors can have a profound effect on our lives as citizens. The amount of money we pay for things like our electricity bills and our university fees are the result of leadership decisions made by others in influential positions in government. Similarly, strategic leadership decisions taken by CEOs can often have significant and far-reaching effects on the livelihoods and employment prospects of organisational members. Alan Joyce's leadership decision at Qantas to slash 5000 jobs over the three-year period to the end of 2016 is an example of this (Meyer & O'Sullivan, 2014).

Is leadership really so important?

Many writers, commentators and observers tend to agree that leadership is highly important to all of us throughout or lives, with some analysts emphasising that leadership has the capacity to shape our organisational careers. However, there are others who argue that the influence of leaders may be overstated in the contemporary literature. Writers such as Pfeffer (1977) and Hout (1999) have put forward the idea that a range of situational factors outside the control of leaders can sometimes have a significant impact on outcomes for both individuals and organisations. This perspective is supported in a report by Jones (2014) on small business failures in Australia. This report indicated that ineffective leadership is the primary cause of business failure in just 44 per cent of cases, while situational factors beyond the influence of leaders were shown to play an important role in most cases.

Others, such as Podsakoff and MacKenzie (1995), have conducted research into the concept of substitutes for leadership. This area of investigation was pioneered by Kerr and Jermier (1978) who suggested that the impact of leadership is lessened and even negated by (1) *subordinate characteristics*, such as high levels of expertise and intrinsic motivation; (2) *task characteristics* such as high degrees of task structure; and (3) *organisational characteristics* such as self-managed work groups and autonomous work teams. Keller (2006), however, calls into question this line of investigation, suggesting that its findings are limited because they are based exclusively on cross-sectional studies (studies conducted at a specific point in time), which provide only a limited snapshot of influencing factors, rather than on longitudinal research (studies conducted over significant time periods).

Although leadership researchers have reached a range of conclusions, some at least agree that leadership behaviour and activity have real potential to influence outcomes under a range of circumstances. Behavioural and organisational psychologists have been studying these influences since the earliest experimental research into leadership styles was conducted by Kurt Lewin and associates in the late 1930s (Lewin, Lippitt & White, 1939).

In contemporary society and in our modern organisational worlds, despite mounting evidence of the ascendancy of economic imperatives, human beings exist and interact in what are ultimately social settings, not merely rational economic settings. In social settings, some form of leadership will always be needed to harness and steer collective human effort. Sometimes this leadership may be highly directive, while at other times it may be more inclusive, participative and empowering. Sometimes it may be expressed through the influence and ascendancy of a single individual, while on other occasions it may be more fluid, shifting and shared. On occasions throughout our lives we may encounter restrictive and even repressive leadership, while on other occasions we may be fortunate enough to experience the potent transforming effects of authentic and inspirational leadership. It is the many faces of leadership that this text seeks to help you to uncover, explore, analyse and understand.

CASE STUDY 1.1

Naomi Simson – Founder, RedBalloon

Naomi Simson is the founding director of RedBalloon, an online gift retailer that sells experiences and memories to individual and corporate clients, including Fuji Xerox, Telstra, Qantas, Westpac and the Commonwealth Bank. Simson began her corporate career as a professional marketing specialist working with a series of large organisations including Ansett Australia, IBM, KPMG and Apple Computers. She launched RedBalloon in 2001 with a personal cash injection of $25 000, and ran the business from her home in Balmain, New South Wales. It took more than two months before she sold her first item, and that earned her a profit of just $9.

The company began to grow its corporate client base six months after it was founded, and the expansion of this business segment led to the creation of RedBalloon Corporate in 2004. Between 2001 and 2012, RedBalloon sold more than 1.7 million gift items, and reported revenue growth of 40 per cent for the financial year to 2012. In 2014 the company had 46 employees, and by 2016 it employed 59 full-time staff.

RedBalloon has won numerous awards and widespread recognition since it was founded just over 15 years ago (Smith, 2012). Between 2005 and 2008, it received four successive Hitwise Awards for the number one website in Australia and New Zealand in the online gift category. Between 2009 and 2013, the company was named in five successive years by *Business Review Weekly* as one of the Great Places to Work, and in 2010 it received the Hewitt Best Employers Award (Smith, 2015). In 2015, RedBalloon became the first Australian company to be nominated by WorldBlu as part of their annual list of Most Freedom-Centred Workplaces.

Simson's strong commitment to employee-centred leadership has helped to develop a culture of dedication and involvement at RedBalloon (Simson, 2013). It is a culture that accounts for much of the company's ongoing success (Smith, 2013). From the outset, Simson approached leadership in a way that she felt would resonate strongly with her employees. For her, recognition for the efforts and achievements of workers as professionals has always been one of the pivotal aspects of what makes a healthy and high performing business:

> For me, engaging both the hearts and minds of people in my business is essential. I want them on board with the vision, living our values and aligned to our goals. To practice gratitude at work is really important (Simson, 2016).

Simson involves her employees in working towards a set of core business objectives which are built around the company's strategic objectives. She reasons that this is a great way to align people to an overarching strategic plan and to ensure that core objectives are agreed on and frequently met. Simson works closely with the leaders of each business unit to establish these core objectives, and then leaves it to each of them to work with their team to set quarterly goals.

Simson believes that leadership at RedBalloon is all about ensuring that people feel productive in their roles in the organisation, and that they get noticed for their accomplishments (Simson, 2016). Ultimately Simson wants her employees to go home at the end of the day feeling proud of what they have achieved and where they work (Walsh, 2014). It is this approach to leadership that has seen Naomi Simson win a range of awards, including the 2005 Westpac NSW Entrepreneur of the Year, The National Telstra Business Women's Award for Innovation in 2008 and the 2013 Lifetime achievement Silver Stevie Award. In 2012, Simson was recognised by LinkedIn as one of the World's Most Influential Thought Leaders, and in 2016 she released her third book, *Ready to Soar*, a publication dealing with entrepreneurial leadership (Simson, 2016).

Critical thinking question
What are the defining characteristics of Naomi Simson's approach to leadership?

COMPARING LEADERSHIP AND MANAGEMENT

In the organisational context, confusion sometimes arises when the terms *leadership* and **management** are used interchangeably to describe the same or very similar observable phenomena. Some organisational writers such as Henry Mintzberg (1975) and Richard Boyatzis (1982) have viewed leadership as a necessary and useful component of management. These writers tend to adhere to the classical view that management is a broader and more complete system of action than leadership. They see leadership as just one of many roles that a **manager** is required to routinely perform (Carroll & Gillen, 1987).

> **Management** – The good stewardship of a range of organisational resources, including human, financial, physical and informational resources.
> **Manager** – A person who organises and controls; one who balances an organisation's human, financial, physical and informational resources; an individual who is responsible for the genesis and progress of change in organisations.

In contrast to this viewpoint, a number of prominent contemporary writers and academics have sought to differentiate leadership from management by emphasising the distinctive elements of effective leadership practice (Kotter, 1990a; Zaleznik, 1992; Bennis, 2009). Warren Bennis captures this perspective with the following salient observation: 'Managers are people who do things right and leaders are people who do the right thing. Both roles are crucial and they differ profoundly' (Bennis, 2009, p. 21). Similarly, John P. Kotter (1990b) argues that leaders are better equipped and more adept than most managers at aligning people. He suggests that leaders are people who have a natural affinity for developing a vision and direction for the future of their team or organisation, and for building commitment to that vision through effective communication. Kotter is well known in the leadership literature for his memorable quote which draws attention to the difference between leadership and management in contemporary organisations: 'Most ... corporations today are over-managed and under-led' (Kotter, 1990a, p. 103).

Writers such as Kotter and Bennis contend that managers frequently struggle to exercise leadership, whereas leaders don't always seek to manage. Indeed, many leaders in society today don't even occupy managerial positions or titles. Leaders of scouting associations, club leaders, church leaders, teachers, sports coaches, school captains, parents and elder siblings are just a few examples of people who demonstrate leadership without occupying a managerial position.

Today, many think that leaders can be more effective than managers at producing lasting change because leaders are able to energise people by motivating them, by building commitment and often by inspiring them. Researchers such as Bennis (2009) and Bernard Bass (1990), author of Bass and Stogdill's definitive *Handbook of Leadership*, suggest that the classical viewpoint of leaders cracking the whip and asking people to jump through hoops is no longer sustainable in today's more egalitarian age. These writers argue that leaders today need to be more like mentors and coaches, and less like military-style drill sergeants. So, contemporary accounts of leadership claim that the styles and approaches of individuals such as Richard Branson (Virgin Group) and Naomi Simson (RedBalloon) are more relevant than the approaches of earlier CEOs, such as Rupert Murdoch (News Corporation) or Jack Welch (General Electric).

Management and leadership: key differences

Although several authors argue that there is considerable overlap between leadership and management, most agree that each mode of action has some distinctive features and some unique areas of emphasis (Fulop, 1992; Hunt, 2006). The differences, as well as the overlapping elements, are:

1. *Leadership is often more intuitive than management.* Both leadership and management represent attempts to get things done through people. Management approaches, however, are often more structured and formal than the approaches and strategies adopted by leaders. Leaders often rely on their personalities and their values systems to guide them in their actions. They are more likely to draw on their intuition, and on their emotions, than on a set of management principles.

2. *Leadership tends to place more emphasis on inspiration, motivation and influence than management.* While both leaders and managers seek to motivate their subordinates to accomplish tasks, the concept of motivation is far more central to leadership practice than it is to managerial endeavour. A leader who is unable to motivate followers is typically considered to be a failure as a leader. In contrast, a manager who doesn't motivate subordinates may still be considered successful if minimum organisational outcomes are achieved. Successful leadership in modern organisations is often judged by whether a leader inspires their followers, but few managers consider it necessary to inspire their subordinates. Both leaders and managers seek to influence those around them, particularly those for whom they are responsible in organisations. The strategies that leaders choose to influence others are often less reliant on positional authority than is the case with managerial influence techniques.

3. *Leadership requires eliciting cooperation and teamwork.* Both managers and leaders aim to enlist the cooperative effort of others to accomplish important goals and tasks. Whereas managers are frequently able to use formal authority to enforce and compel compliance and adherence to procedures, leaders typically approach the task of drawing out cooperative effort rather differently. Leadership is predominantly a process of building cooperative effort over time, often by engaging the hearts and minds of followers. This engagement process is often magnified in strong team-based cultures, where the leader plays a pivotal role in building and developing the team. Managers, by contrast, do not always see it as part of their role to build a team-based culture or a climate conducive to group-oriented effort. Managers can often be successful simply by ensuring that individual efforts meet organisational baseline standards.

4. *Leadership involves having a vision of what an organisation or unit can become.* Much has been written about the importance of vision in modern organisations. From a management perspective, having a vision of what might be achieved in the future, is largely regarded

to be the exclusive province and responsibility of senior executives. Setting a vision is not often considered central to the concerns of mid-level or junior managers. By contrast, leadership is widely regarded as a process of bringing people forward, and part of that process typically involves the capacity to articulate a compelling vision for the future. Leadership today is often about being able to vocalise something that is worth striving for. It is about being able to articulate and emphasise something to focus on for the future and spelling out in broad terms what it is that needs to be achieved.

5. *Leadership deals with change.* Some definitions of leadership equate the concept to the creation of momentum; a surge in the tide, a dynamic approach to harnessing collective effort. In this respect, leadership is often considered to be predominantly concerned with moving people forward and embracing change. Management on the other hand has firm classical roots which suggest that its primary concern is the preservation of order and the adherence to a greater level of stasis. More recent management writings have challenged this perspective, however, suggesting that modern management is very much about the genesis and progress of change (Minkes, 1987). Nevertheless, writers such as Kotter and Heskett (1992) consider leaders to be significantly more adept and more naturally suited to the process of stewarding people through change, particularly tumultuous change that can bring with it varying degrees of upheaval. They reason that leaders tend to be more in tune with the psychological barriers to change, and tend to instinctively work to dismantle these roadblocks, thereby alleviating some of the fears that often give rise to resistance to change in our organisations. Most professional people today would much rather be *led* through change than *managed* through change. Leaders instinctively understand this important difference.

6. *Leadership deals with the interpersonal aspects of a manager's job.* Those who argue that leadership is, in effect, one of several important management undertakings nevertheless acknowledge the pivotal role that leaders play in dealing with the interpersonal dimension of the contemporary working environment (Mintzberg, 1975; Furnham, 1990). These writers also recognise that leadership is not always a role that is well executed by managers. Kotter (2013) maintains that our modern organisations have far too few effective leaders, and that ultimately for organisations to be effective, they need both managers and leaders to play their respective roles.

Four modes of action in modern organisations

One way to understand the differences between leaders and managers in today's organisations is to recognise that there are in fact four distinctive modes of action in the contemporary organisational world, and that individuals often gravitate towards one of these. The four identifiable modes of action are entrepreneurship, leadership, management and administration

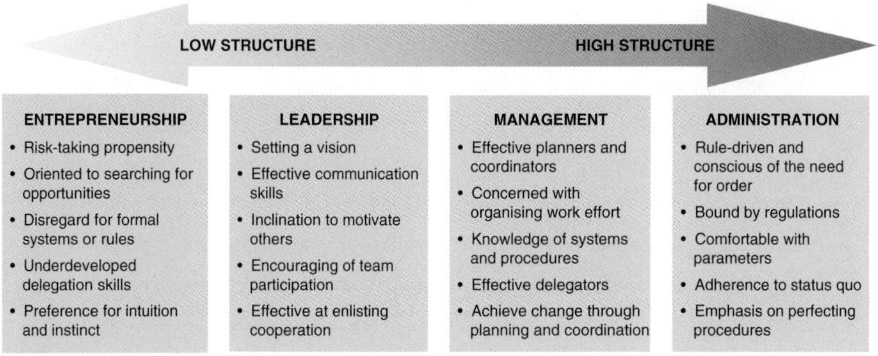

Figure 1.1   Four modes of action in modern organisations

(Figure 1.1). Often, the interplay between a person's preferences, values and cumulative training and experience influences their choice of how to act.

1. *Entrepreneurship*: This mode of action in organisations leads to experimentation and creativity. It leads to testing out new ways of doing things, and trying new approaches. The entrepreneurial mindset, when it appears in modern organisations, often throws out challenges to the status quo and can sometimes be viewed by others as disruptive and unsettling. Individuals who gravitate towards the entrepreneurial mode are often creative thinkers. They tend to approach problem solving in a manner that others might consider to be quite asymmetrical. Many individuals with an entrepreneurial mindset also tend to have tremendous levels of self-belief, and this can sometimes lead them to try to do too much themselves, rather than to delegate effectively.

2. *Leadership*: Those who exercise leadership in our organisations today sometimes tend to share the entrepreneurial distrust for excessive order and routine, preferring to rely on intuition and what feels right in terms of catalysing collective effort and harnessing commitment to achieving goals. On occasions individuals who emerge as leaders can find organisational rules and procedures constraining, and may be tempted to circumvent these, viewing them as guidelines rather than as strict parameters. Leaders tend to rely more on vision statements than on specific short-term goals, and on mobilising human effort through motivational means. In particular, a leader's decision-making process is often quite instinctive and guided by what feels right rather than by a deliberative process of weighing and deciding.

3. *Management*: Effective management in modern organisations essentially entails the good stewardship of a range of organisational resources, such as human, financial, physical and informational resources. Accordingly, those who strongly tend to embrace management practices as their preferred mode of action are normally concerned with 'balancing' organisational resources over time, and increasingly through periods of change. It is

important to note that while all four of these resources can be managed, only one of them can be led: people or human resources. In terms of decision making, managers are often quite deliberate and disciplined in their approach to arriving at and committing to a course of action. Typically, managers prefer to weigh the possible outcomes before taking a decision. Managers tend to feel more comfortable when they believe they have a clear, rational basis for their decisions. This is a pragmatic approach rather than an instinctive one and it remains one of the key differentiators between leaders and managers today.

4. *Administration*: Administration is a mode of action that is predominantly concerned with the preservation of order, and in cases where there is evident disorder, administration focuses on attempting to restore a sense of order. In contemporary organisations, when firms run into serious difficulties, administrators are called in to resolve the situation. *Administration* is a term that was historically used interchangeably with the word *management*, even as late as the 1970s (Katz, 1974). It describes those aspects of management that are predominantly concerned with organisation and control, and the preservation of an ordered, structured system. Administration is not particularly attuned to dealing with the process of change, and it is this point of differentiation that marks it as distinctive from management. As noted earlier, modern managers are required to balance

a range of resources, and this can entail negotiating periods of upheaval and change.

Modern organisations are often quite complex entities. Accordingly, they can derive significant benefits from harnessing the different perspectives and priorities that emanate from entrepreneurship, leadership, management and administration. Each mode of action brings with it some clear competitive strengths. The challenge in modern organisations is for both leaders and managers to develop an understanding of (1) when entrepreneurial mindsets need to be encouraged to unlock opportunities and possibilities, and (2) when administrative modes of action need to be pursued to achieve important efficiency gains.

CASE STUDY 1.2

David Thodey – CEO, Telstra

David Thodey served as CEO at Telstra from May 2009 to April 2015. During this time, he led the Australian telecommunications giant through a series of sweeping changes that saw the transformation of the organisation from a product-centric engineering company to a customer-oriented service provider.

Thodey was born in Perth, Western Australia and educated at Nelson College, New Zealand. He graduated with a Bachelor of Arts degree from Victoria University of Wellington, and pursued postgraduate management studies at the prestigious Kellogg School of Management in Chicago. He held several senior executive roles at IBM throughout the Asia–Pacific region before becoming the Managing Director for IBM Australia in 1999.

Thodey joined Telstra in April 2001 as Group Managing Director, a position which saw him take responsibility for the company's large corporate and government customer base in Australia. In May 2009, Thodey was appointed to the position of CEO at Telstra, following the departure of the American executive Sol Trujillo. Trujillo's four-year term at the helm of the telco giant had been a disaster. He had managed to antagonise and alienate the federal government of the time, who responded by seeking to place limits on Telstra's foreshadowed expansion plans. Trujillo presided over a period during which Telstra lost $25 billion in shareholder value, and customer complaints against the company had risen dramatically (Han, 2016).

Thodey was determined to turn Telstra's fortunes around, and he began by mapping out the company's culture over his first 12 months, in a bid to understand where the problems lay (Kruger, 2010). What he discovered was that the company lacked a strong customer focus and was widely viewed as a poor service provider. Thodey's response was to spend the next five years making important organisational adjustments to lead the company towards building a customer-centric culture.

Telstra adjusted its reward structures and bonus payments to give more weight to customer service quality, and developed a culture of trust in place of the old bureaucracy. The company dispensed with high levels of formalisation, including complex reporting systems requiring pre-approval for travel expenses (Heber, 2014), creating a more open and discretionary system under which employees were given a simple set of principles to follow, based on values of professionalism and honesty.

Thodey realised that the cultural shift would take time to achieve. Initially, some people in the organisation were quite resistant to the new ways of doing things. Thodey spent time reading through customer feedback to demonstrate the importance of the cultural shift towards high-quality customer service. He answered customer calls personally, and frequently visited clients. His leadership by example captured attention, as many of Telstra's employees began to take notice of the important changes Thodey was introducing. According to Thodey:

> The leadership challenge was getting the customer to be the centre of everyone's agenda and thinking more broadly than just 'What is my contribution?' If you make the customer the final arbiter in everything, it actually makes you more responsive to the market, stops internal factionalism and rallies everyone to something that is bigger than any individual (Han, 2016, p. 2).

Thodey's time at the helm of Telstra ultimately paid off for the organisation. A continuous improvement process was put in place and by 2015, customer complaints had diminished considerably. At the same time Telstra's operational costs were reduced by more than $1 billion, and reported employee morale and well-being had improved noticeably in the annual surveys put in place to measure the company's culture. David Thodey's effective approach to leadership had successfully transformed a company that was experiencing significant problems just six years earlier. In August 2015, Thodey left Telstra to take up a five-year appointment as Chairman of the Board at the CSIRO.

Critical thinking question
Why is it important for leaders to understand the culture of their team or their organisation?

THE IMPACT OF LEADERSHIP ON ORGANISATIONAL PERFORMANCE

As noted earlier, leadership has the capacity to impact significantly on organisational performance, and can produce both positive and detrimental effects. This is true of leadership at all levels in organisations, from those who lead small teams or small businesses, such as Naomi Simson, to those who lead global corporate empires, such as Rupert Murdoch. Many of today's most effective leaders show an awareness of the influence they can have in terms of shaping the motivation and productivity levels of their subordinates (Yukl, 2010). From a professional perspective, this awareness is important, because it enables leaders to create environments that are conducive to high levels of performance in others.

Leaders as architects of organisational climate

Leaders create an organisational 'climate' through their actions, behaviours and relationships with people around them, who work and operate within that climate. The term ***organisational climate*** refers to the mood, feeling or perceptual environment cultivated by a leader and experienced by those being led. Volatile and overly aggressive leaders can sometimes quite inadvertently create climates of fear and intimidation, as Steve Jobs discovered in his early years as leader of the Apple Corporation. Leaders who intimidate subordinates tend to preside over organisations and teams that exhibit diminished levels of motivation, and this in turn can adversely affect performance. Leaders who are more attuned to the importance of their working climate tend to deliberately build a sense of confidence and cooperative spirit in others. Leaders who create empowering climates in their working arenas often reap the rewards of more consistent commitment from employees. Larry Page and Sergey Brin have successfully combined as leaders to build a highly innovative and empowering working climate at Google, just as Naomi Simson has done at RedBalloon.

> **Organisational climate** – The mood, feeling or perceptual environment cultivated by a leader and experienced by those being led; the social and psychological environment created by an individual's approach to leadership or management.

LEADERSHIP SKILLS DEVELOPMENT

Effective leaders build commitment in others by drawing out and encouraging collective effort. These capabilities are based on their interpersonal and conceptual skills sets. Interpersonal skills enable leaders to read and understand other people. They enable leaders to relate appropriately to others, to communicate effectively with them, and to motivate them. Interpersonal skills also assist leaders to forge alliances with others who may be in positions of influence, and to build useful networks with them. Conceptual skills in leaders enable them to quickly grasp how organisations operate in the context of their environment. They enable leaders to see possibilities for change and to set an appropriate vision for the future. They enable them to develop meaningful strategies to assist others to play their part in remaining productive and in advancing the organisation.

Emotional intelligence in leaders

Emotional intelligence (EI) –
The capacity of an individual to recognise and manage emotions in themselves and in others.

Researchers such as Salovey and Mayer (1990) and Goleman (1995) have highlighted the importance of **emotional intelligence (EI)** in the contemporary working arena. They see EI as a very important part of social intelligence that determines how adeptly individuals deal with others at the interpersonal level. These authors argue that those who have high levels of EI are better equipped than others to successfully exercise their interpersonal skills in social and organisational settings. EI consists of several aptitudes:

1. *Self-awareness* – the ability to recognise one's own emotions as they arise, and to acknowledge whether an emotion is likely to have a negative or positive impact on one's mood, and on one's effectiveness in relating to others.

2. *Self-regulation* – the ability to regulate and control one's own emotions, including the ability to take active steps to overcome negative emotions such as anger or frustration, which might impede one's ability to operate effectively in social settings.

3. *Recognising emotions in others* – the ability to recognise and acknowledge emotions in others, and to understand the effects that these emotions might have on their behaviour.

4. *Managing the emotions of others* – the ability to influence, regulate and manage emotions in other people; for example, the capacity to placate someone who is angry or to calm someone who is feeling flustered or agitated.

Emotionally intelligent leaders instinctively recognise that their own emotions and the emotions of others can be influenced in a variety of ways. These leaders tend to take active steps to build confidence in themselves and others. They tend to exhibit uplifting emotional energy that can often have a flow-on effect to others around them (Zeidner, Matthews & Roberts, 2012).

Leadership competencies

Leadership competency –
A leader's specific outcome-oriented skills, which can be grouped into meaningful domains or clusters to create a profile, using a framework or model.

Several contemporary writers have noted the strong links between emotional intelligence and **leadership competency** in modern organisations, indicating that EI can assist in the process of leadership skill acquisition and development (Wang & Huang, 2009; Hunt & Fitzgerald, 2013). Researchers such as Hunt (2010) and Müller and Turner (2010) point out that the use of frameworks and models is useful because it helps leaders to recognise their strengths and to identify further skills enhancement opportunities. The six domains of leadership competencies model (Figure 1.2) is one such framework (Hunt, 2002). This model acts as a radar screen, enabling leaders to pinpoint areas for improvement in their skills profile.

This model suggests that effective leadership begins with mastering a series of personal leadership competencies such as self-awareness, achievement orientation and resilience, before attempting to lead others. In other words, the model suggests that self-mastery is an important element in exercising effective leadership. Other important areas or domains of leadership

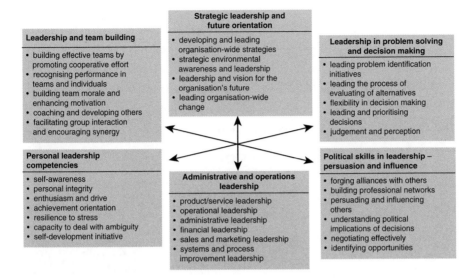

Figure 1.2 Six domains of leadership competence

identified in this model include administrative and operations leadership, team leadership, leadership in problem solving and decision making, political and networking skills in leadership, and strategic leadership. The advantage of these types of models is that they enable leaders to quickly pinpoint areas where they may need to build and develop their skills profile. By grouping leadership skills into meaningful domains, this can assist individuals in their understanding of the major skills sets that underpin effective leadership practice.

LEADERSHIP SELF-ASSESSMENT

The self-initiated quest for continuous improvement is a hallmark of professionalism in any field of endeavour today. Effective leaders tend to take their approach to leadership seriously and often develop the capacity for self-assessment quite early on in their careers. Just as emotionally intelligent individuals have a well-developed ability to recognise their own emotions and to take appropriate steps to regulate them productively, so too are effective leaders quite adept at seizing opportunities for self-improvement. This process of self-development in leaders typically commences with an assessment of their current strengths along with an identification of potential areas for improvement.

The ready availability of various diagnostic instruments makes it easy for leaders to undertake self-assessment. For example, leadership competency frameworks are often accompanied by self-assessment questionnaires which enable individuals to map their current leadership skills profile and to readily identify areas for further development. Other forms of self-diagnostic instrument are available from leading consultancy firms in Australia and internationally, such as Saville & Holdsworth and McKinsey & Co. Leaders can use such instruments to identify their preferred and ideal leadership styles, their preferred conflict-handling modes, their most effective communication strategies, and their capacity for effectively motivating others.

Effective leadership self-assessment takes into account several elements that help to shape the leadership process. As noted earlier, the process of leadership enlists the cooperation of others, typically through the use of influencing strategies designed to motivate and coordinate individual and collective effort. This process revolves around a dynamic relationship between the leader and his or her followers. It is a process that is ultimately focused on achieving results. Figure 1.3 outlines the important elements that relate to this process.

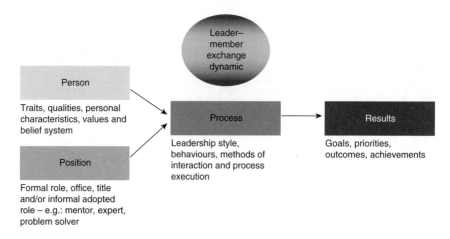

Figure 1.3 Four elements in understanding and defining leadership

Figure 1.3 reminds us that each person brings a unique set of traits, qualities, values and personal characteristics to their role as a leader. Leaders who understand themselves as individuals can capitalise on their strengths and minimise their potential weaknesses as they practise leadership. The figure also draws attention to the fact that leaders are often figureheads and role models in that they occupy a specific position. In large organisations, leaders frequently occupy formal roles or positions, but on other occasions they may exercise leadership and influence without formal authority, as mentors, guides, vision setters or experts. The figure shows that in terms of the leadership process, both the person and the position combine to shape each leader's approach to dealing with others. A leader's handling of this process typically determines the strength and effectiveness of their relationships with others. This in turn influences the goals, priorities and achievements of the leader and the team, with flow-on effects to the whole organisation.

In our contemporary world of organisations, continuous improvement is something that is increasingly expected in all areas of endeavour, and this is particularly so with leadership. Those leaders who dedicate themselves to better understanding their individual capabilities and performances are well positioned to improve on their approach to exercising leadership. It is the profound and far-reaching effect that leadership has on the lives of others – and on the effectiveness of our organisations – that makes it imperative for leaders today to do all they can to improve their capabilities for exercising leadership effectively.

SUMMARY

LEARNING OUTCOME 1: Define the terms *leader* and *leadership*, and explain how leadership differs from management.

A leader is a person who guides, conducts or shows the way; one who exercises influence over others; one who enlists the cooperation of others to achieve specific outcomes; one who sets a vision for the future. Leadership is a principal dynamic process that uses influence and persuasion to motivate and coordinate individual and collective effort. It is the process of enabling or guiding others to achieve goals; the process by which a person leads or shows the way. Leadership differs from management in that it is often more intuitive than management, and tends to place more emphasis on inspiration, motivation and influence. Some writers view leadership as that aspect of a manager's job which deals with the interpersonal aspects of management. Writers such as Kotter and Bennis contend that managers frequently struggle to exercise effective leadership, suggesting that leadership and management are distinctive systems of action in modern organisations.

LEARNING OUTCOME 2: Identify the positive and negative effects of leadership in organisations today.

Leadership in organisations produces positive effects when it lifts the performance of individuals and groups. Leadership is at its most positive when it empowers others, raises their self-esteem, and enables people to contribute to the organisation's overall productivity. The negative effects of leadership include organisational failures and corporate collapse, sometimes resulting in job losses for thousands of employees, having far-reaching effects on their livelihoods.

LEARNING OUTCOME 3: Explain the meaning of the term *organisational climate*, and explain why leaders can be viewed as architects of climate in organisations.

Organisational climate is a term that refers to the mood, feeling or perceptual environment cultivated by a leader and experienced by those being led. Leaders and managers, through their behaviours and in their dealings with others, effectively create a social and psychological environment that can either enhance or impede individual performance and well-being. Leaders are architects or creators of climates that can influence the capacity of others to carry out work tasks, and can shape the effectiveness with which individuals are able to contribute to organisational goals.

LEARNING OUTCOME 4: Define the term *emotional intelligence*, and explain why this is relevant to leadership effectiveness.

Emotional intelligence is an individual's capacity to recognise and manage emotions in themselves and in others. Since leadership requires engaging with others on an interpersonal level, emotional self-awareness and self-regulation can assist leaders to use their emotions positively in their dealings with people. Similarly, the capacity to influence and manage the emotions of others enables leaders to build confidence in subordinates and to create an uplifting environment for themselves and for those around them.

LEARNING OUTCOME 5: Explain the importance of self-assessment for leaders today.

Continuous improvement is a hallmark of professional endeavour. As individuals, leaders have the capacity to engage in a process of refining and enhancing their leadership capabilities. This process often commences with a recognition of where one's strengths and weaknesses lie. Leaders use a range of self-diagnostic instruments to undertake self-assessment, which helps them to work out what they are doing well, and where they can improve. Since leadership can have far-reaching effects on the lives of others, it is particularly important for leaders to actively work on improving their own capacity for effective leadership.

REVIEW QUESTIONS

1. What is the difference between leadership and management? Give examples.

2. What are some of the positive and detrimental effects that leaders can have in organisations today?

3. Why is an understanding of organisational climate of importance to leaders today? What can leaders do to create a positive organisation climate?

4. What is emotional intelligence? Why is EI relevant to leadership effectiveness?

5. What steps can leaders take to assist them in their self-assessment of their leadership behaviours and actions?

CASE STUDY 1.3

Rupert Keith Murdoch – Chairman, News Corporation

Rupert Murdoch is arguably the most influential Australian business leader of all time. As Chairman and CEO of News Corporation (News Corp) and Executive Chairman at 21st Century Fox, Murdoch presides over a vast media empire with interests throughout Europe, the United States and the Asia–Pacific region. Murdoch's unique approach to business and to leadership has attracted significant attention internationally over the past five decades. A polarising figure, Murdoch has been variously described as a brilliant corporate strategist, an entrepreneurial leader with an acute understanding of markets, a manipulative demagogue, a highly directive and detail-oriented autocrat, an amoral opinion leader and even a libertarian (Wolff, 2010).

Born in Melbourne in 1931, Murdoch was educated at Geelong Grammar and Worcester College, Oxford, where he read Philosophy, Politics and Economics. At Oxford, Murdoch was never quite accepted by many of his wealthier peers due to his colonial roots, and felt ostracised at times. This was an experience that shaped his anti-establishment sentiments, and led him to support the Labour Party as well as running for secretary of the University's Labour Club.

Following his father's death, Murdoch returned to Australia at the age of 21 to assume control of the family business, News Limited, which he successfully and aggressively expanded by progressively buying newspapers in Western Australia, New South Wales, Queensland and the Northern Territory.

In the 1960s, Murdoch began to turn his attention to international markets. In 1964, at the age of 32, Murdoch purchased *The Dominion*, a New Zealand daily newspaper. Later that year, he launched Australia's first national newspaper, *The Australian*, which quickly gained a wide readership and proved to be influential in shaping public opinion on political matters at the time.

Murdoch's foray in the UK began in 1968 with his purchase of *News of the World*, a populist tabloid. The following year, he acquired *The Sun*, which he quickly converted into another low-brow newspaper in tabloid format. With these two acquisitions, Murdoch dramatically cut production costs by using the same printing facilities for both papers (Shawcross, 1992). The sensationalist nature of these two papers appealed to the masses, which boosted readership significantly. This popular commercialisation heralded a shift in the newspaper industry in the UK, which bore testimony to Murdoch's willingness to adopt an iconoclastic approach to product marketing.

Since then, Murdoch has continued to build his media empire in Australia and the UK, while also expanding into the US. In 1973 he bought the *San Antonio Express News* and in 1976 he acquired the *New York Post*. In 1981 he acquired both *The Times* and *The Sunday Times* in Britain, and in 1984 he purchased a controlling interest in *20th Century Fox* (Shawcross, 1992).

In 1986, Murdoch began to roll out revolutionary electronic production technology throughout his printing presses in Australia, the UK and the US. The increased levels of automation enabled dramatic reductions in the number of employees required to operate the presses. In the UK, dismissals resulted in job losses for more than 6000 permanent full-time employees and provoked street riots and demonstrations which drew the Thatcher government into a bitter face-off against the British Trade Union Movement (Wolff, 2010). The sacked employees eventually won £60 million in settlements, but the dispute deeply divided public opinion in Britain. Conservatives viewed the Murdoch sackings as a bold, courageous anti-union move, while labour supporters saw the whole affair as evidence of a ruthless foreign mogul costing honest people their jobs, and vilified Murdoch as a callous 'dirty digger'. Independent commentators at the time noted the opportunistic shift in political allegiance, pointing to Murdoch's strong allegiance to the labour movement as a student at Oxford.

In the US, Murdoch launched Fox Broadcasting Company in 1986, an entity which found enormous commercial success with *The Simpsons, The X-Files* and Fox News. Fox News was launched as an antidote to the left-leaning bias Murdoch perceived in CNN and other commercial networks in the United States (Arsenault & Castells, 2008). It quickly gained a strong and loyal audience for its right-of-centre political views. Over the years, Murdoch has never shied away from using his media interests to support particular politicians at both ends of the political spectrum (McKnight, 2012). In the UK his newspapers have been particularly supportive of prime ministers Margaret Thatcher (Conservative, 1979–90), Tony Blair (Labour, 1997–2007) and David Cameron (Conservative, 2010–16).

If nothing else, Murdoch is certainly a highly determined and self-assured decision maker who operates effectively in extremely high-pressure situations. Throughout the late 1980s, Murdoch continued to build his empire by borrowing heavily from no less than 146 banks across four continents. During the recession of the early 1990s, Murdoch's highly leveraged News Corp became vulnerable, having accumulated over $7 billion in debt (Wolff, 2010). Several international creditors began hounding Murdoch – overextended financially, and with his British Satellite Broadcasting Company (BSB) experiencing enormous losses – to make good on overdue interest payments. By early 1991, News Corp was facing the prospect of bankruptcy. The corporation was unable to pay its $2.3 billion debt, and needed an immediate cash injection of $600 million to stay afloat. Through a series of quite harrowing and intense negotiations spanning several months, Murdoch held his nerve and persuaded his creditors to forestall his overdue payments and lend him the additional capital needed to keep News Corp viable (McKnight, 2012).

Having made significant inroads into both the US and UK markets, Murdoch's next expansionary phase led him to focus some of his attention on the Asian region. In 1993, with the worst of the early 1990s downturn behind him, Murdoch acquired Star TV, a Hong Kong business entity founded by Richard Li. This has since provided a platform for News International to broadcast from Hong Kong to Japan, India, parts of China and more than 30 other countries in the region.

In 2004, Murdoch shifted News Corp's headquarters from Adelaide, South Australia to the United States, effectively making the company a US-based firm, thus opening up share trading and investment opportunities for US-domiciled interests. In 2007, Murdoch bought Dow Jones & Company, publishers of the *Wall Street Journal,* for $5 billion. In 2014, Murdoch's 21st Century Fox made a serious bid for the Time-Warner Corporation, which was ultimately unsuccessful. Today Murdoch's business empire includes over 170 newspapers around the globe, television stations on five continents, radio stations, magazines, book publishers, satellite television companies, sports teams, sporting arenas and movie studios.

Admirers describe Murdoch's leadership as ambitious, engaged, decisive and opinion-shaping. In November 2015, he received the Hudson Institute's Global Leadership Award. Never one to shy away from expressing his own view to an international audience, Murdoch referred to Britain's exit from the European Union in 2016 as 'wonderful', comparing the move to 'a prison break' (Martinson, 2016). As a leader, Murdoch has been intensely loyal to a small number of long-serving senior executives, while also creating perpetually high levels of executive turnover in many of his businesses. He describes his best decision as retaining control of News Corp through a network of family trusts, a move that has attracted significant criticism from those who see this approach as a purposeful attempt to diminish accountability from a corporate governance perspective. Ultimately, Murdoch's approach to leadership is at once directive, demanding and opportunistic. A prolific international networker, at 85 years of age Murdoch remains one of the most influential business leaders of our time.

Critical thinking questions

1. Is Rupert Murdoch best described as a manager, a leader or an entrepreneur? Give reasons for your answer.
2. Some critics have argued that Murdoch has gone too far in attempting to shape public opinion through his media holdings. Should business leaders refrain from trying to influence public opinion? Explain your response.
3. Is Rupert Murdoch a positive role model for leaders today? Give examples from the case study to support your answer.

REFERENCES

Arsenault, A. & Castells, M. (2008). Switching power: Rupert Murdoch and the global business of media politics – A sociological analysis. *International Sociology*, 23(4), 488–513.

Bass, B.M. (1985). *Leadership and performance beyond expectations*. New York, NY: Free Press.

—— (1990). *Handbook of leadership: A survey of theory and research*, 3rd edn. New York, NY: Free Press.

—— (1998). *Transformational leadership: Industrial, military and educational impact*. Mahwah, NJ: Erlbaum.

Bennis, W. (2009). *On becoming a leader*. New York, NY: Basic Books.

Boyatzis, R. (1982). *The competent manager*. New York, NY: Wiley & Sons.

Carroll, S. & Gillen, D. (1987). Are the classical management functions useful in describing managerial work? *Academy of Management Review*, 12(1), 38–51.

Fowler, H.W. (1926). *A dictionary of modern English usage*. Oxford: Oxford University Press.

Fulop, L. (1992). *Management for Australian business*. Melbourne: Macmillan.

Furnham, A. (1990). A question of competency. *Personnel Management*, 22(6), 37.

Goleman, D. (1995). *Emotional intelligence: Why it can matter more than IQ*. New York, NY: Bantam Books.

Han, M. (2016). David Thodey says changing Telstra's culture was harder than negotiating the NBN. *Australian Financial Review*, 21 March.

Heber, A. (2014). Six things Telstra's CEO David Thodey is doing to change the company. *Business Insider Australia*, 29 October, n.p.

Hout, T. (1999). Are managers obsolete? *Harvard Business Review*, March–April, 161–2.

Hunt, J. (2002). A comparative analysis of the management and leadership competency profiles reported by German, US and Australian managers. *International Journal of Organisational Behaviour*, 5(9), 263–81.

—— (2006). Key components in the development of senior executives in Australia. *The Business Review, Cambridge*, 15(1), 121–9.

—— (2010). Leadership style orientations of senior executives in Australia. *Journal of the American Academy of Business, Cambridge*, 15(1), 121–9.

Hunt, J. & Fitzgerald, M. (2013). The relationship between emotional intelligence and transformational leadership: An investigation and review of competing claims in the literature. *American International Journal of Social Science*, 2(8), 30–8.

Johnson, S. (1775). *A dictionary of the English language*. London: Knapton Longman Hitch & Hawes.

Jones. K. (2014). Why do businesses fail? *Sydney Morning Herald*, 22 September.

Katz, R.L. (1974). Skills of an effective administrator. *Harvard Business Review*, 52(5), 90–102.

Keller, R.T. (2006). Transformational leadership, initiating structure, and substitutes for leadership: A longitudinal study of research and development project team performance. *Journal of Applied Psychology*, 91, 202–10.

Kerr, S. & Jermier, J.M. (1978). Substitutes for leadership: Their meaning and measurement. *Organizational Behavior and Human Performance*, 22, 375–403.

Klein, E. (1971). *A Comprehensive Etymological Dictionary of the English Language*. Amsterdam: Elsevier Scientific Publishing.

Kotter, J.P. (1990a). What leaders really do. *Harvard Business Review*, 68(3), 103–11.

—— (1990b). *A force for change: How leadership differs from management*. New York, NY: Free Press.

—— (2013). Management is (still) not leadership. *Harvard Business Review*, 9 January.

Kotter, J.P. & Heskett, J.L. (1992). *Corporate culture and performance*. New York, NY: Free Press.

Kruger, C. (2010). Dial T for Thodey. *Sydney Morning Herald*, 16 October.

Lewin, K., Lippitt, R. & White, R. (1939). Patterns of aggressive behaviour in experimentally created social climates. *Journal of Sociology*, 10, 271–99.

Martinson, J. (2016). Rupert Murdoch describes Brexit as 'wonderful'. *The Guardian*, 29 June.

McKnight, D. (2012). *Rupert Murdoch: An investigation of political power*. Sydney: Allen & Unwin.

McSparran, F. (2006). *The Middle English compendium*. Ann Arbor, MI: University of Michigan Press.

Meyer, J. & O'Sullivan, M. (2014). Qantas chief Alan Joyce cuts 5000 jobs. *Sydney Morning Herald*, 27 February.

Minkes, A.L. (1987). *The entrepreneurial manager*. London: Penguin.

Mintzberg, H. (1975). The manager's job: Folklore and fact. *Harvard Business Review*, 53 (4), 49–61.

Müller, R. & Turner, R. (2010). Leadership competency profiles of successful project managers. *International Journal of Project Management*, 28(5), 437–48.

Northouse, P. (2010). *Leadership: theory and practice*, 5th edn. Thousand Oaks, CA: SAGE Publications.

Pfeffer, J. (1977). The ambiguity of leadership. *Academy of Management Review*, April, 104–12.

Podsakoff, P.M. & MacKenzie, S.B. (1995). An examination of substitutes for leadership within a levels-of-analysis framework. *Leadership Quarterly*, 6, 289–328.

Quinn, J. (2008). Lehman Brothers files for bankruptcy as credit crisis bites. *The Telegraph*, 15 September.

Salovey, P. & Mayer, D. (1990). Emotional intelligence. *Imagination, Cognition and Personality*, 9, 185–211.

Shawcross, W. (1992). *Rupert Murdoch: Ringmaster of the information circus*. Chatto & Windus, London.

Simson, N. (2013). Standing up to bullies: Company directors and the elimination of workplace bullying. *Company Director*, 29(6), 42.

—— (2016). Making commercial sense of employee recognition. *Naomi Simson Weblog*, 3 August. Retrieved from: https://naomisimson.com/making-commercial-sense-of-employee-recognition.

Smith, F. (2012). Australia's 20 most popular places to work. *Business Review Weekly*, 24 September.

—— (2013). 50 best places to work in Australia 2013. *Business Review Weekly*, 27 June, 17–21.

—— (2015). RedBalloon named one of the world's most democratic workplaces. *Business Review Weekly*, 10 July.

Speedy, B. (2011). End of story: Borders to close after thirteen years. *The Australian*.

Walsh, B.L. (2014). How unhappy staff taught RedBalloon's founder Naomi Simson her toughest leadership lesson. *The Growth Faculty*, 24 September.

Wang, Y.S. & Huang, T.C. (2009). The relationship of transformational leadership with group cohesiveness and emotional intelligence. *Social Behavior and Personality*, 37(3), 379–92.

Wolff, M. (2010). *The man who owns the news: Inside the secret world of Rupert Murdoch.* Broadway.

Yukl, G. (2010). *Leadership in organizations,* 7th edn. Upper Saddle River, NJ: Pearson.

Zaleznik, A. (1992). Managers and leaders: Why are they different? *Harvard Business Review,* March–April, 126–35.

Zeidner, M., Matthews, G. & Roberts, R.D. (2012). *What we know about emotional intelligence: How it affects learning, work, relationships, and our mental health.* Cambridge, MA: MIT Press.

THEORIES OF LEADERSHIP

James Hunt and Martin Fitzgerald

LEARNING OUTCOMES

After reading this chapter, you should be able to:

1. identify the key contributions of the classical management writers and thinkers to contemporary understanding of leadership

2. distinguish between trait and behavioural theories of leadership

3. explain the contingency approach to understanding leader effectiveness

4. identify six approaches to leadership that have gained increasing attention from contemporary writers and practitioners.

INTRODUCTION

THIS CHAPTER INTRODUCES you to the progression and development of leadership thought from ancient times to the present day. The major phases in leadership research are explained, commencing with trait theories which sought to explore underlying dispositions of prominent leaders. Following this, the chapter provides an examination of behavioural approaches to leadership, and then explores later contingency perspectives. Several prominent leadership models are outlined in this chapter, including Blake and McCanse's leadership grid (1991), Fiedler's contingency theory of leadership (1978), Hersey and Blanchard's situational model of leadership (1982) and House and Mitchell's path–goal theory of leadership (1974).

This chapter draws attention to new and emerging areas of interest in leadership research and practice, noting the many prevalent approaches to leadership that can be identified today. Concepts such as authentic, ethical and servant leadership are defined, and darker areas such as Machiavellian and narcissistic leadership are also explained. The chapter concludes by assessing the applied value of the major leadership theories.

THE EVOLUTION OF LEADERSHIP APPROACHES

Interest in the systematic study of leadership stretches back to ancient times. This section of the chapter provides an account of our progressive understanding of leadership from early history through to our more contemporary perspectives on leadership in the context of the modern organisational world.

Leadership throughout history

From a historical perspective, our earliest conceptions of leadership are derived from the enduring legacies of prominent rulers with an innate capacity to inspire those around them. Individuals such as Alexander the Great, Julius Caesar, Charlemagne, Cleopatra and Joan of Arc all remain in our memories and help to shape our contemporary understanding of what a leader might be. Equally, thought-leaders such as Confucius and Jesus provide us with an understanding of leadership that aligns with current interest in authentic, ethical and servant leaders.

Many of these historical figures bring to mind the idea of a leader with a strength of conviction, and a strategic thinker with a willingness to act decisively, rather than just a commander or figurehead. Historical records tell us that Alexander the Great (356–323 BC) never lost a battle despite being outnumbered on many occasions (Fox, 1997). This remarkable achievement has been attributed to his strong leadership which included a natural ability to command great loyalty from his troops (Martin & Blackwell, 2012). Similarly, Joan of Arc (1412–31) is still upheld today as a young woman of fierce resolve, great courage and uncommon bravery – all potentially important leadership qualities in our contemporary organisational world (Pernoud, Clin & Wheeler, 1999).

Julius Caesar, in his account of the first Roman incursion into Britain, provides evidence of his belief in projecting a clear image of confidence as a leader. When leaping from his ship onto the English shore, Caesar stumbled and found himself laying face-down on the beach. Quickly seizing the moment to turn his apparent clumsiness into an opportunity to inspire his troops, he boldly declared aloud, 'You see – I already have the soil of England firmly in my grasp' (Lewin, 2010; Caesar, 1982).

Other pre-eminent figures from ancient times, such as Confucius (551–479 BC), Jesus (6 BC–30 AD) and Charlemagne (742–814 AD), show us leaders who are intelligent, compassionate, willing to listen to and learn from others, and prepared to challenge the existing order (Barbero, 2004). These leaders, along with Caesar, have also shown us an understanding of the importance of storytelling, demonstrating how compelling narrative can capture the attention of followers and convey a strong enduring message.

Taken together, these lessons illustrate various ideas that prevail in shaping our conceptions about leadership practices and qualities today. Authenticity, decisiveness, determination, resolve, courage, intellectual curiosity and a capacity to foster loyalty and to inspire others – these are all characteristics that emerge in current leadership research and writings, and are reported to be among some of the most sought-after attributes in modern leaders today (Ling, Liu & Wu, 2017; Hunt 2010).

Leadership in classical management writings

Early classical writings tended to view leadership as one part of the broader practice of management, and emphasised the efficiency gains that could be expected to flow from decisive goal-driven leadership. Max Weber, the German sociologist, saw rational organisational design as a quintessential part of effective leadership, while US industrial engineer Frederick Winslow Taylor saw leaders as instrumental in systematically establishing structured work processes (Weber, 1947 [1924]; Kanigel, 1997; Conger, 1993). Taylor firmly believed that the most effective organisations had leaders who put in place detailed work practices and procedures, and where responsibilities were clearly divided. He advocated a form of distributed leadership whereby one person would be placed in charge of operational efficiency, another would be responsible for monitoring quality control, and yet another would be charged with taking corrective action (Taylor, 1911).

Writing in 1917, the French administrative theorist Henri Fayol lent support to the emerging 'pursuit of efficiency' theme that typified leadership thinking at the time. Fayol qualified his thinking, however, by drawing attention to the importance of promoting team spirit to build harmony and unity within organisations (Fayol, 1917). This consideration gained momentum in the 1930s with the work of Elton Mayo, an Australian-born Harvard professor who founded the human relations school of management (Smith, 1998). Both Elton Mayo and his contemporary, Mary Parker Follet, offered fresh perspectives on leadership which captured the importance of team dynamics, motivation and empowerment (Metcalf & Urwick, 1940). Their work provided an important bridge to the later landmark studies that emerged in the second half of the twentieth century.

Writings by Douglas McGregor, David McClelland and Edgar Schein began the long process of exploring the depths of human nature and motivation, by drawing attention to the idea that leadership is as much about empowering others as it is about setting clear goals and standards for others to follow. In *The Human Side of Enterprise* (1960), McGregor emphasised the role of leadership in participatory management practices, while McClelland and his co-author provided new insights into the motivational profiles of leaders and workers. Schein further developed these ideas in his exploration of the relationship between leadership and organisational culture (McGregor, 1960; McClelland & Burnham, 1995; Schein, 2010).

Peter Drucker (1954, 1964, 1966) in his writings on management, lent support to the growing recognition of the value of the human element in modern organisations. Although best known for his work advancing management by objectives, Drucker also called for greater decentralisation in hierarchical enterprises, and at the same time cautioned against over-reliance on the command-and-control model of management. Implicit in Drucker's early writings was an understanding that a new form of management was required. This paved the way for an increasing interest in leadership, which would soon become a central concern of modern organisational writers.

Twentieth-century leadership studies

Trait theory – Trait theory in leadership is an approach that seeks to identify underlying dispositional characteristics that are thought to typify successful leaders. Trait theory investigations dominated the leadership research literature in the first half of the twentieth century.

Twentieth-century leadership studies progressed through several distinctive but overlapping phases, commencing with the early **trait theories** and moving progressively through behavioural approaches, situational and contingency perspectives, and culminating with a strong research interest in transformational leadership from 1980 onwards. Figure 2.1 presents this sequence of theory development and research interest. Early trait theories sought to identify a constellation of innate characteristics that were thought to underlie great leaders and define their unique temperament. The mixed results from these empirical studies led researchers from the late 1940s onwards to focus instead on observable behaviours of effective leaders. Researchers noted how these behaviours differed from one leader to another in terms of the degree of emphasis on task-oriented and people-oriented behaviours (Stogdill, 1974).

In the period after 1970, various contingency theories of leadership emerged which sought to specify the range of conditions under which particular leadership styles and practices might be most appropriate. While the insights afforded by contingency theories are noted in the leadership literature today (Bass, 1990), the complexity of some of these theories has made them difficult to apply in a practical sense.

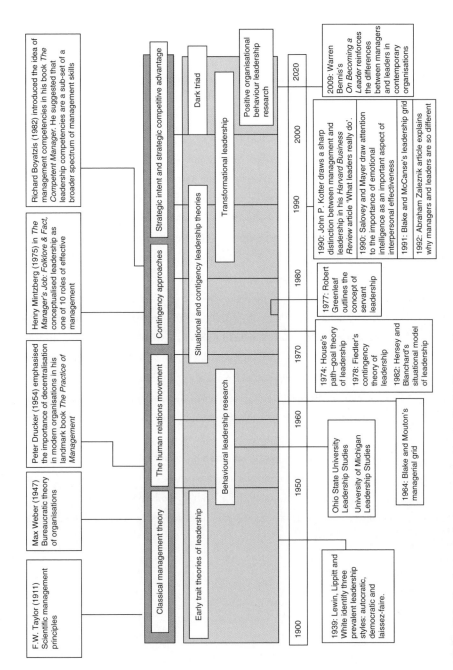

Figure 2.1 Development of management and leadership thinking over time

Psychopathic leadership – Sub-clinical psychopaths have been shown to be cruel and callous in their interactions with others. Leaders who show signs of sub-clinical psychopathy are typically unmoved by the psychological pain and suffering they inflict on others.

Narcissistic leadership – An approach to leadership characterised by the leader's inflated sense of self and an accompanying tendency to overreach. These leaders have a diminished capacity for empathy, making genuine engagement with others challenging.

Machiavellian leadership – An expedient and self-serving approach to leadership that typically employs lies and deceit to achieve end goals.

Ethical leadership – An approach to leadership governed by a clear set of principles underpinned by a firm set of values which act to guide behaviour and enable the leader to determine what is right and wrong.

Authentic leadership – An approach to leadership practised by individuals who have a strong sense of self and who establish clear and transparent relationships with others, thereby avoiding the pursuit of hidden agendas.

Servant leadership – An approach to leadership where by the leader places the interests of followers before his/her own needs. Servant leaders see their primary role to be 'clearing the path' to enable their followers to excel.

From 1980 onwards, a strong interest in the motivational potency of energetic visionary leaders grew steadily, and was captured in the concept of transformational leadership. Transformational leadership is an approach to leadership which elicits high levels of cooperation and commitment from followers, typically through behaviours such as individualised consideration and inspirational motivation. This concept will be covered in greater depth in Chapter 3.

Leadership studies today

At the turn of the twenty-first century, interest in transformational leadership remained strong, with several researchers showing renewed enthusiasm for exploring the underlying personality traits that correlate with certain transformational leader behaviours (Dinh & Lord, 2012). Alongside this, a growing fascination with the darker side of leadership has increasingly consumed the attention of contemporary researchers and managers alike. Narcissistic and Machiavellian leadership constructs continue to be explored, as some prominent corporate figures and CEOs are thought to exhibit aspects of these behaviours (Maccoby, 2000, 2007). Together with **psychopathy**, **narcissistic** and **Machiavellian leadership** form what is known as the dark triad of leadership research. Juxtaposed against this is another emerging stream of contemporary leadership research generated by scholars aligned to the Positive Organisational Behaviour school (Seligman & Csikszentmihalyi, 2000; Luthans, 2002). These researchers explore concepts such as responsibility, altruism, courage, perseverance and civility, a focus which has led to renewed interest in **ethical leadership**, **authentic leadership** and **servant leadership**. Additional contemporary areas of leadership research interest that will be covered in later chapters include followership, fluid, shifting and shared leadership, leader–member exchange dynamics, and emerging leadership in self-managed teams.

CASE STUDY 2.1

Indra Nooyi – CEO, Pepsi

Indra Nooyi has been the CEO at Pepsi since 2006, and its chairperson since 2007. She is considered one of the world's most outstanding corporate leaders, respected not only for her strategic acumen and relentless pursuit of excellence, but also for her natural inclination to empower others and elicit the best from those around her. Viewed as charismatic and engaging, she has won widespread international recognition for her corporate successes and her tireless leadership in various public service roles.

Nooyi was educated at Madras Christian College, India, where she graduated in 1974 with a BSc in Chemistry, Physics and Maths. Two years later, she completed a postgraduate diploma in Finance and Marketing at the Indian Institute of Management in Calcutta. Her early corporate career unfolded at Johnson & Johnson in India, where she held the position of Product Manager.

In 1978, Nooyi was admitted to Yale School of Management in the US, and during this time she completed a summer internship at managing consulting firm Booz, Allen & Hamilton. Graduating in 1980 with a Master's degree in Public and Private Sector Management, Nooyi accepted an offer to join the prestigious Boston Consulting Group as Director of International Corporate Strategy Projects, a position she held for six years (Sharma & Kumar, 2016). She then joined Motorola as a senior executive, where in 1988 she was promoted to the position of Vice-President and Director of Corporate Strategy and Planning. This was followed by a stint at the Swiss-Swedish conglomerate Asea Brown Boveri (ABB) as Director of Corporate Strategy and Marketing.

By 1994, Indra Nooyi's infectious resolve and strategic acuity gained the attention of several of America's most influential CEOs. Both Jack Welch (General Electric CEO) and Wayne Calloway (Pepsi CEO) tried to woo her to their respective senior executive teams. In the end Calloway won the day, and Nooyi joined PepsiCo as the company's chief strategist.

By the time Nooyi joined Pepsi, she had already developed a reputation as an excellent communicator and a clear-headed strategic thinker, highly adept at enlisting the cooperation of others to achieve outstanding results in a team-centred environment. In 2001, she was promoted to the position of CFO at Pepsi, and five years later she became the company's fifth CEO in its 44-year history (Davidson, 2009, p. 368).

Since then, Nooyi has succeeded in growing the company from a producer of carbonated beverages to a more diversified but streamlined organisation, making several key acquisitions (Sokol, 2017).

In addition to her strategic repositioning of PepsiCo in a highly competitive and saturated market, Nooyi has worked diligently as a leader on the world stage. She serves as a member of the Foundation Board of the World Economic Forum's International Rescue Committee, is the chairperson of the US–India Business Council and a board member of the Eisenhower Fellowships Trust, which runs an international leadership exchange program. Her public service responsibilities also include board membership at Yale University and the Lincoln Centre for Performing Arts. Fortune has rated Nooyi as one of the three most influential women in business globally every year since 2006, and in 2016 Forbes listed her among the 20 most powerful women in the world, along with Angela Merkel and Hillary Clinton (Belstrom, 2015; Sellers, 2012). The same year, Nooyi accepted an invitation to join President Trump's newly formed Business Council (Kell, 2016).

Nooyi's leadership style is inclusive, collegial, hard-working and considerate (Davidson, 2009, p. 386). She has won widespread recognition for her repeated demonstration that results-oriented leadership and decisiveness are not incompatible with humanistic and empowering management practices.

Critical thinking questions
1. What are the defining features of Indra Nooyi's approach to leadership?
2. Would you consider Indra Nooyi to be an appropriate role model as a leader in today's business environment? Give reasons for your answer.

THE TRAIT APPROACH TO LEADERSHIP

Early trait-based investigations into leadership spanned a period of more than four decades (1904–47) and produced a significant body of empirical research. These studies used the term 'trait' in a broad sense to refer to a range of variables, including age, height, weight and scholastic achievement, as well as many aspects of personality and temperament. Early studies by Goodenough (1930), Sward (1933) and Middleton (1941) are indicative of this period of investigation in that they concentrated on one or more dimensions of personality. Each of these studies explored the relationship between introversion-extraversion and leadership. Similarly, studies by Webb (1915), Cox (1926) and Drake (1944) investigated the trait of dominance in terms of its impact on leadership. It is difficult to derive overarching conclusions from these and similar studies from this early period because of the persistently contradictory evidence that emerged from the research. For example, Middleton (1941) found that leaders scored lower than non-leaders on the trait of extraversion, while Drake (1944) found no significant correlation between extraversion and leadership. This high level of contradiction eventually led many scholars to label trait-based leadership research as inconclusive (Jenkins, 1947; Stogdill, 1948).

Many decades later, a comprehensive meta-analysis of these early trait-based studies has revealed that they may have been prematurely dismissed. Lord, DeVader and Alliger (1986) found that significant relationships between personality and leadership were in fact evident in a number of these early studies. Further investigation by Bass (1990, pp. 75–84) into this nascent body of research has demonstrated that a significant number of studies had shown positive correlations between traits such as energy, enthusiasm, dominance, conviction, adaptability and mood control and either leader behaviour or leader emergence. This new perspective on the early studies sparked a renewed interest in research on **trait leadership**, which continues to this day, for example in the work of Judge and co-authors (2002), and Khoo and Burch (2008). Nevertheless, the trait approach to leadership research was widely dismissed in the decades following the 1940s, and although it was never completely abandoned, it progressively gave way to an emerging interest in behavioural leadership studies.

Trait leadership – A view of leadership that takes into account a range of variables such as age, height, weight and scholastic achievement, as well as many aspects of personality and temperament.

THE BEHAVIOURAL APPROACH TO LEADERSHIP

The **behavioural approach** to understanding and explaining leadership focuses not on individual traits or specific skills sets but on the exhibited and observable behaviours of leaders, and on explanations as to how those behaviours affect followers. Behavioural leadership research represented a significant advancement in the leadership field in that it heralded an important departure from earlier trait-based investigations.

Behavioural theory – Behavioural theory in leadership is a broad approach to understanding the range of observable behaviours that combine to determine an individual's general leadership style. Studies in this area have focused on task-centred and people-centred approaches to leadership.

The basic conceptual premise underpinning behavioural research draws attention to the relative weight that a leader places on task-oriented behaviours and relationship-oriented behaviours. The notion that leaders assign varying levels of importance to production (task-oriented behaviour) versus people (relationship-oriented behaviour) has been supported in subsequent empirical studies (Yukl, 2013).

The nature of this behavioural research has been dominated by three landmark studies. These are the Ohio State University studies and the University of Michigan studies conducted in the late 1940s, and the subsequent work of Blake and Mouton in developing their managerial grid (Blake & Mouton, 1964, 1978, 1985) which was later developed and renamed the leadership grid (Blake & McCanse, 1991). Collectively these investigations focused on two types of leadership behaviours: people or relationship behaviours and task or production behaviours.

These studies showed that leaders who demonstrate strong people or relationship behaviours tend to have a propensity and a desire to focus on the followers and their needs. In this respect behaviours that seek to encourage participation and heighten motivation are prevalent in these leaders. Their leader behaviours therefore tend to emphasise group processes rather than specific targets or outcomes.

In contrast, these studies provided evidence that leaders who display task or production behaviours tend to focus on goal accomplishment and repeatedly emphasise specific targets to ensure that followers meet predetermined objectives.

These behavioural research initiatives sought to observe, record and explain how leaders combine people and task orientations to influence followers and to enhance performance.

University of Michigan studies

In the late 1940s, Rensis Likert led a team of researchers at the University of Michigan who undertook a series of studies designed to examine the effect of leadership behaviour on group performance. This research identified two general leadership behaviours: task-centred leadership and employee-centred leadership. These orientations were conceptualised as lying at opposite ends of the same continuum (Stogdill, 1974).

Employee-centred leadership behaviour focused on the development of cohesive group relationships and on elevating employee motivation and morale. Task-centred leadership behaviour placed emphasis on adhering to specific work procedures and emphasised targets and objectives. This research was considered fruitful in that it drew attention to observable and measurable behaviours which could be explored in terms of their relative impact on things such as productivity and employee morale in the context of group performance.

Ohio State University studies

In contrast to the Michigan studies, the Ohio State University studies focused primarily on seeking to more accurately describe leadership behaviours. Shartle (1951) and his colleagues developed a research instrument designed to capture distinctive individual differences in leadership preferences and actions. Results from their Leader Behaviour Description Questionnaire (LBDQ) led to the identification of two types of leadership behaviours: consideration and initiating structure. These closely paralleled what the University of Michigan studies termed employee-centred leadership and task-centred leadership respectively, and bore similarities with earlier notions of autocratic versus democratic leadership styles (Lewin, Lippit & White, 1939). See Chapter 3 for more on these leadership styles.

Researchers in the Ohio State University project team regarded these two variables as independent of each other and unrelated. Accordingly, a leader who was high on initiating structure could equally be high on consideration. This meant that these two behavioural orientations did not form part of a single continuum. This conceptualisation represented a breakthrough in understanding leadership because it signalled a move away from the narrower view that a leader was either autocratically inclined or democratically oriented.

While the University of Michigan researchers initially conceptualised employee-centred and job-centred leadership as opposite ends of the same continuum, they later revised this conceptualisation and proffered a model of leadership behaviour that was much more closely aligned to that proposed by the Ohio State University studies team.

Over the next 20 years, much research was undertaken to identify which combination of behaviours was best suited to different situations, to maximise the satisfaction and performance of followers. Unfortunately, much of this research was inconclusive and several writers have considered the findings from these studies to be either contradictory or unclear (Yukl, 2013). Nevertheless, as a means of better capturing the thrust and intention of leader behaviour, these studies provided useful insights into the various orientations and behavioural styles that are evident in modern organisations.

The leadership grid

In the 1960s, what are now the best known of the behavioural leadership models emerged. The model originally referred to as the managerial grid (Blake & Mouton, 1964, 1978, 1985) was revised several times to become what is now widely known as the leadership grid (Blake & McCanse, 1991).

This model originally sought to provide organisations and their leaders with deeper insights into how institutional goals might be achieved over time, and to show how organisational renewal processes might be put into effect. Grid organisational development emerged as a long-term approach to organisational revitalisation. Leadership was considered an important part of this overall renewal process. Specifically, the grid model suggests the desirability of a strong dual focus on the part of leaders at all levels. The model draws attention to the possibility of maintaining high levels of concern for production and people.

The distinctiveness of the leadership grid, as with its predecessor the managerial grid, lies in the fact that it unites the two dimensions into a grid structure, where concern for production is plotted on the horizontal axis and concern for people is plotted on the vertical axis. Figure 2.2 illustrates this configuration and reveals that leader behaviours can be rated along each dimension from 1 (minimum) to 9 (maximum).

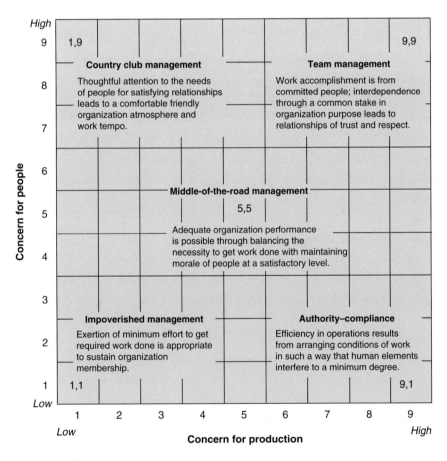

Figure 2.2 The leadership grid
Source: Blake & McCanse (1991, p. 29)

The grid is a practical leadership model that gives a framework for leaders to assess their own behaviours. The authors of this model believed that every leader has a dominant leadership behavioural orientation which they will be inclined to adopt, as well as a secondary back-up style which they revert to when they are under pressure (Blake & McCanse, 1991).

The plotting of task orientation against relationship orientation reveals five major leadership behavioural styles which are labelled on the grid.

Authority–compliance (9,1)

This form of leadership emphasises control and the achievement of performance through efficiency. This leader directs and dominates and seeks to minimise interference of relationships in the pursuit of task performance. Work is arranged so that the human element has minimal interference with performance goals.

Country club management (1,9)

This form of leadership centres on relationship management. This leader focuses on creating a nurturing environment where positive relationships are developed, with minimal concern for task performance in the first instance.

Impoverished management (1,1)

This form of leadership behaviour is about indifference. This leader is neither concerned with task performance nor with relationships. The leader tends to minimise her or his involvement with both people and production issues and is often withdrawn from the task or team.

Middle-of-the-road management (5,5)

This form of leadership behaviour is about compromise. This leader seeks to balance concern for production and people by seeking to achieve moderate levels of performance and satisfactory relationships by avoiding or reducing conflict.

Team management (9,9)

This form of leadership behaviour is about high-performance teamwork. Here the leader invests heavily in developing relationships while focusing on task completion to a high standard. This leader stimulates, clarifies, encourages, involves and enables performance.

The leadership grid is commonly interpreted as a model that provides a visual and spatial representation suggesting that team management (9,9) might be the optimal leadership behaviour. Yukl (2013) argues that it is this normative approach that represents one of the weaknesses of the model, and suggests that it is the situation that often determines the most appropriate leadership style.

Interestingly, Blake and McCanse (1991) identified two further leadership behavioural styles while developing their leadership grid. These are outlined below.

Paternalism or maternalism

This leadership behaviour uses the country club management approach (1,9) and the authority-compliance approach (9,1) simultaneously but in a non-integrated way. Followers are treated as a 'means' to achieving a performance 'end' and so country club management behaviours are employed with the single objective of achieving a performance 'end'.

Opportunism

This leadership behaviour uses each of the five approaches but with the single objective of placing personal advancement ahead of any other goal. These leaders are highly political in orientation, they tend to be self-serving, and are viewed as 'strategic' or 'manipulative' by their peers.

The leadership grid is viewed by many as a highly useful self-diagnostic tool. Due to its visual appeal and the ease with which it can be understood and applied, it presents itself as one of the more accessible leadership models. Today, it is still widely referred to in leadership training programs, university business courses, consultancy development initiatives and performance review processes.

CASE STUDY 2.2

Melinda Smith – Founding Director, Melinda Smith Consulting

Melinda Smith is the Director and Principal of her own corporate communications consultancy firm headquartered in the Hunter Region of NSW. She has an established reputation as an expert in cultivating business partnerships, developing company profiles, strengthening commercial brands and nurturing team-based leadership initiatives. Drawing upon her extensive professional network, Melinda uses her natural people skills as a leader to build relationships and to encourage managers to achieve results by tapping into the energies and enthusiasm of their employees. She views leadership as her most important undertaking, saying that 'I believe leadership is a privilege, and that good leaders have a great responsibility'.

Melinda graduated from Tamworth High School in 1984 where she was School Captain and Dux. During her school years, she was a member of the senior debating team, winning several inter-collegiate competitions, and an active participant in a range of team sports, including swimming, basketball and hockey. During this time, Melinda also studied piano and flute, and involved herself in local theatre company productions. She was also involved in a range of fundraising initiatives for organisations such as the Red Cross and the Smith Family, and she continues to contribute her time to charitable causes to this day.

In 1985, Melinda began her career in journalism with a cadetship at NBN Television News, which helped her to hone her professional communication skills. In 1988, she was appointed to the position of Public Relations Manager with the Hunter Technology Development Centre, a role which enabled her to draw upon her natural capacity to engage others. In this position she worked to increase the start-up organisation's profile across the community and strengthened its relationship with stakeholders.

In 1990, Melinda joined ABC Radio as a breakfast news presenter, and was also given her own evening program. At the same time, in recognition of her organisational capabilities, she was appointed to manage the station's publicity campaigns.

Between December 1992 and March 2010, Melinda developed a long and successful career as the leading news presenter and senior journalist with NBN Television. In 2003, she won awards for Best TV Journalist and Best TV Feature, and in 2005, she was nominated for a Logie Award for Best Documentary Feature on Australian Television.

Between February 2006 and March 2010, Melinda took on the additional responsibilities that came with her appointment to the position of Corporate Projects Manager at NBN. This enabled her to focus on strategic management and development, marketing, sponsorship arrangements, and relationship-building across five major corporate and community welfare areas.

In 2010, Melinda joined the Hunter Valley Training Company as Senior Executive Manager of Corporate Affairs and Communications. In this role, she was responsible for the leadership and management of the organisation's strategic communications across its ten NSW regional branches. During her five years in this position, Melinda developed and strengthened the company's marketing position and business offering by leading an entire corporate rebranding project. She established valuable productive relationships with consultants and revitalised partnerships through a new engagement strategy. Melinda also helped to actively build the organisation's culture through targeted internal communications. Alongside these achievements, Melinda managed to complete a master's degree in Business, graduating with distinction in 2012.

In 2015, Melinda established her own corporate communications consultancy firm to assist businesses with professional relationship building, employee engagement initiatives, and the development of company profile through the creation of brand value-building strategies. She describes her approach to business as collaborative and decisive. For her, effective management is built on integrity, trust and maintaining respect for others. When asked about her views on what makes an effective leader, Melinda suggested the following:

> Authenticity is one of the most important traits underpinning leadership on every level. As a leader, being willing to show openness and vulnerability is needed before requiring others to take the same approach. That's when real growth happens. The most effective leaders create a safe space, nurture trust and have an absolute belief in potential.

Melinda remains active in a range of community service and charitable causes, performing as MC for multiple major awards evenings, including the Westpac Rescue Helicopter Service Ball and the Hunter Business Chamber Awards. She was made a life member of the Hunter Youth Mentor Collaborative in 2011, and became an Australia Day Ambassador in 2012. In 2014, she was appointed to the board of directors of the Maitland Mutual Building Society, a position she holds to this day.

Critical thinking questions

1. What are the defining characteristics of Melinda Smith's approach to leadership?
2. How would you describe her leadership style?

CONTINGENCY APPROACHES TO LEADERSHIP

The limitations exposed by the early trait and behavioural theories in explaining the relevance and impact of leadership approaches in different contexts led to the development of a range of contingency theories. These theories are founded on the premise that leadership effectiveness is determined by the contingencies of the situation that the leader faces. We have seen how path–goal theory (House & Mitchell, 1974) and situational leadership theory (Hersey & Blanchard, 1982) dealt with these variables. Fiedler's contingency model of leadership (1967) takes a different approach again.

Fiedler's **contingency theory** is a 'leader-match' theory that seeks to align the natural style of the leader to the specific situation. In contrast, the path–goal theory centres not on matching a leader to a situation but focuses on a leader adapting her or his leadership style to certain situational variables to maximise motivation from followers. In Hersey and Blanchard's situational theory, the same focus on adapting leadership styles to the situational context is present but, rather than adapting to elevate follower motivation, this theory requires the leader to adapt to the follower's developmental level.

> **Contingency theory** – A theory that specifies that something is dependent on or determined by one or more other things. Fiedler's contingency theory of leadership posits that the effectiveness of any leadership style will depend on how well that style matches several other variables.

In general, each theory assumes that the leader can diagnose the situation they face and identify the right leadership style required of the situation to improve outcomes. Except for Fiedler's contingency theory, the other theories assume that the leader can adapt their style to the demands of the situation.

Fiedler's contingency theory

Contingency theories are leader-match theories in that they match the leader's natural style to an appropriate environmental setting (Fiedler & Chemers, 1974) and they consider style orientation as an internal trait.

Fiedler (1967) believed that adapting leadership style to changing situations was difficult and therefore either (1) leaders should be chosen so that their leadership style matches the situational context; or (2) the leadership situational context needs to be modified. If neither occurred, suboptimal performance would result. Fiedler explained that this resulted because leaders working in an unfavourable situational context would suffer stress from operating in a mismatched setting. Consequently, their decision making would become increasingly ineffective (Fiedler, 1995a, 1995b).

As such, Fiedler's theory can be described as a predictive theory which requires organisations and individuals to match the most appropriate leadership style to a given situation to increase the probability of success. In doing so, it places a responsibility on organisations to either match or move a leader or change the workplace situation if successful outcomes are to result.

To measure leadership behavioural styles, Fiedler developed his 'least preferred co-worker' (LPC) scale. This scale was incorporated into the LPC questionnaire, which Fiedler used to gather attitudinal information about leader preferences. Leaders with high scores were judged to be primarily relationship oriented, while those with low scores were judged to be primarily task oriented.

Fiedler then developed another framework, in which he made empirically supported generalisations about which styles of leadership were best and worst for different organisational settings. In his contingency framework, Fiedler sought to determine the 'favourableness' of an environmental setting for either task-oriented or relationship-oriented leadership behaviours. He achieved this by using three situational variables, prioritised in a hierachy as follows:

1. *leader–member relations:* ranging from very good to very poor
2. *task structure:* ranging from very high structure (clear) to very low structure (ambiguous)
3. *the leader's position power:* ranging from very low authority and influence to very high authority and influence.

For Fiedler leader–member relations were twice as important as task structure, which in turn, was twice as important as position power. The order of importance was based on the perceived contribution of each situational variable to the leader's sense of control in a leadership situation – which he termed 'situational favourability'. The most favourable of environmental settings were considered those with the highest scores against all three situational variables.

In order of importance, a high positive score in leader–member relations indicated a positive leader-follower culture and loyal followers who were attracted to and had confidence in the leader. A high score in the level of task structure indicated that the requirements of the task and its execution were clear and known to the followers. This would be a task with only a finite number of alternative solutions and a task where a successful outcome could be easily measured. The least important variable was the position power of leader. A high score in position power indicated a high level of authority on the part of the leader to reward and punish followers. According to Fiedler's research, the preferred leadership style to be adopted in an environmental setting depended on the blend of these three variables. Figure 2.3 illustrates this.

Over time, Fiedler has recognised that his earlier articulation of his theory was an over-simplification and he has since suggested that the theory might be better explained through a motivation hierarchy.

That is, leaders do not *only* focus on their LPC-score behavioural orientation but are *primarily* motivated to. For example, low-scoring LPC leaders would focus on relationships but only after they were satisfied that the task was being satisfactorily performed since the task was typically their primary motivation. The opposite applied to high-scoring LPC leaders: task motivation was secondary to their primary relationship orientation but would still be an area of focus once the primary motivation was satisfied.

Fiedler believed that, in unfavourable or moderately favourable situations, leaders would satisfy their primary motivation first. Accordingly, low-LPC leaders focused on the task, while

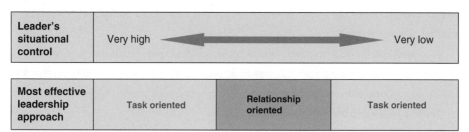

Leader–member relations	Good	Good	Good	Good	Poor	Poor	Poor	Poor
Task structure	High	High	Low	Low	High	High	Low	Low
Position power	Strong	Weak	Strong	Weak	Strong	Weak	Strong	Weak

Leader's situational control	Very high ←——————————————→ Very low

Most effective leadership approach	Task oriented	Relationship oriented	Task oriented

Figure 2.3 Fiedler's contingency theory of leadership
Source: Adapted from Fiedler (1967); Fiedler & Chemers (1974)

high-LPC leaders focused on relationships. In contrast, when in highly favourable situations, leaders (knowing their primary motivation is already being satisfied) could focus on their secondary motivation.

For leaders who were not necessarily high or low on the LPC scale, Fiedler recognised that they could not be easily classified in his hierarchical model. Others, however, have since argued that intermediate leaders are more likely to be interpreted as equally motivated by task or relationship work and thereby can readily switch between the two, depending on the situation (Kennedy, 1982).

Fiedler's contingency theory is regarded as a conceptually grounded and reasonably robust model and empirical studies have since demonstrated this (Strube & Garcia, 1981; Fiedler & Chemers, 1982; Fiedler & Garcia, 1987; Ayman, Chemers & Fiedler, 1995). However, the conceptual nature of the model has elsewhere been criticised (Peters, Hartke & Pohlmann, 1985). Fiedler himself recognised in his later writings that there was a need to attempt to explain why certain styles succeed in some situations but not in others. He termed this the 'black box problem' (Fiedler, 1993).

Perhaps the biggest criticism of Fiedler's contingency theory lies not in its empirical or conceptual validity, but in its processual complexity and consequent inaccessibility as an applied tool to assist managers in making sense of their environment. The three layers of 'situational favourableness' require leaders to process a complex set of variables, a mental juggling act which contemporary organisational settings are not particularly conducive to (Northouse, 2016).

Hersey and Blanchard's situational approach

Hersey and Blanchard's (1982) situational leadership model draws on the same task and relationship constructs of behaviour that were advanced in the Ohio State and Michigan studies, and supports the idea that these variables are independent of each other and capable of combining in multiple ways. This model extends the previous work by proposing that the optimal leadership style will be determined by the situational context facing the leader. Hersey and Blanchard's paradigm therefore introduces a third dimension to the model that accounts for this situational context. This third dimension was referred to initially as 'follower maturity', and then 'follower readiness'.

As originally conceived, leadership effectiveness would increase across the four behavioural dimensions but would be contingent on the readiness level of the individual to perform the task. The four behaviours were different combinations of task- and relationship-oriented leadership behaviours.

The four leadership behaviours were identified as:

S1	Telling	High-task/low-relationship behaviours
S2	Selling	High-task/high-relationship behaviours
S3	Participating	Low-task/high-relationship behaviours
S4	Delegating	Low-task/low-relationship behaviours

In this model, follower 'readiness' was defined as the 'ability and willingness' to execute the task. It was not a measure of personality but simply readiness to perform. Four levels of readiness were considered:

R1	Unable	Unwilling/Insecure
R2	Unable	Willing/Insecure
R3	Able	Unwilling/Confident
R4	Able	Willing/Confident

Each level of readiness matched the corresponding number relating to the identified leadership behaviour. For example, for someone with the lowest level of readiness (R1), a leader would adopt a S1 (Telling) leadership style.

Thus, it was the expectation that the leader would vary their style of leadership to match the situation facing them, along a continuum from directive (task-oriented) leadership behaviours to supportive (relationship-oriented) leadership behaviours.

Despite its intuitive appeal, there is not a strong body of research supporting the theoretical basis of this model's third dimension, and several studies have criticised it on conceptual grounds (Graeff, 1983; Fernandez & Vecchio, 1997; Graeff, 1997; Vecchio & Boatwright, 2002; Thompson & Vecchio, 2009).

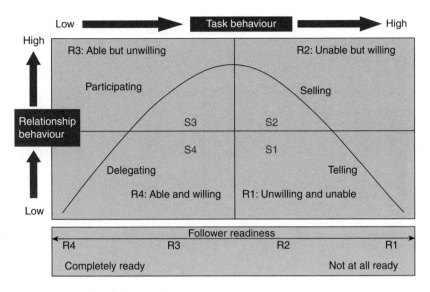

Figure 2.4 Situational leadership model

Source: Adapted from Hersey & Blanchard (1982); Hersey, Blanchard & Johnson (2001)

Situational leadership II (SLII)

Blanchard and various co-authors further developed the situational leadership approach, leading to the creation of the '**situational leadership** II' model in 1985. This was the culmination of his work with others (Blanchard, 1985; Blanchard, Zigarmi & Zigarmi, 1985). The broad structure and assumptions of SLII were the same as the original theory but there was an important adjustment. Readiness level 1 (the subordinate who is both unwilling and unable) was replaced with Developmental level 1 (the subordinate who is highly willing, but unable – referring to someone with low competence but high commitment). Whereas the earlier model suggests that a telling style of leadership is appropriate for someone who is unwilling and unable, the revised model suggests that the telling or directive style is more appropriate for someone with higher commitment but lower competence.

> **Situational leadership** – An approach to leadership which draws attention to situational variables as determinants of the most appropriate leadership style to be adopted in the prevailing circumstances. Hersey and Blanchard's model is an example of this approach.

The SLII model prescribes that the leader should engage in a blend of directive and supportive behaviours. In this model, directive leadership behaviours will involve largely one-way communication, with clear goal setting. In contrast, supportive leadership behaviours involve the leader engaging in emotionally intelligent, socially supportive two-way communication with subordinates. These two types of behaviours create four possible categories of approach for the situational leader. Table 2.1 details the classification and features of each of these approaches.

The key dimension of the SLII model is the developmental level of the employee. The developmental level represents the competence and skill of the employee to execute the identified task, as well as their level of confidence and motivation in performing it successfully. (Blanchard, 1985; Blanchard, Zigarmi & Nelson, 1993; Blanchard, 2007).

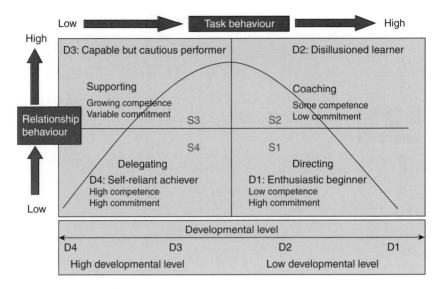

Figure 2.5 SLII

Source: Adapted from Blanchard (1985); Blanchard, Zigarmi & Nelson (1993)

Table 2.1 SLII behavioural styles

Category	Style	Features
High directive – Low support	Directing	Focus is on the communication of goal achievement. The leader provides clear instructions and undertakes close supervision.
High directive – High support	Coaching	Focus is on the communication of goals while also meeting employee's support needs. The leader directs but does so after seeking employee input and offering employee encouragement.
Low directive – High support	Supporting	Focus is on facilitating employee execution of work function within a supportive environment. The leader invites participation, actively listens and supports, provides constructive feedback and is always available for higher-order problem solving.
Low directive – Low support	Delegating	Focus is on giving control and autonomy to the employee. The leader agrees with 'what needs to be done and by when' but leaves it to the employee to decide on how it is to be done. The leader remains in the background to provide task advice or support but does not impose it.

As conceived, the developmental level pertains to a particular task, not to the employee generally. For example, a senior, experienced middle manager may be considered developed (D4) in managing departmental staff, but might be considered as developing (D1) in another area such as leading a major organisation-wide change initiative. The introduction of the term 'developmental level' (see Table 2.2) cleared up the ambiguity of the terms 'maturity' and 'readiness' used in earlier versions of this model.

The model rests on the assumption that employees differ in their task-related motivational strength and in their task-related skills level.

Table 2.2 SLII developmental levels

Developmental level	Competence level for task at hand	Commitment level for task at hand	Features
D1	Low	High	Little competence but charged with initial enthusiasm for the new task
D2	Low – Moderate	Low	Initial enthusiasm waned but some competence in evidence for task
D3	Moderate – High	Low	Competent but lacking confidence/motivation to execute
D4	High	High	Competent and confident

Once the leader has correctly identified the developmental level of each subordinate, the SLII model can be used to indicate which leadership style should be adopted in each case. So D1 corresponds with S1; D2 aligns with S2; D3 matches S3; and D4 fits with S4.

A major challenge to this model relates to the basis of its conceptualisation. Yukl has been a persistent critic of the initial model and the SLII model (Yukl, 2013). Others have questioned the relationship between motivation and confidence which form the components of 'commitment', and ask why commitment starts high at the D1 level, then dips during the D2 and D3 levels, only to rise again by the D4 level (Northouse, 2016). Blanchard and co-authors have articulated the need for further research into how competence and commitment might be conceptualised and weighted across each developmental level (Blanchard et al., 1993). Despite these criticisms, the situational leadership theory remains both easier to use in practice and more readily understood than Fiedler's contingency theory.

House's path–goal theory

A further contingency theory of leadership, path–goal theory, was first developed by Robert House in the early 1970s (House, 1971; House & Dressler, 1974; House & Mitchell, 1974; House, 1996). It is based on the expectancy theory of motivation, which states that followers will be motivated if the following three conditions are satisfied:

1. followers believe they are capable of performing the work if they put in the required effort
2. followers can see that their work will result in an expected outcome
3. followers perceive the outcomes of their work to be of value to them as individuals.

House's path–goal theory is based on the premise that followers will be motivated if the leader increases the pay-offs (rewards) associated with accomplishing work tasks, and smooths the path to those rewards with such activities as induction, training, mentoring, praise, support, direction and encouragement. Thus, path–goal theory proposes that a follower's motivation towards their work depends on their assessment as to whether their effort will lead to good performance, whether that performance will produce the kind of reward they want, and whether that reward is perceived to be of significant value to the follower.

The role of the leader using goal–path theory, therefore, is to adopt a leadership style that best meets the motivational needs of the employee. This model proposes that a leader should make available valued rewards to motivate action (the 'goal' in path–goal theory) and that they should assist the follower to find the best way of getting there (the 'path' in path–goal theory) by aiding them in avoiding obstacles, negotiating roadblocks and supporting the follower throughout the journey. This model suggests that leaders will need to adapt their behavioural style to suit the motivational needs of the followers in relation to the task at hand.

As a leadership theory, the path–goal approach has intuitive appeal because it recognises that different behavioural styles are needed, and that the right choice depends on both employee contingencies and environmental factors.

Path–goal leadership styles

This theory identifies four leadership behavioural styles that can affect a follower's motivation. They are directive, supportive, participative and achievement-oriented behaviours. House and Mitchell (1974) considered these four styles as non-exclusive and were open to further styles being added over time.

Directive

This style is characterised by the same directive approach illustrated in Hersey and Blanchard's situational leadership model. Here the leader tells the employee precisely what tasks to undertake, how to accomplish them, and when to execute them. With this approach, the leader articulates clear standards of performance and typically maintains a close supervisory presence to ensure the task is satisfactorily completed. This approach also mirrors what was described as the 'initiating structure' in the Ohio State University studies.

Supportive

The supportive behavioural style resembles what the Ohio State University studies referred to as 'consideration behaviour' where the leader attends to the emotional needs and psychological well-being of the employee. Leaders who adopt this style are approachable, supportive and respectful towards subordinates, and tend to treat employees as equals.

Participative

The participative behavioural style invites the employee to be part of the decision-making process, integrating their views into how the work of the individual, group or organisation is carried out. In this approach, the leader tends to encourage and facilitate genuine employee involvement.

Achievement-oriented

The achievement-oriented behavioural style involves the leader challenging employees to achieve higher goals. It establishes an environment of continuous improvement, where ambitious goals are set and where the leader continuously encourages the employees by demonstrating confidence in their ability to achieve. Here, the leader emphasises the achievement of peak performance in subordinates.

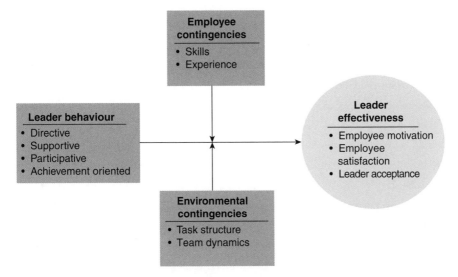

Figure 2.6   Path–goal theory
Source: Adapted from House (1971, 1996)

The path–goal model suggests that leaders are most effective when they can select the appropriate behavioural style to match each situation. The model also allows for the use of two or more leadership styles in conjunction with one another, if the situation requires it.

Employee and environmental contingencies

According to path–goal theory, success as a leader is dependent on two principal contingencies. These are employee contingencies and environmental contingencies. Employee contingencies include the needs of each subordinate, their level of experience, their skills and competency profiles, their perceived abilities, their satisfaction levels, their anxiety levels and their locus of control. Environmental contingencies refer to characteristics of the work environment that are beyond the direct control of the employee. These include aspects such as task structure and team dynamics.

In one of its early inceptions, this model proposed two follower variables as worthy of consideration by leaders, namely follower satisfaction levels and follower self-perception of abilities (House & Dressler, 1974). Critics of this model have pointed out that there is only so much a leader can do to increase satisfaction because satisfaction also depends on the personality traits of the follower (Mitchell, 1974; Yukl, 2013). Nevertheless, studies relating to the personality construct of 'locus of control' have found that different leadership behaviours will motivate various 'locus of control' profiles in distinctive ways (Mitchell, Smyser & Weed, 1975).

For those with a strong internal locus of control, who firmly believe they play a determining role in their life's direction, participative leadership is preferred in this model, because this allows followers to play a decisive role in their work life. In contrast, for those with a strong external locus of control, who tend to believe that outside forces determine their fate, directive leadership is preferred because the subordinate typically views direction as both welcome and reassuring.

A follower's perception of their own abilities can also affect the impact of particular leadership behaviours. For example, an employee confident in their own ability is less likely to accept or be motivated by a directive leader, and more likely to be receptive to participative leadership. Similarly, an employee who holds a self-perception of limited or insufficient competence is likely to welcome the greater level of structure that the directive leader would bring to their relationship.

With respect to environmental contingencies, the path–goal model suggests that when a task is unclear or non-routine, leaders should assume a directive style as this will minimise role ambiguity. When employees undertake routine tasks that are well defined and highly structured, though, the directive style is often ineffective and employees may view it as unnecessarily interfering and demotivating. This model suggests that a supportive leadership approach is more suited to very routine tasks, because it can help employees to come to terms with repetitive or mundane work.

Assessing path–goal theory

With four behavioural styles and two broad contingencies, path–goal theory is potentially complex. Indeed, not only can the employee contingencies and the environmental contingencies impact leader behaviours, they can also impact each other. For example, an ambiguous task can affect a follower's perception of their ability. This complexity can make the model difficult to use in practice.

Additional criticism of path–goal theory points to the fact that there is little empirical evidence to support several of the contingencies given in the model (McShane et al., 2016). According to Schriesheim and Neider (1996), other contingencies posited in this model have not been empirically tested at all.

Despite these criticisms path–goal theory certainly provides a set of assumptions about how different leadership behaviours can interact with employee and environmental contingencies to better motivate followers and to improve performance. In this respect the model is viewed as a useful reflective tool for leaders seeking to gain insights into how their leadership behaviour can be adapted to enhance work outcomes (Schreischeim & Schreischeim, 1980). Table 2.3 is a simplified depiction of how leadership styles can align with situational variables.

Subsequent research studies testing this theory's validity have been equivocal (House & Mitchell 1974; Schriesheim & Neider, 1996; Stinton & Johnson, 1975; Wofford & Liska, 1993).

Table 2.3 Path–goal theory: Aligning situational variables to leader behaviours

Situational variable	Leadership style	Influence on follower
Role, task or job ambiguity or complexity	Directive leadership	Precise articulation and clarification of paths to rewards
Lack of confidence on the part of the follower	Supportive leadership	Communicating a can-do attitude increases the confidence of the follower
Inappropriate rewards offered to follower	Participative leadership	Leader clarifies follower's motivational drives and provides appropriate rewards
Lack of perceived challenge in the tasks undertaken or lack of desire to produce high-quality work	Achievement-oriented leadership	Influences aspiration levels and sets challenging goals

There is some support for the path–goal model, but no consistent position has been established with respect to the validity of the theory's basic assumptions, nor the correlation between its respective variables. The theory does not clearly explain why certain leadership behaviours motivate or demotivate followers in different contingent settings. A further criticism is that the theory mentions some contingencies but ignores others (Osborn, 1974). For example, factors other than motivation which can ultimately improve follower performance are not considered, such as recruitment and development strategies and work-design initiatives. The model also fails to recognise political, strategic and other influences on leader behaviour and does not sufficiently account for such factors as work culture and stress climate or the level of technological support. The external environment has changed significantly since the theory's early development and, as such, contemporary settings present challenges for those seeking to use this model. It does not consider the economic, political, legal and regulatory, societal, technological and ecological environmental factors that affect any business in a globalised economy today.

Despite these concerns, path–goal theory does provide a practical framework to enable leaders to choose their behaviour with the specific intention of motivating their followers towards better performance. This reminds them that an integrative part of their role as leaders is to inspire, support, praise and coach followers towards better performance.

CONTEMPORARY APPROACHES TO LEADERSHIP

Leadership practices today can still be understood through the analytical lenses of the behavioural and contingency theories examined in this chapter. Nevertheless, our understanding of the manifestations of leadership have broadened significantly, particularly in the past 20 years. There is a heightened awareness now of the darker, more exploitative side of leadership practices. This has given rise to an area of leadership research focusing on what has been termed the '**dark triad** of personality': narcissism, Machiavellianism and psychopathy (Paulhus & Williams, 2002). See also Chapter 3 for more on the dark triad of leadership styles.

> **Dark triad** – The manifestations of leadership that reveal darker and exploitative practices according to Paulhus and Williams (2002): narcissism, Machiavellianism and psychopathy.

Exploitative and ethical leadership approaches

Self-concept – The combination of attitudes and beliefs that we have about ourselves. These include our level of self-esteem as well as our level of optimism and pessimism.

Narcissistic leaders are individuals with a grandiose and often unrealistically inflated **self-concept**. They can be extremely ambitious and driven, but have a persistent tendency to overreach. A defining characteristic of narcissistic leaders is their diminished capacity for empathy, making them poor one-on-one motivators who are prone to exploiting others (Rosenthal & Pittinsky, 2006). Machiavellian leaders have strong self-serving inclinations and tend to favour manipulation and deceit to advance their own careers. These leaders tend to have an uncompromising focus on end goals and will often do whatever it takes to achieve those goals, even if this includes engaging in behaviours that others might consider quite unethical. Leaders with psychopathic tendencies are often ruthless and can be cruel in their dealings with peers and subordinates. They are unmoved by suffering in others, and when in positions of power they can be enormously difficult to work for. Several recent studies have noted the surprising prevalence of these three types of leaders among the ranks of today's senior corporate executives (Ressick et al., 2009; Maccoby, 2007).

In contrast to these somewhat sinister leaders, there has been renewed interest in authentic, ethical and servant leadership approaches in contemporary organisations (Giampetro-Meyer et al., 1998; Mayer, Bardes & Piccolo, 2008; Kiersch & Byrne, 2015).

Servant leadership was first proposed by Greenleaf (1977) and describes leaders who unselfishly put the needs of their subordinates before their own. Servant leaders see themselves as enablers whose role it is to clear the way for their subordinates to flourish professionally. Servant leaders have been shown to facilitate and develop extremely high levels of job commitment on the part of followers.

Authentic leaders are individuals who pride themselves on their transparency, shunning hidden agendas and instead developing frank, open and legitimate relationships with their subordinates. Studies have shown that authentic leaders are generally viewed very positively by others and can elicit high levels of commitment from their subordinates who often readily embrace their leader's vision for the future (Harter, 2002).

Ethical leaders are individuals with a strong sense of integrity who establish a clear framework articulating what constitutes acceptable and unacceptable behaviour. Their behaviours and dealings with others adhere closely to this framework. Ethical leaders are often greatly admired and are seen to fit with broad notions in modern society of how our organisational leaders ought to conduct themselves.

Each of these approaches to leadership capture quite distinctive manifestations of observable behavioural styles. A more detailed account of these approaches will be provided in Chapter 3, along with an assessment of their relative prevalence in today's organisations.

APPLICATION OF LEADERSHIP THEORIES

Kurt Lewin, one of the most prominent social and organisational psychologists in the modern era, proclaimed that there is nothing so practical as a good theory (Lewin, 1999; first published 1943). This is a timely reminder that the ultimate value of any leadership theory lies in the insights it can provide for leadership practice in the real world.

The Ohio State and Michigan studies discussed earlier in this chapter paved the way for the development of the leadership grid, a model which demonstrates that concern for people and concern for production need not be mutually exclusive aspects of a leader's role. Many managers and leaders today view the leadership grid as a useful applied tool that provides a clear visual representation of five potential approaches to practising leadership.

The various contingency theories discussed in this chapter provide deeper insights into the range of conditions which can determine the effectiveness of a leadership approach. Fiedler's contingency theory suggests that the success or otherwise of any leadership style may rest upon such factors as leader–member relations, task structure, and the relative positional power of the leader. For some, these insights may hold considerable applied value, while for others, the model's relative complexity may make it difficult to use.

Some also consider Hersey and Blanchard's situational model of leadership of limited applied value due to its complexity across three dimensions. Others, however, see the model as having practical applications because it alerts leaders to the need to match their approach to the overall development level of their subordinates. Similarly, many think that House's path–goal theory is too complex and difficult to apply in any practical sense, although it does present leaders with several indicators they can use to align their leadership style to various situational factors. It therefore facilitates leaders' thinking in terms of the impact that their leadership approach has on employee motivation, and on the extent to which subordinates are likely to accept them as leaders in the first place.

Ultimately the applied value of any theory lies in its perceived utility as a barometer for determining leadership effectiveness. For some, contingency theories provide useful guidelines to refine their chosen leadership style. For others, contingency approaches seem too complex and one or more of the behavioural theories might provide greater insights into effective leadership practice. In the final analysis, each leader has the responsibility to decide for themselves what is useful and what is not, from the array of theoretical models and paradigms available in the literature.

SUMMARY

LEARNING OUTCOME 1: Identify the key contributions of the classical management writers and thinkers to contemporary understanding of leadership.

Classical writers tended to view leadership as one aspect of the broader responsibility of management. Max Weber (1947 [1924]) emphasised the need for leaders to create well-defined structures in their organisations. Frederick Taylor (1911) advocated the establishment of clear work practices, to be overseen by leaders. Henri Fayol (1917) indicated the need to adhere to specific management principles, one of which was the promotion of team spirit by leaders. Later, the narrow classical perspective on leadership became less popular, and writers drew greater attention to the human element in organisations. Increasingly, they described leaders as individuals who have the opportunity to establish participatory management practices in organisations.

LEARNING OUTCOME 2: Distinguish between trait and behavioural theories of leadership.

Trait theories of leadership prevailed in the management literature from 1904 to 1947. These theories sought to identify the defining characteristics of successful leaders, including aspects of temperament and personality. Traits such as dominance, adaptability and mood control were shown to correlate with effective leadership. Behavioural theories of leadership moved away from a focus on leaders' dispositions, seeking to identify observable behavioural patterns in their actions instead. Behavioural studies led to the identification of a range of distinctive leadership approaches, centred on whether the leader was either task or people oriented, or whether the leader adopted some combination of both.

LEARNING OUTCOME 3: Explain the contingency approach to understanding leader effectiveness.

Contingency approaches to leadership, emerging from the 1970s onwards, started with the premise that no single behavioural style is suited to all situations. The assumption of these theories therefore is that a range of variables will combine to determine the most appropriate and most effective leadership approach in each circumstance. Contingency theories seek to alert leaders to the unique characteristics of each situation, and suggest appropriate leader behaviours that are expected to align favourably with the situational contingencies identified in each circumstance.

LEARNING OUTCOME 4: Identify six approaches to leadership that have gained increasing attention from contemporary writers and practitioners.

The 'dark triad' research into the psychology of narcissistic, Machiavellian and psychopathic leader behaviours (Paulhus & Williams, 2002) has attracted growing interest from writers and practicing managers over the past 20 years. From the Positive Organisational Behaviour research school, closely associated with the work of Seligman and Csikszentmihalyi (2000), interest in authentic, ethical and servant leadership has mounted, capturing the attention of students, scholars, consultants, executive trainers and practising managers today.

REVIEW QUESTIONS

1. What specific traits did early trait-based leadership research show to have positive correlations with either leader behaviour or leader emergence?

2. What two basic behavioural orientations did the University of Michigan and Ohio State University studies have in common?

3. Explain how, in your view, a manager might alter his or her leadership style from a 5,5 position to a 9,9 position on the leadership grid. How challenging do you think achieving this change would be, in practice?

4. What are some criticisms of House's path–goal theory of leadership? To what extent is this theory of leadership still relevant today?

5. Explain why some people consider one or more of the contingency theories of leadership to be difficult to apply in practice.

CASE STUDY 2.3

Jack Ma – Founder and Executive Chairman, Alibaba Group

Jack Ma is the co-founder and executive chairman of China's enormously successful business-to-business web-based company, Alibaba. Considered both charismatic and inspirational, Ma has consistently emphasised a set of core values that have guided his approach to leadership at Alibaba. These values include teamwork, passion, commitment and integrity, and Ma prides himself on championing these values in everything he does. Teamwork is particularly important to Ma. He attributes the success of his organisation to the cooperative spirit that the company has carefully nurtured and developed from its beginnings. He believes that teamwork enables ordinary people to do extraordinary things.

Heralded by some business commentators as China's answer to Steve Jobs, Ma was born in Zhejiang Province, China in 1964. He had a deep interest in English language from an early age and took every opportunity to practise his spoken English with international business representatives. For nine years, he acted as an informal tour guide for English-speaking guests at a hotel close to his home, so that he could engage executives in conversation and improve his own vocabulary and pronunciation. In 1988, Ma graduated with a BA in English from Hangzhou Teacher's College, and went on to lecture in English and International Trade at Hangzhou Dianzi University (Liu & Avery, 2009).

During a visit to the United States in 1995, where he acted as interpreter for a Chinese trade delegation, Ma observed the early power and reach of the Internet. When he got a chance to play around on it one evening, he was very surprised to find absolutely no content relating to China. Upon returning home, Ma began creating his own Chinese webpages and quickly started to receive email enquiries from interested individuals. This prompted him in April 1995 to launch China's first Internet company, China Yellow Pages, which developed professional websites for businesses. Within the first three years, his company had generated an income stream of just under US$1 million (Rose, 2015).

In 1998, Ma became the director of an IT company established by the Chinese Ministry of Foreign Trade and Economic Cooperation. In 1999, he resigned from that position to start his own business-to-business web-based company, and Alibaba was created. Despite the enormous difficulties the firm encountered in its early years, the company survived by attracting more than US$25 million in venture capital investment (Liu & Avery, 2009). This early growth period was nevertheless a painful time for Ma, who struggled with challenges such as the need to make substantial layoffs (Alibaba News, 2009).

By 2003, Alibaba's fortunes had begun to reverse. The outbreak of SARS greatly restricted domestic commercial travel within China, but significantly boosted the demand for e-commerce transactions, lifting Alibaba's business traffic considerably (Davidson, 2009). The company's growing profits enabled Ma to invest some of the capital in launching China's equivalent to eBay: an online auction business, Taobao, which targeted ordinary consumers. This was paired with a newly developed online payment platform called Alipay, offering similar services to PayPal (Rusli, 2011).

In 2005, Ma bought out Yahoo! China, which brought in more than US$1 billion in investment for Alibaba. In the same year, *Fortune* nominated him as one of the 25 most powerful businesspeople in Asia. Just three years later, Ma's unique leadership style had captured the attention of international business analysts. In 2008, he was nominated by *Barron's Investment Magazine* as one of the world's 30 best CEOs, winning widespread recognition for his energetic and enthusiastic leadership. In 2009, *Time Magazine* nominated Ma as one of the 100 most influential people in the world, paying tribute to his visionary leadership (Ignatius, 2009). In a candid interview, Ma explained his three-pronged growth strategy for Alibaba: 'Win eBay, buy Yahoo, and stop Google' (Gallardo, 2015). In 2010, Google pulled out of China, leaving behind an online market that was more than twice the size of their US customer base (Waddell, 2016). This move meant that Ma had achieved all three of his key strategic intentions.

Ma has an overriding sense of mission to change the way business is conducted in China and to restore his country's sense of pride and culture. He sees Chinese businesses as being responsible for setting a vision for improving the lives of all employees as well as the greater community (Gallardo, 2015). Alibaba employees see him as highly approachable and easy to relate to. When he visits his employees in their offices, he likes to joke and lighten the mood for them, often handing out spray-cans of silly string. Although he is both tenacious and persistent, for Ma work should not be all-consuming, as he has said on several occasions:

> We are born here not to work but to enjoy life. We are here to make things better for one another … if you are spending your whole life working, you will certainly regret it (Kux, 2016).

Ma considers authentic leadership one of the most crucial aspects of successful organisations today. It is not about uniting an organisation under the vision of a single person but about uniting people in service to a common goal; the vision is far more important than the leader.

Ma's broader vision is for China to become a leader in the e-commerce world (Popovic, 2014). In September 2014, Alibaba raised more than US$25 billion in an initial public offering on the New York Stock Exchange, making it one of the most valuable Internet companies globally (China National News, 2014). Ma currently serves as Executive Chairman of the Alibaba Group, having stepped down from the role of CEO in 2013.

Alibaba is a holding company with 10 major subsidiaries including Alibaba.com, Alibaba Cloud Computing, Taobao.com, Tmall.com, Juhuasuan.com, 1688.com, AliExpress, Ant Financial Services (which includes Alipay), Cainiao Logistics Network and Alimama, a marketing technology platform. The holding company is governed by a 30-member steering committee consisting of managers from the Alibaba Group. Ma explains that this structure enables the team of executives to collaborate better and to avoid the pitfalls of bureaucracy. He says it permits the businesses to focus on long-term growth, rather than getting caught up in short-term shareholder interests. Nine of the 30 governing members are women. Alibaba Group thus has a better gender balance in its corporate leadership team than either Google or Twitter (McGregor, 2014).

Critical thinking questions

1. How would you describe Jack Ma's approach to leadership? Is it an approach that others might easily copy and adopt? Explain your answer.
2. What might explain the relatively high proportion of female executives on the Alibaba Group's steering committee? What advantages might this give the organisation?
3. Is Ma a positive role model for leaders today? Give reasons to support your answer.

REFERENCES

Alibaba News (2009). An interview with Jack Ma. *Alibaba News Report*, 6 December.

Ayman, R., Chemers, M.M. & Fiedler, F.E. (1995). The contingency model of leadership effectiveness: Its levels of analysis. *Leadership Quarterly*, 6(2), 147–67.

Barbero, A. (2004). *Charlemagne: Father of a continent*. London: Folio Society.

Bass, B.M. (1990). *Bass and Stogdill's handbook of leadership: Theory, research and managerial applications*. New York, NY: Free Press.

Belstrom, K. (2015). Fortune's most powerful women list. *Fortune*, 15 September.

Blake, R.R. & McCanse, A.A. (1991). *Leadership dilemmas: Grid solutions*. Houston, TX: Gulf Publishing Company.

Blake, R.R. & Mouton, J.S. (1964). *The managerial grid*. Houston, TX: Gulf Publishing Company.

—— (1978). *The new managerial grid*. Houston, TX: Gulf Publishing Company.

—— (1985). *The managerial grid III*. Houston, TX: Gulf Publishing Company.

Blanchard, K.H. (1985). *SLII: A situational approach to managing people*. Escondido, CA: Blanchard Training and Development.

—— (2007). *Leading at a higher level*. Upper Saddle River, NJ: Prentice Hall.

Blanchard, K.H., Zigarmi, D. & Nelson, R. (1993). Situational leadership after 25 years: A retrospective. *Journal of Leadership Studies*, 1(1), 22–36.

Blanchard, K.H., Zigarmi, P. & Zigarmi, D. (1985). *Leadership and the one minute manager: Increasing effectiveness through situational leadership*. New York, NY: William Morrow.

Caesar, J. (1982). *The Conquest of Gaul*. Harmondsworth, UK: Penguin.

China National News (2014). IPO launch of Alibaba pushed back by a week. *China National News*, 1 September.

Conger, J.A. (1993). Max Weber's conceptualization of charismatic authority: Its influence on organizational research. *Leadership Quarterly*, 3–4, 277–88.

Cox, C.M. (1926). *The early mental traits of three hundred geniuses*. Stanford, CA: Stanford University Press.

Davidson, A. (2009). *1000 CEOs*. London: Dorling Kindersley.

Dinh, J. & Lord, R. (2012). Implications of the dispositional and process views of traits for individual difference research in leadership. *Leadership Quarterly*, 23, 651–69.

Drake, R.M. (1944). A study of leadership. *Character and Personality*, 12, 285–89.

Drucker, P. (1954). *The practice of management*. New York, NY: Harper & Brothers.

—— (1964). *Managing for results*. New York, NY: Harper & Row.

—— (1966). *The effective executive*. New York, NY: Harper Collins.

Fayol, H. (1917). *Administration industrielle et generale: Prevoyance, organisation, commandement, coordination, controle*. Paris: H. Dunod et E. Pinat.

Fernandez, C.F. & Vecchio, R.P. (1997). Situational leadership theory revisited: A test of an across-jobs perspective. *Leadership Quarterly*, 8(1), 67–84.

Fiedler, F.E. (1967). *A theory of leadership effectiveness*. New York, NY: McGraw-Hill.

—— (1978). The Contingency Model and the dynamics of the leadership process. *Advances in Experimental Social Psychology*, 11, 59–112.

—— (1993). The leadership situation and the black box in contingency theories. In M.M. Chemers & R. Ayman (eds), *Leadership, theory, and research: Perspectives and directions* (pp. 1–28). New York, NY: Academic Press.

—— (1995a). Cognitive resources and leadership performance. *Applied Psychology: An International Review*, 44(1), 5–28.

—— (1995b). Reflections by an accidental theorist. *Leadership Quarterly*, 6(4), 453–61.

Fiedler, F.E. & Chemers, M.M. (1974) *Leadership and effective management*. Glenview, IL: Scott, Foresman.

—— (1982). *Improving leadership effectiveness: The leaders match concept*, 2nd edn. New York, NY: Wiley.

Fiedler, F.E. & Garcia, J.E. (1987). *New approaches to leadership: Cognitive resources and organisational performance*. New York, NY: Wiley.

Fox, R.L. (1997). *Alexander the Great*. London: Folio Society.

Gallardo, L. (2015). Four lessons in leadership from Jack Ma, CEO of Alibaba. Linkedin article, 6 February. Retrieved from: www.linkedin.com/pulse/4-lessons-leadership-from-jack-ma-ceo-alibaba-luis-gallardo.

Giampetro-Meyer, A., Brown, T., Browne, M. & Kubasek, N. (1998). Do we really want more leaders in business? *Journal of Business Ethics*, 17, 1727–36.

Goodenough, F.L. (1930). Inter-relationships in the behaviour of young children. *Child Development*, 1, 29–48.

Graeff, C.F. (1983). The situational leadership theory: A critical review. *Academy of Management Review*, 8, 285–96.

—— (1997). Evolution of situational leadership theory: A critical review. *Leadership Quarterly*, 8(2), 153–70.

Greenleaf, R.K. (1977). *Servant leadership*. New York, NY: Paulist Press.

Harter, S. (2002). Authenticity. In C.R. Snyder & S.J. Lopez (eds), *Handbook of positive psychology* (pp. 382–94). Oxford: Oxford University Press.

Hersey, P. & Blanchard, K.H. (1982). *Management of organizational behaviour: Utilizing human resources*, 4th edn. Englewood Cliffs, NJ: Prentice Hall.

Hersey, P., Blanchard, K.H. & Johnson, D. (2001). *Management of organizational behaviour: Leading human resources*, 8th edn. Englewood Cliffs, NJ: Prentice Hall.

House, R.J. (1971). A path–goal theory of leader effectiveness. *Administrative Science Quarterly*, 16(3), 321–28.

—— (1996). Path–goal theory of leadership: Lessons, legacy, and a reformulated theory. *Leadership Quarterly*, 7(3), 323–52.

House, R.J. & Dressler, G. (1974). The path–goal theory of leadership: Some post hoc and ad hoc tests. In L. Hunt & L. Larson (eds), *Contingency approaches in leadership* (pp. 29–55). Carbondale: Southern Illinois University Press.

House, R.J. & Mitchell, R.R. (1974). Path–goal theory of leadership. *Journal of Contemporary Business*, 3, 81–97.

Hunt, J. (2010). Leadership style orientations of senior executives in Australia. *Journal of the American Academy of Business, Cambridge*, 16(1), 207–17.

Ignatius, A. (2009). The 2009 TIME 100: Jack Ma. *TIME*, 30 April.

Jenkins, W.O. (1947). A review of leadership studies with particular reference to military problems. *Psychological Bulletin*, 44, 54–79.

Judge, T., Bono, J., Ilies, R. & Gerhardt, M. (2002). Personality and leadership: A qualitative and quantitative review. *Journal of Applied Psychology*, 87(4), 765–80.

Kanigel, R. (1997). *The one best way: Frederick Winslow Taylor and the enigma of efficiency*. New York, NY: Viking.

Kell, J. (2016). Pepsico CEO Indra Nooyi Joins Trump's Business Council. *Fortune*, 14 December.

Kennedy, J.K. (1982). Middle LPC leaders and the contingency model of leader effectiveness. *Organizational Behaviour and Human Performance*, 30, 1–14.

Khoo, H.S. & Burch, G. (2008). The 'dark side' of leadership personality and transformational leadership: An exploratory study. *Personality and Individual Differences*, 44(1), 86–97.

Kiersch, C.E. & Byrne, Z.S. (2015). Is being authentic being fair? Multilevel examination of authentic leadership, justice, and employee outcomes. *Journal of Leadership and Organizational Studies*, 22, 292–303.

Kux, S. (2016). Eight keys to success from Jack Ma, self-made billionaire and CEO of Alibaba. *Lifehack – Work*. Retrieved from: www.lifehack.org/articles/work/8-keys-success-from-jack-self-made-billionaire-and-ceo-alibaba.html.

Lewin, K. (1999). Psychology and the process of group living (1943). In M. Gold (ed.), *The complete social scientist: A Kurt Lewin reader* (pp. 333–45). Washington, DC: American Psychological Association.

Lewin, K., Lippitt, R. & White, R. (1939). Patterns of aggressive behaviour in experimentally created social climates. *Journal of Sociology*, 10, 271–99.

Lewin, T. (2010). *The invasion of Britain by Julius Caesar*, 2nd edn. London: Longman, Green, Longman & Roberts.

Ling, Q., Liu, F. & Wu, X. (2017). Servant versus authentic leadership: Assessing effectiveness in China's hospitality industry. *Cornell Hospitality Quarterly*, 58(1), 53–68.

Liu, S. & Avery, M. (2009). *Alibaba: The inside story behind Jack Ma and the creation of the world's biggest online marketplace*. New York, NY: HarperCollins.

Lord, R.G., DeVader, C.L. & Alliger, G.M. (1986). A meta-analysis of the relation between personality traits and leadership perceptions: An application of validity generalization procedures. *Journal of Applied Psychology*, 71, 402–10.

Luthans, F. (2002). Positive organizational behaviour: Developing and managing psychological strengths. *Academy of Management Executive*, 16(1), 57–72.

Machiavelli, N. (2007). *Niccolo Machiavelli's The Prince on the art of power*. London: Duncan Baird Publishers.

Maccoby, M. (2000). Narcissistic leaders. *Harvard Business Review*, 78, 68–77.

—— (2007). *Narcissistic leaders: Who succeeds and who fails*. Random House, 1–300.

Martin, T.R. & Blackwell, C.W. (2012). *Alexander the Great: The story of an ancient life*. New York, NY: Cambridge University Press.

Mayer, D., Bardes, M. & Piccolo, R. (2008). Do servant leaders help satisfy follower needs? An organizational justice perspective. *European Journal of Work and Organizational Psychology*, 17, 180–97.

McClelland, D.C. & Burnham, D.H. (1995). Power is the great motivator. *Harvard Business Review*, 73, 126–39.

McGregor, D. (1960). *The human side of enterprise*. New York, NY: McGraw-Hill.

McGregor, J. (2014). Five things to know about Alibaba's leadership. *Washington Post*, 18 September.

McShane, S., Olekalns, M., Newman, A. & Travaglione, T. (2016). *Organisational behaviour: Emerging knowledge, global insights*, 5th Asia–Pacific edn. North Ryde, NSW: McGraw-Hill.

Metcalf, H.C. & Urwick, L. (1940). *Dynamic administration: The collected papers of Mary Parker Follett*. New York, NY: Harper & Brothers.

Middleton, W.C. (1941). Personality qualities predominant in campus leaders. *Journal of Social Psychology*, 13, 199–210.

Mitchell, T.R. (1974). Expectancy models of job satisfaction, occupational preference, and effort: A theoretical, methodological, and empirical appraisal. *Psychological Bulletin*, 81, 1053–77.

Mitchell, T.R., Symser, C.M. & Weed, S.E. (1975). Locus of control: Supervision and work satisfaction. *Academy of Management Journal*, 18, 623–30.

Northouse, P.G. (2016). *Leadership: Theory and practice*, 7th edn. Thousand Oaks, CA: SAGE.

Osborn, R.N. (1974). Discussant comments. In J.G. Hunt & L.L. Larson (eds.), *Contingency approaches to leadership* (pp. 56–59). Carbondale: Southern Illinois University Press.

Paulhus, D.L. & Williams, K.M. (2002). The dark triad of personality: Narcissism, Machiavellianism, and psychopathy. *Journal of Research in Personality*, 36(6), 556–63.

Pernoud, R., Clin, N.V. & Wheeler, B. (1999). *Joan of Arc: Her story*. New York, NY: St Martin's Press.

Peters, L.H., Hartke, D.D. & Pohlman, J.T. (1985). Fiedler's contingency theory of leadership: An application of the meta-analysis procedures of Schmidt and Hunter. *Psychological Bulletin*, 97, 274–85

Popovic, S. (2014). Jack Ma: The man leading the Chinese e-commerce market. *Hot Topics*, 4 May.

Ressick, C., Whitman, D., Weingarden, S. & Hiller, N. (2009). The bright side and dark side of CEP personality: Examining core and self evaluations, narcissism, transformational leadership and strategic influence. *Journal of Applied Psychology*, 94(6), 1365–81.

Rose, C. (2015). Alibaba's Jack Ma on early obstacles, his ambitions. *Bloomberg*, 29 January.

Rosenthal, S.A. & Pittinsky, T. (2006). Narcissistic leadership. *Leadership Quarterly*, 17(6), 617–33.

Rusli, E. (2011). Yahoo and Alibaba resolve Alipay dispute. *New York Times*, 29 July.

Shartle, C.L. (1951). Leader behaviour in jobs. *Journal of Counselling and Development*, 30(3), 164–6.

Schein, E. (2010). *Organizational culture and leadership*, 2nd edn. San Francisco, CA: Jossey-Bass.

Schriesheim, C.A. & Neider, L.L. (1996). Path–goal leadership theory: The long and winding road. *Leadership Quarterly*, 7 (3), 317–21.

Schriesheim, J.R. & Schriesheim, C.A. (1980). A test of the path–goal theory of leadership and some directions for future research. *Personnel Psychology*, 33, 349–70.

Seligman, M.D. & Csikszentmihalyi, M. (2000). Positive psychology. *American Psychologist*, 55, 5–14.

Sellers, P. (2012). Forbes magazine's list of the world's 100 most powerful women. *Forbes*, 2 October.

Sharma, M. & Kumar, A. (2016). Indra Nooyi: Woman of focus. *Asia One*, October–November, 60–3.

Smith, J. (1998). The enduring legacy of Elton Mayo. *Human Relations*, 51(3), 221–49.

Sokol, M. (2017). The strategic leader's roadmap: 6 steps for integrating leadership and strategy. *People and Strategy*, 40(1), 58–60.

Stinton, J.E. & Johnson, R.W. (1975). The path–goal theory of leadership: A partial test and suggested refinement. *Academy of Management Journal*, 18, 242–52.

Stogdill, R.M. (1948). Personal factors associated with leadership: A survey of the literature. *Journal of Psychology*, 25, 35–71.

—— (1974). *Handbook of leadership: A survey of theory and research*. New York, NY: Free Press.

Strube, M.J. & Garcia, J.E. (1981). A meta-analytic investigation of Fiedler's contingency model of leadership effectiveness. *Psychological Bulletin*, 90, 307–21.

Sward, K. (1933). Temperament and direction of achievement. *Journal of Social Psychology*, 4, 406–29.

Taylor, F.W. (1911). *The principles of scientific management*. New York, NY: Harper & Row.

Thompson, G. & Vecchio, R.P. (2009) Situational leadership theory: A test of three versions. *Leadership Quarterly*, 20, 837–48.

Vecchio, R.P. & Boatwright, K.J. (2002). Preferences for idealised style of supervision. *Leadership Quarterly*, 13, 327–42.

Waddell, K. (2016). Why Google quit China – and why it's heading back. *The Atlantic*, 19 January.

Webb, U. (1915). Character and intelligence. *British Journal of Psychology*, 1(3), 99.

Weber, M. (1947). *The theory of social and economic organisation* (1924). Trans. and eds A.M. Henderson & T. Parsons. New York: Free Press.

Wofford, J.C. & Liska, L.Z. (1993). Path–goal theories of leadership: A meta-analysis. *Journal of Management*, 19(4), 857–76.

Yukl, G. (2013). *Leadership in organizations*, 8th edn. Englewood Cliffs, NJ: Prentice Hall.

STYLES OF LEADERSHIP

James Hunt and Martin Fitzgerald

LEARNING OUTCOMES

After reading this chapter, you should be able to:

1. identify the main established leadership styles (autocratic, democratic and laissez-faire) and explain their advantages and disadvantages

2. distinguish between charismatic and transformational leadership styles

3. identify and define leadership styles explained by the dark triad research into personality

4. identify leadership styles that have gained increasing attention from Positive Organisational Behaviour researchers.

INTRODUCTION

THIS CHAPTER INTRODUCES a range of leadership styles, commencing with the earliest established distinctions between autocratic, democratic and laissez-faire approaches. The advantages and disadvantages of each style are outlined, and the conditions under which each style is likely to be most effective are presented. Tannenbaum and Schmidt's (1958) leadership continuum is explained, and its usefulness as a reflective tool for managers is discussed.

This chapter also provides a detailed coverage of the charismatic and transformational leadership styles, pointing out their similarities and differences. The leadership styles described in brief in Chapter 2 are investigated further in this chapter: first, the dark triad of personality (narcissism, Machiavellianism and psychopathy), and then servant leadership and authentic leadership, building on research in the field of Positive Organisational Behaviour (POB). The chapter concludes with an overview of psychologist Daniel Goleman's six leadership styles, along with an indication of how each impacts an organisation's climate.

EARLY CONCEPTIONS OF LEADERSHIP STYLES

The way in which individual leaders deal with and relate to their followers can vary significantly. Most leaders, however, show some measure of consistency and regularity over time in their interactions with followers, giving rise to noticeable patterns of behaviour. These behavioural consistencies enable others to interpret the leader's modus operandi or preferred way of doing things – their leadership style. Terms such as 'authoritarian', 'militaristic' and 'dictatorial' are often used to describe leaders who exhibit a pattern of behaviours that highlights their desire for order and control. Such leaders are commonly referred to as having an autocratic leadership style. In contrast, terms such as 'consensus-seeking', 'empowering' and 'employee-centred' are frequently used to describe leaders who adopt a more inclusive approach in their interactions with subordinates. These leaders are typically referred to as having a democratic leadership style. Other references to leaders in modern organisations include expressions such as 'highly disengaged', 'relaxed', 'permissive', 'in holiday-mode' and 'retired-on-the-job'. These descriptions capture the type of individual who has a laissez-faire leadership style, a term derived from the French expression for 'non-interference'.

Each of these three fundamental leadership styles has profoundly different effects on group dynamics and on individual follower motivation, and each style can produce a different outcome in terms of a team's productivity level. These leadership styles are all readily identifiable in our modern organisations. An account of Lewin, Lippitt and White's early investigations into these three styles is presented below. This is followed by a more thorough explanation of each style, along with an evaluation of the circumstances in which it is most relevant.

AUTOCRATIC, DEMOCRATIC AND LAISSEZ-FAIRE LEADERSHIP STYLES

A landmark study by Lewin, Lippitt and White (1939) produced one of the earliest explorations into the relative effects of different leadership styles on human subjects. These researchers conducted an experimentally controlled investigation into the influences and outcomes produced by **autocratic**, **democratic** and **laissez-faire leadership**. They defined autocratic leaders as highly directive individuals who act in an authoritarian and deterministic manner. Democratic leaders were defined as participative individuals who readily engage group members in discussions and involve them in the decision-making process. Democratic leaders were seen to balance order with freedom. Laissez-faire leaders were defined as individuals who leave group members entirely to their own devices. Figure 3.1 illustrates these three leadership styles, along with their relative emphasis on freedom and order.

Autocratic leadership – A leadership style that emphasises an authoritarian control-oriented approach to dealing with subordinates.
Democratic leadership – A leadership style that emphasises consultation and involvement of followers in the decision-making process.
Laissez-faire leadership – A leadership style that involves minimal exertion of effort by the leader. Subordinates are afforded maximum latitude to determine their work priorities.

Findings from this study indicated that social relations were least aggressive and most conducive to group harmony among subjects led by a democratic leader, whereas subjects who were led by either an autocratic or a laissez-faire leader tended to become involved in more socially aversive behaviour, exhibiting hostility and aggression towards other group members. Although this study was conducted on subjects who were children, the findings were thought to be worthy of further investigation to determine whether they could be generalisable to adult populations in the working arena (White & Lippitt, 1960).

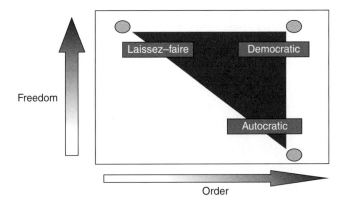

Figure 3.1 Three leadership styles
Source: Lewin et al. (1939)

The autocratic leadership style

Autocratic leaders are individuals who have a strong desire to establish and maintain order and control. They tend to be task-focused rather than relationship-oriented, and are inclined to engage in behaviours that seek to regulate and constrain the actions of their subordinates.

They also tend to have authoritarian personalities, indicating their high regard for the principle of obedience to those in positions of superior authority. Rank, status, title and formal position are particularly important to them. As leaders in organisations they expect their followers to adhere to their directives without questioning or challenging them. Autocratic leaders are disinclined to interact openly with subordinates in a participative manner, preferring to limit their exchanges to providing direction and maintaining control. They are often highly assertive individuals who can be uncompromising disciplinarians and domineering in their desire to assert their will over others. These leaders can be highly effective in situations where they have superior knowledge and experience in comparison to their followers, but tend to be resented when leading very experienced and highly competent teams. Examples of leaders with an autocratic propensity from today's business world include Rupert Murdoch, Bill Gates and the late Kerry Packer. Table 3.1 provides an overview of the advantages and disadvantages of this leadership style.

Table 3.1   Advantages and disadvantages of autocratic leadership

Advantages	Disadvantages
Enables fast, decisive action to be taken	Fails to draw out follower suggestions and insights into problems and issues
Useful when decision urgency is high, for example in times of crisis	May be viewed as overly constraining and restrictive by followers
Useful when a team or group is new and diverse and therefore requires initial direction and the setting of clear parameters	Not useful when dealing with highly motivated experts who expect input into the decision-making process
Particularly useful when the situation is complex and when the leader has far greater experience and expertise than followers	Misses the opportunity to build a climate of openness and support

The democratic leadership style

Democratic leaders tend to be lower on uncertainty-avoidance than autocrats, and typically have non-authoritarian personalities. This enables them to feel comfortable adopting a participative approach to leading others, readily seeking the ideas and opinions of followers and involving them in the decision-making process. Democratic leaders have been shown to be far more objective in their evaluations of follower performance than their autocratic counterparts, and tend not to play favourites to the same degree that autocratic leaders do (Korten, 1962, p. 226). Democratic leaders are often adept consensus-builders. This stems from their inclination to seek consensus in the first place, to build motivation and heighten commitment on the part of their followers. They value collective effort and typically enjoy working with rather than above their subordinates. Richard Branson typifies this approach. Often described as people-centred leaders, effective exponents of the democratic style use their interpersonal skills to encourage employees to willingly exert effort and assume responsibility. This style of leadership works well when followers are experienced, competent and motivated to contribute. It is a style that is less effective when followers lack experience and require explicit direction. Table 3.2 provides an overview of the advantages and disadvantages of this leadership style.

Table 3.2 Advantages and disadvantages of democratic leadership

Advantages	Disadvantages
Often seen as empowering by followers which can elevate individual motivational levels	May be seen as an inefficient or time-wasting approach to leadership, particularly by those seeking clear direction
Encourages deeper involvement on the part of followers which can lift morale and commitment	Not useful when subordinates lack the experience or expertise to contribute meaningfully to discussions or decisions
Enables a greater array of ideas and suggestions to be put on the table, thereby expanding the decision options available to the leader	Not useful when a decision is urgent and needs to be made immediately
Affords opportunities to build a climate of cooperative effort that is conducive to mutual support among followers	Not useful when a group is deeply divided or suspicious and disinclined to discuss issues openly

Comparing autocratic and democratic leadership styles

Table 3.3 provides a summary of the contrasting behaviours exhibited by autocratic and democratic leaders. Early conceptualisations of these two leadership styles treated them as separate and distinctive modes of action, determined predominantly by the disposition and value preferences of the leader.

Table 3.3 A comparison of autocratic and democratic leadership behaviours

Autocratic leadership	Democratic leadership
All policies are determined solely by the group leader	All policies are a matter for group discussion and decision, which is encouraged and assisted by the leader
Techniques and activity steps are dictated by the leader, one at a time, so that future steps are uncertain	General steps to achieving goals are sketched by the leader, but the leader is likely to suggest alternatives and encourage individual ideas
Leader dictates work tasks and work companions of each member	Members are usually free to work with whoever they choose. Division of tasks is often left to the group to decide
Leader tends to be 'personal' in praise and criticism of the work of each member	Leader tries to be 'objective' in praise and criticism of the work of each member
Leader remains aloof from active group participation, except when demonstrating tasks to members	Leader participates as an active group member without doing too much of the work

Source: White & Lippitt (1960)

The laissez-faire leadership style

Due to the laissez-faire leader's minimal exertion of effort, this style of leadership is generally viewed as less desirable than either of the other styles. In most circumstances, this leadership style is inappropriate and tends to produce significantly reduced levels of performance in followers. There are however some notable exceptions to this. Laissez-faire leadership can be a highly effective approach when certain conditions prevail. For example, when a team comprises highly motivated experts who are clear about their tasks and goals, and when the team members place a high value on mutually supportive behaviour including openly sharing information, a laissez-faire leader can let the team members get on with their job. The leader can also spend time outside the team, potentially acting as a spokesperson or figurehead, networking and winning additional resources for the team. This was precisely how former President Ronald Reagan ran the White House during his eight years in office. He was essentially a figurehead and spokesperson, who left many of the administrative and executive duties to senior members of his White House team, thus practising laissez-faire leadership. Reagan is perceived by some historians to be the most successful and popular US President and leader in modern history.

A related set of behaviours that can enable a designated leader to succeed while adopting a laissez-faire style concerns the dynamic of shifting or fluid leadership. Here, a team adopts a self-organising approach as its principal dynamic, whereby leadership flows to whoever is the most competent and qualified person to lead the project or group at any given time. This self-organising dynamic is particularly prevalent in expert teams. Even where a project manager is given formal authority to lead the team, the exercise of leadership may nevertheless be fluid within the group, which at times can permit the formally designated leader to take a back seat. Consultancy teams, product and software design groups and advertising campaign task forces can sometimes operate very successfully in this way.

The autocratic–democratic continuum

Tannenbaum and Schmidt (1958) put forward a model depicting autocratic and democratic leadership styles along a continuum ranging from boss-centred leadership on the left to subordinate-centred leadership on the right. This model represented an important departure from previous conceptions of autocratic and democratic styles, which tended to view the two approaches as an either-or proposition. These authors developed their model to provoke mangers to think critically about the prospect of adjusting their leadership style to suit a range of circumstances, including the level of capability of their subordinates and the leader's own capacity to alter his or her style in the first place.

Tannenbaum and Schmidt suggested that their model helped to shed light on the question that was present in the minds of many managers of the time: how to be democratic in developing relations with subordinates while maintaining expected authority and control. The authors suggested that different circumstances will present the manager with different degrees of latitude to exercise seven possible leadership approaches, from simply deciding and announcing the decision, at one extreme, through to permitting subordinates to make decisions within limits, at the other end of the continuum.

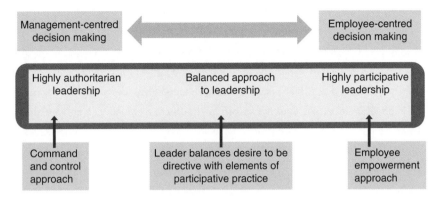

Figure 3.2   The leadership continuum concept from authoritarian to participative leadership

Tannenbaum and Schmidt believed that successful leaders are those who behave according to their own assessment of the prevailing situation. So, in circumstances where direction is called for, the leader would adopt a highly directive approach, and in situations where participative freedom is desirable, the leader would provide that freedom. However, the authors noted, not every manager can use the full range of leadership styles in the continuum, suggesting that leaders need to weigh up not only the confidence they have in their subordinates, but also their own leadership inclinations and their feelings of security when faced with uncertain situations. These researchers referred to the leader's 'tolerance for ambiguity' as an important consideration to be evaluated. In other words, they suggested, for managers with a low tolerance for ambiguity, moving towards the subordinate-centred end of the continuum many not be a viable option. The greatest advantage of this model is that it has strong intuitive appeal. Due to its lack of conceptual complexity, it is readily understood and can easily be applied to the working arena.

Interest in autocratic and democratic approaches to leadership continued for several decades beyond these early seminal studies, and only in the 1980s did research interest shift its focus to other styles of leadership. At the forefront of these new styles were charismatic and transformational approaches to leadership.

CASE STUDY 3.1

Kyle Loades – Chairman, NRMA

Kyle Loades joined the Board of Directors of the National Roads and Motorists' Association (NRMA) in 2005, and served as its Chairman between 2014 and 2017. During this time, he has been active in leading this iconic 98-year old Australian organisation through a period of significant transformation and revitalisation. Working closely with the organisation's new CEO, Kyle has helped to reposition the NRMA by developing the organisation's capability to respond to the needs of its 2.5 million members, while simultaneously unlocking its capacity to anticipate the growing disruption that is prevalent in today's world of enterprise.

As a leader, Kyle is known as much for his foresight and clear strategic vision as he is for his easy-going nature which he blends with a strong determination to achieve results. Drawing on his natural inclination to connect with people at all levels, Kyle has demonstrated a rare ability to effectively align others and build enormous team commitment. He is particularly adept at cultivating a sense of camaraderie in those he leads, through his own enthusiasm and authenticity. Described by followers as down-to-earth, intelligent and consensus-building, his natural instincts and years of experience have won him a reputation for being one of Australia's most successful and most inclusive leaders.

Prior to his tenure as Director and Chairman of the NRMA, Kyle launched and developed his own independent car-broking business, which he ran as a successful enterprise for nearly 15 years. He eventually sold the business to a large listed company, to free up time to devote to community service.

Kyle has, for several decades, been interested in a range of endeavours aimed at improving the quality of community services and infrastructure. An active and longstanding member of his local Surf Life Saving Club in NSW, Kyle served for a time as its President. He has also held the role of Director of the Westpac Rescue Helicopter Service and is a past president of the Hunter Business Chamber. Currently, Kyle serves as Chairman of the Hunter Medical Research Institute.

Kyle's leadership has variously been referred to as energetic, people-oriented, facilitative, deeply engaging and decisive. His capacity to connect with others has enabled him to motivate his followers and to elicit high levels of cooperative effort.

Kyle has complemented his leadership experiences by engaging in formal learning opportunities along the way. While serving as a Director at the NRMA, he also managed to complete his MBA at the University of Newcastle, along with a Disruptive Strategy course at Harvard Business School. Kyle is a Fellow of the Australian Institute of Company Directors, and is currently taking part in a Transformational Management Fellowship course at ANU.

Critical thinking question

How would you describe Kyle Loades's leadership approach, using Tannenbaum and Schmidt's leadership continuum?

CHARISMATIC LEADERSHIP

While definitions of **charismatic leadership** vary in the literature, there is nevertheless an underlying consistency in our understanding of the concept. Identifying the commonalities in these definitions enables us to see charismatic leadership as a useful construct, worthy of deeper consideration. *Charisma* is a Greek word that refers to 'a divinely inspired gift'. In the field of leadership, charisma signals a special constellation of personal qualities that combine to confer on an individual a heightened sense of attractiveness in the eyes of followers, which in turn differentiates them from other leaders. Charisma is an elusive concept in that it is based, as Weber (1947 [1924]) suggested, on the perceptions of others. It is rare that any leader today will be perceived as charismatic by all their followers. Former US presidents Bill Clinton and Barack Obama are cases in point, as is former Australian prime minister Bob Hawke. While these leaders

Charismatic leadership – A leadership style based on the strong personal appeal of a leader who tends to be greatly admired by followers.

were in office, many voters viewed them as charming and charismatic, but equally, each had their vocal critics and detractors. Charismatic leadership theory, then, rests on widespread (rather than universal) follower perceptions of the leader as an extraordinary individual. Weber referred to charismatic leaders as individuals who enjoy a remarkable degree of influence over followers. Charismatic theories of leadership trace this influence to heightened follower perceptions of outstanding or exceptional qualities in the leader.

In the decades following Weber's early work, more current and contemporary ideas and theories have emerged to further our understanding of charismatic leadership (House, 1977; Conger & Kanungo, 1998; Howell & Shamir, 2005). Several researchers have used attribution theory to develop an understanding of the circumstances in which leaders are most likely to be perceived by followers as charismatic. A study by Conger, Kanungo and Menon (2000) found that leaders were viewed by followers as charismatic when the leader:

- articulates a vision that challenges the status quo, but that also fits with follower perceptions of what is acceptable
- is willing to take risks and make personal sacrifices to achieve their vision
- is viewed by subordinates as primarily motivated by concern for others rather than by self-interest
- is viewed as confident, energetic, and enthusiastic
- uses emotive language and passionate appeals to deliver inspiring messages that elevate follower enthusiasm and commitment.

These findings reinforced the conclusions reached in an earlier study by Halpert (1990). This study found that the effects of charismatic leaders on followers were more profound and enduring when the leader was perceived to have both **referent** and **expert power**. Referent power is conferred on an individual who is seen in a positive light. A person who is liked will have some referent power, while someone who is deeply admired or revered will have a great deal of referent power. Both Richard Branson (Virgin) and Andrea Jung (Avon) are seen to have strong referent power, and are often referred to as charismatic. Expert power refers to a leader's capacity to influence others due to their specialist knowledge or abilities. The late Apple CEO Steve Jobs, who in the 1990s returned to lead the company he co-founded after being ousted in the mid-1980s, was seen to have enormous expert power. In the decade after his return, he drew on his expertise to harness collective effort to transform three separate industries, with the introduction of iPhones, iTunes and iPads. Jobs's expert power led some commentators to view him as a charismatic leader who successfully revitalised a struggling corporation.

Referent power – Power that flows to a leader because they are liked, admired, revered or adored by followers.

Expert power – Power that flows to a leader because their followers believe the leader has expertise in a particular area.

Common research themes in charismatic leadership

While various researchers in this field have put forward different definitions of charismatic leadership, there remain several common themes that run through these definitions. First, there is a concurrence that charismatic leaders have strong convictions and high levels of self-confidence. Second, there is a consensus that charismatic leaders are dynamic and energetic individuals. Third, there is an agreement that followers tend to greatly admire and even idolise charismatic leaders (Yukl, 2010). Conger (1989) explains that the common element in charismatic leadership is the very strong influence process that flows from the leader to the followers, one that is based on personal identification. This is to say that followers identify strongly with their leader, to the point where they have a deep desire to please and imitate them. Further research studies (House & Howell, 1992; Conger & Kanungo, 1998) point to several behaviours that they propose are characteristic of charismatic leaders:

- communicating high expectations of followers along with expressions of optimism and confidence in followers
- managing followers' perceptions of the leader, placing emphasis on positive emotions such as optimism, enthusiasm and personal drive
- cultivating and nurturing social identification within the group, so that members develop deeply-held shared values.

Additional behaviours identified in subsequent research by Greer (2005) include the capacity to exercise tact and diplomacy in social settings, and the tendency to engage in self-promoting activities. The first of these behaviours emerges from the charismatic leader's natural ability to read and respond to the emotions of others, while the second stems from a desire to raise personal visibility on the part of the charismatic leader. Tact and diplomacy are the hallmarks of the behaviour of Jack Ma, Ricardo Semler and Oprah Winfrey, while self-promoting behaviours are evident in the actions of both Richard Branson and Donald Trump. All these individuals have been referred to as charismatic leaders at various points in their respective careers (DuBrin, 2010).

Charismatic leaders and the use of narrative

Additional studies (Conger, 1991; Guber, 2007) have noted the potency of charismatic leaders in an era where dictatorial management approaches are increasingly being replaced by inspiring leadership practices. Conger's research (1991) has drawn attention to the prevalence of the use of illustrative anecdotes and analogies by charismatic leaders, as well as their capacity to use language that suits specific audiences. Guber (2007) has shown that the use of 'stories' by leaders to convey meaning is a technique that can accentuate interest in the leader's message and heighten its impact. The famous challenge that the late Steve Jobs issued to Pepsi executive John Sculley, as part of a bid to lure Sculley to Apple, illustrates the power of compelling narrative. When Jobs saw Sculley's hesitation at moving from the global corporate giant Pepsi to Apple – then a fledgling four-year-old start-up – he simply said, 'Do you want to sell sugar water for the rest of your life, or do you want to come with me and change the world? (O'Reilly, 2011).

Evidence from studies by Conger (1991) and Guber (2007) points to the natural affinity that charismatic leaders have for developing expressive and compelling narrative. This research indicates that these leaders frequently use storytelling as a technique to draw attention to their messages, and to throw out compelling challenges intended to motivate others.

Positive and negative charismatic leaders

One of the difficulties presented by various charismatic leadership theories is that they don't necessarily differentiate between what we might refer to as positive and negative charismatics. In history, for example, figures such as Winston Churchill and Adolf Hitler are both considered to be charismatic leaders. Indeed, some charismatic leaders may have both positive and negative qualities, and the impact they have on followers may also range from very favourable to extremely unfavourable. Musser (1987), House and Howell (1992), and Howell and Shamir (2005) all acknowledged this problem, and therefore attempted to establish clear criteria for distinguishing between positive and negative charismatics. They based the distinction on the power motives of the charismatic leader, suggesting that these leaders would gravitate towards either personalised power or socialised power.

Negative charismatics – Leaders who are fascinated by and preoccupied with personalised power.
Positive charismatics – Leaders who develop a sense of devotion to their vision or mission, rather than cultivating personal reverence or adoration.

For these researchers, **negative charismatics** are those leaders who are fascinated by and preoccupied with personalised power. They tend to cultivate and encourage a high level of devotion to themselves as leaders, and they typically use coercion and rewards to manipulate followers and to create strong levels of dependency from them. They sometimes achieve this dependency by overemphasising the magnitude of external threats to their organisation.

By contrast, **positive charismatics** have a socialised power motive. These leaders develop a sense of devotion to their vision or mission, rather than cultivating personal reverence or adoration. Leading through a process of role-modelling and setting a clear example for others to follow are key features of this approach. For them, building commitment to shared values is more important than follower commitment to the leader as an individual.

Potential unfavourable outcomes from charismatic leadership

Research into positive versus negative charismatics has led to the identification of certain actions related to charismatic leaders, and of the unfavourable outcomes that can arise from them (Finkelstein, 2003; Yukl, 2013). For example:
- high levels of reverence and admiration for the leader reduce the likelihood of alternative suggestions and ideas being put forward by followers
- follower desire for acceptance and approval stifles constructive criticism of the leader, preventing possible adjustments to risky strategies

- unrealistic and inflated levels of self-assurance on the part of the leader often prevent necessary corrective or adaptive behaviour
- a leader's attraction to bold, risky undertakings increases chances of overreaching and eventual failure
- a leader's inclination towards non-conformity and impulsiveness can create opposition as well as support.

The biggest limitation of charismatic leadership theory is that it rests largely on the perceptions of followers, and because these perceptions can change over time charismatic leadership presents itself as a somewhat transitory phenomenon (Yukl, 2010). Subsequent research into the relevance and impact of charisma on leadership has tended to treat the concept as one element of a broader pattern of leader behaviour, referred to as transformational leadership.

TRANSFORMATIONAL LEADERSHIP

Transformational leadership is one of the most popular and most widely investigated styles of leadership, as it has been now for some 30 years (Hunt & Fitzgerald, 2014; Northouse, 2016). Once heralded as the new leadership paradigm, it signalled a departure from the longstanding focus on autocratic and democratic leadership styles which had dominated the management literature since the 1940s. Building on the narrower construct of charismatic leadership, the emergence of transformational leadership marked an important turning point in our understanding of leadership practice and helped to rejuvenate the field of leadership research (Hunt, 2010).

> **Transformational leadership** – A leadership style comprising four elements: idealised influence, inspirational motivation, intellectual stimulation and individual consideration.

Transformational leadership represents an approach that emphasises the leader's capacity to elicit extraordinarily high levels of cooperation and commitment from followers. What defines transformational leaders is their capacity to command unusually high degrees of influence over their subordinates, which enables them to elevate both individual and group performances beyond normal levels of expectation (Bass & Avolio, 1990a).

Downton (1973) was one of the first writers to point to the magnifying effect that leaders can have on their followers when they engage deeply with them on an emotional level to articulate worthwhile goals based on deeply shared values. Burns (1978) further developed the concept, using the term 'transforming leadership' to describe the impact that leaders can have on follower engagement. Transforming leaders were seen by Burns to enhance motivational drive in their subordinates by elevating their morale and heightening their levels of aspiration. In other words, these leaders had a transforming effect on their followers' desire to achieve. To illustrate the magnitude of this effect, Burns drew a sharp distinction between 'transforming leaders' and 'transactional leaders', arguing that the latter produced noticeably lower levels of engagement and commitment in their followers. This was attributed to the reduced impact of a less emotionally invested exchange between the transactional leader and her or his followers.

Bass and his colleagues significantly refined these ideas during the 1980s (Bass, 1985; Hater & Bass, 1988; Seltzer, Numerof & Bass, 1989). They put forward the idea that transformational and transactional styles of leadership, although distinct, were not mutually exclusive, instead proposing a single continuum encompassing both. Transformational leadership was therefore conceived as an 'augmentation' of the more routine but necessary transactional leader exchanges that take place on a regular basis.

The four elements of transformational leadership

Bass and his colleagues conducted quantitative studies that enabled the construct of transformational leadership to be operationalised (Seltzer, Numerof & Bass, 1989). Through confirmatory factor analysis, their studies demonstrated that transformational leadership has an underlying four-dimensional factor structure. In other words, transformational leadership could be described by four important defining elements:

1. *Idealised influence*: The leader's inclination and capacity to act as a role model, and to evoke from followers a powerful emotional identification with, and attachment to, the leader, stemming from subordinates' strong feelings of trust, respect and admiration for the leader. This element is akin to charisma.

2. *Inspirational motivation*: The leader's capacity to use emotive messages to express challenging and compelling goals for the future, as well as the communication of high expectations of followers. Inspirational motivation results when these messages elicit enthusiasm from subordinates and produce elevated levels of cooperative effort.

3. *Intellectual stimulation*: The leader's inclination to challenge conventional thinking and to encourage followers to reconsider established ways of doing things. This process heightens follower self-efficacy by stimulating subordinates' ideational fluency (their ability to generate new ideas) and encourages them to develop their capacity for creative problem solving.

4. *Individualised consideration*: The leader's inclination and desire to interact with subordinates as individuals, and to respond accordingly to their unique needs for guidance, support, encouragement and recognition. This enables the leader to create a climate of recognition and acknowledgement, thereby signalling to followers their unique value to the team and to the organisation.

Measuring transformational leadership: The Multifactor Leadership Questionnaire

Bass and Avolio's (1990b, 1995) Multifactor Leadership Questionnaire (MLQ) is a quantitative research tool that has been designed to measure a leader's transformational qualities, and remains the most widely used instrument of its kind in the field of leadership (Hunt & Fitzgerald,

2014, p. 86). Several studies have evaluated the validity of the MLQ (Tejeda, Scandura & Pillai, 2001; Antonakis, Avolio & Sivasubramaniam, 2003), many of them finding support for the clear distinction between transformational and transactional leadership, indicating that they are indeed separate leadership styles (Yukl, 2010, p. 279). However, results from efforts to differentiate between the component behaviours of transformational leadership have not always been consistent in these investigations. This has led some researchers to call for fundamental re-evaluation of the elements that define transformational leadership, and of the construct itself (van Knippenberg & Sitkin, 2013).

Transformational leadership and its influence on followers

Transformational leadership is notable for the strength and impact of its influence on followers (Bass, 1985; Bass & Avolio, 1990a; House & Howell, 1992; Ergeneli, Gohar & Temirbekova, 2007). According to this strand of research, a leader can be called transformational when he or she behaves in ways that influence followers'

- perceived connection to and identification with the leader
- degree of emotional and motivational arousal
- experience of a heightened sense of valence towards the goals or vision articulated by the leader
- sense of self-esteem and self-efficacy
- level of trust and confidence in the leader.

Additional research by Bass and Avolio (1990a), House and Howell (1992), and Polychroniou (2009) suggests that the impact of the influence factors listed above is heightened when transformational leaders articulate and express:

- a convincing pathway towards a better long-term future for the group, team or organisation
- a strong can-do attitude conveying high self-confidence as well as high confidence in followers
- the importance of the mission and goals of the group, team or organisation
- the importance of the collective identity, and conveying the message that the achievements sought can only be attained through collaborative effort
- the personal worth and value of each follower as an individual contributor who is instrumental in helping to realise the broad vision.

On the international stage, individuals such as Nelson Mandela, Mother Theresa, Martin Luther King and John F. Kennedy are often cited as iconic examples of transformational leaders. Many consider that Kennedy's famous line 'My fellow Americans: ask not what your country can do for you, ask what you can do for your country' had a transformational impact on many US citizens in the early 1960s (Humphreys, 2014, p. 115). Similarly, Martin Luther King's 'I Have a Dream' speech is widely regarded as one of the most moving and transformational speeches of the twentieth century. Dr King challenged the values of the day and painted a picture of a better future state in which people would be able to live together in harmony and not be judged solely by the colour of their skin. From our modern world of organisations, global corporate leaders such as Indra Nooyi (PepsiCo), Ricardo Semler (Semco Corporation, Brazil) and Andrea Jung (formerly of Avon) are all considered to be transformational leaders, due to their demonstrated capacity to get the best from their followers. In the Asia–Pacific region, Stan Shih (Acer Computers), Jack Ma (Alibaba) and Gerry Harvey (Harvey Norman) are similarly considered to be transformational leaders due to the positive impact that each has had on their followers.

Limitations of the transformational leadership perspective

While transformational leadership remains the most popular perspective on leadership today, it does have several limitations. The first is that transformational leadership is often defined in terms of its effects on followers, rather than in terms of the specific behaviours that give rise to those effects. The second is that transformational leaders are often defined by their personal characteristics, such as being energetic, visionary, insightful and emotionally intelligent. These personal qualities and characteristics may well be valid predictors of transformational leadership in some cases, but none of them are sufficient in themselves as descriptors of transformational leadership behaviour. The third limitation is that the transformative style is often held up as universally applicable; one that is useful in any circumstance. Bass (1997) has argued, for example, that transformational leadership is applicable across cultures and situations. The theory is limited in that it does not point to the circumstances under which transformational leadership might be most ineffective. Subsequent studies have provided evidence that transformational leaders are less effective in stable organisational environments where change is not required, and that these leaders can have limited impact on teams of highly motivated experts (Yukl, 2010).

CASE STUDY 3.2

Heidi Alexandra Pollard – CEO, UQ Power

Heidi Alexandra Pollard is the CEO and founder of UQ Power, a company that provides specialist coaching and strategic advice to corporate leaders, boards of directors, and human resource professionals. An expert communicator, Heidi has a reputation for being highly empowering, deeply engaging, collaborative, honest, insightful, generous, and authentic in her dealings with others. Her colleagues frequently describe her as a real people-person who is enjoyable to be around. Heidi has built a career and a company around assisting organisations to revitalise their corporate culture by nurturing and developing employee talent and self-esteem.

Heidi completed her Bachelor of Arts degree at the University of Newcastle in 1995, majoring in Communication Studies, before pursuing a corporate career as a public relations manager. In 2003, she was appointed to the position of Manager of Marketing and Public Affairs at a large public-sector institution. Nine months later, she became Director of Communications at WorkCover NSW. At the same time, she completed her Master's degree in Public Relations and Professional Communication at the University of Southern Queensland.

In 2005, Heidi founded Leading Ladies International, an organisation that provides assistance and career advice to female executives. In 2013, she founded UQ Power, a company that seeks to empower professionals in senior positions to excel in their roles as leaders and to foster healthy, productive corporate cultures throughout their working environments.

Heidi works closely with senior executive teams and leaders to help them to understand and enhance their personal communication style. Her wealth of knowledge around the key areas of leadership, culture and branding enable her to empower other professionals to unleash their personal strengths so they can perform at their very best.

Heidi believes that high-calibre employees are not necessarily drawn to companies with the best services or products, but are attracted to businesses that have positive contemporary cultures. She sees culture as an important business enabler:

> In our experience at UQ Power, we've found that a culture of genuine trust, ownership and accountability is the key driver of growth and success in any industry or organisation.

On her corporate website, which provides business-relevant content in the form of videos, podcasts and articles, there is an interview with Sir Richard Branson titled 'Lessons from Necker Island'. In the prelude to this video, Heidi reveals her own views on what is most needed from leaders today:

> What we need is a new era of leaders, expander leaders who resonate at a higher level and who look to be of service to the world around them.

The importance of providing service to others is a defining characteristic that typifies Heidi's own approach to leadership. In addition to her role as CEO at UQ Power, Heidi has served as a foundation member of the Hunter Medical Research Institute (2006–16), chair of the Professional Communicators Network, and director of a group of residential property investors who seek to provide affordable housing for low-income families. In 2016, Heidi co-founded Human Power, which brings together business, government, not-for-profits and the broader community to address issues such as aged care, homelessness, housing and healthcare.

Today, Heidi remains a strong advocate for the importance of health and well-being and works tirelessly with others to create happier and healthier workplaces. Described as an inspirational leader who speaks with authority, conviction and experience in a warm and compassionate way, Heidi's dynamism and energy are infectious. Her desire to serve others and to make a difference in people's lives are evident in the way she conducts herself personally and professionally.

Critical thinking questions

1. What are the defining characteristics of Heidi Pollard's approach to leadership?
2. How would you describe her leadership style?

THE LEADERSHIP ORIENTATION PARADIGM – AN INTEGRATIVE FRAMEWORK

In the leadership literature, transformational, autocratic, democratic and laissez-faire leadership styles remain among the most prevalent and most widely researched, and in our modern organisations each of these styles can be readily observed in practice. Hunt (2017) argues that these four leadership styles can be understood in terms of the relative underlying dispositional drives in the leaders who exhibit them. This is to say that democratic versus autocratic inclinations in leaders may be understood in terms of the strength of the trait of authoritarianism in the leader (Adorno et al., 1950). Similarly, a leader's propensity for transformational practice may be related to the strength of their underlying personal drive and value conviction. This model, referred to as the **leadership orientation paradigm**, provides a conceptual depiction of the four pre-eminent leadership styles, along with a proposed representation of four 'blended' styles; the energetic task-master, the inspiring team leader, the authoritarian bureaucrat and the excessive delegator.

> **Leadership orientation paradigm** – A model comprising four primary leadership styles and four 'blended' styles. The model consists of two dimensions: authoritarianism and personal drive. These dimensions are shown to shape and define an individual's leadership orientation.

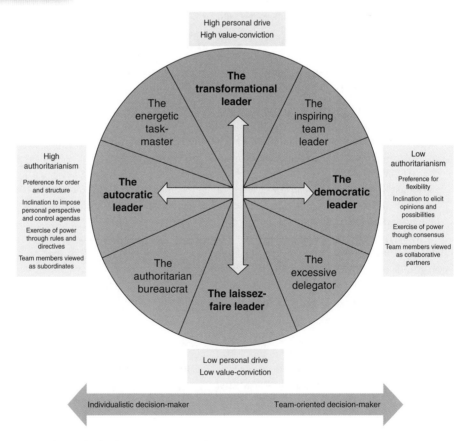

Figure 3.3 The leadership orientation paradigm
Source: Hunt (2017)

This model suggests that transformational leadership need not be viewed as a separate style that has no relationship with any of the other prominent leadership styles. The model draws attention to the fact that some transformational leaders tend to be quite autocratic – the energetic task-masters Steve Jobs and Jack Welch are notable examples. Other transformational leaders are decidedly more democratic in their approach to leadership – the inspiring team leaders Ricardo Semler, Richard Branson, Elon Musk and the late Anita Roddick are prominent examples. Others are neither particularly autocratic nor democratic, and yet they nevertheless show transformational qualities – examples are Indra Nooyi (PepsiCo), and Gail Kelly (formerly of Westpac). The model further suggests that not all laissez-faire leaders will simply be laissez-faire. Some may have an inclination, however marginal, towards either a democratic or an autocratic approach when interacting with subordinates and dispensing with their duties as leaders. This model is useful because it provokes leaders to consider their inclination towards either democratic or autocratic practices, along with their propensity towards either transformational or laissez-faire leadership behaviours. The model suggests that by considering these two 'orientations' simultaneously, a leader is able to gain a much richer picture of their actual leadership style.

THE DARK TRIAD OF LEADERSHIP

The research of Paulhus and Williams (2002) first drew attention to the dark triad of personality, consisting of three distinct but overlapping constructs: narcissism, Machiavellianism and psychopathy (see Chapter 2). Subsequent research by Babiak and Hare (2006), Cohan (2009) and Kets de Vries (2012) has identified the prevalence of these personalities in individuals holding senior corporate positions in contemporary organisations. At the same time, several authors have established connections between dark triad personality manifestations and particular distinctive styles of leadership (Babiak, 2007; Maccoby, 2007; Ouimet, 2010). Each of these styles of leadership is outlined below.

Narcissistic leadership

Narcissism from a clinical perspective is a personality disorder first identified by Ellis (1898) and later refined in successive studies by Freud (1931) and Horney (1939). Narcissists feel a sense of entitlement, dominance, superiority and supreme self-confidence. The narcissistic personality is prone to harbouring delusions of grandeur, cultivating an inflated sense of self-importance, and indulging in self-admiration, combined with a strong desire to be admired by others. Subclinical narcissism refers to narcissistic tendencies and traits that are not sufficiently pronounced to warrant the diagnosis of a clinical personality disorder. It is at the subclinical level that narcissistic personalities typically exhibit behaviours associated with narcissistic leadership in modern organisations.

According to Rijsenbilt and Commandeur (2013, p. 421), narcissistic leaders are selfish, preoccupied with their own ascendance, seized with the acquisition of power and open to using aggression as a means to achieve their goals. These tendencies have led to a disproportionate representation of leaders with narcissistic inclinations at the top of large organisations (Maccoby, 2000; Brown & Sarma, 2007; Ouimet, 2010).

Duchon and Drake (2009) link narcissistic leadership to unethical behaviour and the desire to exploit others. Rijsenbilt and co-authors (2013) have demonstrated that CEOs with high levels of subclinical narcissism are more likely to display deceitful and fraudulent behaviours. They cite Joseph Nacchio (Qwest CEO, 1997–2002) and Jean Marie Messier (Chairman and CEO of Vivendi, 2000–2) as examples of senior executives who displayed clear narcissistic leadership behaviours. Nacchio was convicted on 42 counts of securities fraud, while Messier was forced to resign when it was revealed that he used corporate funds to purchase a $17.5 million private apartment in New York for his own personal use.

Narcissistic leaders in practice

Maccoby (2000) has proposed that there are in fact two types of narcissistic leaders in our modern organisations: productive narcissists and unproductive narcissists. He suggests that productive narcissists can be very successful leaders if they learn to temper the darker side of their personalities and concentrate on their strengths, citing Bill Gates (formerly of Microsoft) and Andy Grove (former CEO and Chairman at Intel) as examples of such leaders. Research by Maccoby (2000, 2004), Rosenthal and Pittinsky (2006), and Ressick and co-authors (2009) have refined our understanding of the narcissistic leadership concept by providing a clearer recognition of the strengths and weaknesses of this leadership style. Table 3.4 provides a summary of these findings.

Table 3.4   Strengths and weaknesses of narcissistic leaders

Strengths	Weaknesses
Very high confidence levels	Poor listeners, remote
Dynamic, energetic communicators	Reduced capacity for empathy
Results-oriented goal achievers	Overly sensitive to criticism
Intense competitive drive	Obsessed with own importance
Willing to take difficult decisions	Lacking in emotional competence
Can engage and inspire followers	Tendency to overreach

Maccoby (2007) points out that narcissistic leaders are generally not comfortable with their own emotions. Although they seek approval and admiration from others, they show little inclination to engage in meaningful or lasting relationships with co-workers or subordinates. They are prone to engaging in exploitative behaviour and can be emotionally distant. They are however, energised by the prospect of success, particularly when it is attached to financial rewards or status gains, and can demonstrate tremendous drive in the pursuit of personal accomplishments. If they can rein in their manipulative tendencies, Maccoby (2000) suggests, narcissistic leaders can achieve great things in organisations, pointing to Jack Welch (former CEO at General Electric) and George Soros (investor) as examples of individuals who typify the strong results orientation typical of productive narcissists. In contrast, Volvo's Pehr Gyllenhammar is an example of an unproductive narcissist (Maccoby, 2000). Gyllenhammar presided over a risky and value-destroying merger with Renault, demonstrating the tendency of narcissistic leaders to overreach. In Australia, examples of destructive narcissists who presided over failed organisations include Steve Iliopoulos (former CEO of the Viking Group), Rodney Adler (former director at HIH Insurance) and Ray Williams (former HIH CEO). All three men were handed jail sentences following convictions relating to corporate criminal offences (Gannon, 2016).

Ultimately, then, the narcissistic leadership style is a double-edged sword. Narcissistic leaders bring with them enormous confidence, great energy, genuine enthusiasm and drive, and a strong desire to accomplish success, all of which can draw people to them. Their energetic disposition means that they have no trouble attracting followers. On the other hand, their desire to succeed can lead to overly aggressive leadership, and their self-centred sense of entitlement can alienate their followers

Machiavellian leadership

Unlike the concept of narcissism, which developed from its roots in clinical psychology, Machiavellianism has its origins in the writings of Niccolo Machiavelli, a sixteenth-century Italian courtier and confidant of the influential Medici family. Machiavelli advocated a set of principles emphasising the use of duplicity and cunning as a legitimate and natural means to acquire and build influence. His ideas centred on the acquisition of power, and he reasoned that the ultimate goal should be considered paramount and that any means necessary might be used to achieve it, including deceit and manipulation (Machiavelli, 2007).

In psychology, Machiavellianism is a term that personality researchers use to describe individuals who are highly manipulative, self-interested and self-promoting, with a corresponding capacity to deal with others in a cool and calculating manner. Machiavellians are not incapable of showing empathy to others when they see it as a way of heightening their influence over them, but are able to suspend such feelings in favour of viewing people for their instrumental value. Machiavellianism is commonly measured using the Mach IV 20-item questionnaire (Christie & Geiss, 1970).

Machiavellian leaders in practice

The Machiavellian leadership style is one that, not surprisingly, individuals with strong Machiavellian personalities readily adopt. This leadership style is often viewed as cynical and unprincipled in its use of intentionally manipulative behaviours to elicit cooperation and compliance from followers. Machiavellian leaders are just as ambitious as narcissistic leaders, but they are far less impulsive, preferring to exercise patience and develop a clear strategy to achieve their end goals. Their higher level of emotional control and their much lower desire to be admired enables Machiavellian leaders to be very calculative in their interactions with others. Research into this leadership style has shown that they move effortlessly between hard (coercive) and soft (ingratiating) manipulative tactics (Jonason, Slomski & Partyka, 2012). They are also less prone to temptation than the other two dark triad leadership styles, which enables them to be more deliberate and cautious in their exhibited behaviours as leaders.

Kessler and co-authors (2010) have demonstrated significant correlations between counterproductive workplace behaviour and Machiavellian leadership. More recent research has shown that Machiavellian leaders are more likely to be involved in white-collar crime than those who adopt a narcissistic leadership style (Furnham, Richards & Paulhus, 2013). The Machiavellian style of leadership is generally viewed as socially aversive, and therefore once identified it becomes unsustainable in terms of harnessing cooperative effort, largely because followers will avoid or abandon leaders they know to be manipulative or deceitful. The prevalence of Machiavellian leaders in today's organisations has been suggested by several researchers (Rauthmann, 2012); however, their ubiquity is difficult to determine, since their duplicitous nature makes Machiavellian leaders highly skilled tacticians adept at concealing their true intentions and identities.

Psychopathic leadership

Psychopathy is a personality disorder characterised by emotional coldness, an incapacity for empathy and high impulsiveness (Black, 2011). While there is a correlation between criminality and clinically diagnosed psychopathy (Skeem & Cook, 2010), at the subclinical level individuals may exhibit certain psychopathic traits and behaviours without being clinically classifiable as psychopaths. Hare and Neumann (2010) have proposed that subclinical manifestations of psychopathy relate to the tendency to exhibit antisocial behaviour rather than criminal behaviour. The term psychopathic leadership, therefore, typically refers to individuals in corporate positions who display subclinical psychopathic tendencies.

Psychopathic leaders in practice

Psychopathic leaders tend to be emotionally void, high on impulsiveness, reckless, manipulative and deceitful. They often come across as being cold, callous, self-centred, exploitative and even parasitic (Babiak, Neumann & Hare, 2010). An important defining characteristic of psychopathic leaders is their emotional distance. They do not typically experience feelings of remorse, guilt or responsibility for the suffering they may cause others (Babiak, 2000; Basham, 2011). This, together with their social boldness, enables them to take tough, even ruthless decisions as leaders, while remaining impervious to the harm that their actions may cause others.

Boddy (2011) notes that psychopathic leadership has established itself in the management literature as a dark, dysfunctional form of leadership that is evident in modern organisations. Babiak and co-authors (2010) have conducted research into the leadership styles of 203 corporate professionals, investigating the prevalence of subclinical psychopathy in these individuals. Their findings indicated that possessing psychopathic traits does not necessarily impede a leader's career path. Further, their survey results showed that those individuals with the highest scores on psychopathy were perceived by others to be high on strategic thinking capability, high on effective communication and high on innovative capacity.

Historically prominent leaders who have been shown to exhibit the psychopathic leadership style include Adolf Hitler and Joseph Stalin. Examples of leaders from the corporate world who have been identified as psychopathic leaders include Richard Fuld (former CEO of Lehman Brothers), Sir Fred Goodwin (CEO of the Royal Bank of Scotland, 2001–09), as well as Bernie Madoff, Ken Lay and Jeffrey Skilling (Basham, 2011; Kets de Vries, 2012; Cranston, 2017).

LEADERSHIP STYLES FROM THE FIELD OF POSITIVE ORGANISATIONAL BEHAVIOUR

The constructs of authentic leadership and servant leadership, together with the broader concept of ethical leadership, have risen to prominence within the fields of Positive Psychology and **Positive Organisational Behaviour** or POB (Luthans, 2002; Cameron, Dutton & Quinn, 2003). This research stream seeks to develop an understanding of how human well-being can be enhanced in modern organisations (Cameron et al., 2003). The heightened attention received by authentic and servant leadership styles over the last 10 years has coincided with revelations of corporate corruption and scandals in organisations at the senior executive level (Avolio & Gardner, 2005; Kiersch & Byrne, 2015). Authentic and servant leadership styles therefore represent a response to the challenges emerging from the prevalence of unethical behaviour in today's business world (Blanch et al., 2016).

> **Positive Organisational Behaviour (POB)** – A research stream that focuses on exploring and understanding ways in which organisations can promote productive, uplifting and healthy experiences and positive social relations. Studies in authentic, servant and ethical leadership form an important part of this research.

Authentic leadership

Authentic leadership stems from the longstanding interest in authenticity in human behaviour, a concept that has roots in the writings of the ancient Greek philosophers (Kernis & Goldman, 2006). Authentic leadership theory proposes that leader effectiveness can be heightened by projecting qualities and behaviours that demonstrate honesty, authenticity and transparency. According to this theory, authentic leaders are individuals who typically have high self-awareness. They tend to use this clarity of self-insight to create open and frank relationships with others, and their co-workers and followers view them as genuine and legitimate leaders (Clapp-Smith, Vogelgesang & Avery, 2009).

The term 'authentic leadership' has its origins in the 1960s, when it was initially used to explore how organisations could develop and establish productive and fruitful relations among employees (Seeman, 1966; Rome & Rome, 1967). More recently, the seminal work of George (2003) and Luthans and Avolio (2003) has fleshed out the authentic leadership concept by aligning it to the emerging body of POB research.

Authentic leadership has continued to develop as a concept to represent the expression of a range of positive leader emotions such as self-confidence, hope and optimism. These are understood to combine favourably with a deep sense of self-awareness, which enables leaders to readily articulate their priorities and values with a level of transparency that in turn lends authenticity to their developing relationships with followers.

Recent scholarship in this field has seen a rapid increase in published works, giving rise to the development of new definitions and theories. Nevertheless, the construct of authentic leadership remains in its early stage of conceptual development. There is greater agreement about the strength of the values and convictions held by these leaders, than there is about their specific behaviours. For example, George (2003) and Gardner and co-authors (2005) posit that authentic leaders engage in behaviours that empower subordinates and encourage follower self-determination, which suggests a participative approach to leadership. By contrast, Avolio, Luthans and Walumbwa (2004) state that authentic leaders can be either participative or directive, depending on the circumstances. According to Shamir and Eilam (2005), specific behaviours cannot easily be used to identify and describe authentic leaders. Rather, they argue, authentic leadership is characterised by a strong self-knowledge and the expression of a clear and consistent value set, which in turn signals relational transparency to others.

While the precise definition of authentic leadership varies from one theorist to another, there is common agreement that at the core of these leaders there is a strong sense of consistency and continuity in their espoused values and in their actions. Authentic leadership theories suggest that it is this 'individual authenticity' that enables these leaders to develop trusting relationships with their followers (Yukl, 2010, p. 344).

Theories of authentic leadership are normative in nature – that is, they all put forward a set of characteristics thought to describe the ideal leader. One such theory is that posited by Walumbwa and co-authors (2008), who have proposed a four-dimensional model that clarifies the foundational elements of authentic leadership and shows how the concept of authentic leadership can be operationalised. The four dimensions of this model are:

1. *self-awareness*: possessing insight into one's own strengths and limitations, and understanding the influence that one's behaviour has on followers
2. *balanced processing*: weighing information objectively and being comfortable seeking advice from followers before taking decisions
3. *relational transparency*: sharing information and being open to full disclosure, as well as being able to express genuine thoughts and emotions with others
4. *internalised moral perspective*: setting definitive standards for moral behaviour and adhering to a clear ethical code of conduct.

According to Avolio and Gardner (2005), authentic leadership is a 'root construct' that underpins a range of leadership styles including charismatic, transformational and servant leadership. Some researchers have suggested that authentic leadership should simply be viewed as an extension of transformational leadership, while others see it as a style that fits within the broader contextual framework of ethical leadership approaches (Yukl, 2010, p. 346). In contrast to this perspective, Ling, Liu and Wu (2017) maintain that authentic leadership is a distinct construct and therefore represents a definitive leadership style.

Measuring authentic leadership

Several instruments have been designed to measure authentic leadership including the Leader Authenticity Scale (LAS) (Henderson & Hoy, 1983), the Authentic Leadership Questionnaire (ALQ) (Walumbwa et al., 2008), and the Authentic Leadership Inventory (ALI) (Neider & Schriesheim, 2011). Concerns have been raised about the generalisability of the LAS, because its creators used only a small and homogeneous sample. The validity of the ALQ has also been questioned since a published paper that reported statistically incorrect results relating to this instrument was retracted (Paulus, 2016). In contrast, the ALI provides a more rigorously developed and substantiated measure of authentic leadership behaviours (Neider & Schriesheim, 2011).

Authentic leadership: A unique and distinctive style

Although still in the early stages of conceptual development, there is now sufficient empirical evidence to suggest that authentic leadership can sensibly be viewed as a unique and independent leadership style (Algera & Lips-Wiersma, 2012; Walumbwa et al., 2008). While authentic leadership may share certain elements that are evident in other leadership styles, it nevertheless represents a conceptually distinct style. For example, authentic leaders do not share the strong altruistic devotion to serving followers that is evident in servant leaders, and their high self-awareness and balanced processing capabilities distinguish them from the sometimes more instinctive styles exhibited by charismatic and transformational leaders.

Servant leadership

Robert Greenleaf (1977) first proposed the concept of servant leadership as a way of helping followers to pursue healthier and more fulfilling organisational lives. His ideas have their foundations in Christian teachings of humility and servitude towards others. For Greenleaf, a servant leader is someone who exhibits qualities such as integrity, selflessness and altruism, and who upholds these ideals when leading others. Greenleaf proposed that leadership is at its most effective when leaders see their first responsibility to be serving and supporting their followers. Unlike authentic leaders, who are true to themselves first, the servant leader sees service to followers as the primary objective in the exercise of leadership. According to this perspective servant leaders are 'enablers' and 'path clearers' who strive to ensure that their followers are supported both psychologically and with the appropriate organisational resources.

For Greenleaf, the ultimate responsibility of the servant leader is to empower followers to willingly take complete responsibility for their work, and to eventually become servant leaders themselves. Greenleaf argued that organisational leaders should adhere to clear ethical principles, and be guided by a moral compass that enables them to determine what is right and wrong. He then proposed that servant leaders must always place the interests of their followers first, even if this might not be in the best financial interest of the firm (Yukl, 2010, p. 340).

Although these ideas have existed in the leadership literature for more than four decades, servant leadership has attracted only marginal interest from researchers until recently. Following the corporate scandals of the early 2000s (Enron, WorldCom, HIH Insurance), and the global financial crisis of 2007–09, with its revelations of widespread recklessness on the part of CEOs internationally, there is renewed interest in servant leadership as a possible antidote to these corrupt practices (van Dierendonck, 2011).

Recent research by van Dierendonck and Nuijten (2011) has helped to operationalise the concept of servant leadership, providing a clearer understanding of its practices and demonstrating its relevance to today's organisational world. These authors position servant leadership beyond its roots in Christian ethics by explaining the concept in broader, secular terms. They identify eight key characteristics that combine to define servant leadership, and have used this as a basis for the development of a validated multidimensional survey instrument designed to measure the construct. The defining characteristics of servant leadership posited by these researchers are:

- *empowerment*: enabling others and developing them to readily take responsibility for their own actions and achievements
- *accountability*: holding themselves and others accountable for achieving worthy and meaningful goals
- *enabling*: resisting the temptation to interfere in the work accomplishments of others, letting others take the credit for their achievements
- *humility and self-awareness*: rejecting the trappings of hubris, shunning self-glorifying behaviours
- *authenticity*: developing transparent relationships with others, being authentic in communicating with followers
- *courage*: being willing to challenge unjust or unethical practices within the organisation
- *empathy and healing*: understanding followers' needs and concerns through active listening, expressing regenerative psychological messages that promote healing and growth in others
- *stewardship*: focusing on the common good above self-interest, placing primary emphasis on the needs of others.

Recent research (Kiersch & Peters, 2017; Ling, Liu & Wu, 2017) has helped to affirm the view that servant leadership is an identifiable and distinct style of leadership that can increase follower loyalty and trust in the context of modern working environments. Contemporary examples of servant leaders include James Goodnight (co-founder of the SAS Institute, a software company) and Arne Sorenson (current President and CEO of the Marriott International Group). Goodnight (CEO at SAS, 1976–2011) rejected several highly lucrative acquisition bids for his company, hoping to protect the employee-centred organisational culture that he had helped to build over more than 30 years. Described as utopian by business analysts, Goodnight exemplifies the servant leader's primary concern for the well-being of followers. Arne Sorenson also displays many of the characteristic behaviours of the servant leader. Heading the Marriott Group since 2012, Sorenson has progressively nurtured and developed a culture that has had an uplifting effect on employee morale. As a leader, he sees his primary role as an enabler of employees, seeking to continuously empower them through the creation and preservation of a culture conducive to the provision of service to others.

Yukl (2010, 2013) argues that despite recent developments, servant leadership is still in its infancy as a construct. He suggests that several unanswered questions about this style of leadership remain. The first of these concerns the relationship between personality and servant leadership. Yukl points out that it remains unclear whether certain personalities might more readily practise servant leadership than others. The second question relates to the relationship between organisational culture and servant leadership. According to Yukl, it is uncertain whether servant leadership can exist and survive in aggressive profit-oriented corporations, and whether its expression as a leadership style might be restricted to atypical or unique organisational cultures.

Ethical leadership

Ethical leadership is not so much a specific style of leadership as an overarching philosophical framework. Ethical leadership is a broad approach that helps to define what a leader sees as right and wrong. A leader with a strong ethical code uses this as a guiding set of parameters to underpin their chosen leadership style. Accordingly, ethical leaders may adopt a range of styles, from highly participative and democratic to more directive and even autocratic approaches. Ethical leaders adopt a principled approach to their dealings with others. They tend to have very clear views about what is and isn't acceptable behaviour, and are more likely than other leaders to be outspoken when they sense an injustice has been done, either to themselves or to others. Ethical leaders are also likely to expend considerable effort in maintaining their sense of integrity. They are unwilling to compromise on issues that might challenge their values, and tend to be guided by a strong overarching sense of responsibility to their team, department, organisation and community. Ethical leaders are often seen as favourable role models in contemporary organisations. This is thought to be due to their willingness to actively espouse their core values, and to consciously model desirable behaviours through the consistency of their conduct (Dineen, Lewicki & Tomlinson, 2006). James McNerney, Chairman and CEO at Boeing for a decade up to 2015, exemplifies this approach to leadership. He is widely recognised for his integrity, ethical initiative and effective personal leadership style (Davidson, 2009, p. 85).

GOLEMAN'S SIX LEADERSHIP STYLES

Daniel Goleman (2000) has put forward a model that identifies six distinctive leadership styles, which he links to the emotional competencies of the leader. His model suggests that each leadership style has a clear impact on the organisation's climate, and that the style itself is an expression of the emotional competencies that underpin it. The six styles are:

1. *The coercive style*: The leader demands compliance and emphasises direct control over followers. This style comes from the emotional desire to achieve and to exercise initiative. Emotionally, these leaders have high levels of self-control, according to Goleman's research. His studies found that the overall impact of this leadership style on the organisational climate is negative. (This style is akin to autocratic leadership.)

2. *The authoritative style*: The leader adopts a 'come with me' approach, setting a vision and mobilising effort while seeking to maximise commitment. This is not the same as an authoritarian or autocratic approach. The authoritative style is built on the emotional competencies of leader self-confidence and empathy for followers. Goleman found that this approach has the strongest and most positive effect on the organisation's climate. (This approach shares some similarities with transformational leadership.)

3. *The affiliative style*: The leader puts people first, paying particular attention to increasing morale and building team harmony. This style is based on the emotional competencies of empathy and building relationships. Goleman found that the affiliative leadership style has a strong positive effect on an organisation's climate, second only to that produced by the authoritative style. (This approach is linked to both the democratic style of leadership, and to servant leadership.)

4. *The democratic style*: The leader seeks to involve followers in the decision-making process, encouraging new ideas and building organisational flexibility. This style rests on the emotional desire to be collaborative and to build open relationships. Goleman's research shows that the effect of this style on the organisation's climate is positive, but that it is not as strong as the effects produced by the authoritative and affiliative styles.

5. *The pacesetting style*: The leader sets extremely high-performance standards for followers. This works well for highly competent self-starters but can leave other employees feeling overwhelmed, exploited and stressed. This leadership style is based on the emotional drive to achieve, underpinned by a strong sense of conscientiousness. Goleman found that the overall impact on organisational climate produced by this leadership style is negative. (This approach encompasses elements of narcissistic leadership as well as certain aspects of transformational leadership.)

6. *The coaching style*: The leader focuses on the personal development of followers, and takes a long-term view of building competence within the organisation. This leadership style is based on the emotional competencies of self-awareness and empathy, and is

driven from a strong desire to develop others to be the best they can be. Goleman found that the coaching style of leadership has a positive effect on the organisational climate of the same magnitude as the effect produced by the democratic leadership style. (This approach has some similarities with servant leadership.)

Goleman's model is useful for two reasons. First, it encourages leaders to think about the effect that their leadership style might have on the climate of their team or organisation. Second, it identifies the underlying emotional competencies that drive leaders to express a particular behavioural style of leadership. Goleman's research also posits a range of circumstances in which each leadership style is likely to be effective, and suggests developing the capacity to switch between authoritative, affiliative, democratic and coaching styles (the four styles that he identifies a having a positive effect on organisational climate).

SUMMARY

LEARNING OUTCOME 1: Identify the main established leadership styles (autocratic, democratic and laissez-faire) and explain their advantages and disadvantages.

Autocratic leadership is a command-and-control leadership style, best suited to urgent situations and those where followers require close guidance; it is less appropriate in cases where participative practices are necessary, such as with expert teams. Democratic leadership is a participative leadership style best suited to surfacing ideas and building consensus, and less suited to circumstances where there is a high degree of decision urgency or where subordinates lack the experience to participate meaningfully. Laissez-faire leadership is a hands-off approach to leadership, generally not well suited to a wide range of situations. In cases where followers are prepared to exercise self-direction, this style can sometimes work reasonably well.

LEARNING OUTCOME 2: Distinguish between charismatic and transformational leadership styles.

Charismatic leadership is based on the strong personal appeal of the leader, while transformational leadership is a more clearly defined behavioural style that encompasses not only idealised influence (charisma), but also inspirational motivation, intellectual stimulation and individualised consideration.

LEARNING OUTCOME 3: Identify and define leadership styles explained by the dark triad research into personality.

Narcissistic leadership is characterised by the leader's inflated sense of self-concept which finds expression in a strong drive to achieve along with a sense of entitlement and a tendency to overreach. Machiavellian leadership is characterised by the leader's strong self-serving and manipulative inclinations, including a tendency to be deceitful and exploitative. Psychopathy in leadership is demonstrated by an inclination towards ruthlessness and cruelty. All three dark triad leadership styles are regarded as socially aversive. This means that they are not conducive to creating climates of social harmony, but instead often provoke feelings of wariness and suspicion among subordinates.

LEARNING OUTCOME 4: Identify leadership styles that have gained increasing attention from Positive Organisational Behaviour researchers.

Authentic leadership emphasises the leader's need to project a genuine and transparent self-identity to followers, and to therefore develop open trusting relationships with them. Servant leadership places the needs of followers above all else. These leaders see themselves as path clearers and enablers, and have a strong desire to serve their followers.

REVIEW QUESTIONS

1. What are three conditions under which autocratic leadership is likely to be useful? What are three conditions under which this style is likely to be less effective?

2. What are three conditions under which democratic leadership is likely to be useful? What are three conditions under which this style is likely to be less effective?

3. Explain the difference between a charismatic leader who uses personalised power, and one who uses socialised power.

4. Of the four dimensions of transformational leadership, which two do you think are most important, and why?

5. What is servant leadership? Provide two examples of servant leaders from your own experience or your knowledge of historical figures.

CASE STUDY 3.3

Andrew Forrest – Chairman, Fortescue Metals Group

Andrew Forrest is a highly respected businessman and philanthropist admired as much for his leadership in the corporate arena as for his passionate devotion to several humanitarian causes on the world stage. In his 30s, Forrest founded Anaconda Nickel, a company that is now one of Australia's largest mineral exporters. As the former CEO and current Chairman of Fortescue Metals Group, a company valued at A$16 billion, Forrest is one of Australia's wealthiest businessmen, and the nation's leading philanthropist. In 2017 alone, he donated over A$400 million to charitable causes.

Born in Perth, Western Australia in 1961, Forrest was educated at Christ Church Grammar School and the Hale School. He spent his early years working as a jackaroo at Minderoo Station, a property managed by his father, located in the Pilbara region of Western Australia. As a young man, Forrest attended the University of Western Australia, majoring in economics and politics.

Following his graduation, he worked for a time as a stockbroker at Kirke Securities before becoming the founding CEO of Anaconda Nickel. In 2003, he acquired a controlling interest in Allied Mining and Processing, renaming it the Fortescue Metals

Group. The group has dominant interests in the Pilbara region, an area rich in iron ore, with active sites at Mount Nicholas, Christmas Creek, Cloudbreak and Tongolo. In 2007, Forrest further expanded his interests in the mineral resources sector by acquiring Niagara Mining which has operations in Laverton, Western Australia. In 2011, Forrest was named by Ernst & Young as the western region's Entrepreneur of the Year.

Forrest's expansion into the cattle industry began in 2009, when he bought back Minderoo Station. This was the property he had spent time on as a youngster – and which had been sold by his father in 1998 out of necessity, due to insurmountable debt caused by a severe drought. In 2014, Forrest purchased several nearby cattle stations, including Nanutarra and Uaroo, bringing his total pastoral property holdings to more than 7000 square kilometres. The same year, Forrest purchased Harvey Beef, a meat processing firm, for A$40 million. The company is the largest beef exporter in Western Australia, with a significant market in China. In 2015, Forrest purchased two more stations, Brick House and Minilya, lifting his total pastoral land holdings to more than 10 000 square kilometres. In 2017, Andrew Forrest's net worth was A$6.84 billion, making him the sixth richest person in Australia, and placing him in the top 300 wealthiest individuals worldwide (Stensholt & Tadros, 2017).

Unlike many other successful business leaders, Forrest sees no value in the accumulation of wealth, unless the money can be used to improve the human condition. In 2011, it was estimated that he spent more than 50 per cent of his time and energy on indigenous projects. Accordingly, he decided it was time to step down from his role as CEO at Fortescue Metals, while remaining as the Group's chairman. This move freed him up to concentrate on a series of charitable causes and humanitarian endeavours. He has subsequently devoted more and more of his time to these undertakings over the last eight years (Weber, 2011).

As an ambassador to the Australian Indigenous Education Foundation, and co-founder with his wife Nicola of the Australian Children's Trust, Forrest has been able to raise significant sums of money for civic initiatives. This money has flowed into programs designed to improve the lives of others by creating regenerative opportunities for many disadvantaged citizens. As early as 2007, Forrest had donated A$90 million to his children's charity, and in 2013 alone he donated A$65 million towards higher education scholarships in Western Australia. His private philanthropic organisation, the Minderoo Foundation, has donated A$270 million to philanthropic causes since 2001. The A$400 million he donated to charitable causes in 2017 is without precedent in Australia.

Critical thinking questions

1. How would you describe Andrew Forrest's approach to leadership? Is it an approach that might easily be replicated by others? Explain your answer.
2. What is Andrew Forrest's primary motivation in his exercise of leadership on the world stage?
3. Is Andrew Forrest a significant role model for corporate leaders today? Give reasons to support your answer.

REFERENCES

Adorno, T.W., Frenkel-Brunswick, E., Levinson, D.J. & Sanford, R.N. (1950). *The authoritarian personality*. New York, NY: Harper & Row.

Algera, P.M. & Lips-Wiersma, M. (2012). Radical authentic leadership: Co-creating the conditions under which all members of the organization can be authentic. *Leadership Quarterly*, 23(1), 118–31.

Antonakis, J., Avolio, B.J. & Sivasubramaniam, N. (2003). Context and leadership: An examination of the nine-factor full-range leadership theory using the multifactor leadership questionnaire. *Leadership Quarterly*, 14, 261–95.

Avolio, B.J. & Gardner, W.L. (2005). Authentic leadership development: Getting to the root of positive forms of leadership. *Leadership Quarterly*, 16(3), 315–38.

Avolio, B.J., Luthans. F. & Walumbwa, F.O. (2004). *Authentic leadership: Theory building for veritable and sustained performance*. Lincoln, NE: Gallup Leadership Institute.

Babiak, P. (2000). Psychopathic manipulation at work. In C.B. Gacono (ed.), *The clinical and forensic assessment of psychopathy: A practitioner's guide* (pp. 287–311). Mahwah, NJ: Erlbaum.

—— (2007). From darkness into the light: Psychopathy in industrial and organizational psychology. In H. Herve' & J.C. Yuille (eds), *The psychopath: Theory, research, and practice* (pp. 411–28). Mahwah, NJ: Erlbaum.

Babiak, P. & Hare, R.D. (2006). *Snakes in suits: When psychopaths go to work*. New York, NY: HarperCollins.

Babiak, P., Neumann, C.S. & Hare, R.D. (2010). Corporate psychopathy: Talking the walk. *Behavioral Sciences and the Law*, 28, 174–93.

Basham, B. (2011), Beware corporate psychopaths – they are still occupying positions of power. *The Independent*, 29 December.

Bass, B.M. (1985). *Leadership and performance beyond expectations*. New York, NY: Free Press.

—— (1997). Does the transactional-transformational paradigm transcend organisational and national boundaries? *American Psychologist*, 52, 130–9.

Bass, B.M. & Avolio, B.J. (1990a). The implications of transactional and transformational leadership for individual, team and organizational development. *Research in Organizational Change and Development*, 4, 231–72.

—— (1990b). *Multifactor Leadership Questionnaire*. Palo Alto, CA: Consulting Psychologists Press.

—— (1995). *Multifactor Leadership Questionnaire for research*. Menlo Park, CA: Mind Garden.

Black, P. (2011). Fact sheet: The dark triad. *European Association of Psychology and Law*, June, 1–4.

Blanch, J., Gil, F., Antino, M. & Rodriguez-Munoz, A. (2016). Positive leadership models: Theoretical framework and research. *Papeles de Psicologo*, 37(3), 170–6.

Boddy, C.R. (2011). The corporate psychopaths theory of the global financial crisis. *Journal of Business Ethics*, 102, 255–9.

Brown, R. & Sarma, N. (2007). CEO overconfidence, CEO dominance and corporate acquisitions. *Journal of Economics and Business*, 59(5), 358–79.

Burns, J.M. (1978). *Leadership*, New York, NY: Harper & Row.

Cameron, K.S., Dutton, J.E. & Quinn, R.E. (2003). Foundations of positive organizational scholarship. In K.S. Cameron, J.E. Dutton, & R.E. Quinn (eds), *Positive organizational scholarship* (pp. 3–13). San Francisco, CA: Berrett-Koehler.

Cameron, K.S., Dutton, J.E., Quinn, R.E. & Wrzensniewski, A. (2003). Developing a discipline of positive organizational scholarship. In K.S. Cameron, J.E. Dutton & R.E. Quinn (eds), *Positive organizational scholarship* (pp. 361–70). San Francisco, CA: Berrett-Koehler.

Christie, R. & Geis, F.L. (1970) How devious are you? Take the Machiavelli test to find out. *Journal of Management in Engineering*, 15(4), 17.

Clapp-Smith, R., Vogelgesang, G.R., & Avery, J.B. (2009). Authentic leadership and positive psychological capital: The mediating role of trust at the group level of analysis. *Journal of Leadership and Organizational Studies*, 15, 227–40.

Cohan. W.D. (2009). *House of cards: A tale of hubris and wretched excess on Wall Street*. New York, NY: Doubleday.

Conger, J.A. (1989). *The charismatic leader: Behind the mystique of exceptional leadership*. San Francisco, CA: Jossey-Bass.

—— (1991). Inspiring others: The language of leadership. *Academy of Management Executive*, February, 39, 31–45.

Conger, J.A. & Kanungo, R.N. (1998). *Charismatic leadership in organisations*. Thousand Oaks, CA: SAGE Publications.

Conger, J.A., Kanungo, R.N. & Menon, S.T. (2000). Charismatic leadership and follower effects. *Journal of Organizational Behavior*, 21, 747–67.

Cranston, K. (2017). Which of our leaders are psychopaths? A voter and shareholder guide, *World Post, Online*. Retrieved from: www.huffingtonpost.com/kim-cranston/which-of-our-leaders-are-_b_752833.html

Davidson, A. (2009). *1000 CEOs*. London: Dorling Kindersley.

Dineen, B.R., Lewicki, R.J. & Tomlinson, E.C. (2006). Supervisory guidance and behavioural integrity: Relationships with employee citizenship and deviant behaviour. *Journal of Applied Psychology*, 91(3), 622–35.

Downton, J. (1973). *Rebel leadership: Commitment and charisma in the revolutionary process*. New York, NY: Free Press.

DuBrin, A.J. (2010). *Leadership: Research findings, practice and skills*, 6th edn. Mason, OH: South-Western Cengage Learning.

Duchon, D. & Drake, B. (2009). Organizational narcissism and virtuous behaviour. *Journal of Business Ethics*, 85(3), 301–8.

Ellis, H. (1898). Auto-eroticism: A psychological study. *Alienist and Neurologist*, 19, 260–99.

Ergeneli, A., Gohar, R. & Temirbekova, Z. (2007). Transformational leadership: Its relationship to culture value dimensions. *International Journal of Intercultural Relations*, 31(6), 703–24.

Finkelstein, S. (2003). *Why smart executives fail*. New York, NY: Portfolio.

Freud, S. (1931). *Standard edition of the complete psychological works of Sigmund Freud*, vol. 21. London: Hogarth Press/Institute of Psychoanalysis.

Furnham, A., Richards, S.C. & Paulhus, D.L. (2013). The dark triad of personality: A 10-year review. *Social and Personality Psychology Compass*, 7(3), 199–216.

Gannon, G. (2016). Former Viking CEO jailed for $33.5 m fraud. News.com.au, 9 August.

Gardner, W.L., Avolio, B.J., Luthans, F., May, D.R. & Walumbwa, F.O. (2005). Can you see the real me? A self-based model of authentic leader and follower development. *Leadership Quarterly*, 16(3), 343–72.

George, B. (2003). *Authentic leadership: Rediscovering the secrets of creating lasting value*. San Francisco, CA: Jossey-Bass.

Goleman, D. (2000). Leadership that gets results. *Harvard Business Review*, 78(2), 78–90.

Greenleaf, R.K. (1977). *Servant leadership*. New York, NY: Paulist Press.

Greer, M. (2005). The science of savoir faire. *Monitor on Psychology*, January, 28–39.

Guber, P. (2007). The four truths of the storyteller. *Harvard Business Review*, December, 56. Retrieved from: https://hbr.org/2007/12/the-four-truths-of-the-storyteller.

Halpert, J.A. (1990). The dimensionality of charisma. *Journal of Business Psychology*, 4(4), 399–410.

Hare, R.D. & Neumann, C.S. (2010). The role of antisociality in the psychopathy construct: Comment on Skeem & Cooke (2010). *Psychological Assessment*, 22(2), 446–54.

Hater, J. & Bass, B. (1988). Supervisors' evaluations and subordinates' perceptions of transformational and transactional leadership. *Journal of Applied Psychology*, 73, 695–702.

Henderson, J.E. & Hoy, W.K. (1983). Leader authenticity: The development and test of an operational measure. *Educational and Psychological Research*, 3(2), 63–75.

Horney, K. (1939). *New ways in psychoanalysis*. New York, NY: Norton.

House, R. (1977). A 1976 theory of charismatic leadership. In J.G. Hunt and L.L. Larson (eds), *Leadership: The cutting edge*. Carbondale, IL: Southern Illinois University Press.

House, R.J. & Howell, J.M. (1992). Personality and charismatic leadership. *Leadership Quarterly*, 3, 81–108.

Howell, J.M. & Shamir, B. (2005). The role of followers in the charismatic leadership process: Relationships and their consequences. *Academy of Management Review*, 30, 96–112.

Humphreys, E. (2014). *Great speeches: Words that shaped the world*. London: Acturus Publishing.

Hunt, J. (2010). Leadership style orientations of senior executives in Australia. *Journal of the American Academy of Business, Cambridge*, 16(1), 207–17.

—— (2017). The Leadership Orientation Paradigm II: Assessing leadership styles in the context of dispositional propensities towards authoritarianism and personal drive. *Working Paper Series*, School of Business, University of Newcastle, 1, 1–10.

Hunt, J. & Fitzgerald, M. (2014). An evidence-based assessment of the relationship between emotional intelligence and transformational leadership. *International Journal of Arts and Commerce*, 3(9), 85–100.

Jonason, P.K., Slomski, S. & Partyka, J. (2012). The dark triad at work: How toxic employees get their way. *Personality and Individual Differences*, 52(3), 449–53.

Kernis, M.H. & Goldman, B.M. (2006). A multicomponent conceptualization of authenticity: Theory and research. In M.P. Zanna (ed.), *Advances in experimental social psychology*, vol. 38 (pp. 283–357). San Diego, CA: Academic Press.

Kessler, S.R., Bandeii, A.C., Spector, P.E., Borman, W.C., Nelson, C.E. & Penney, L.M. (2010). Re-examining Machiavelli: A three-dimensional model of Machiavellianism in the workplace. *Journal of Applied Social Psychology*, 40, 1868–96.

Kets de Vries, M.F.R. (2012). The psychopath in the C suite: Redefining the SOB. *INSEAD Working Papers*, 2012/119/EFE. Retrieved from: http://dx.doi.org/10.2139/ssrn.2179794

Kiersch, C.E. & Byrne, Z.S. (2015). Is being authentic being fair? Multilevel examination of authentic leadership, justice, and employee outcomes. *Journal of Leadership and Organizational Studies*, 22, 292–303.

Kiersch, C. & Peters, J. (2017). Leadership from the inside out: Student leadership development within authentic leadership and servant leadership frameworks. *Journal of Leadership Education*, 16(1), 148–68.

Korten, D.C. (1962). Situational determinants of leadership structure. *Journal of Conflict Resolution*, 6(3), 222–35.

Lewin, K., Lippitt, R. and White, R. (1939). Patterns of aggressive behaviour in experimentally created social climates. *Journal of Social Psychology*, 10, 271–99.

Ling, Q., Liu, F. & Wu, X. (2017). Servant versus authentic leadership: Assessing effectiveness in China's hospitality industry. *Cornell Hospitality Quarterly*, 58(1), 53–68.

Luthans, F. (2002). The need for and meaning of positive organizational behaviour. *Journal of Organizational Behavior*, 23, 695–706.

Luthans, F. & Avolio, B. (2003). Authentic leadership: A positive development approach. In K.S. Cameron, J.E. Dutton, & R.E. Quinn (eds), *Positive organizational scholarship: Foundations of a new discipline* (pp. 241–61). San Francisco, CA: Berrett-Koehler.

Maccoby, M. (2000). Narcissistic leaders. *Harvard Business Review*, 78, 68–77.

—— (2004). *The productive narcissist: The promise and peril of visionary leadership*. New York, NY: Broadway Books.

—— (2007). *Narcissistic leaders: Who succeeds and who fails*. New York, NY: Random House.

Machiavelli, N. (2007 [1532]). *Niccolo Machiavelli's The Prince on the art of power*, ed. C. Westhorpe. London. Duncan Baird Publishers.

Musser, S.J. (1987). *The determination of positive and negative charismatic leadership*. Working paper, Mesiah College, Grantham, PA.

Neider, L.L. & Schriesheim, C.A. (2011). The Authentic Leadership Inventory (ALI): Development and empirical tests. *Leadership Quarterly*, 22(6), 1146–64.

Northouse, P.G. (2016). *Leadership: theory and practice*, 7th edn. Thousand Oaks, CA: SAGE Publications.

O'Reilly, T. (2011). Steve Jobs 1955–2011. *Nature: International Weekly Journal of Science*, 479(42), n.p.

Ouimet, G. (2010). Dynamics of narcissistic leadership in organizations: Towards an integrated research model. *Journal of Management Psychology*, 25(7), 713–26.

Paulhus, D.L. & Williams, K.M. (2002). The dark triad of personality: Narcissism, Machiavellianism, and psychopathy. *Journal of Research in Personality*, 36(6), 556–63.

Paulus, S. (2016). Concerns attached to three more papers by retraction-laden management researcher. *Retraction Watch*, 1 April. Retrieved from: retractionwatch.com/category/by-author/walumbwa.

Polychroniou, P.V. (2009). Relationship between emotional intelligence and transformational leadership of supervisors: The impact on team effectiveness. *Team Performance Management*, 15(7–8), 343–56.

Rauthmann, J.F. (2012). The dark triad and interpersonal perception: Similarities and differences in the social consequences of narcissism, Machiavellianism, and psychopathy. *Social Psychological and Personality Science*, 3(4), 487–96.

Ressick, C., Whitman, D., Weingarden, S. & Hiller, N. (2009). The bright side and dark side of CEO personality: Examining core and self evaluations, narcissism, transformational leadership and strategic influence. *Journal of Applied Psychology*, 94(6), 1365–81.

Rijsenbilt, A. & Commandeur, H. (2013). Narcissus enters the courtroom: CEO narcissism and fraud. *Journal of Business Ethics*, 117(2), 413–29.

Rome, B.K. & Rome, S.C. (1967). Humanistic research on large social organizations. In J.F. Bugental (ed.), *Challenges of human psychology* (pp. 181–93). New York, NY: McGraw-Hill.

Rosenthal, S.A. & Pittinsky, T.L. (2006). Narcissistic leadership. *Leadership Quarterly*, 17(6), 617–33.

Seltzer, J., Numerof, R. & Bass, B. (1989). Transformational leadership: Is it a source of more or less burnout or stress? Conference paper presented at Academy of Management, New Orleans, LA.

Seeman, M. (1966). Status and identity: The problem of inauthenticity. *Pacific Sociological Review*, 9(2), 67–73.

Shamir, B. & Eilam, G. (2005). What's your story? A life stories approach to authentic leadership development. *Leadership Quarterly*, 16(3), 395–417.

Skeem, J.L. & Cooke, D.J. (2010). Is criminal behavior a central component of psychopathy? Conceptual directions for resolving the debate. *Psychological Assessment*, 22, 433–45.

Stensholt, J. & Tadros, E. (2017). AFR rich list 2017. *Australian Financial Review*.

Tannenbaum, R. & Schmidt, W. (1958). How to choose a leadership pattern. *Harvard Business Review*, 36(2), 95–101.

Tejeda, M.J., Scandura, T.A. & Pillai, R. (2001). The MLQ revisited: Psychometric properties and recommendations. *Leadership Quarterly*, 12, 31–52.

van Dierendonck, D. (2011). Servant leadership: A review and synthesis. *Journal of Management*, 37, 1228–61.

van Dierendonck, D. & Nuijten, I. (2011). The servant leadership survey: Development and validation of a multidimensional measure. *Journal of Business Psychology*, 26, 249–67.

van Knippenberg, D. & Sitkin, S.B. (2013). A critical assessment of charismatic-transformational leadership research: Back to the drawing board? *Academy of Management Annals*, 7(1), 1–60.

Walumbwa, F.O., Avolio, B.J., Gardner, W.L., Wernsing, T.S. & Peterson, S.J. (2008). Authentic leadership: Development and validation of a theory-based measure. *Journal of Management*, 34, 89–125.

Weber, D. (2011). Andrew Forrest stands down as Fortescue CEO. *ABS News Online*, 1 June. Retrieved from: www.abc.net.au/pm/content/2011/s3233015.htm.

Weber, M. (1947). *The theory of social and economic organisation* (1924). Trans. and eds A.M. Henderson & T. Parsons. New York, NY: Free Press.

White, R K. & Lippitt, R. (1960). *Autocracy and democracy: An experimental inquiry*. New York, NY: Harper & Brothers.

Yukl, G.A. (2010). *Leadership in organizations*, 7th edn. Upper Saddle River, NJ: Prentice Hall.

—— (2013). *Leadership in organizations*, 8th edn. Englewood Cliffs, NJ: Prentice Hall.

4

ETHICS, VALUES AND RESPONSIBLE LEADERSHIP

Mario Fernando

LEARNING OUTCOMES

After reading this chapter, you should be able to:

1. understand the need for responsible leadership

2. develop an awareness of the factors influencing ethical leadership behaviour

3. appreciate why ethical decision making matters in leadership

4. understand moral leadership and virtuous leadership

5. appreciate the real challenges of leading ethically.

INTRODUCTION

IN THE CONTEMPORARY business context, values and leadership are inextricably mixed. Some argue that values are not just embedded in the leadership process, but central to it. Increasingly, unethical corporate practices have been reported across the globe, particularly in the forms of bribery and corruption, fraud, discrimination, sexual harassment and unfair competition. Such practices highlight the disparity between drive to profit-making objectives and social responsibilities. For example, Commonwealth Bank, Volkswagen, HIH, James Hardie, Nike, Enron, JP Morgan, Parmalat and WorldCom have all gained attention and criticism for permitting – or even committing – scandalous behaviour. Due to these and other high-profile corporate scandals across the globe, there has been a growing demand for leadership geared towards responsibility and ethics. Do such instances of corporate misconduct reflect ineffective, irresponsible or unethical leadership? This chapter explores the ethical issues contemporary leaders face in leading business organisations.

THE NEED FOR LEADING RESPONSIBLY

Leading responsibly has emerged as one of the newest forms of leadership that attempts to integrate different notions of responsibility. Some view responsible leadership as old wine in a new bottle. Traditionally, 'good' leadership has been assumed to be responsible. However, responsible leadership seems to place a heavier emphasis on **responsibility**. According to Pless (2007), responsible leadership is a 'values-based and thorough ethical principles-driven relationship' of leaders and stakeholders (p. 438). It is laden with **values** and **ethics**. Maak and Pless (2006) identify responsible leadership as a relational approach to leading, which includes both internal and external stakeholders. The responsible leader is characterised as someone who can excel at developing and maintaining relationships with both internal and external parties to an organisation (stakeholders). They should be able to weave a web of relationships to deliver better outcomes to both business and society.

> **Responsibility** – a requirement of being answerable to someone
> **Values** – at an individual level, values demonstrate what is important in life
> **Ethics** – principles that guide individual activity

Leaders are expected to operate businesses in a responsible manner. Responsibility is attributed to assign answerability for actions in several ways. Role responsibility relates to the role attached to a person; for example, a company's CEO is held liable for harm that the company does during their tenure. Causal responsibility requires one to be answerable to others due to an event like a chemical or nuclear leak into a community. Capacity responsibility assigns answerability based on the person's ability, or capacity, to have influenced the event. Liability responsibility it based on who is determined to be legally responsible in the situation.

In the leader–follower relationship, followers see leaders as role models, and seek to interpret and emulate their actions. Hence, if leaders encourage or overlook unethical behaviour in the workplace, their followers are likely to engage in similar behaviour. So, although leaders may perceive their own actions as harmless, unethical actions that influence their followers could give rise to legal action against a company. The unethical practices of leaders could threaten the survival of the firm and threaten the job security of followers (Knights & O'Leary, 2006). So, leaders have also been asked to follow principles of ethical leadership.

Ethical leadership can be defined formally as the 'demonstration of normatively appropriate conduct through personal actions and interpersonal relationships, and the promotion of such conduct to followers through two-way communication, reinforcement, and decision-making' (Brown et al., 2005, p. 120). Under this definition, corporate leaders are expected to be the custodians of their corporations' **morals**. Due to the continuing spate of corporate scandals and unethical activities in corporations, businesses have lost credibility and trust with society. By leading in an ethical manner, leaders can rebuild the lost credibility and trust of business in society.

> **Ethical leadership –** Normatively appropriate conduct of a leader who uses ethics in their personal actions and work relationships, to foster and reinforce ethical decision making in an organisation.
> **Morals –** The principles that help individuals to reflect and determine between right and wrong actions.

Ethical leadership in corporations promotes social behaviours that foster the good of the society. Ethical leadership within corporations also encourages workers to

CASE STUDY 4.1

James Hardie

Australia is known to have one of the highest number of asbestos-related lung cancer cases; asbestos causes a kind of lung cancer called mesothelioma. A building products manufacturer, James Hardie, which used asbestos in the course of its construction work, was held responsible for more than half of these cases. Some estimate that as many as 7000 Australians have died from mesothelioma since 1945 and this is expected to increase to 18 000 in 2020 (Murray, 2005). Because the cancer can be detected only around 40 years after a person was exposed to asbestos, planning for compensation has been a difficult task for the company. The company leadership was blamed for mismanaging and misleading communication on the funding available to pay victims of this cancer (Fernando & Sim, 2011). The issue was a high-profile business scandal featured in the Australian media, with state and federal governments weighing in on the corporate social irresponsibility of the company leadership.

Critical thinking questions
Research the James Hardie asbestos story, and answer the following questions.
1. What were the ethical challenges of leading James Hardie during this period?
2. In what ways did James Hardie fail its stakeholders?
3. Applying the principles of responsible leadership, explain how the company executives should have developed a responsible resolution for the asbestos victims.

'blow the whistle' and bring the attention of senior management to unethical practices. More attractively from the point of view of the corporate leaders, ethical leadership has been found to promote the performance of the organisations, and increase the level of employees' commitment to the organisation. Ethical leadership makes employees do the 'right thing' within and outside organisations. Thus, engaging in ethical leadership brings about not only improved firm performance but a host of other individual, organisational and social benefits as well.

FACTORS INFLUENCING ETHICAL LEADERSHIP BEHAVIOUR

The study of how leaders should behave morally draws mostly from the business ethics literature. Business ethics is about doing the right thing. It is established that the 'rightness' of an action depends on what the larger society expects its outcome will be, and how this outcome compares with what the society considers normal or correct; in other words, the society's ethical norms. To lead with ethics, leaders must make decisions with ethical norms in mind, including an intention not to harm others. Business decisions are normally based on corporate ethical codes, situational factors and the individual leader's values framework. Overall, a leader can strive to become ethical by influencing individual, organisational and other contextual factors.

Individual factors

Moral person view – The view that a leader's goodness or moral character influences their ethical behaviour.

A leader can make decisions based on various individual factors such as religion, values, family and cultural background, personality, gender and age. According to the **moral person view**, a leader's goodness or moral character influences his or her ethical behaviour. The characteristics that demonstrate goodness or virtue include humanity, honesty, justice, care for the interests, wishes and needs of others, respect for human dignity and rights, and altruism. Leaders who are virtuous and have a moral character reflect these in their personal and professional behaviours. Individual personality has also been found to influence behaviour (Fernando, Dharmage & Almeida, 2008). How we behave and think have been characterised in organisational behaviour research through the 'Big Five' personality traits: agreeableness, conscientiousness, emotional stability, being open to experience, and extraversion. Each of these personality traits could influence how we behave in varying degrees.

There is research to suggest that a critical measure of leadership excellence should be based on leaders' integrity, trust and human dignity (Sankar, 2003). A leadership approach that is studied comprehensively is transformational leadership. It aims to transform the followers, not only to enable the company to achieve what it wants, but also to facilitate and promote corporate ethics.

Demographic factors like gender and age have also been found to affect leaders' ethical outcomes. There is debate about whether men or women make better ethical leaders. Some studies (e.g. Bernardi et al., 2009) have shown that females exhibit higher levels of ethical behaviour, as they tend to consider societal, corporate and environmental ethics more important than do men. Some researchers (e.g. Fernando, Dharmage & Almeida, 2008) have proposed the superior caring nature of women could mean that they would be better ethical leaders in our workplaces. Women leaders are more likely to project a caring and communal character than men, and to be more concerned about harm coming to others in ethically challenging decision-making situations. However, other researchers (e.g. Sun et al., 2011; Roozen et al., 2001; Smith et al., 2013) have found little or no evidence of difference between men and women in their ethical attitudes.

There is a view that, as they age, leaders tend to become more ethical and less concerned with material growth than with their own personal growth. For example, Singhapakdi and co-authors (1999) found that as older managers are more exposed to a variety of ethical problems, they become more sensitive to the harm that ethical violations can inflict on organisations and their stakeholders. Thus, gender and age may also determine ethical leader behaviour in some contexts.

Situational factors

A large body of literature suggests that organisational factors, such as an organisation's ethical values, can influence a leader's ethical decision making (e.g. Ferrell & Gresham, 1985; Trevino et al., 2014; Trevino, 1986). Hunt, Wood and Chonko (1989) define corporate ethical values as an aggregate of the individual ethical values of employees and the formal and informal ethical rules and regulations. For example, organisational climate and culture have been found to promote value-based practices and professional integrity in the army (Allen, 2015). However, there is some research to suggest that a climate of ethical behaviour is not in itself enough to promote ethical behaviour (Copeland & Potwarka, 2016); it needs to be supplemented and supported by ethical codes and policies and the individual's value framework.

Just as organisational climate can be influenced by national and cultural factors external to the organisation, the social context and other cultural influences can affect leaders' ethical behaviour. Performance pressures common in an organisation's culture, such as the importance of meeting quality and quantity standards, time deadlines and the attitude of 'win at all costs', have been found to lead to unethical decisions (Malhotra & Bazerman, 2008). For example, an energy company that promotes economic responsibilities over ethical responsibilities to the environment is likely to compromise on its ethical responsibilities in protecting the environment for a future generation. In the Australian context, investment in coal seam gas operations on rural land across Australia has increased rapidly. However, farmers have raised concerns over loss of their farmland. What would an ethical business leader do under this context? These types of situations will challenge the ethical decision making of leaders based on situational factors. Other scholars (e.g. Koh, Fernando & Spedding, 2017; Fernando, Dharmage & Almeida, 2008) have found that culturally based aspects such as how the leader handles interpersonal conflict, the leader's decision-making autonomy, the type of ethical issue at hand, and how the leader is expected to respond to others' level of authority in interactions affect the quality of ethical decisions.

ETHICAL DECISION MAKING IN LEADERSHIP

Organisations and leaders often face ethical dilemmas, particularly when multiple stakeholders, interests and values conflict with each other. When leaders are faced with these dilemmas, they are required to engage in ethical decision making because their decisions will have consequences for the health, safety and well-being of all stakeholders, including consumers, employees, the environment, communities and society. A well-known theory called the **stakeholder theory** asserts that those who have decision-making power in organisations are responsible to all stakeholders involved (Pless & Maak, 2011). As corporate scandals and executive misconduct reach media headlines across the globe on a regular basis, it has become clear that the established ethical codes in business organisations have no effect in discouraging unethical behaviour. Since having a well-formulated ethics code is not a guarantee for corporate ethical behaviour, it is important to understand the complexities of responsible decision making and what drives leaders to engage in either responsible or irresponsible decision making.

> **Stakeholder theory** – A theory that those who have decision-making power in organisations are responsible to all stakeholders involved (Pless & Maak, 2011).

A responsible decision from an ethical standpoint needs to be in line with both the legal and moral standards of the surrounding community (Jones 1991). Over the years, scholars have developed several decision-making models to explain ways to make responsible and ethical decisions. Prominent among these are Rest's (1986) four-component model, Ferrell and Gresham's (1985) contingency framework for ethical decision making and Jones's (1991) issue-contingent model of ethical decision making. Rest (1986) developed a four-step model for ethical decision making and behaviour, within which the leader recognises the moral issue, makes a moral judgement, decides to place moral concerns over other concerns (establishing moral intent) and acts on these moral concerns. Rest argued that each step of the process is conceptually different and that a leader may succeed in one step while struggling with other steps.

Craft (2013) later reformulated this model, replacing Rest's steps with new ones: awareness, judgement, intent and behaviour. According to this new approach:

> moral awareness is the ability to interpret a situation as being moral. Moral judgement is the ability for the decision maker to decide which course of action is morally correct. Moral intent is the ability to prioritise moral values over other values. Moral behaviour is the application of the moral intent to the situation (Craft 2013, p. 221).

During the 1980s and 1990s, many ethical models were developed and advanced based on Rest's (1986) ethical decision-making model.

Ferrell and Gresham's (1985) framework for decision making identifies individual and organisational based factors that affect the decision maker (Jones, 1991). Individual contingent factors include knowledge, values, attitudes and intentions; organisational contingent factors include significant actors and opportunities. In Ferrell and Gresham's (1985) framework, an ethical decision arises out of the context of individual and organisational factors to generate an action. This action is then evaluated, with the results feeding back to the individual and organisational factors, which then influence the next decision.

Jones's (1991) issue-contingent model of decision making has six elements:

1. *magnitude of consequences:* the total amount of harm or benefit a moral act has on those involved
2. *social consensus:* the level of social agreement on whether a suggested act is good or bad
3. *probability of effect:* the probability that the act will actually happen and will harm or benefit those involved
4. *temporal immediacy:* the amount of time between the present and proposed act
5. *proximity:* the feeling of nearness to those involved
6. *concentration of effect:* how significant the consequences will be for those involved.

Fundamental to Jones's issue-contingent model is the concept of moral intensity: 'a construct that captures the extent of issue-related moral imperative in a situation' (1991, p. 372). This model of decision making focuses on the specific moral issue, rather than the moral agent or organisational context. Jones (1991) argues that aspects of moral decision making and processes become unimportant if a person fails to recognise that a moral issue is even happening.

Scholars have suggested several ways to improve leadership decision making in ethically challenging situations. For example, Thiel and co-authors (2012) propose that leaders could use emotional regulation, self-reflection, forecasting and collecting information to increase the effectiveness of a leader's decisions. In addition, researchers have found that thinking critically, asking the right questions and applying a self-test (Langvardt, 2012), rewards or lack of rewards (Selart & Johansen, 2011), and open communication and employee innovation (Clayton & van Staden, 2015) promote and support leaders' ethical decision making.

MORAL AND VIRTUOUS LEADERSHIP
Moral leadership

According to Bass (1985), moral leaders should help followers not only to discover how their own values conflict, but also how their personal values and behaviours may conflict as they encounter different work contexts. He introduced a leadership approach called transformational leadership which he claimed as a moral leadership style, distinct from ethical leadership. It is distinct from ethical leadership in that, while both leadership styles focus on doing the 'right thing', morals come from within the person, and moral leadership is more concerned with the values and character of the person without examining concrete actions, whereas ethics considers the action itself and its effects.

The benefits of moral leadership have been well documented. Moral leaders:

- allocate rewards and responsibilities fairly
- apply organisational policies accurately and consistently
- promote representation and understanding among supervisors and subordinates (Long, 2015)
- positively implement the effectiveness of top management team decisions (Chen et al., 2015)
- increase the intrinsic task motivation of followers (Li et al., 2012)
- give employees a voice (Chan, 2014)
- foster employee identification with the leader and facilitate creativity (Gu et al., 2013).

Virtuous leadership

Virtuous leadership has been defined as:

> distinguishing right from wrong in one's leadership role, taking steps to ensure justice and honesty, influencing and enabling others to pursue righteous and moral goals for themselves and their organisations and helping others to connect to a higher purpose (Pearce et al., 2006, p. 62).

Virtues are a more or less stable set of positive traits. Cameron (2011) explains virtuous leadership as enabling organisations to achieve the most ethical outcome that humanity could aspire to. A virtuous leader in an ethically challenging situation should ask, 'What would my role model do in this situation?' The role model in this instance is someone who the leader believes to have strong morals and a high level of integrity.

Virtuous leadership is often compared with moral leadership, responsible leadership and other value-based leadership styles, but uniquely among these styles it incorporates six characteristics: character, competence, commitment, courage, clarity and compassion (Caldwell et al., 2015). Thus, virtuous leadership require leaders to lead with virtuous characteristics. Several ways have been proposed to enact these virtues in business organisations.

Morales-Sánchez and Cabello-Medina (2015) propose a typology of approaches to enact virtuous leadership: the philosophical approach (virtues), the psychological approach (character strengths) and the management approach (competencies). Virtue ethics is based on practices that form habits (Fernando & Moore, 2015), which can have an impact on ultimate leadership performance. According to MacIntyre (2007), when leaders strive to embody a virtuous character, this can lead to effectiveness and excellence in leadership. Virtues are 'dispositions not only to act in particular ways but also to feel in particular ways. To act virtuously … is to act from inclination formed by the cultivation of the virtues' (MacIntyre, 2007, p. 149). Not only doing, but feeling – the emotional side to leadership – is important in virtuous leadership.

Why should leaders bother with virtuous leadership? What are the benefits of engaging with virtuous leadership? Some of the benefits of enacting virtuous leadership are more ethical leader behaviour, leader happiness, life satisfaction and leader effectiveness (Hackett & Wang, 2012); higher concern for equity, justice and right behaviour (Pearce et al., 2006); and balancing the interests of stakeholders and shared learning (Pearce et al., 2006).

CASE STUDY 4.2

Caliber Collection

The US firm Caliber Collection (www.calibercollection.com) is dedicated to the manufacture and sale of jewellery for a social good. It works on the theme 'Jewellery for a Cause', and clearly operates on some of the key values-based leadership principles outlined in this chapter. Its founder and CEO, Jessica Mindich, uses parts from illegal guns and brass shell casings that the Newark Police Department confiscates in Newark, New Jersey. Some of the proceeds of Caliber's sales are given back to the police department and, according to police reports, the crime rate in the area has dropped because these sale proceeds are used to remove more guns from the streets.

Critical thinking questions

1. Using the various types of ethical leadership covered in this chapter, how would you describe Jessica Mindich's leadership style? Explain your response.
2. If you were the CEO at Caliber Collection, how would you develop the business further to promote virtuous leadership?
3. What moral leadership messages do you find in the Caliber Collection case?

CHALLENGES IN LEADING ETHICALLY

Leading ethically involves several challenges. A key challenge in ethical leadership is the need to balance various stakeholder needs with the leader's moral and ethical value framework in a particular situation. For instance, in some business situations, because of the leader's strict moral standards, they would not engage in bribery and this could lead to their companies losing the market share due to others engaging in bribery to attract lucrative contracts. So, Western companies operating in national cultures where there are strict standards of engaging in these types of corrupt practices could be at a disadvantage in parts of the world where these practices are tolerated as part of engaging in business. However, research strongly supports the idea that, in the long run, ethical leadership practices generate positive performance outcomes for companies, as they generate reputational goodwill and foster staff retention (Doh et al., 2011; Haque et al., 2017). Therefore, ethical leaders must identify the principles they are willing to compromise on, and understand to what extent they can do so, to stay true to their ethical goals. There is no single guideline or strategy that leaders can apply to every situation that demands ethical leadership because pressures resulting from social norms and expectations placed on leaders could lead to unethical leadership outcomes. Therefore, it is imperative for ethical leaders to discover an optimum balance between their moral foundation and those of their followers and organisations.

Leaders' increasing responsibility for their organisations' impact on the climate is also becoming a challenge for ethical leadership. Climate change and resource scarcity are becoming critical decision-making concerns for ethical leaders (Eisenbeiss, 2012). Maak and Pless (2006) call for ethical and responsible leaders to safeguard the natural resources for the benefit of an unknown future generation.

Another key challenge for ethical leadership is the growing complexity of business. In an increasingly borderless world, many business organisations conduct a growing share of their business online. Instead of leading a group of followers in a geographically bound space, the ethical leader has the challenge of now leading followers spread across the globe. Such borderless leadership creates enormous challenges associated with setting corporate values across ethical, legal and social dimensions, in multiple countries and among multiple cultures, each of which has its own norms and expectations (Fernando, 2016). For example, due to globalisation, multinational firms are exposed to more corrupt practices along the value chain (Hauser & Hogenacker, 2014). The challenge for ethical leaders in these globalised business contexts is to determine the intention of specific activities in a cross-cultural context (Hauser & Hogenacker, 2014).

SUMMARY

LEARNING OUTCOME 1: Understand the need for responsible leadership.

Traditionally, good leadership has been assumed to be responsible. However, the newer form of leadership, responsible leadership, seems to heavily emphasise 'responsibility', and has a strong focus on values and ethics. There is a need for responsible leadership because it assigns accountability in different forms to different stakeholders, ensures that values and ethics are always present, and results in better outcomes for both the business and society. There are different types of responsibility, including role responsibility, causal responsibility, capacity responsibility and liability responsibility.

LEARNING OUTCOME 2: Develop an awareness of the factors influencing ethical leadership behaviour.

Business decisions are normally based on corporate ethical codes, situational factors and the individual leader's values framework. Individual factors include religion, values, family and cultural background, personality, gender and age. From a 'moral person' viewpoint, a leader's inherent goodness or moral character may also influence his or her ethical leadership behaviour. Organisational factors include the ethical codes and values of an organisation. These codes can often be influenced by cultural and societal factors external to an organisation, so the situational factors may have significant influence on behaviour.

LEARNING OUTCOME 3: Appreciate why ethical decision making matters in leadership.

Organisations and leaders will often face ethical dilemmas, given the multiple stakeholders, interests and values that may come into conflict. Leaders are required to make ethical decisions in these situations, as their choices will have consequences for the health, safety and well-being of all stakeholders, including consumers, employees, the environment, communities and society. There are several frameworks through which a leader may reach an ethical decision, including Rest's (1986) four-step model, Craft's (2013) revised version of this model, Ferrell and Gresham's (1985) framework and Jones's (1991) issue-contingent model.

LEARNING OUTCOME 4: Understand moral leadership and virtuous leadership.

Moral leadership is distinct from ethical leadership in that morals speak to the values and character of the leader, while ethics considers the leader's actions and their consequences. The benefits of moral leadership are well documented, and moral leaders are seen to be fair, consistent and motivational and to foster positive environments. Virtuous leadership is often compared to moral leadership and other value-based leadership styles, but distinctively it has a stable set of six positive characteristics: character, competence, commitment, courage, clarity and compassion. Virtuous leadership is one of the most aspirational forms of practice that humanity can aspire to, in ensuring ethical outcomes.

LEARNING OUTCOME 5: Appreciate the real challenges of leading ethically.

Leading ethically raises several challenges in practice, particularly in an increasingly globalised world where online technology is influencing how business works. A key challenge in ethical leadership is the need to balance various stakeholder needs with that of the leader's moral and ethical value framework in any situation. It is important that leaders find a balance while remaining ethical. There is no one guideline of strategy that a leader can apply to every situation, which can provide a challenge in and of itself. The leader must remember always to be ethical. Modern issues such as the environment, climate change and the Internet ensure that leaders will be constantly confronted with new ethical dilemmas.

REVIEW QUESTIONS

1. Identify three reasons why leaders should act responsibly. Explain your response.

2. How can situational factors influence a leader's decision-making outcomes?

3. Discuss how one of the ethical decision-making models in this chapter might help a leader who needs to decide on actions that support profit-making, but which may also risk increased environmental harm.

4. What is moral leadership? Explain why it is important in today's business context.

5. Identify two challenges that ethical leaders may face in practice. Explain why you chose these challenges.

CASE STUDY 4.3

The collapse of HIH Insurance

The collapse of HIH brought the issue of directors' duties into the spotlight. Publicly listed companies have a board of directors who sit above the CEO and are responsible for corporate oversight or what is referred to as good corporate governance. Directors are under legal obligations to act in good faith and to represent the interest of the shareholder. In fact, directors are under what is known as a 'fiduciary obligation' to their shareholders. This means that the directors are under a legal obligation to act in the best interests of another person or group of people, in this case the shareholders.

A failure to uphold these obligations is not only illegal but raises serious questions about the nature of business ethics and conceptions of responsible leadership. Many of the directors involved in the HIH collapse received either civil or criminal sentences for their part in orchestrating the collapse. A Royal Commission, established in August 2001, investigated breaches of both Australian Corporations Law and the NSW Crimes Act 1900. A total of 56 breaches were found and referred to the Australian Securities and Investments Commission (ASIC), which filed suit against various company managers and directors.

As one of Australia's largest corporate failures, the liquidation of HIH Insurance on 15 March 2001 shook public confidence and dismantled community expectations relating to good corporate governance. The company's liquidation was a major contributor to the subsequent insurance industry crisis, inflicting considerable hardship on the Australian community. The Australian community expected that good corporate governance, auditing and regulation would trigger early warning signs of crisis.

The Royal Commission focused on several key issues, notably:

- when HIH became unable to pay its debts on time
- whether the board or management withheld information from, or misled, shareholders, the Australian Prudential Regulatory Authority (APRA) or potential investors
- what caused the collapse
- what was the extent of the loss
- who should be held accountable for the events leading up to HIH's collapse.

The Royal Commission found that corporate extravagance and overspending, based on an incorrect assumption of the company's financial situation, contributed to the financial insecurity of HIH. While the Commission did not find adequate evidence to substantiate claims of fraud and embezzlement against HIH directors, it did highlight that there had been an attempt to conceal the vulnerabilities that HIH had developed after overspending on acquisitions. The major reason for the collapse, however, was found to be a gross underestimation of the finance needed to pay off insurance claims. Past claims had not been properly priced, leading to a funding shortfall estimated to be in the billions of dollars.

HIH had failed to act with due diligence in relation to its core business activity of providing insurance. In its report the Royal Commission raised concerns relating to the moral and ethical duties of those who govern large corporations:

> all those who participate in the direction and management of public companies as well as their professional advisors need to identify and examine what they regard as the basic moral underpinning of their system of values (Bailey, 2003, p. 1).

The Royal Commission found that a culture of not questioning leadership decisions had evolved within HIH, so that employees did not question poor commercial decisions. Before the collapse, HIH attempted to re-enter the American market, acquired FAI Insurance and expanded its UK operations. The Royal Commission was critical of these moves and argued that the model of corporate governance used by HIH was out of date and not responsive to the changing insurance industry requirements. Further, the Commission found that at the time of the collapse, all three insurance arms of HIH had been operating below the minimum solvency requirements pursuant to the Insurance Act 1973 and APRA stipulations.

The HIH case highlights the need for company leaders to act with diligence in conducting business operations. The case further shows how corruption and a lack of ethics within a company can cripple an entire industry.

Source: Adapted from Bailey (2003)

Critical thinking questions

1. Who was affected by HIH's collapse?
2. Why did HIH fail?
3. What lessons can be learned from, and responses made to, the HIH experience?
4. How could the leaders at HIH have avoided the company's collapse?

REFERENCES

Allen, C.D. (2015). Ethics and army leadership: Climate matters. *Parameters*, 45(1), 69–83.

Bailey, B. (2003). Report of the Royal Commission into HIH Insurance. Research Note No. 32, 13 May. Department of the Parliamentary Library, Australia.

Bass, B.M. (1985). *Leadership and performance*. New York, NY: Free Press.

Bernardi, R.A., Bosco, B.M. & Columb, V.L. (2009). Does female representation on boards of directors associate with the 'Most Ethical Companies' list? *Corporate Reputation Review*, 2, 270–80.

Brown, M.E., Treviño, L.K. & Harrison, D.A. (2005). Ethical leadership: A social learning perspective for construct development and testing. *Organizational Behavior and Human Decision Processes*, 97(2), 117–34.

Caldwell, C., Hasan, Z. & Smith, S. (2015). Virtuous leadership – insights for the 21st century. *Journal of Management Development*, 34(9), 1181–200.

Cameron, K. (2011). Responsible leadership as virtuous leadership. *Journal of Business Ethics*, 98, 25–35.

Chan, S.C.H. (2014). Paternalistic leadership and employee voice: Does information sharing matter? *Human Relations*, 67(6), 667–93.

Chen, L., Yang, B. & Jing, R. (2015). Paternalistic leadership, team conflict, and TMT decision effectiveness: Interactions in the Chinese context. *Management and Organization Review*, 11(4), 739–62.

Clayton, B.M. & van Staden, C.J. (2015). The impact of social influence pressure on the ethical decision making of professional accountants: Australian and New Zealand evidence. *Australian Accounting Review*, 25(4), 372–88.

Copeland, R. & Potwarka, L.R. (2016). Individual and contextual factors in ethical decision making: A case study of the most significant doping scandal in Canadian University sports history. *Sport Management Review*, 19(1), 61–8.

Craft, J. (2013). A review of the empirical ethical decision-making literature: 2004–2011. *Journal of Business Ethics*, 117(2), 221–59. doi:10.1007/s10551-012-1518-9.

Doh, J.P., Stumpf, S.A. & Walter, T.G., Jr. (2011). Responsible leadership helps retain talent in India. *Journal of Business Ethics*, 98(1), 85–100.

Eisenbeiss, S.A. (2012). Re-thinking ethical leadership: An interdisciplinary integrative approach. *Leadership Quarterly*, 23, 791–808.

Fernando, M. (2016). *Leading responsibly in the Asian century.* New York, NY: Springer.

Fernando, M., Dharmage, S.C. & Almeida, S. (2008). Ethical ideologies of senior Australian managers: An empirical study. *Journal of Business Ethics*, 82(1), 145–55.

Fernando, M. & Moore, G. (2015). MacIntyrean virtue ethics in business: A cross-cultural comparison. *Journal of Business Ethics*, 132(1), 185–202.

Fernando, M. & Sim, A.B. (2011). Strategic ambiguity and leaders' responsibility beyond maximizing profits. *European Management Journal*, 26(6), 504–13.

Ferrell, O.C. & Gresham, L.G. (1985). A contingency framework for understanding ethical decision making in marketing. *Journal of Marketing*, 49(3), 87.

Gu, Q., Tang, T.L.P. & Jiang, W. (2013). Does moral leadership enhance employee creativity? Employee identification with leader and leader–member exchange (LMX) in the Chinese context. *Journal of Business Ethics*, 126(3), 513–29

Hackett, R.D & Wang, G. (2012). Virtues and leadership: An integrating conceptual framework founded in Aristotelian and Confucian perspectives on virtues. *Management Decision*, 50(5), 868–99.

Haque, A., Fernando, M. & Caputi, P. (2017). The relationship between responsible leadership and organisational commitment and the mediating effect of employee turnover intentions: An empirical study with Australian employees. *Journal of Business Ethics*, https://doi.org/10.1007/s10551-017-3575-6

Hauser, C. & Hogenacker, J. (2014). Do firms proactively take measures to prevent corruption in their international operations? *European Management Review*, 11(3/4), 223–37.

Hunt, S.D., Wood, V.R. & Chonko, L.B. (1989). Corporate ethical values and organizational commitment in marketing. *Journal of Marketing*, 53(3), 79–90.

Jones, T. (1991). Ethical decision making by individuals in organizations: An issue-contingent model. *Academy of Management Review*, 16(2), 366–95.

Knights, D. & O'Leary, M. (2006). Leadership, ethics and responsibility to the other. *Journal of Business Ethics*, 67(2), 125–37.

Koh, C., Fernando, M. & Spedding, T. (2017). Exercising responsible leadership in a Singapore context. *Leadership and Organization Development Journal*, Online first, 1–17.

Langvardt, A.W. (2012). Ethical leadership and the dual roles of examples. *Business Horizons*, 55(4), 373–84.

Li, C., Wu, K., Johnson, D.E. & Wu, M. (2012). Moral leadership and psychological empowerment in China. *Journal of Managerial Psychology*, 27(1), 90–108.

Long, C.P. (2015). Mapping the main roads to fairness: Examining the managerial context of fairness promotion. *Journal of Business Ethics*, doi:https://doi.org/10.1007/s10551-015-2749-3

Maak, T. & Pless, N.M. (2006). Responsible leadership in a stakeholder society – a relational perspective. *Journal of Business Ethics*, 66(1), 99–115.

MacIntyre, A. (2007). *After virtue*, 3rd edn. London: Duckworth.

Malhotra, D. & Bazerman, M.H. (2008). Psychological influence in negotiation: An introduction long over due. *Journal of Management*, 34(3), 509–31.

Morales-Sánchez, R. & Cabello-Medina, C. (2015). Integrating character in management: Virtues, character strengths, and competencies. *Business Ethics*, 24(S2), S156–S174.

Murray, A. (2005). *Asbestos-related claims (management of commonwealth liabilities), Bill 2005*. Australian Democrat speeches, Senator Andrew Murray Portfolio: Workplace Relations. Retrieved from: http://parlinfo.aph.gov.au/parlInfo/download/chamber/hansards/2005-06-14/toc_pdf/3966-5.pdf;fileType=application%2Fpdf#search=%22chamber/hansards/2005-06-14/0115%22

Pearce, C.L., Waldman, D.A. & Csikszentmihaly, M. (2006). Virtuous leadership: A theoretical model and research agenda. *Journal of Management, Spirituality and Religion*, 3(1/2).

Pless, N.M. (2007). Understanding responsible leadership: Role identity and motivational drivers. *Journal of Business Ethics*, 74(4), 437–56.

Pless, N. & Maak, T. (2011). Responsible leadership: Pathways to the future. *Journal of Business Ethics*, 98, 3–13. doi:10.1007/s10551-011-1114-4.

Rest, J.R. (1986). *Moral development: Advances in research and theory*. New York, NY: Praeger.

Roozen, I., De Pelsmacker, P. & Bostyn, F. (2001). The ethical dimensions of decision processes of employees. *Journal of Business Ethics*, 33(2), 87–99.

Sankar, Y. (2003). Character not charisma is the critical measure of leadership excellence. *Journal of Leadership and Organizational Studies*, 9(4), 45–55.

Selart, M. & Johansen, S.T. (2011). Ethical decision making in organizations: The role of leadership stress. *Journal of Business Ethics*, 99(2), 129–43.

Singhapakdi, A., Vitell, S.J. & Franke, G.R. (1999). Antecedents, consequences, and mediating effects of perceived moral intensity and personal moral philosophies. *Journal of the Academy of Marketing Science*, 27(1), 19–35.

Smith, R.D., Debode, J.D. & Walker, A.G. (2013). The influence of age, sex, and theism on ethical judgments. *Journal of Management, Spirituality and Religion*, 10(1), 67–89.

Sun, J., Liu, G. & Lan, G.T. (2011). Does female directorship on independent audit committees constrain earnings management? *Journal of Business Ethics*, 99(3), 369–82.

Thiel, C.E., Bagdasarov, Z., Harkrider, L., Johnson, J.F. & Mumford, M.D. (2012). Leader ethical decision-making in organizations: Strategies for sensemaking. *Journal of Business Ethics*, 107(1), 49–64.

Trevino, L.K. (1986). Ethical decision making in organizations: A person–situation interactionist model. *Academy of Management Review*, 11(3), 601–17.

Trevino L.K., den Nieuwenboer N.A. & Kish-Gephart J.J. (2014). (Un)Ethical behavior in organizations. *Annual Review of Psychology*, 65, 635–60.

AUTHOR'S ACKNOWLEDGEMENT

I am grateful for the research assistance provided by Dr Nadeera Ranabahu and Ms Casidhe Sternbeck-Rutte in chapters 4–6 and 11.

5

FOLLOWERSHIP

Mario Fernando

LEARNING OUTCOMES

After reading this chapter, you should be able to:

1. explain the psychology of followers in relation to leadership

2. discuss how followers and leaders interact to generate effective leadership outcomes

3. demonstrate an awareness of the types of followers and their role in the leadership process

4. explain followership theory and practice

5. explain the challenges of followership.

INTRODUCTION

THIS CHAPTER WILL introduce the little-understood role of **followers** in achieving effective leadership outcomes. Most research in leadership is devoted to the leader, situation or goal factors in the leadership process. Only recently has research on **followership** caught the attention of scholars. Without good followers, even the most skillful leadership will be ineffective. Historically, followers have been projected in the business literature as either passive or defiant. There is increasing attention to the importance of building healthy leader–follower relationships in developing effective leaders as well as leaders.

> **Followers** – People who grant certain behaviours that allow them to be led by others.
> **Followership** – A role in relation to a leader that is determined by the context of the leadership process and the leadership style.

As ways of organising contemporary work and organisations change, newer leadership styles such as emergent, participatory and distributed leadership approaches place more emphasis on followers. For example, when organisational structures become less hierarchical, the distinction between leaders and followers gradually decreases. In this light, the absence of scholarly research work on the notion of followership is surprising (Lapierre & Carsten, 2014). In this chapter, we will identify the role and types of followers in the leadership process. We will also look at followership theory and how it could be practised. There are some leadership styles that better accommodate the focus on followership; we will examine these in particular. To conclude, the chapter will examine various challenges to followership.

THE PSYCHOLOGY OF FOLLOWERS

Leadership theory is concerned with examining the leadership process, which includes the leader, their followers, the achievement of goals and the situation or context. However, the literature around leadership is mainly focused on the leader and the behaviours of an effective leader (Bass & Bass, 2008; Burns, 1978; Bryman, 1992). Followers have attracted much less attention. Moreover, leader-centric approaches tend to assume that all followers will recognise and react the same way to a leader. This is not the case. A leader may inspire different reactions across their base of followers.

Followership has become increasingly important as organisations move away from the traditional, taller hierarchical organisational structures to flatter organisational structures. The flatter organisational structures of modern organisations increase the importance of followers in the leadership equation. According to leadership scholars (e.g. Uhl-Bien & Pillai, 2007; Kellerman, 2008; Kelley, 1988), organisations must have leaders who encourage healthy levels of dissent and allow their followers to both express concerns and disagree with the leader.

Followership has been defined in several ways (Baker, 2007). Some scholars define it as a relationship, others as a role, some others as a submissive role to a leader and as a role to achieve common goals. Followership implies 'deferring to the directives, decisions, or desires of another, thereby giving another higher status and legitimacy in determining the course of events' (Uhl-Bien & Pillai, 2007, p. 196). A useful definition of followership is: 'A role in relation to a leader that is conceived of differently by followers and is dependent on contextual variables, such as leadership style and organisational climate' (Carsten et al., 2010, p. 559). Based on this definition, followership, like many other management concepts, can be influenced by the context or situation. The nature of the team goals, the personality of the leader and the industry in which the team is operating are some of the contextual variables that can have an impact on followership.

According to Bligh (2011), leaders do not derive authority merely from their power to give orders. The authority of the leader comes from the responses of the people to whom the orders are directed. From this perspective, followers hold significant power in the leader–follower relationship, furthering the argument that there can be no leadership without followership. At some stage of their career or at any given point in a working day, most employees will be followers.

Whether you're a student working in a graduate program with multiple supervisors, a senior executive in a company or even the CEO, someone will most likely always be leading you in some way or another. Recent literature has studied the importance of followers in the leadership equation (Palmer, 2013; Uhl-Bien et al., 2013; Bligh, 2011). The term 'followers' refers to the group of people over whom the leader exerts influence. Followers can be passive or active. The way that a follower thinks and ultimately acts in their followership, which can be driven by the psychology of followership, is important. Lapierre and Carsten (2014) argue that followers should adapt their leadership style depending upon their stage of adult development, organisational context and the leadership style of the leader. For example, the leadership process can take place only when there is at least a follower. Drucker (1993) defines a leader simply in terms of whether he or she has followers. Imagine an Australian prime minister with no cabinet ministers to direct, or no nation to lead.

Some theorists believe that a charismatic leader can greatly influence the attitudes and behaviours of the follower (Howell & Shamir, 2005). A charismatic leader is seen as 'extraordinary and treated as endowed with supernatural, superhuman, or at least specifically exceptional powers or qualities' (Weber, 1968, p. 241). According to Hummel (1975), followers feel bound to obey this leader, expressing themselves as loyal and devoted followers. Charisma and the response it produces among followers can be dangerous. For example, Hitler was a charismatic leader, able to invoke massive support among his followers for unethical actions. Weber (1968) described charisma as being so strong and powerful that it can challenge and transform traditional and rational values and norms. A leader's charisma can affect followers' psyches and behaviours.

Khurana (2002) draws on the example of Jeff Skilling of Enron, who was a charismatic leader. Leaders like Skilling can bend rules and even reject rules outright and behave in an unregulated manner, because of their high levels of power and authority. The Enron board allowed Skilling to engage in investments outside the bounds of the company ethics code (Khurana, 2002). These leaders are therefore in a capacity to manipulate their followers, to the extent that the followers blindly follow the leader, granting full surrender.

It may not be only charismatic leaders who can influence the mindset of followers. Palmer (2013) argues that unethical behaviour in followers is influenced by the behaviour of the leader. Similarly, ethical leaders act as role models for ethical conduct. Followers may look to emulate their leaders' actions (Lipman-Blumen, 2005; Palmer, 2013). A follower who observes their leader engaging in either ethical or unethical conduct can use this to rationalise their own behaviour. Followers have been observed by scholars (e.g. Bandura et al., 2000) to copy the unethical behaviour of the leader and rationalise their actions as acceptable because the leader is doing or has done the same thing; this is referred to as moral disengagement.

According to Palmer (2013), a follower may use the leader's response to an ethical dilemma as an opportunity for learning. The follower may watch how the leader operates, and this may directly influence the way the follower will operate or rationalise behaviours in different circumstances. For example, it was recently uncovered that 7-Eleven was committing wage fraud in Australia: 7-Eleven franchise holders were found to be exploiting workers by paying well below the minimum wage (Branley, 2015). The leadership of the organisation did not monitor the franchisees and allowed them to perpetuate the unethical conduct. The franchisees may have rationalised their unethical and illegal behaviour as acceptable because many others in the organisation were doing the same thing.

Other studies have shown how followers' perceptions of the ethics of their leaders influence followers' commitment to the organisation (e.g. Sharif & Scandura, 2013). Scholars have found that followers who perceived their leader to be ethical responded with higher levels of what is referred to as organisational citizenship behaviour (Podsakoff et al., 1990). Elements of organisational citizenship include altruism, good sportsmanship and courtesy (Organ, 1988). On the other hand, when followers view their leader as unethical, they are likely to exhibit lower levels of organisational citizenship.

Other researchers have used the notion of power bases (such as expert, referent, coercive, technical and information) to explain a follower's motivation to follow the leader (Lapierre & Carsten, 2014; French & Raven, 1960). How the leader uses power influences how the follower views the leader, and affects their commitment to the leader and organisation. Similarly, how the follower perceives the leader's motives for their actions affects how they see the leader. Some studies have shown that followers can tell the difference between an authentic and inauthentic leader. If the leader is perceived not to be authentic, the follower may respond by reducing their work effort and no longer taking initiative. The psyche of the follower can be greatly influenced not only by the actions and behaviours of the leader, but also by how the follower perceives the leader's motives behind their actions.

FOLLOWER AND LEADER INTERACTIONS

We have identified the leader, situation, goals and follower as key variables in the leadership process. Earlier, we noted that scholars have focused mostly on the first three variables of leadership, giving scant attention to the role of followers in influencing leadership outcomes. There are several reasons for this. The extent of the achievement attributed to the leader during organisational success is one key reason (Uhl-Bien & Pillai, 2007). The leader is singled out for praise when organisational bottom lines and targets are met, while the follower's role in achieving these outcomes may be hardly noted. The role of the follower is also perceived to be a passive role: the leader's instructions are followed and the follower's actions exert little overt influence on the ultimate leadership outcomes. This is reflected in the literature through the definitions of followership that identify the followership process as a duty. However, leaders cannot deliver effective leadership outcomes without followers who are not only loyal, but also skilled and capable of carrying out their leader's instructions (Chaleff, 1995; 2003).

According to Kelley (1988), effective followers share four common characteristics: they are self-managers who are capable, committed, effective and focused. The power of effective followers is in their ability and willingness to challenge their leader and think critically about the organisation and what is going on around them. When the leader–follower relationship is a two-way exchange and where there is trust between the leader and followers, the followers have the power to affect, and even constrain, the leader's actions (DeRue & Ashford, 2010). This is particularly important where the leader's actions are unethical or even dangerous (Reynolds & Jones, 2017). Leaders need to lead with integrity and make profits without compromising basic human principles. Passive followers allow leaders to assume power, and they just go along with what they are told. These types of followers sit back and watch as bad leadership decisions lead to destructive outcomes.

Followers need to be distinguished from subordinates. Although the academic literature uses these terms interchangeably at times, the manager–subordinate relationship has a formal basis to it (Tepper et al., 2006). There are rules and regulations governing such a relationship. However, in the leader–follower relationship, the roles are quite informal. The follower can opt to be an active follower or a very passive follower, and the relationship has little structure. In this light, it is important to remember that leaders and followers are roles that individuals fulfil at various places and times; they do not necessarily speak to the inherent attributes of an individual.

Given the low prominence granted to followers, Barbuto (2000) asked why anyone would want to follow rather than lead, and placed the reasons into three categories, based on power, relationship and values. For example, a follower might choose to follow because the follower is attracted to the power of, and likes to be associated with, the leader. Another follower might follow a leader because they place importance on what they see as the nature of their relationship with that leader. Others still might feel aligned with the leader's values and admire how the leader demonstrates those values in the execution of their role.

TYPES OF FOLLOWER AND THEIR ROLE IN THE LEADERSHIP PROCESS

Scholars have found that, just as there are types of leaders, there can be follower types (Collinson, 2006). Prominent among these are the contributions of Kelley (1988), who compared active versus passive followers and dependent/uncritical thinkers versus independent/critical thinkers. Active followers and critical thinkers engage in the leadership process more and provide critical input to the leader. On the other hand, passive and uncritical thinkers take a more 'hands-off' approach and participate in the leadership process only when called upon to do so. Based on these dimensions, Kelley's (1988) study proposed five types of followers (see Figure 5.1):

1. Passive and dependent uncritical thinkers – 'Sheep'
2. Active but dependent and uncritical thinkers – 'Yes people'
3. Partially active/independent, critical thinkers – 'Survivors'
4. Critical independent thinkers but passive – 'Alienated followers'
5. Active and independent critical thinkers – 'Effective followers'.

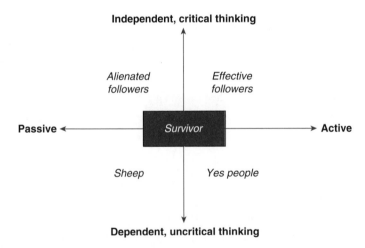

Figure 5.1   Kelley's five types of followership
Source: Adapted from Kelley (1988)

Sheep

These followers are passive and uncritical in their followership. They do not take initiative, instead focusing on the task given, completing it and going no further. For example, suppose you work at a supermarket and your boss tells you to operate the checkout for three hours. A 'sheep' follower would stand at the checkout and merely serve customers, not looking for other jobs to do in between serving, such as refilling the lollies at the counter or cleaning their work area.

Yes people

These followers are typically more active, but are like 'sheep' in that they do not take initiative, instead relying on the leader to inspire and motivate. Bosses without strong convictions tend to like this type of follower (Kelley, 1988). 'Yes people' tend to go along with what the leader says. They are unquestioning and yield to the will of the leader easily. This type of follower can be problematic in situations where they do not express their disagreement with the leader, instead just trying to win favour by always agreeing with them. For example, suppose a leader decides to launch an aggressive expansion strategy that will incur huge costs. Perhaps the follower is an accountant who knows that the business's financial position is not strong enough to support such a strategy. Instead of raising the issue with the boss, the 'yes person' follower goes along with the strategy because they see that the boss supports it.

Survivors

These followers can be more active than 'sheep' and 'alienated followers', but they can be both partially independent, critical thinkers and as well as dependent, uncritical thinkers. In other words, they sit in the middle of the passive/active scale and the independent, critical thinking/ dependent, uncritical thinking scale. 'Survivors' have a mix of traits from the other four types of followers.

Alienated followers

'Alienated followers' are independent thinkers who are critical of their surroundings. However, this type of follower for some reason has become disenfranchised, even cynical. They can become increasingly disgruntled in their workplaces. This type of follower may be difficult to motivate.

Effective followers

These followers are independent and critical thinkers. They carry out their tasks with enthusiasm and assertiveness. This type of follower will take risks, solve problems and be seen as effective by their peers and leaders. This type of follower can succeed even when there is no strong leader to guide them. According to Kelley (1988), '[s]elf-confident followers see colleagues as allies and leaders as equals'. It is active and effective followers who have power. For example, Ba Banutu-Gomez (2004) writes, '[f]ollowers can evaporate a leader's mask of power merely by disbelieving in it'. Perhaps you can remember having a teacher who could not control a classroom. You would assume that they have authority and power over their students because of their position as the teacher. Yet some teachers struggle to hold their students' attention and gain their trust and cooperation. This could be explained by the followers (the students) taking the power from the teacher (leader) by not believing or acting as if the teacher has any power, thus making room for more power for the students.

Moreover, it is almost a certainty that followers will outnumber leaders. By banding together, followers can exert power over the leader by using strength in numbers. This strategy can be useful where there is a mix of active and passive followers. The fact that there is a group of people working together to communicate with the leader may help those followers who are uneasy about, or even frightened of, being active in their followership.

Another useful followership model was developed by Blackshear (2003). This model focused on examining whether 'the highest followership stages of the Followership Continuum provides a diagnostic and prescriptive approach for improving workforce productivity' (p. 25). The model was presented in a continuum with five distinct stages – see Figure 5.2. The first stage is that of the ordinary employee, delivering the services required by the job role. The second stage is when the employee demonstrates more commitment to the organisation, mission and goals of the job. The third is when the employee becomes an active and engaged follower, often delivering service beyond the call of duty. At the fourth stage, the follower demonstrates how he or she can be capable and dependable at work. The last stage is when the follower demonstrates skills and ability of performing the leadership role but supports the leader to achieve the set goals.

CASE STUDY 5.1

Passive versus active followers

In 2013, a host of Australian apparel companies were implicated in the Rana Plaza building collapse. Rana Plaza was a clothing factory operating in Bangladesh. The factory used child and forced labour and put bars over the windows and entry and exit points to stop workers from going home if the quotas set by the Australian companies were not met. It is arguable that the followers within Australian brands such as Forever New and Kmart did not have the courage to blow the whistle on their companies' complicity in human rights abuses. The followers would have known that their operation was unethical, yet the practice of exploitation continued until an international scandal. The followers were arguably passive and unwilling to speak up. An effective follower in this situation could have had the power – and, just as importantly, *seen themselves* as having the power – to change the situation by encouraging others to join them in raising concerns about exploitation with their employer. Followers who are active and critical thinkers uphold their values even at work, and stand up when their values are compromised by their organisations. Because of actions by active followers, McDonald's and Burger King now have strict guidelines for their egg suppliers to allow more wing room and fresh air for egg-laying hens and to provide the hens with extra water.

Critical thinking questions
1. Explain the difference between passive and active followers.
2. Why would active followers take a riskier path to reporting unethical behaviour?
3. What attributes of a passive follower limits them to be active followers?
4. In an ethically challenging situation, would you be a passive or active follower? Why?

Employee	Committed follower	Engaged follower	Effective follower	Exemplary follower
Stage 1	Stage 2	Stage 3	Stage 4	Stage 5

Figure 5.2   Blackshear's followership continuum

Source: Adapted from Blackshear (2003)

Figure 5.2 shows how a normal employee work role can change and evolve based on the context. Blackshear (2003) presented this model as a continuum, based on the idea of realising the actual potential of employees: that is, enabling each employee to reach the effective follower stage, where they show readiness to take on leadership roles. Organisations should promote a suitable organisational culture to realise these individual abilities of each employee.

FOLLOWERSHIP-CENTRED LEADERSHIP MODEL (SHAMIR, 2007)

Shamir (2007) focuses on followers on a continuum of passive to active and categories and proposes a model of five types of followership-centred leadership, with constructors, recipients, moderators, substitutes and followers as leaders.

Constructors

In this type of followership, the followers actively create leadership. They become co-constructors of the leadership process, so that the leadership process is primarily centred on followers. Thus, leadership is essentially in the eye of the follower (Jackson & Parry, 2008).

Recipients

Under this type, the passive role of follower is emphasised. The traditional and dominant view of the follower as the passive and inactive party in the leadership process is accentuated through followers' granting or receiving behaviour.

Moderators

In this follower type, their role in the leadership process is somewhat recognised. Several leadership theories including contingency theories of leadership recognise that individual follower characteristics influence followers' attitudes and performance. Although the moderating role of the follower characteristics on leadership influence is recognised, as moderators of leadership these follower types are still passive followers (Shamir, 2007; Jackson & Parry, 2008).

Substitutes

Followers in this category play a more dominant role than moderators. Kerr and Jermier (1978) argue that under certain conditions, followers can neutralise or even substitute the influence of leaders over followers. When the leadership influence is neutralised, the leader's task or relationship-based activities fail to make any influence on the follower. When substituted, the leader's role and influence can become largely unnecessary (Jackson & Parry, 2008).

Followers as leaders

Shamir (2007) proposed that followers are co-producers of leadership. They were not merely passive followers of leader directions but take an active part in charting the leadership course. Interestingly, the last category suggests that some followers can be leaders as well. This phenomenon of followership will be examined later in the chapter.

KELLERMAN'S TYPOLOGY OF FOLLOWER ENGAGEMENT

Another prominent study of follower types is from Kellerman (2008), who also identified five follower types. The basis for the follower categories in this study is the extent of engagement. She developed the typology based on two extremes: followers who feel and do absolutely nothing on the one hand, to being passionate and committed and deeply involved in their roles on the other. From least to most engaged, Kellerman's five types are isolates, bystanders, participants, activists and die-hards.

Isolates

Followers who can be identified as isolates are not involved in the leadership process in any way. They support the status quo, and in effect support the leader's view be taking a hands-off approach. They can be found mostly in large organisations, where they can disappear and be lost from the main thrust and drive of the leadership process. There can be several reasons why followers choose to be isolates. They could be stressed over their jobs, they could be disgruntled employees, they could be in some way not satisfied with their jobs and the job tasks are not aligned with their values.

Bystanders

Unlike isolates, bystanders know what is going on in the leadership process. However, they deliberately choose not to engage in the leadership process. Sometimes, when it suits them, they might engage to serve their personal needs. Like isolates, their inaction also supports the status quo and the leader's agenda. Bystanders can be found in large organisations where it is easier to go unnoticed. Like isolates, bystanders can also have several reasons for failing to engage in the leadership process including job stress, job dissatisfaction and misalignment of personal values with organisational values.

Participants

These types of followers are engaged in some way. Even if they don't like their leaders, these followers contribute to the leadership process because they are driven by passion and commitment to the organisation. Participants are motivated to engage in some way in the leadership process due to their link to an idea or person, because they mean something to them.

Activists

Activists are more engaged than the participants. These followers go out of their way to perform. They have loyalty to the leader and/or the organisation. In a typical organisation there are only a few activist followers. They are very motivated to the cause or the leader.

Die-hards

These types of followers are prepared to sacrifice what most wouldn't for the sake of engaging in the leadership process. Whistleblowers are a good example of die-hard followers. Even with the likelihood of losing their jobs, whistleblowers would rather engage in the process by bringing the attention of the public to a corporate scandal. Die-hards take this approach because of their deep commitment and identification with a cause or because of their deep loyalty to the leader.

In all these types of follower typologies, what is clear is that some followers engage in the leadership process more than others. And that this involvement can also vary based on the given context.

CASE STUDY 5.2

Susan as a follower
Susan is a manager of human resources and participates in a weekly senior meeting chaired by her CEO. She rarely contributes at these meetings, but outside of a meeting she diligently works on any matters that have been assigned for her action at the meeting. Outside of a meeting she also has personal chats with the CEO about the matters discussed at the meeting. Susan feels that meetings are a waste of time and people who talk big at meetings rarely do the actual hard work required to achieve company goals.

Critical thinking question
How would you describe the behaviour of Susan as a follower, drawing on the typologies by Kelley (1988) and Shamir (2007)?

FOLLOWERSHIP THEORY AND PRACTICE

We identified earlier that leadership as a process involves several key variables. The leader, follower, situation or context and goals are central to understanding the leadership process: leaders do the leading and followers do the following, in a particular context, to achieve a common set of goals. Leaders and followers perform specific roles in the social process of leadership.

Accordingly, scholars have identified two key types of followership theories (Uhl-Bien et al., 2013). The first type is role-based. These theories consider followers as fulfilling a formal or informal role in the leadership process. A follower could be anyone who is reporting to a manager (in other words, a subordinate) or anyone in a following relationship of any kind to a leader. In the role-based view of followership, the follower is the person who causes the leadership process to work. The follower, not the leader, is at the heart of the leadership process.

These theories tend to focus more on the attributes, personality and character of followers in determining how leadership can be more effective. They try to answer the question of which mix of follower traits and attributes will more strongly influence leadership outcomes. Shamir (2007) characterises these theories as 'reversing the leader lens' because the follower in effect takes the attention usually given to the leader. The follower becomes the instigator and initiator of leadership action.

The other type of followership theory is based on the relational aspects of followership. At the centre of these theories are the interactions between leaders and followers, which take place in a particular context. Leadership outcomes are viewed as the result of a social process. One critical aspect in these theories is the notion that for leaders to be effective leaders, followers should have 'granting' behaviours. That is, to accommodate leader directions and demands, followers should have a suitable set of behavioural traits that accommodate the leader's demands. Sometimes followers may disagree with leader viewpoints, and on occasions some leaders might accept those followers' viewpoints. With these types of interactions, relationship-based followership theories propose that the leadership outcomes are co-created by both leaders and followers (Uhl-Bien et al., 2013).

Based on the social-interaction-driven followership theory, an alternative viewpoint of followers as leaders is emerging in the academic literature. This view is more prominent in new leadership approaches such as **emergent leadership** and **distributed leadership**.

Emergent leadership

The emergent leadership approach asserts that leadership is not role-focused, but instead depends on the situation, which is a critical factor in the notion of emergent leadership. Although, for example, there can be formal leaders appointed in sporting teams and work projects, others take leadership of certain situations because they are more experienced or more skilled, or simply because others in the team are willing to be influenced by the emergent leaders. One definition of emergent leadership is that of Baruch (1998), who says that emergent leadership occurs 'when individuals are ready and willing to be influenced by another individual' (p. 134). Thus, in effect, any follower can become a leader.

> **Emergent leadership –** Leadership that is vested in someone due to his or her expertise, skill or because others let the individual influence them.
> **Distributed leadership –** Leadership that is shared or vested in more than one person at a given time.

Distributed leadership

Distributed leadership advocates a position where the leadership role is fluid, and depends on the context and skills of the team members at a given time in the project. The best team members, those who meet the demands of a particular context, are considered to be the leaders in that context. This allows for the possibility of more than one leader operating at a given point in time. This distributed leadership style, sometimes referred to as shared leadership, is also based on episodes or situations. Thus, the role of the follower as leader becomes more pronounced in the emergent and distributed types of leaders as any follower at a given point could become the leader.

Implicit followership theory

In implicit followership theory (IFT), an individual forms assumptions as they observe another person's traits and behaviours, and acts accordingly (Sy, 2010; Martin, 2015). Sy (2010) studied the typical attributes of followers and found that leaders will try to work out who their followers may be, based on alignment between their own personal attributes and those of potential followers. Based on this impression, the leaders will make decisions about engaging the follower in the leadership process. Thus, a leader may recognise potential in followers who fit with their implicit model of an ideal follower, and engage them accordingly.

CASE STUDY 5.3

Peter's leader–follower dilemma

Peter Chin works in a Telstra telecommunication project in Victoria. His project team is responsible for the National Broadband Network (NBN) rollout in the state. The team has seven specialists, and each tends to take the leadership role based on the stage of a particular project. Peter is a data communication specialist, and he is the only non-white Australian in the team. When he is in a following role, he gives his fullest support to the leader, but he feels that when he is leading the team, he is unable to attract the same support from his team. He feels that his inability to be seen and behave 'like an Australian' is affecting his leadership outcomes. Peter wants your help as a leadership consultant to remedy the situation.

Critical thinking questions
1. Explain how a distributed leadership approach might help Peter to resolve the challenge he has identified.
2. Using implicit follower theory (IFT), explain how you would ensure that Peter achieves his desired leadership outcomes.
3. Analyse what may be informing Peter's perception that not behaving 'like an Australian' is affecting his leadership outcomes.

CHALLENGES OF FOLLOWERSHIP

This chapter began by pointing out how followers are a neglected group in leadership research. In both the scholarly literature and leadership practice, the greater attention has been paid to, and romance associated with, the leaders. Although we know that leadership can't exist without followers, why would anyone want to follow? You might have come across people who are not comfortable with taking the initiative and being in the spotlight. They actually prefer to be in the shadow of the leader. However, followership is not easy and has its fair share of challenges.

The type of follower can indicate certain associated challenges for leaders and organisations. For example, from Kelley's (1988) typology of followers, those followers who are classified as 'sheep' can cause problems for leaders who value creativity and initiative. A group of followers passively following the leader, neither thinking critically about the ramifications of the leader's actions nor speaking up and voicing their opinions, are classic examples of Kelley's 'sheep' followers. In a group of followers, having a few or many 'sheep' in the group can lead to destructive outcomes or ethical dilemmas (Fernando & Sim, 2011); bosses engaged in dubious behaviour tend to like 'sheep', as they just go with the flock. The danger of having a group of uncritical followers who do not feel a sense of responsibility to the leader, organisation or greater community is that wrongs or ethical violations are likely to go unchallenged or undisclosed (Kelley, 2008). Ethical violations can occur when followers do not speak up and work together with, or even oppose, the leader.

On the other hand, followers classified as 'alienated' pose a different set of challenges to leaders and organisations. As we have discussed, alienated followers are often cynical and disgruntled. They can affect the morale of the organisation through their observable apathy. The issue with alienated followers is that they are critical and independent thinkers, and these are skills that any organisation can benefit from if the followers have a stake in the organisation and are committed to working alongside the leader in the achievement of organisational goals and targets (Kelley, 2008). Alienated followers can challenge the leader and organisation through their lack of motivation and reluctance to engage positively with the organisation. For example, a Qantas engineer who has worked for the company for 30 years has witnessed major changes to the organisation: the loss of market share, the moving of manufacturing to low-cost centres in Asia. This employee has survived these changes, but many of his colleagues have not. He feels angry at the organisation for the way his colleagues were treated and believes that he has very little control over his work situation. Instead of functioning as a motivated and enthusiastic team member, as he once did, the engineer approaches his work with apathy and is cynical about both Qantas as a company and his position within the organisation. This type of follower challenges leadership by not actively seeking to achieve goals despite a clear ability to give input and be assertive.

The challenges posed by 'yes people' can be problematic for the organisation and for other staff who are not similarly uncritical and lacking in independence of thought. 'Yes people' accept leaders, looking to them for inspiration. The challenges created by 'yes people' grow when the leader is not strong in their convictions, and perhaps lacks a certain level of confidence. These types of leaders tend to form alliances with 'yes people', as they can make the leader feel powerful, validated and smart. Such alliances can work against the good of the organisation by overpowering followers with independent thoughts and opinions who seek genuine reciprocity between themselves and the leader, and who see themselves as the leader's colleagues and allies. It is important that leaders who are surrounding themselves with 'yes people' recognise it as soon as possible and take steps to listen to a broader range of comments and suggestions. An example of a prominent leader wishing to surround herself with 'yes people' is the late Margaret Thatcher; as UK prime minister she once said, 'I don't mind how much my ministers talk, as long as they do what I say' (Savoie, 2010). 'Yes people' can become more prevalent when the organisation bases performance evaluations on subjective criteria (Prendergast, 1993).

Similarly, other types of followers can have their own challenges because of the idiosyncrasies of their personalities, roles and contribution to the leadership process. However, at the core of all these challenges is the requirement that followers have granting behaviours, even while remaining critical and independent thinkers who support the quality of the leadership outcomes.

CASE STUDY 5.4

James and Geoff
James is a human resources manager at a prominent Sydney-based telecommunications company, reporting to a team of senior managers. He is 45 and has always lived in Sydney. Although he has an MBA from University of Sydney and has worked for 20 years in human resource management, he is not comfortable with leadership positions. He doesn't like to be in the limelight, always preferring to be in the shadow of a more prominent person. His CEO, Geoff, is a dominant personality who is very vocal and follows an authoritative leadership style. They have been working together for more than three years. While James's colleagues find working with Geoff very difficult, James finds it easy and works effectively with him. He is able to accommodate Geoff's mannerisms, which his co-workers disparage as 'macho'.

Critical thinking questions
1. Using Kelley's typology of followers (1988), explain why James finds it easier to work with Geoff than his other colleagues do.
2. Which follower type would you assign to James, based on Kelley's typology (1988)?
3. Explain the impact on Geoff's leadership outcomes if James were an active and independent critical thinker.

SUMMARY

LEARNING OUTCOME 1: Explain the psychology of followers in relation to leadership.

Leadership is a complex process and only recently has attention been drawn to the role, characteristics and underpinning psychology of different types of followers. Just as good leaders must have certain desirable traits, scholars are now conducting studies about the nature of followership and the desirable qualities of good followers. A key element in good followership is the ability to accommodate the influencing behaviour of leaders. Followers need to adopt 'granting' behaviours.

LEARNING OUTCOME 2: Discuss how followers and leaders interact to generate effective leadership outcomes.

Leadership is a process and the leader, follower, situation and goals are key variables in this process. It's important to make a distinction between followers and subordinates. The interactions between leaders and followers generate leadership outcomes.

LEARNING OUTCOME 3: Demonstrate an awareness of the types of followers and their role in the leadership process.

Among the various follower typologies, Kelley's (1988) typology is most frequently cited in the academic literature. However, all typologies underscore the idea that some followers engage with the leadership process more than others. A follower who is taking part at least minimally in the leadership process is more effective in helping achieve leadership outcomes than a follower who chooses not to participate at all.

LEARNING OUTCOME 4: Explain followership theory and practice.

The academic literature points to two main followership theories. First are those that focus on followership as a role-centred process, defining the follower as anyone who occupies a following role. Such theories actually reverse the leadership process, placing the follower, not the leader, at the centre of any examination of leadership. The second set of theories on followership focuses on followership as a social interaction between the leader and follower, asserting that the leadership process and outcomes are co-created.

LEARNING OUTCOME 5: Explain the challenges of followership.

Just as leadership is not for everyone, followership is not for everyone. There are certain qualities that make people good followers. Effective followers are good at accommodating the leader's influencing behaviour, and provide valuable input into the leadership outcomes by being active and critical in the leadership process. However, not all followers can be active, critical contributors to the leadership process, and followers face several challenges in practice.

REVIEW QUESTIONS

1. Define the term 'followership'.

2. What are the three key attributes of a 'good' follower'? Justify your response.

3. Explain the conditions that enable a follower to become a leader.

4. Identify three key challenges that followers encounter, and explain how these may be overcome.

5. Think of an exemplary follower from your own experience or from your knowledge of historical figures. Compare and contrast your own attributes with those of the follower you have chosen, and discuss what you learn about your preferred follower style.

CASE STUDY 5.5

Toni Hoffman – a follower and a whistleblower

Toni Hoffman, Nurse-in-Charge at the Intensive Care Unit (ICU) at Bundaberg Base Hospital, Queensland, blew the whistle on a medical scandal at her hospital. Toni's decision to blow the whistle on the clinical incompetence of surgeon Dr Jayant Patel was years in the making. Toni raised a series of concerns regarding the conduct of Dr Patel to no avail. According to other nurses, Toni's actions were brave and 'fairly incredible'. Former theatre nurse unit manager Jenny White believes that Toni's actions were probably an Australian first. The risks involved in pursuing allegations of unsafe practice could have ended Toni's career.

Toni began nursing with a desire to help people. After completing her nursing training in Australia, Toni relocated to the UK and worked in a private intensive care facility. While in the UK she studied midwifery, then moved on to Saudi Arabia during the Gulf War. Upon arrival back in Australia, Toni took up a unit manager role at the ICU at Bundaberg Base Hospital in 2002. Dr Patel began at Bundaberg as a surgeon in 2003.

One of Toni's earliest interactions with Dr Patel was marred by issues with Patel's decision to operate on a man whom other doctors had advised would not survive the surgery. Dr Patel completed the surgery and the patient passed away in ICU after five days. At this stage, Toni wrote to the Medical Director with concerns regarding the small hospital's capacity to perform such operations. She was informed that nothing was going to change.

Dr Patel worked long hours, often 6.30am to 9.00pm, and rarely offered medical opinions that did not involve a recommendation of surgery. According to Toni, he was a dream for hospital executives, who allowed him pretty much free reign over his practice. However, while the executive saw a valuable money-making asset, other medical professionals saw problems. Dr Patel's patients had high complication rates following surgery; he allegedly prescribed 'old-fashioned' medications; and he made mistakes in his patients' charts. After noticing incorrect information displayed in patients' charts, Toni again contacted her medical director, but was again ignored.

Due to Dr Patel's behaviour and his bullying of Toni in the hospital, she began to show symptoms of psychological distress. According to her mother, she stopped going out, wouldn't sleep and was uncharacteristically quiet. Toni spent much of her time away from work contemplating how to deal with the surgeon. She soon discovered that not only was Dr Patel not writing up any surgery complications on his own patients' charts, but he was also advising the junior doctors in the ICU to do the same. While these medical malpractices were occurring, executive management did not intervene; Dr Patel was making them too much money. According to Toni, '[i]t wasn't just that we were dealing with difficult people, it was that we were dealing with clinical incompetence and we needed someone to pay attention and listen'.

More shockingly, anaesthetists who were allowing this doctor to continue to operate, when questioned about their faith in Dr Patel, responded that they wouldn't let him operate on them. Although the doctors were in a position to do something about this clinical incompetence, they did nothing.

A major incident occurred with Dr Patel, which further encouraged Toni to do something about his malpractice: he cancelled the planned transfer of a patient who needed better care at a larger hospital. The patient had been injured when a caravan rolled onto his chest, and the Bundaberg staff discovered that he had 3 litres of blood in his lungs. The patient was approved for a transfer to Brisbane Hospital, but Dr Patel cancelled the transfer and the patient later passed away.

Following the incident, Toni made an appointment to see the Director of Nursing at Bundaberg but was put off for two weeks. She then called the coroner and the police department, to raise the issues she was encountering at the hospital. After seeking advice from the Queensland Nurses Union, Toni decided to speak to the District Manager and District Director of Nursing, hoping to gain their support for her challenge to Dr Patel. Toni was aware that without the support of higher-ranking staff, her challenge could be fruitless.

At the stage of her meetings, knowing the seriousness of her allegations, Toni's aim was to have Dr Patel audited based on 14 cases she felt needed to be looked over. After the managers reassured Toni that something would be done, she found that Dr Patel had been awarded Employee of the Month. Then, suddenly, representatives from the Ethical Standards Branch at the corporate office delivered a presentation where they threatened that staff could be jailed if they passed certain information over to their unions. This sequence of events scared Toni.

Following yet more deaths of Dr Patel's patients, the Chief Health Officer for Queensland Health arrived to investigate Toni's allegations. Despite the fact-finding mission, plans were being made to renew Dr Patel's contract for another five-year term.

By the time Toni made the decision to speak to her local MP, she'd attempted to raise her concerns with no less than 12 people. The MP used his parliamentary privilege to assert that 14 patients at Bundaberg Base Hospital had suffered serious complications following treatment by Dr Patel. The hospital's management demanded the MP make a public apology.

Perhaps more shockingly, the Australian Medical Association (AMA) issued a press release condemning the MP's actions as 'irresponsible'. When the story finally broke to the public, hospital staff thought it was Toni who had made the leak and accused her of just wanting her '15 minutes of fame'. A senior doctor threatened that she would be lucky to keep her job after the story broke, and the District Manager visited the hospital staff, professing that he was furious and appalled at the whistleblower's behaviour. A few days after the story, Dr Patel left the country.

Later, the Queensland Minister for Health and Director-General of Queensland Health visited the hospital, arguing that Dr Patel had not been afforded natural justice and decided against releasing the audit findings. The staff were furious that Dr Patel had got away with so much and had been protected by those who had the power to stop him but did not. These high-level staff members went even further than turning a blind eye to actively hiding the details of his incompetence.

The journalist who picked up the story was stunned at what had transpired. Dr Patel had been practising medicine for between 25 and 30 years, so the journalist decided to look into the matter. After a basic Google search, he found that Dr Patel had been severely disciplined and forced to surrender his licence just two years before being employed at Bundaberg Base Hospital. For Toni, this made the whole situation '10 times worse'. Patel's behaviour at Bundaberg was not an isolated event, it had been happening since 1982.

After this information came to light, the State Medical Board apologised for allowing a foreign doctor to practise in Queensland despite being struck off for negligence in the US. In his two years at Bundaberg, Dr Patel treated 1200 patients, of which some 90 deaths were thought to be related to his care.

A Royal Commission later found that Dr Patel should be charged with murder. Detectives from Queensland's homicide division worked to collect evidence and applied for Dr Patel to be extradited to Australia to face murder charges. Toni Hoffman said (ABC, 2005):

> we've been bullied and intimidated for so long now that I have no idea what the future holds. I probably have made some enemies because of this, but I did have to be a patient advocate. I think that I'll just keep going to work and I'll probably have some time off at the end of the year and go overseas and, I don't know, I don't know. I can't ... I have no idea ... just get some normality back in my life. That would be good, I think.

Source: Adapted from ABC (2005)

Critical thinking questions

1. Conduct your own research online to find the latest news updates on Dr Patel and Toni Hoffman.
2. Giving examples from the case study, compare and contrast the attributes of a follower and whistleblower.
3. Using Kelley's (1988) typology, what kind of follower is Toni Hoffman? Explain your response.
4. From a leader's perspective, would you prefer to have critical and independent followers or passive and uncritical followers? Explain your response.

REFERENCES

Australian Broadcasting Corporation (ABC) (2005). *Australian Story: At death's door.* Retrieved from www.abc.net.au/austory/content/2005/s1402495.htm.

Ba Banutu-Gomez, M. (2004). Great leaders teach exemplary followership and serve as servant leaders. *Journal of American Academy of Business*, 4(1–2), 143–151.

Baker, S.D. (2007). Followership: Theoretical foundation for a contemporary construct. *Journal of Leadership and Organizational Studies*, 14(1), 50–60.

Bandura, A., Caprara, G.V. & Zsolnai, L. (2000). Corporate transgressions through moral disengagement. *Journal of Human Values*, 6, 57–63.

Barbuto, J.E, Jr. (2000). Influence triggers: A framework for understanding follower compliance. *Leadership Quarterly*, 11(3), 365–87.

Baruch, Y. (1998). Leadership – is it what we study? *Journal of Leadership Studies*, 5, 100–24.

Bass, B.M. & Bass, R. (2008). *The Bass handbook of leadership: Theory, research, and managerial applications.* New York, NY: Free Press.

Blackshear, P.B. (2003). The followership continuum: A model for increasing organizational productivity. *Public Manager*, 32(2), 25–30.

Bligh, M.C. (2011). Followership and follower-centered approaches. In A. Bryman, D. Collinson, K. Grint, B. Jackson & M. Uhl-Bien (eds), *SAGE handbook of leadership* (pp. 425-436). London: SAGE Publications.

Branley, A. (2015). *7-Eleven staff work twice as long at half pay rate, investigation reveals: Four Corners.* Australian Broadcasting Corporation. Retrieved from: www.abc.net.au/news/2015–08-29/7-eleven-half-pay-scam-exposed/6734174.

Bryman, A. (1992). *Charisma and leadership in organizations.* London: SAGE Publications.

Bryman, A., Collinson, D., Grint, K., Jackson, B. & Uhl-Bien, M. (eds) (2011). *The SAGE handbook of leadership.* London: SAGE Publications.

Burns, J.M. (1978). *Leadership.* New York, NY : Harper & Row.

Carsten, M.K., Uhl-Bien, M., West B.J., Patera J.L. & McGregor, R. (2010). Exploring social constructions of followership: A qualitative study. *Leadership Quarterly*, 21(3), 543–62.

Chaleff, I. (1995). *The courageous follower: Standing up to and for our leaders.* San Francisco, CA: Berrett- Koehler Publishers.

—— (2003). The courage to follow: The term 'follower' need not imply weakness or docility. Powerful followers are necessary to support powerful leaders. *Security Management*, 47(9), 26–30.

Collinson, D. (2006). Rethinking followership: A post-structuralist analysis of follower identities. *Leadership Quarterly*, 17, 179–89.

DeRue, S. & Ashford, S. (2010). Who will lead and who will follow? A social process of leadership identity construction in organizations. *Academy of Management Review*, 35(4), 627–47

Drucker, P.F. (1993). *Management: Tasks, responsibilities, practices.* New York, NY: Harper Business.

Fernando, M. & Sim, A.B. (2011). Strategic ambiguity and leaders' responsibility beyond maximizing profits. *European Management Journal*, 29(6), 504–13.

French, J. & Raven, B. (1960). *The bases of social power.* In D. Cartwright and A. Zander, *Group Dynamics*. New York, NY: Harper & Row.

Howell, J.M. & Shamir, B. (2005). The role of followers in the charismatic leadership process: Relationships and their consequences. *Academy of Management Review*, 30, 96–112.

Hummel, R.P. (1975). Psychology of charismatic followers. *Psychological Reports*, 37, 759–70.

Jackson, B. & Parry K. (2008). *A very short, fairly interesting and reasonably cheap book about studying leadership.* London: SAGE Publications.

Kellerman, B. (2008). *Followership: How followers are creating change and changing leaders.* Boston:Harvard Business School Publishing.

Kelley, R.E. (1988). In praise of followers, *Harvard Business Review*, 66(6), 141–8.

—– (2008). *Rethinking followership. The art of followership – how great followers create great leaders and organizations.* San Francisco, CA: Jossey-Bass.

Kerr, S. & Jermier, J.M. (1978). Substitutes for leadership: Their meaning and measurement. *Organizational Behavior and Human Performance*, 22, 375–403.

Khurana, R. (2002). The curse of the superstar CEO, *Harvard Business Review*, 80(9) (September 2002).

Lapierre, L. & Carsten, M. (2014). *Followership: What is it and why do people follow?* London:Emerald Group Publishing.

Lipman-Blumen, J. (2005). *The allure of toxic leaders: Why we follow destructive bosses and corrupt politicians – and how we can survive them.* Oxford: Oxford University Press.

Martin, R. (2015). A review of the literature of the followership since 2008: The importance of relationships and emotional intelligence. *SAGE Open*, October–December 1–9.

Organ, D.W. (1998). *Organisational citizenship behaviour: The good soldier syndrome,* Lexington, MA: Lexington Books.

Palmer, N. (2013). The effects of leader behavior on follower ethical behavior: Examining the mediating roles of ethical efficacy and moral disengagement. *Dissertations and Theses from the College of Business Administration.* paper 40. Retrieved from: http://digitalcommons.unl.edu/businessdiss/40.

Podsakoff, P.M., MacKenzie, S.B., Moorman, R.H. & Fetter, R. (1990). Transformational leader behaviors and their effects on followers' trust in leader, satisfaction, and organizational citizenship behaviors. *Leadership Quarterly*, 1, 107–42.

Prendergast, C. (1993). A theory of yes men. *The American Economic Review*, 83, 4.

Reynolds, G. & Jones, P. (2017). Trumping distrust in the corporate world. *The Stand*. Retrieved from: http://stand.uow.edu.au/trumping-distrust-in-the-corporate-world.

Savoie, D. (2010). *Power: Where is it?* Montreal: McGill-Queen's University Press.

Shamir, B. (2007). From passive recipients to active co-producers. In B. Shamir, R. Pillai, M.C. Bligh & M. Uhl-Bien (eds), *Follower-centered perspectives on leadership* (pp. ix–xxix). Greenwich, CT: Information Age.

Sharif, M. & Scandura, T. (2013). Do perceptions of ethical conduct matter during organizational change? Ethical leadership and employee involvement. *Journal of Business Ethics*, 124(2), 185–196.

Sy, T. (2010). What do you think of followers? Examining the content, structure, and consequences of implicit followership theories. *Organizational Behavior and Human Decision Processes*, 113, 73–84.

Tepper, B.J., Uhl-Bien, M., Kohut, G.F., Rogelberg, S.G., Lockhart, D.E. & Ensley, M.D. (2006). Subordinates' resistance and managers' evaluations of subordinates' performance. *Journal of Management*, 32(2), 185–209.

Uhl-Bien, M. & Pillai, R. (2007). The romance of leadership and the social construction of leadership. In B. Shamir, R. Pillai, M.C. Bligh & M. Uhl- Bien (Eds). *Follower-centered perspectives on leadership* (pp. 187–210). Greenwich, CT: Information Age.

Uhl-Bien, M., Riggio, R., Lowe, K.B. & Carsten, M.K. (2013). Followership theory: A review and research agenda. *Leadership Quarterly*, 25, 1–22.

Weber, M. (1968). *Economy and society*. New York, NY: Bedminster Press.

6

CROSS-CULTURAL LEADERSHIP

Mario Fernando

LEARNING OUTCOMES

After reading this chapter, you should be able to:

1. understand how culture can affect leadership

2. demonstrate an awareness of cultural frameworks and leadership

3. understand the relationship between cultural values and leadership

4. explain and discuss international leadership skills

5. explain the challenges of cross-cultural leadership.

INTRODUCTION

THIS CHAPTER WILL introduce the key situational factors that influence leadership, demonstrating that leadership doesn't take place in a vacuum. Both internal and external contexts influence the practice of leadership, and they can affect leaders, followers and the leadership process itself. Internal factors may include the organisation's culture, life-cycle stage, number of employees, internal politics and profitability. External factors may include the industry in which the organisation operates, the state of the economy, national cultural attributes and social expectations. Cultural factors such as values, norms and beliefs, at both national and organisational levels, affect leadership styles, decisions and leadership practices. This chapter examines the key influences that culture may exert over leadership, and outlines the skills that leaders need to effectively lead in culturally challenging situations.

HOW CULTURE CAN AFFECT LEADERSHIP

The contemporary business landscape is becoming increasingly complex and multicultural, and leaders must be ready to perform across a range of cultures. **Culture** is the common understanding of the members of a society. It is their collective understanding of events and activities as they have evolved over time, as projected through language, behaviour and 'artefacts' (things that symbolise a society). Culture can play a significant role in influencing leadership style.

> **Culture** – The collective mental programming of a group of people that distinguishes them from other groups.

The importance of culture in leadership can be understood by considering an example. Imagine a leadership situation where an Australian who was qualified through an American business school is required to lead the subsidiary of an Indian firm operating in Africa. The challenge for this leader would be to identify the best leadership attributes to suit the local cultural conditions. Several researchers have studied how culture can influence leadership (Kong & Volkema, 2016; Barker, 2002; Hage & Posner, 2015; Hofstede, 1980, 1991). They have noted that the cultural norms, traditions and values can have an impact on how leaders form their attitudes, and ultimately their leadership behaviour. Cultural norms set out rules and guidelines for acceptable or unacceptable behaviour that people in a society are expected to follow. The rules explain what outsiders to the society, as well as locals, can and can't do. Cultural values are deeply held beliefs about what is important to a society.

Australian cultural attributes

A study conducted by Karpin (1995) found that lack of vision, short-termism and not paying enough attention to strategy, teamwork, people skills and cross-cultural skills all contribute to poor leadership in Australia (O'Neill, 1996; Barker, 2002). Australian studies (e.g. Ashkanasy & Falkus, 1997) have found that the cultural attributes of **egalitarianism** and individualism can influence leadership. Egalitarianism is based on the idea that Australians hold strong values of equality, and that leaders in Australia should pay

> **Egalitarianism** – A belief that all individuals are equal.

attention to ensuring equitable outcomes from their leadership behaviours. This idea of equality stems from the early experiences of Australian society, where members of the new convict colonies needed to cooperate to survive in a vast and difficult terrain (Ashkanasy & Falkus, 1997). The evolving Australian society at the time disregarded the class system and bureaucracy of the 'mother country' (Great Britain) and, as the members of the society saw themselves as convicts fighting the system, they considered all as equals in the struggle. The concept of 'mateship' developed in Australian society at that time and quite visibly persists today. Any individual who attempted to stand out by achieving a higher level of performance was criticised and brought down to the level of the 'group'; this is still referred to as 'tall poppy syndrome', whereby any member of a society who distinguishes themselves is 'cut down'. Individualism is also linked to the preference for equality and the tendency to value having a 'fair go' at success in life. Thus, to be effective in Australia, a leader needs to pay attention to ensuring equality in outcomes and develop opportunities for all to have a fair chance of success at work.

Like national culture, organisational culture can also influence leadership style. For example, Ahammad and co-authors (2014) found that organisational cultural differences have a negative effect on the acquisition of companies across several countries. Meng (2015) found in a study conducted in England and Singapore that leadership attributes and skills in corporate communications are driven by the immediate organisational context, a supportive organisational culture and the flexible nature of the organisation.

Influence of cultural attributes on leadership

Cultural acceptance and public endorsement of antisocial behaviours such as corruption can generate leaders with a tendency to behave in a self-serving style, with highly self-centred and autocratic behaviour. Kong and Volkema (2016) used data from 53 societies to find that cultural endorsement or acceptance of self-serving leadership, where the public expects leaders to achieve self-interest at the expense of collective welfare, was positively related to corruption, and that this relationship was strengthened in cases where the leader was wealthy. Other scholars such as Resick and co-authors (2006) found that integrity is highly valued among Nordic societies, and is consequently expected from leaders. In contrast, Middle Eastern countries tend to place less emphasis on transparency and equity, which is reflected in their leaders' behaviours.

Religious values may also affect leadership in cross-cultural settings (Fernando, 2011). For example, Wong (2001) found that Chinese culture and leadership are strongly influenced by Buddhism and Confucianism. Moreover, religion is an integral part of Arab cultures, and, as Hage and Posner (2015) found, the religious convictions of Arab managers and other leaders affect the way they interact with subordinates. They studied 384 organisational leaders in Lebanon and found that Muslim leaders were less transformational, with more autocratic leadership styles than their Christian counterparts. Hage and Posner conclude that these Muslim leaders may have been influenced by a strict adherence to Qur'anic principles, which stipulate that followers must obey those who are in authority. Similar trends are found in Muslim-majority countries such as Turkey, Kuwait, Egypt, Morocco and Qatar (Kabasakal & Bodur, 2002) and the United Arab Emirates (UAE) (AlMazrouei & Pech, 2015).

CULTURAL FRAMEWORKS FOR LEADERSHIP

Culture-specific traditions and philosophy can have a major impact on the leadership style within an organisation. Although they have limited applicability, some theoretical frameworks have been developed to measure different aspects of cross-cultural leadership and to describe the attributes of various cultures. Managers find these frameworks useful when dealing in unfamiliar cultures.

Hofstede's cultural dimensions

Geert Hofstede, a prominent scholar who conducted a series of studies on how cultural differences influence organisations, treated culture as the 'collective programming' of a group of people that distinguishes that group from others. He found what he labelled 'dimensions of culture' were common across groups of cultures (Hofstede, 1980; 1991).

Power distance

The power distance dimension groups those cultures that are more willing to accept inequality between followers, who have less power, and leaders, who have greater power. In countries like Australia, where egalitarianism is more prevalent, a low power distance was evident in the studies: followers were not willing to accept inequality and lack of power distribution in society. On the other hand, in countries such as China and Japan, followers were found to be more likely to accept inequality and lack of power distribution due to the long-term centralisation of authority.

Individualism and collectivism

The dimension of individualism versus collectivism groups cultures by the extent to which people are likely to live in close-knit groups. Most Western countries are high in individualism and low in collectivism, because of their relatively informal ties to others and a tendency to focus on 'I' as opposed to 'we' (Hofstede, 1980). In Hofstede's dimensions, Australia has been found to lie at the individualistic end of this scale.

Uncertainty avoidance

Another dimension that Hofstede (1980) found was uncertainty avoidance, which shows the extent of a society's tolerance for ambiguity. Cultures with high uncertainty avoidance prefer to follow strict codes and rules; Singapore is an example. A lower uncertainty avoidance is found in cultures like Australia's, which is more accepting of creative ideas and opposing viewpoints. These cultures tend to embrace change and contrasting viewpoints, which may allow them to flourish in a rapidly changing economic and social global environment.

Masculinity and femininity

Hofstede found a dimension across what he termed 'masculine' and 'feminine' attributes. In more 'masculine-dominant' cultures, attributes such as success, heroism and assertiveness are prominent. More 'feminine-dominant' cultures tend to value modesty, caring for the weak and improving quality of life. In Australia, there are more of what Hofstede called 'masculine-dominant' attributes, as opposed to what he called 'feminine-dominant'.

Long-term and short-term orientation

Hofstede also found that some cultures preferred to organise their communities with a long-term perspective, whilst others preferred a short-term perspective. This long-term versus short-term dimension examines societies' connection to the past, present and future. A society at the short-term end of the scale values links to the past, honours traditions and has relatively little concern for the future. Those cultures that score toward the long-term end organise their communities more with the present, and aim to determine absolute truth.

Later developments in Hofstede's cultural dimensions

Later studies of Hofstede's cultural dimensions include indulgence: the extent to which members of a society attempt to control their desires and impulses. In this way, cultures can be identified as indulgent or restrained. A culture where relatively weak control is exerted is more indulgent, and one where relatively strong control is exerted is more restrained.

Hofstede's framework in an Australian context

What Hofstede's study findings mean to Australian leadership effectiveness can be explained by looking at where Australia stands in terms of the dimensions in relation to another country, namely China. (You can use this comparison tool to compare the cultural dimensions of other countries: https://www.hofstede-insights.com/country-comparison/australia,china/.) Compared to China, Australia scored low on power distance, suggesting that leaders should be accessible and use both formal and informal communication with followers, and that followers expect to be consulted in key decisions (see Figure 6.1).

Australia's high individualism score suggests that leaders in Australia, unlike in China, will be effective if they respect followers' individual rights. High masculine scores in both countries suggest that in Australia, leaders need to recognise that the society is driven by competitiveness, a merit-driven ethos and success, expressed by a 'winner takes all' mentality. Australia received an average score on uncertainty avoidance; thus, this dimension is relatively stable in the Australian context. Unlike China, Australia scored high on the short-term dimension, suggesting relatively little concern for the future, with a short-term approach to solving problems. Compared to China, Australia can be classified as an indulgent culture where people have a tendency to enjoy life; Australians value leisure time, and wish to live their lives as they choose.

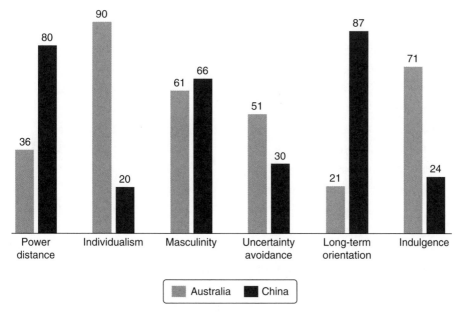

Figure 6.1 Hofstede's dimensions – Australia and China compared

Source: Hofstede et al. (2010), © Geert Hofstede B.V., quoted with permission

Global Leadership and Organizational Behavior Effectiveness (GLOBE) study

More recently, to respond to complex, culture-driven leadership situations, Robert House and his team from the Wharton School of the University of Pennsylvania conducted the Global Leadership and Organizational Behavior Effectiveness (GLOBE) study (House et al., 2004). The study analysed data gathered from 62 societies and from 17 300 middle managers in 951 organisations, across various manufacturing and services sectors. They found that 'one size does not fit all', and recommended that a set of leadership attributes should be employed to suit the local conditions of cultural norms and expectations. Thus, although a leader might be known to be charismatic, under certain cultural conditions they might have to adjust their style to suit the notions of charisma that apply in the local business context. The GLOBE study findings are often used to identify which leadership attributes are required to succeed in a particular culture. House and co-authors (2004, p. 30) established nine cultural dimensions to capture the similarities and/or differences in cultural norms, beliefs and practices in societies to assess leadership effectiveness across cultures. These are:

1. *performance orientation*: The degree to which a community encourages and rewards group members for performance improvement and excellence

2. *power distance*: The degree to which members of a community expect power to be distributed equally

3. *humane orientation*: The degree to which a society, organisation or group encourages and rewards individuals for being fair, altruistic, generous, caring, and kind to others

4. *collectivism I (institutional):* The degree to which organisational and societal institutional practices encourage and reward collective distribution of resources and collective action

5. *collectivism II (in-group):* The degree to which individuals express pride, loyalty and cohesiveness in their organisations or families.

6. *uncertainty avoidance*: The degree to which a society, organisation or group relies on social norms, rules and procedures to alleviate unpredictability of future events

7. *assertiveness*: The degree to which individuals are assertive, confrontational and aggressive in their relationships with others

8. *gender egalitarianism*: The degree to which a collective minimises gender inequality

9. *future orientation*: The extent to which individuals engage in future-oriented behaviours such as delaying gratification, planning, and investing in the future.

Based on the similarities and differences of these dimensions across the 62 societies, the GLOBE study then grouped similar cultures together and found six common leadership styles across the cultures. The first is the performance-oriented style or charismatic/value-based style. It emphasises achieving for high-quality outcomes, with decisiveness and innovation. This style inspires people around a vision and creates a passion among them to perform. The team-oriented style focuses on cohesiveness and group-oriented approaches to problem solving with loyalty at the core of the group's activity. While the participative style seeks to promote an inclusive approach to decision making and equality, the humane style places compassion and generosity as the most important aspects to focus on. This leadership style ultimately is concerned about followers' well-being. The promotion of ego is at the centre of the autonomous style. It is driven by a desire for an individualistic approach to leadership. The last leadership style is the self-protective (and group-protective) style. The protection of the individual (or group) is at the core of this leadership style. It uses rules and regulations to protect the image of the leader (and the group).

Global Leadership and Organizational Behavior Effectiveness (GLOBE) study and Australia

What do the GLOBE study findings mean to leadership effectiveness in Australia? According to Ashkanasy and Falkus (1997), the first type of leadership attribute, visionary, suggests a style of leadership that presents followers with a clear goal to motivate and influence them in a collegial, but firm and strategic, manner. The second, narcissistic, suggests self-centred leadership behaviour that will reduce leadership effectiveness; leaders should avoid it. The third attribute, egalitarianism, stems from the Australian culture and represents an unselfish and collaborative approach to work. It emphasises the importance of working in teams led by a benevolent and compassionate leader. The last attribute, bureaucratic, like egalitarianism, stems from the Australian culture; however, unlike egalitarianism, it will impede leader effectiveness because of Australians' tendency to resent overbearing authority and to value individuality. Thus, the GLOBE study findings presented two attributes that promote leadership effectiveness and two that impede it.

While the GLOBE study confirms the long-held view that a visionary leadership style promotes leadership effectiveness regardless of culture-specific attributes, egalitarian leadership should be considered as an additional attribute to lead effectively in Australia. Thus, in essence, Australian leaders need to learn skills to balance the demands of visionary leadership with egalitarianism.

Association of Southeast Asian Nations' Perspective on Excellence in Leadership (APEL) framework

Some scholars (e.g. Selvarajah et al., 1995) have suggested that the Association of Southeast Asian Nations' Perspective on Excellence in Leadership (APEL) is a framework that incorporates a cross-cultural dimension in leadership. The framework, which is used to identify perceptions of excellence in leadership in both private and public sectors in the Association of Southeast Asian Nations (ASEAN) countries, includes four dimensions: personal, managerial, organisational and environmental. Personal qualities refer to values, skills, beliefs, attitudes and qualities such as morality, religion and interpersonal relationships and communication that affect the behaviour of managers (De Waal et al., 2015; Fernando & Nilakant, 2008; Selvarajah et al., 1995). Managerial behaviours refer to values, attitudes, actions and styles of management specific to the performance of managerial tasks. Organisational demands refer to how managers respond to organisational goals, rules, structures, demands, pressures and rewards. Environment influence explains the factors outside the organisation that affect operational success. APEL is often used to examine leadership effectiveness across several cultures. It has been used and validated in follow-up studies in several ASEAN countries, including Singapore, Thailand, China, Cambodia and Malaysia (Selvarajah & Meyer, 2006, 2008). The APEL framework is considered valid in some developed countries, such as in the Netherlands and the UK, as well as in South Africa (Shrivastava et al., 2014).

Some researchers also use the Leadership Competency Framework (LCF), which discusses universal competencies, to identify why some leaders are successful across countries. However, this is considered problematic due to the 'great person' view portrayed in the theories underpinning it, because it raises the question of how great the person is (Hollenbeck et al., 2006). Further, Wang and co-authors (2014) point out that the framework does not highlight cultural values associated with transformational and charismatic leadership.

Suresh goes to Australia

Suresh Patel, born in India, has been posted to the Sydney office of an information technology multinational company as the CEO. Suresh lived in India until he was 33, when he moved to the United States to undertake his MBA. Soon after graduating, he returned to India. He has never travelled to Australia and, apart from sharing a passion for the game of cricket, he has little in common with Australian culture.

Suresh was brought up in a very conservative Hindu family, where paternalism and collectivist group behaviour were valued. Suresh is a humble and quiet character, preferring to speak only when spoken to. He is very religious and visits the Hindu temple on a weekly basis. Suresh has learned that his office is based in Sydney's central business district, and that the 120 employees he is expected to lead are mostly of Caucasian origin. He is now quite anxious about how he will be received by his colleagues at the Sydney office.

Critical thinking questions

1. Using Hofstede's cultural dimensions, analyse the key cultural differences between India and Australia.
2. How might these key differences affect Suresh's leadership as the CEO of the Australian branch?
3. What advice would you give Suresh to help him lead his Australian team?

CULTURAL VALUES AND LEADERSHIP

Leadership styles are linked with culture, as people from different cultures have different assumptions and beliefs about the characteristics that are effective for leadership (Jogulu, 2010). Studies on culture and leadership have found that cultural values shape leadership styles in different ways: they can directly influence the leadership style, moderate the leadership effect and provide a substitute for the leadership function when leader behaviour is absent.

There is evidence across the globe to suggest that national cultural values can influence a leadership style. In China, business leadership styles are related to Confucian principles: for example, as Wong (2001) shows, Chinese business leaders tend to emphasise moral aspects of leadership. Mingzheng and Xinhui (2014) note that this is not only true for private business organisations: Chinese public leadership is also based on moral concepts and relationships influenced by the Confucian tradition. Wang and co-authors (2012), using data from Chinese high-tech private enterprises in the medical device sector, found that benevolent leadership based on Confucianism was the main leadership style.

There is also evidence from other countries that leadership style is directly correlated with culture. For example, in Germany, the culture is structured and individualistic, with a place and purpose for everything (Richardson et al., 2014). Thus, the leadership style is straightforward and aggressive, with no tolerance for mistakes. In Japan, however, the relationship orientation reflects the cultural values of collectivism, long-term orientation and strong and stable relationships

(Mujtaba & Isomura, 2012). In Russia, the influence of the national cultural heritage stemming from the Stalin regime and communist principles is clear from the most common leadership style, which is centralised, and followers have a preference for strong direction (Richardson et al., 2014). In contrast, in Australia, with freedom and autonomy being fundamental values, leaders often demonstrate transformational leadership styles (Jogulu & Ferkins, 2012).

Scholars have found that cultural values can serve as a substitute for leadership when leadership behaviours do not reflect any task- or relationship-oriented focus (Hartnell et al., 2016). Culture provides cues on accepted behaviours, norms and practices in relational or task-oriented cultures. Hartnell and co-authors (2016) point out that organisational leadership is ineffective when the leadership style is high-relational or task-oriented with high levels of corresponding cultural values.

National values can also influence the leadership in certain cultures, as they can affect the 'power base' that leaders use to influence their followers. For example, Mittal and Elias (2016) found that managers are more likely to activate expert, referent, informational, legitimate and personal-reward powers in cultures that are loose, collectivistic and low in power distance, masculinity and uncertainty avoidance. In these countries, for example, Israel and the Netherlands, leaders tend to use 'soft' power to gain compliance from followers (i.e. persuasive power based on cultural and other factors). Cultures that are tight, short-term-oriented and high in power distance and uncertainty avoidance (e.g. Turkey and South Korea) influence followers through 'hard' power, such as the power that comes from authority and the power to reward and punish.

INTERNATIONAL LEADERSHIP SKILLS

Cross-cultural leadership skills are essential for the international success of a business. Understanding culture is important for leaders because of the various approaches to staffing that global companies use. There are various organisational approaches to working with people from different cultures.

Cross-cultural staffing approaches

Ethnocentric staffing policies focus more on the parent-company control and tend to appoint leaders from the culture of the parent company. The desire to maintain the superiority of the culture where the parent company is located is a key feature in these cultures. An expatriate leader who is operating in a host culture would be required to use home-country cultural norms and values in leading the operations overseas. Such a leader would not try to adopt a style that is aligned with the local customs and traditions. In **polycentric staffing**, the focus is more on focusing on the host-country culture. An expatriate leader under these circumstances would be expected to pay a great deal of attention to local customs and norms.

Ethnocentric staffing – The tendency to focus more on home-country cultural values in international staffing policies.

Polycentric staffing – the tendency to focus more on the host-country cultural values in international staffing policies.

The **geocentric staffing** approach appears to hold no bias towards either the home- or host-country cultures. Instead, the leader is selected on the level of competence for the job and is expected to adopt a leadership approach that considers the best interests of the company, and will take whatever action necessary to further the company's goals. These three prominent cross-cultural staffing approaches can influence how leaders effectively deal with cross-cultural challenges.

Essential intercultural competencies

Intercultural competencies are the essential skills that leaders must have to practise effectively across cultures. Important intercultural competencies include:

- adopting a global mindset in addressing complex issues
- adaptability
- cultural and cross-cultural awareness
- the ability to lead and motivate a diverse workforce
- communication
- empathy
- conflict management.

Global mindset

Global mindset is defined as an individual's capability to influence others unlike themselves (Javidan & Bowen, 2013, p. 1). Three types of capital are essential components of the global mindset:

1. global intellectual capital, which includes global business savvy, cognitive complexity and cosmopolitan outlook
2. global psychological capital, which includes passion for diversity, quest for adventure and self-assurance
3. global social capital, which includes intercultural empathy, interpersonal impact and empathy.

A global mindset is considered an essential skill for leaders who need to solve problems effectively in complex and multicultural situations.

Adaptability

Leadership in international settings also requires leaders to adapt to new cultural contexts (Deal, 2003). Adaptability in leaders is associated with emotional resilience, which is the ability to withstand high levels of pressure and stay emotionally stable under stressful conditions. Being adaptable also includes achieving goals through hard work and reliability. To be adaptable, leaders should be aware of the local conditions: specifically, the customs, laws and traditions of the culture in which they are operating.

Cultural and cross-cultural awareness

Cultural and cross-cultural awareness is another skill that can help leaders perform effectively in cross-cultural settings. Being aware of the attitudes and behaviours of the local people can help leaders operate with authority in business matters. A high level of cultural awareness can help leaders to decide how power and authority can be exercised, and to understand the behaviour of the local people.

Adaptability and cultural awareness are closely linked with cultural intelligence: a person's ability to interact, adapt and perform in diverse cultural contexts (Alon et al., 2016; Crowne, 2008). The number of countries a person has lived in for more than six months, level of education and number of languages spoken contribute to increasing levels of cultural intelligence. A leader with high cultural intelligence is able to identify cultural cues, and thus to operate more effectively in diverse situations.

Leading and motivating a diverse workforce

Scholars have found that international leaders require the ability to motivate a diverse workforce. For example, an operation in the oil and gas sector could involve a migrant work team consisting of locally sourced employees and contractors from Indonesia, the Philippines and East Timor. The leadership could be from a Western country such as Australia or the US. The diverse group of workers might have different perceptions of safety measures. Some workers might not report operational errors due to their perceptions of reporting faults. Where there are different expectations about safety-measure reporting, a leader's ability to motivate the team could be a critical factor in ensuring consistent action across the multicultural team. Under these conditions, international business leaders could motivate a diverse team by becoming initiators, role models, coaches and strategists.

Communication

Effective international leaders also require the ability to communicate across cultures. Scholars have found that in many instances, the high rate of failure in multinational operations is due to lack of effective cross-cultural communication. Numerous scholars have found that trustworthy, strategic and ethical leaders who can articulate a message clearly across cultures are crucial to business success. Leaders' ability to effectively communicate in cross-cultural settings is particularly important in high-risk industries such as oil and gas, where lack of effective communication could lead to serious harm to workers' health and safety (Casey et al., 2015).

Empathy

When working with employees from various nationalities, it is important for leaders to understand that what is manifestly obvious in follower behaviour is likely to be deeply rooted in cultural traditions and habits. Habits and value systems shape our behaviour. In the contemporary workplace, where leaders can come across followers with an array of cultural backgrounds, leaders need to have the patience and empathy to understand followers' rationale for behaviour in terms of their cultural background and value systems.

Conflict management

Leaders need to have highly developed conflict management skills. These skills include abilities to accommodate, compromise, avoid, collaborate and other traits. Due to the higher levels of unknowns involved, conflict management issues when leading in international settings can be more complex and challenging.

CASE STUDY 6.2

Jenny's communication skills in China

Jenny has just arrived in China and two weeks ago started a new job with an Australian-owned oil and gas company as team leader of a small of group of Chinese workers responsible for safety on oil rigs. As she has no knowledge of Mandarin, she finds it hard to be an effective leader. Jenny is becoming increasingly frustrated that she can't lead the way she wants to, particularly as there is only one-way communication with her team. Jenny meets with her team, using an interpreter, and asks how she can help them to perform better and whether there are issues that she needs to resolve. Nobody speaks in response to her question.

Critical thinking questions
1. What advice would you give Jenny about being more effective in her communication skills?
2. How do you think cultural differences are affecting the situation that Jenny is facing?
3. If you were Jenny, how would you address this issue?

CHALLENGES IN CROSS-CULTURAL LEADERSHIP

The role of the cross-cultural leader is to motivate and drive a culturally diverse workforce to achieve a common goal. However, leading in cross-cultural settings can be difficult and complex, and it's important to be aware of the key challenges leaders could face.

Familiarity with norms, values and cultural artefacts

To be effective in cross-cultural settings, leaders should first be familiar with the norms, values and cultural artefacts in cross-cultural settings. This could be a challenge to leaders, depending on how different their own cultural background is from that of their organisation. For example, in the UAE, Islamic religious principles and practices and Arab culture could play a key role in determining how effective organisational leadership is. A leader from the West might initially find it quite difficult to adjust to such conditions, and the underlying cultural values that drive corporate behaviour could create misunderstandings in organisational change processes. Thus, leaders who cannot or do not gain a deeper understanding of the host culture's norms, beliefs and attitudes may fail to achieve effective leadership outcomes.

Blending with local cultural expectations

To be effective in cross-cultural settings, leaders must adopt a leadership style that blends with local cultural expectations. For example, in countries such as Australia, with a relatively low power distance on the Hofstede dimensions, leaders have the opportunity to use effective communication skills to gain more access to their followers than they could in societies with a high power distance, such as the Middle Eastern countries, where leaders are expected to be more controlling and less approachable, and to delegate less (Dickson et al., 2003). Further, in the Australian context, leaders must accept that they are operating within a culture that appreciates freedom and autonomy as cultural values. The need to have a flexible leadership approach that accommodates local conditions could be challenging for some leaders.

Resolving conflict between culture and management

Leaders in cross-cultural settings can be exposed to issues arising from conflicting practices between cultural norms and organisational management practices. For example, in Arab cultures, where authoritarianism and over-protectionism are dominant, followers may expect leaders to protect them from adverse business situations. In some other cultures, a collective mindset and an emphasis on group relationships could be more dominant. Under these circumstances, some Western management practices such as performance evaluations and 360-degree feedback, where bosses are evaluated by followers, would likely not achieve the expected outcomes. Thus, balancing the best organisational management practices with culture-specific practices may be challenging for a leader.

Navigating discrimination and maintaining diversity

Cultural norms and discrimination practices may challenge the effectiveness of leadership in certain cross-cultural settings. For example, an Australian leader appointed to head the operations in an Arab culture may find it difficult to negotiate the gender differences prevalent in these cultures. The participation of women in positions of authority is limited, and the Australian leader who is used to the principles of egalitarianism and autonomy may find it confronting to lead in such circumstances. Scholars have found that in the UAE, expatriate managers who are not accustomed to that society's female dress code, which sometimes includes covering the face, may feel intimidated or uncomfortable (AlMazrouei & Pech, 2015). These leaders may find dealing with males relatively easier, and thus may have a subconscious bias towards males. Thus, cultural and organisational norms and practices may challenge leaders to maintain diversity.

Understanding cross-cultural ethics

In cross-cultural settings, differences in perceptions of standards of ethics and transparency could pose some challenges to leaders. For example, integrity and transparency are highly valued in Nordic societies, and these values are expected to be reflected in business leadership. On the other hand, in Middle Eastern countries business leaders are not expected to display the same level of transparency and equity (Resick et al., 2006). There may also be significant perception differences regarding ethical practices due to cultural differences in the BRIC countries (Brazil, Russia, India and China). Corruption is one area where perception differences could raise problems for leaders in cross-cultural settings. In countries such as some African states, corruption is widespread and 'normalised'. Leading and managing corruption-free workplaces across borders may be challenging for leaders. More generally, leaders could find it difficult to manage a workforce with different perceptions and standards on ethics, integrity and transparency.

CASE STUDY 6.3

Emprise IT – the challenge of cross-cultural leadership
Emprise IT is a global information technology company with offices in New Zealand, China, Australia, the UAE and Kenya. The group CEO of the company, Meena Reza, is Australian-born of Jordanian ancestry. She is a devout Muslim. She speaks English fluently with an Australian accent. No one would notice her Muslim or Jordanian background unless she were to speak about it. Meena often has virtual meetings with her country managers over Skype and finds it difficult to understand the different cultural values and norms underlying the country managers' demands and expectations. She wants your advice as a cross-cultural leadership consultant on how to be an effective leader across all her operational sites.

Critical thinking questions
1. Meena wants to implement a global human resource system applicable to all her operational sites. Identify and explain three challenges that Meena would face in the implementation of the global human resource system.
2. If you were Meena, how would you overcome these challenges?
3. Explain how having a global mindset would help Meena to be an effective leader.

SUMMARY

LEARNING OUTCOME 1: Understand how culture can affect leadership.

This chapter has examined how leadership can be influenced by cultural values and norms. Leadership is a complex process that doesn't transpire in a vacuum. The context of each leadership process influences the leadership outcomes. Culture is embedded in any leadership situation and it can influence the leadership outcomes directly or indirectly.

LEARNING OUTCOME 2: Demonstrate an awareness of cultural frameworks and leadership.

Of the available cultural frameworks, the GLOBE study is the most significant when it comes to understanding the cross-cultural dimensions of leadership effectiveness. It employs the findings of Hofstede and others to develop six effective leadership styles to be used across cultures.

LEARNING OUTCOME 3: Understand the relationship between cultural values and leadership.

Studies have found that cultural values can directly determine what leadership style is effective in a culture. National cultural values can influence organisational culture and, in turn, the leadership process.

LEARNING OUTCOME 4: Explain and discuss international leadership skills.

A parent company's international staffing policies across cultures may consider individual leader skills before posting staff to leadership positions overseas. Leader effectiveness may depend on the alignment between the parent company's international staffing approaches and ethnocentric, polycentric or geocentric approaches.

LEARNING OUTCOME 5: Explain the challenges of cross-cultural leadership.

Leadership is a complex process. The ability to lead effectively can be more challenging in cross-cultural settings. Appreciating these challenges is a step towards becoming an effective leader in cross-cultural settings.

REVIEW QUESTIONS

1. How can cultural attributes influence leadership behaviour?

2. Explain Hofstede's cultural dimensions.

3. What are the GLOBE study findings about leadership effectiveness in Australia?

4. Why are cross-cultural leadership skills important for the international success of a business?

5. Explain the challenges of cross-cultural leadership.

CASE STUDY 6.4

Leading Kookaburra Books in Indonesia

Having captured much of the domestic market for the supply of books to school libraries, Australian book retailer Kookaburra Books is seeking to expand its business into new markets overseas that have a growing demand for English-language books for schools. One of Australia's most proximate northern neighbours, Indonesia, represents a potentially lucrative expansion option: its economy is predicted to grow to become the world's seventh largest in the next decade; English is taught universally in its schools; and it has a burgeoning middle class with growing expendable income.

Despite these challenging differences, Indonesia represents an alluring proposition for growth-oriented Australian companies. The economic growth prospects for Indonesia are very positive. Indonesia has the largest economy of the 10 ASEAN countries. Of particular interest to Kookaburra Books is the fact that education is Australia's number one 'services' export to Indonesia ($585 million). The requirement for the supply of English-language books to support education and training programs in Indonesia represents a clear business opportunity.

Additionally, there is significant movement of students and teachers between the two countries through exchanges, partnerships and paid tertiary study. Indonesia is the most popular destination for students under the Australian Government's New Colombo Plan, an initiative to encourage young Australians to work and study in the region. Over 13 000 Indonesian students enrolled in over 17 100 courses in 2013, making Indonesia the seventh largest source of international students in Australia. Each of these fora represents a possible opportunity for the supply of English-language books.

Whilst the economic opportunity in Indonesia is apparent, Kookaburra Books will need to exercise a great deal of care with its first foray into unfamiliar territory. It is through the prism of Geert Hofstede's Dimensions of National Cultures Model that this report explores Indonesia's cultural complexities for an Australian business.

Dimension #1: Power distance

Power and wealth are distributed unequally in Indonesia. The inequality is starkly apparent when visiting the Indonesian capital, Jakarta, where towering skyscrapers, home to some of the world's biggest corporations, adjoin desperately-poor kampung (villages) where day-to-day subsistence is the only pursuit. The juxtaposition of rich and poor is universally accepted as a way of life by Indonesians, and the relative harmony of Indonesian society, despite the stark disparity, is often incomprehensible to Westerners.

Indonesian society is ordered hierarchically at all levels – the family unit (with the *Bapak* or father as head of the family), the village (*desa*), school (the teacher, or *guru*, is a revered figure), business, and local, provincial and national government. Not only is *Bapak* the word for father, but it is also used to address any person in a position of authority. The commonly used Indonesian phrase '*asal Bapak senang*' (or 'keep the boss happy') is indicative of the cultural predominance of the father figure in Indonesia. Those at the top of the hierarchy wield considerable power and there are clear inequalities between top elites and those on the lower rungs of society. Unlike Australian society, many upper and middle-class families in Indonesia utilise the services of one or more *pembantu* (a helper or maid) from the lower classes and it is not uncommon for Western expatriates living in Indonesia to have at least a driver and a house-maid.

In business, a high power distance means that employees unfailingly do what they are told by those in higher positions. Subordinates expect to receive direction, they do not question authority and their superiors expect unconditional compliance. Managers are respected for the position they hold, not for their individual managerial or leadership capabilities. There is little direct communication between manager and employee, and negative feedback is not expressly stated. Business dealings are typically conducted in a highly formal manner, with the ritual exchange of business cards and an extended period of pleasantries before engaging in business discussion. Handshakes are limp and prolonged. Small tokenistic gifts are often given – always with the right hand – as a sign of respect. Being deferential, soft tones, an open stance and a friendly demeanour are critical, regardless of the situation.

Dimension #2: Individualism versus collectivism

Recognised in both the Hofstede model and other cultural models is the dimension of individualism versus collectivism. This dimension recognises the degree of interdependence a society maintains among its members, and the degree to which individuals are integrated into groups.

Indonesia is a collectivist society. There is a clearly defined social framework and hierarchy in which individuals must operate, and conformity is expected by the collective. Individual pursuits are subordinated to those of the group and there is an emphasis on 'we' and 'us', rather than 'I' or 'me'. Accordingly, the directive style of management and communications that is appropriate in the West is not effective in Indonesia. Decision making frequently occurs through consensus and senior managers are inclined to discuss rather than direct. The resultant lack of clear direction often brings about issues and incidents that are unacceptable to Western managers – a lack of punctuality, early departures from work, absenteeism, non-adherence to safety procedures, and in some cases theft and misuse of equipment or stock to supplement wages.

Dimension #3: Masculinity versus femininity

In Indonesia, hierarchical status and the trappings that accompany high office in society are sought after and revered. With increased economic development and capitalist pursuits in Indonesia, this trend to Hofstede's conception of 'masculinity' will continue, particularly among the country's elites.

However, as a society at large, Indonesia tends more to the 'feminine': people work to live; they are focused on family first; individuals are comfortable with their lot; managers seek consensus in decision making; conflicts are resolved through compromise and negotiation; work flexibility and free time are favoured over material rewards.

Dimension #4: Uncertainty avoidance

Uncertainty avoidance, according to Hofstede, is a society's tolerance for uncertainty and ambiguity, and to what extent a culture programs its members to feel either uncomfortable or comfortable in uncertain situations. Uncertainty-avoiding cultures try to minimise uncertainty through the imposition of strict laws and rules. People in uncertainty-avoiding cultures are characterised by strong emotions and nervous energy.

Uncertainty-accepting cultures, on the other hand, are more tolerant of alternative viewpoints and have fewer laws and rules to constrict this freedom. People in these cultures are more comfortable in their being and less likely to express strong emotions. Hofstede's study suggests that Indonesians have a low preference for avoiding uncertainty and that this is essentially on a par with Australians (51 versus 48). Indonesians do generally prefer stable and predictable conditions over ambiguity.

Regardless of whether an Indonesian feels anger, he/she will remain polite and continue to smile, bottling up any emotions internally to avoid conflict. In business, workplace harmony is extremely important and any situation that threatens the status quo will be suppressed or avoided. Western managers have traditionally found it very difficult to 'read' the sentiment of their Indonesian subordinates, as there is no outward indication of dissatisfaction, but often faux contentment instead.

Dimension #5: Long-term versus short-term orientation

Hofstede's findings indicate that Indonesia is a long-term oriented society, although evidence points to the contrary. Despite recent development and modernisation, Indonesia remains a traditional, hierarchically ordered society with communitarian values and national pride that stems from its historical struggle for independence. Indonesians, especially the sizeable Javanese ethnic group, are a very traditional, proud and face-saving people. Care must be taken to ensure that an Indonesian is not singled out or humiliated in front of others, as this represents the most galling and demoralising of circumstances for an Indonesian. Indonesians will do everything in their power to avoid such situations, even if it means lying or absconding.

The need to 'save face' is evident in routine conversations between managers and subordinates: asking an Indonesian if they have completed an assigned task will always elicit an affirmative response, even if the task has not been completed. Indonesians are inclined to respond in the affirmative or in an indirect manner when asked a yes/no question, to avoid further scrutiny or to bring attention to failings. Indonesians are more inclined to answer 'not yet' (*belum*) when quizzed about task completion, rather than the more definitive response of 'no' which infers that the individual has missed a deadline and is at fault. Australians working in Indonesia need to adopt a questioning technique that elicits the necessary information without singling out the individual.

Another trait of Indonesian society which can be attributed to ingrained tradition is the propensity to engage in official corruption. Corruption remains a major issue in

Indonesia and Australian companies that do business in that country may encounter ethically challenging situations where corruption is present.

Source: Wehner (2016), reproduced with permission from
Clayton Wehner and Blue Train Enterprises

Critical thinking questions
1. If you were the Australian CEO of Kookaburra Books, what four critical steps would you take to lead the company effectively in Indonesia?
2. Using the GLOBE study findings, identify which of the study's six leadership styles would best support effective leadership in this case. Explain your response.
3. Using the GLOBE study findings, identify three key Indonesian cultural norms that would challenge an Australian CEO to lead effectively in Indonesia. Explain your response.

REFERENCES

Ahammad, M.F., Tarba, S.Y., Liu, Y. & Glaister, K.W. (2014). Knowledge transfer and cross-border acquisition performance: The impact of cultural distance and employee retention. *International Business Review*, 25, 66–75.

AlMazrouei, H. & Pech, R.J. (2015). Working in the UAE: Expatriate management experiences. *Journal of Islamic Accounting and Business Research*, 6(1), 73–93.

Alon, I., Boulanger, M., Elston, J.A., Galanaki, E., Martínez de Ibarreta, C., Muñiz-Ferrer, M., Meyers, J. & Velez-Calle, A. (2016). Business cultural intelligence quotient: A five-country study. *Thunderbird International Business Review*, doi:10.1002/tie.21826.

Ashkanasy, N.M. & Falkus, S. (1997). The Australian enigma. *Globe Anthology*, 1, Brisbane.

Barker, C. (2002). *Making sense of Cultural Studies: Central problems and critical debates*. London: SAGE Publications.

Casey, T.W., Riseborough, K.M. & Krauss, A.D. (2015). Do you see what i see? Effects of national culture on employees' safety-related perceptions and behavior. *Accident Analysis and Prevention*, 78, 173–84.

Crowne, K.A. (2008). What leads to cultural intelligence?. *Business Horizons*, 51(5), 391–9.

De Waal, A.A., Van der Heijden, B.I.J.M., Selvarajah, C. & Meyer, D. (2015). Comparing Dutch and British high performing managers. *Journal of Management and Organization*, 22(3), 349–66.

Deal, J.J. (2003). Cultural adaptability and leading across cultures. *Advances in Global Leadership*, 3, 149–66.

Dickson, M.W., Den Hartog, D.N. & Mitchelson, J.K. (2003). Research on leadership in a cross-cultural context: Making progress, and raising new questions. *Leadership Quarterly*, 14(6), 729–68.

Fernando, M. (2011). 'Spirituality and leadership'. In A. Bryman, D. Collinson, K. Grint, B. Jackson & M. Uhl-Bien (eds), *The SAGE handbook of leadership* (pp. 483–94). London: SAGE Publications.

Fernando, M. & Nilakant V. (2008). The place of self-actualisation in workplace spirituality: Evidence from Sri Lanka. *Culture and Religion*, 9, 233–49.

Hage, J. & Posner, B.Z. (2015). Religion, religiosity, and leadership practices: An examination in the Lebanese workplace. *Leadership and Organization Development Journal*, 36(4), 336–412.

Hartnell, C.A., Kinicki, A.J., Schurer Lambert, L., Fugate, M. & Doyle Corner, P. (2016). Do similarities or differences between CEO leadership and organizational culture have a more positive effect on firm performance? A test of competing predictions. *Journal of Applied Psychology*, doi:http://dx.doi.org/10.1037/apl0000083.

Hofstede, G. (1980). *Culture's consequences: International differences in work related values*. Beverly Hill, CA: SAGE Publications.

—— (1991). *Cultures and organizations: Software of the mind*. London: McGraw-Hill.

Hofstede, G., Hofstede G.J. & Minkov, M. (2010). *Cultures and organizations: Software of the mind. Revised and expanded*, 3rd edn. New York, NY: McGraw-Hill.

Hollenbeck, G.P., McCall, M.W., Jr. & Silzer, R.F. (2006). Leadership competency models. *Leadership Quarterly*, 17(4), 398–413.

House, R.J., Hanges, P.J., Javidan, M., Dorfman, P.W. & Gupta, V. (eds.) (2004). *Culture, leadership, and organizations: The GLOBE Study of 62 societies*. Thousand Oaks, CA: SAGE Publications.

Javidan, M. & Bowen, D. (2013). The 'global mindset' of managers: What it is, why it matters, and how to develop it. *Organizational Dynamics*, 42(2), 145–55.

Jogulu, U.D. (2010). Culturally linked leadership styles. *Leadership and Organization Development Journal*, 31(8), 705–19.

Jogulu, U. & Ferkins, L. (2012). Leadership and culture in Asia: The case of Malaysia. *Asia Pacific Business Review*, 18(4), 531–49.

Kabasakal, H. & Bodur, M. (2002). Arabic Cluster: A bridge between East and West. *Journal of World Business*, 37(1), 40–54.

Karpin, D. (1995). Australia industry task force on leadership and management skills. In *Enterprising nation: Renewing Australia's managers to meet the challenges of the Asia–Pacific century*. Report. Canberra: Australian Government Publishing Service.

Kong, D.T. & Volkema, R. (2016). Cultural endorsement of broad leadership prototypes and wealth as predictors of corruption. *Social Indicators Research*, 127(1), 139–52.

Meng, J. (2015). Cultural congruence as reflected in communication leaders' decision-making: A convergent view from London and Singapore. *Leadership and Organization Development Journal*, 36(4), 346–59.

Mingzheng, X. & Xinhui, W. (2014). Chinese leadership. *Public Integrity*, 16(2), 165–72.

Mittal, R. & Elias, S.M. (2016). Social power and leadership in cross-cultural context. *Journal of Management Development*, 35(1), 58–74.

Mujtaba, B.G. & Isomura, K. (2012). Examining the Japanese leadership orientations and their changes. *Leadership and Organization Development Journal*, 33(4), 401–20.

O'Neill, M. (1996). The Karpin Report, *Business Date*, 4(2), 1–5.

Resick, C.J., Hanges, P.J., Dickson, M.W. & Mitchelson, J.K. (2006). A cross-cultural examination of the endorsement of ethical leadership. *Journal of Business Ethics*, 63(4), 345–59.

Richardson, J., Millage, P., Millage, J. & Lane, S. (2014). The effects of culture on leadership styles in China, Germany and Russia. *Journal of Technology Management in China*, 9(3), 263–73.

Selvarajah, C. & Meyer, D. (2006). Archetypes of the Malaysian manager: Exploring ethnicity dimensions that relate to leadership. *Journal of Management and Organization*, 12(3), 251–69.

—— (2008). One nation, three cultures: Exploring dimensions that relate to leadership in Malaysia. *Leadership and Organization Development Journal*, 29(8), 693–712.

Selvarajah, C.T., Duignan, P., Suppiah, C., Lane, T. & Nuttman, C. (1995). *In search of the ASEAN Leader: An exploratory study of the dimensions that relate to excellence in leadership*, 35(1), 29–44.

Shrivastava, S., Selvarajah, C., Meyer, D. & Dorasamy, N. (2014). Exploring excellence in leadership perceptions amongst South African managers. *Human Resource Development International*, 17(1), 47–66.

Wang, C.L., Tee, D.D. & Ahmed, P.K. (2012). Entrepreneurial leadership and context in Chinese Firms: A tale of two Chinese private enterprises. *Asia Pacific Business Review*, 18(4), 505–30.

Wang, L., James, K.T., Denyer, D. & Bailey, C. (2014). Western views and Chinese whispers: Re-thinking global leadership competency in multi-national corporations. *Leadership*, 10(4), 471–95.

Wehner, C. (2016). Australian companies doing business in Indonesia: A cross-cultural analysis using Hofstede's Six Dimensions of National Cultures model. *Blue Train Enterprises*. Retrieved from: http://bluetrainenterprises.com.au/blog/2016/03/11/australian-companies-doing-business-in-indonesia-a-cross-cultural-analysis-using-hofstedes-six-dimensions-of-national-cultures-model.

Wong, K-C. (2001). Chinese culture and leadership. *International Journal of Leadership in Education*, 4(4), 309–19.

7

CREATING ORGANISATIONAL CULTURE

Ali Intezari and Bernard McKenna

LEARNING OUTCOMES

After reading this chapter, you should be able to:

1. describe organisational culture and explain how it is different from organisational climate

2. identify the internal and external factors that affect organisational culture

3. describe the process of organisational culture change

4. analyse the existing culture of an organisation

5. explain the process of defining the desired culture

6. explain the process of implementing and sustaining the organisational culture change.

INTRODUCTION

AMONG ALL THE aspects and concepts that are discussed in association with organisations, organisational culture is one of the most challenging. It is not easy to define the terms *culture* in general and *organisational culture* in particular. Assessing an organisation's culture is difficult because cultures are complicated and multi-layered phenomena. Further, each culture may be interpreted in various ways, as an organisation's people may perceive its culture differently than people outside the organisation do. Organisational culture differentiates the people working for an organisation from those who work for another. An organisation's culture affects the way that people in the organisation think, behave, perform their job and interact with the surrounding environment. The culture is embedded in the core values of its employees and influences how people act in the organisation.

There is more involved in the success or failure of an organisation than factors such as organisational structure, competitive advantage or financial performance. Whereas factors such as organisational hierarchical structure, rationality in work design and operation and formality in communication may to some extent represent how people operate in an organisation, organisational culture can better explain employee's organisational behaviour. Leadership plays a critical role in the emergence and reinforcement of the organisational culture.

WHAT IS ORGANISATIONAL CULTURE?

There is no consensus among scholars and practitioners about the meaning of **culture**, and it follows that it is difficult to come up with a globally accepted and unified definition of organisational culture too. This is because culture is a complex phenomenon. Generally, culture refers to the collective values and beliefs of a group of people who have something in common and, as a result, interact socially. Culture connotes a strong group process with prevailing values, vision, languages, assumptions, beliefs and habits, which guide people or an organisation (Martin, 2002). **Organisational culture** can be defined as 'the shared values, beliefs, assumptions, and patterns of behavior within an organisation' (Riggio, 2015, p. 419). According to Edgar Schein (2010), a foremost scholar in the field, organisational culture is

> a pattern of shared basic assumptions learned by a group as it solved its problems of external adaptation and internal integration, which has worked well enough to be considered valid and, therefore, to be taught to new members as the correct way to perceive, think and feel in relation to those problems (p. 18).

Culture enables its members to deal with the changes in the environment within which the people are operating. More importantly, drawing on shared values and beliefs, the culture enables the members to retain their integrity while dealing with

> **Culture** – The collective values and beliefs of a group of people who have something in common, and interact socially as a result.
>
> **Organisational culture** – 'A pattern of basic assumptions – invented, discovered, or developed by a given group as it learns to cope with its problems of external adaptation and internal integration – that has worked well enough to be considered valid and, therefore, to be taught to new members as the correct way to perceive, think and feel in relation to those problems' (Schein, 1985b, p. 9).

the external environment. Some pioneering scholars in organisational culture studies are Ouchi (1983), Schein (1985a, 1985b), Pascale and Athos (1981), Peters and Waterman (1982) and Deal and Kennedy (1982).

According to Schein (2010), there are four main categories of culture:

- macro-cultures
- organisational cultures
- sub-cultures
- micro-cultures.

Macro-cultures refer to the cultures that exist at the national or global levels, such as national culture, or a prevailing culture in a multinational enterprise. Sub-cultures and micro-cultures refer to the values and beliefs that are shared by groups within an organisation. Micro-cultures are the subset of sub-cultures. Peoples bring their own cultures to their organisations. The newcomers then affect and are affected by the organisation's culture. The culture in one department may or may not be significantly different from the culture of another department. The same is the case with the organisational levels. The culture among operational managers may be different from the culture prevailing at the strategic level. This difference could be due to the nature of the job, which in turn affects the culture of the group, or it may be culture that the group members have created.

Brown (1995) defines organisational culture as:

the pattern of beliefs, values and learned ways of coping with experience that have developed during an organisation's history, and which tend to be manifested in its material arrangements and in the behaviours of its members (p. 8).

Schein (1985b) defines organisational culture as:

a pattern of basic assumptions – invented, discovered, or developed by a given group as it learns to cope with its problems of external adaptation and internal integration – that has worked well enough to be considered valid and, therefore, to be taught to new members as the correct way to perceive, think and feel in relation to those problems (p. 9).

Deal and Kennedy (1982) describe organisational culture as 'the social glue' that holds together the whole organisation. Hofstede and co-authors (1990), however, note that many of the diverse definitions of organisational culture share the same assumptions:

that they are related to history and tradition, have some depth, are difficult to grasp and account for and must be interpreted; that they are collective and shared by members of groups and primarily ideational in character, having to do with values, understandings, beliefs, knowledge and other intangibles; and that they are holistic and subjective rather than strictly rational and analytical (p. 2).

Organisational culture can be simply described as the ways things are done in an organisation (Schneider, 2000). Shared norms, values and goals form an organisation's culture (O'Reilly & Chatman, 1996).

Organisational culture and organisational climate

Organisational culture is sometimes used interchangeably with organisational **climate**. Climate and culture are organisational constructs that are often linked together but can be conceptually differentiated from each other (Ashkanasy & Härtel, 2014). The interrelationship is informed by the similarities between the two concepts. The two concepts involve observation of the actions and experience occurring in the workplace, and both are interested in social systems.

> **Climate** – A momentary manifestation of culture, and unlike culture is more quantitatively measurable.

However, organisational culture gives the organisation a personality (Kilman, Saxton & Serpa, 1985), while climate is a kind of momentary manifestation of culture, and is more quantitatively measurable (Denison, 1996).

In addition, while culture characterises an organisation, climate defines the organisational atmosphere and environment. Unlike organisational culture, organisational climate is shorter term and is easier to assess and alter. Another notable difference between the concept of climate and that of culture is that climate is a more individual or local based issue that can be addressed by altering local practices and rewards, whereas culture is a more organisationally focused construct. Burke (2013) developed an analogy for comparing these two concepts by describing culture as the personality, and climate as the behaviour of an organisation. Culture is an enduring, slow-changing core characteristic of organisations, while climate is a temporary set of attitudes, feelings and perceptions of individuals in the organisation (Schneider, Ehrhart & Macey, 2013).

Aspects of organisational culture

Organisational culture is unique and has multiple elements (Cameron, 2003; Kotter, 1995; Schneider et al., 2013; Weick & Quinn, 1999). In the simplest view, organisational culture is the specific way that things are done in the organisation, in response to external changes and otherwise.

- *Multilevel phenomenon*: Cultures are multifaceted. As mentioned above, organisational culture can be analysed at different levels, core values, underlying assumptions and artefacts. Moreover, organisational culture relates to individuals, groups and the organisational level. Individuals joining organisations take with them their own culture. Therefore, the impact of an organisation's culture on individual, group and organisational performance is not a one-way process. Individuals affect the organisational culture too.
- *Dynamism of culture*: A clear attribute of culture is its dynamism. Cultures are not static. They are dynamic and evolve over time. Organisational culture is an emerging and revisable phenomenon. The shared values and beliefs of the members of the organisation are alterable for the greater good of the organisation.
- *Structural stability*: Although organisational culture can be revised and altered, cultures show the characteristics of stability. Organisational culture survives even when a group

member leaves or exits the organisation. Once an organisation's culture is created and stabilised over time, the culture represents people's values and beliefs, and people identify themselves with the culture. Since people's underlying values and beliefs are constructed and formed over time, they are to a certain extent stable, which makes a culture highly stable. For this reason, changing an organisation's culture is very challenging.

- *Cultural depth and breadth*: As many scholars such as Schein (2010) argue, culture is the deepest, often unconscious part of a group. Organisational culture is inextricably tied with people's underlying assumptions and worldviews, and, as a result, has profound impact on employees' perceptions and behaviours. It is the embeddedness of culture that lends stability to the organisation. Another characteristic of culture that emerged from Schein's work is the breadth of culture. This indicates that once culture is developed, it covers all the organisation's functioning. Hence, culture is perceived to be pervasive, influencing every dimension of organisational operations: task, performance, competitions and general internal operations.
- *Patterning and integration*: Schein (2010) also argues that organisational culture integrates individual values, characters and behaviours into a coherent whole. Weick and Quinn (1999) believe that this integration ultimately comes from people's need to make the environment sensible and orderly.
- *Measurement of culture*: Although it is not easy, organisational culture can be measured (Denison & Mishra, 1995). Measuring means assessing the level of the impact of an organisation's culture on other aspects of the organisations. For example, an organisation's culture can be assessed in terms of whether, and to what extent, the culture is supporting or hindering, creating, sharing and implementing knowledge across the organisation (Intezari, Taskin & Pauleen, 2017).
- *Central role of leadership in culture*: Leadership plays a critical role in creating and reinforcing an organisation's culture. In an organisation, a leader's words and deeds represent to a certain level the culture that the organisation values. Leadership is originally the source of the beliefs and values that propels the organisation in achieving its goals, and dealing with its internal and external challenges (Schein, 2010; Yagil, 2014). In addition to leaders, the founders of an organisation, who could also be the leaders, drive the organisational culture (Schneider, Brief & Guzzo, 1996).
- *Enabling organisational outcomes*: Organisational culture has impact on performance and effectiveness (Denison & Mishra, 1995).

Level of cultural analysis

Organisational culture is a multidimensional phenomenon that spans across three levels: artefacts, espoused beliefs and values and basic underlying assumptions (see Figure 7.1) (Schein, 2010). Artefacts are the visible aspect of a culture. Artefacts include things that can be

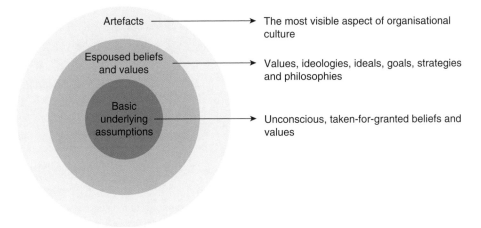

Figure 7.1 Analytical levels of culture
Source: Adapted from Schein (2010)

seen, heard and felt when facing an unfamiliar culture. Elements such as physical environment, buildings, décor and office layouts, dress codes, stories, myths and behaviour patterns are examples of artefacts. Schein (2010) further categorises artefacts into five analytical levels: physical manifestations, language, stories, technology and traditions. The best way to examine artefacts is observation. Artefacts are in fact the manifestations of the deeper values and underlying assumptions that are invisible yet influential in terms of guiding people's thinking and behaviours.

Espoused beliefs and values deal with the normative character of the group. The values are the public statements of values and goals. Espoused beliefs refer to what the organisation, groups or people think are highly important for the organisation (examples are goals, ideals and aspirations). These beliefs are what members of an organisation say about situations, and not necessarily about what they will do in the situations (Schultz, 1995). Espoused values are reflected in the organisation's philosophies, strategies and goals.

The deepest level refers to the basic, unconscious, taken-for-granted assumptions that underlie and determine employees' perception, thoughts, feelings and actions (Schein, 2010). This level of culture is the least visible aspect of culture compared to the values and artefacts aspects of a culture. However, it profoundly affects the individuals' and organisation's performance. By identifying employees' underlying assumptions and core values, the leader can find out why employees think, feel and act the way they do about certain issues (Schein, 2004).

Like Schein's classification of cultural layers, Hofstede and co-authors (1990) argue that an organisation's culture manifests itself in four layers (from deep to shallow respectively): values, rituals, heroes and symbols. Values represent the deepest layer of culture. It is values that form the core of a culture: for example, people's feeling and understanding of the concepts such as good and evil, selfishness and altruism, and greed and generosity. Rituals refer to people's collective activities that are carried out for their own sake. Another layer of an organisation's culture is 'heroes'. Heroes represent either real or imaginary people who serve as behavioural models for people. The most visible layer of a culture is the 'symbols'. Symbols are pictures, words, objects and gestures that carry particular meanings within the culture. According to Hofstede et al. (1990), as rituals, heroes and symbols are the visible aspects of a culture, they can be regarded as in some way representing the practices of the culture.

Organisational culture represents the shared beliefs, collective values, perceptions, behavioural patterns as well as expectations and priorities of individuals in an organisation. Organisational culture distinguishes one organisation as a unique social system from another (Needle, 2010). Because of the emerging values, beliefs and norms, organisational culture can be assumed to be the personality of the organisation. Culture is concerned with both individual and corporate identity as well as collective integrity. Thus, it is very important to understand the main characteristics of organisational culture.

WHY CHANGE ORGANISATIONAL CULTURE?

Organisational culture codifies organisation members' perceptions of themselves and the surrounding environment, and, as a result, clarifies the organisational goals and preferred values (Schein, 1992). As Williams, Dobson and Walters (1993) state:

> Culture provides the decision-making and problem-solving processes of the organisation. It influences the goals, means and manner of action. It is a source of motivation and demotivation, of satisfaction and dissatisfaction. In short, culture underlies much of the human activity in an organisation (p. 12).

Organisational culture is a key factor in organisational performance, efficacy, growth and development as it provides the organisation with fitness and stability in the face of the rapidly changing environment in the twenty-first century. At the individual level, organisational culture affects employees' morale, job satisfaction, commitment, productivity and retention. Organisations cannot survive if they fail to adapt themselves to their changing environment. Central to these changes is culture change. If the dominant values and beliefs in the organisation do not change, no real changes happen. Organisational culture can support or suppress an organisation's ability to use its full capacity and ability to perform effectively and efficiently. Culture makes organisations unique, and **organisational culture change** is concerned with how this uniqueness originates, evolves and operates (Needle, 2010).

Organisational culture change – A process through which the organisation's existing culture is critically evaluated, the desired values and beliefs are envisioned, the preferred culture is implemented, and the cultural changes are reinforced and sustained for a period deemed appropriate by the organisations.

Advances in technology, the information explosion and big data have led to the emergence of new forms of organisation, such as virtual organisations. These are digitally enabled organisations, which form a network of cooperating entities and make resources available to each other in order to support a particular product or service. In virtual organisations, employees work in dispersed geographical places. Activities and communication are coordinated and supported by information communication technologies, as globalisation and political and social issues contribute to making organisational culture change pervasive. As Denison (1996, 2000) points out, organisational culture involves codes or logics that organise the behaviour of the people within the organisation, and the lessons learned in the past that may be important enough to pass on to the next generation. Hence, organisational culture has a great impact on the daily behaviour of members of the organisation, and the organisational performance. The shared values and beliefs of the organisational members are alterable for the greater good of the organisation. Otherwise, culture ends up altering people's individual values and beliefs within the group or organisation.

The impact of organisational culture on performance and long-term effectiveness of the organisation has been documented by many researchers (Ashkanasy & Härtel, 2014; Burke, 2013; Liao & Chuang, 2007; Schein, 2010; Schneider et al., 2013). For this reason, it is critically important for organisations to be able to assess their organisational cultures and change the culture if the internal and or external environment warrant.

There are several reasons why understanding organisational culture change is vital in today's business world, including:

- Organisational culture is formed from, and provides an organisational narrative (Schneider, Erhart & Macey, 2011). Organisational culture is a point of differentiation between otherwise indistinguishable companies. It gives the organisation a different subjective impression, 'feel' (Schein, 1992).

- Today's business world is characterised as being volatile and complex. Adaptation is essential for an organisation's survival (Greenwood & Hinings, 1996; Martins, 2011; Nutt & Backoff, 1997). Such an adaptation is not achievable unless organisations have the capacity to change their cultures as necessary.

- The fit of culture and strategy is central to the success of organisations (O'Reilly, 1989). Because organisational culture provides a framework for implementing business strategies, it is critically important for leaders and senior managers in an organisation to be conscious of the culture of their organisations. If cultural values in an organisation involve flexibility, openness and responsiveness, the organisation is more likely to grow, expand and innovate. If cultural values involve consistency and adherence to mission, the organisation is more likely to be productive and profitable (Denison & Mishra, 1995; Naranjo-Valencia, Jimenez-Jimenez & Sanz-Valle, 2011).

- Organisations' cultures vary in strength (O'Reilly, 1989), and having a positive organisational culture can improve performance (Collins & Smith, 2006) and long-term effectiveness of individuals and the organisation.

- Culture plays a critical role in creating and maintaining a level of commitment among employees (O'Reilly, 1989; Ouchi, 1983). A company that enjoys the reputation of a good organisational culture can better recruit talent (Catanzaro, Moore & Marshall, 2010).

- Organisational culture change is one of the most challenging tasks that leaders and managers encounter. Senior managers and CEOs are fired most commonly for failure to manage change appropriately (Hempel, 2005).

The impetus for organisational culture change could be internal or external (Joyce, 1999).

Internal and external influences on organisational culture

The way that organisational culture comes into existence can be illustrated on one single continuum. At one extreme, an organisation's culture emerges naturally from social interactions among a group of people working towards shared goals; at the other, culture emerges from people's deliberate efforts to develop new values and beliefs. Neither of these extremes are likely in the real world; most organisational cultures come about through both emergence and manipulation.

Before we examine the process of organisational culture change it is important to understand what factors affect an organisation's culture. There are two primary factors that influence organisational culture: internal and external factors.

Internal factors

Internal factors play an important role in affecting organisational culture. These are factors that exist within the organisation, and are associated with the organisation and or people and tasks in the organisation. Examples are the organisational structure, leadership style, tasks (processes and procedures, complexity of the task, the level of stress) and communication.

- *Members' values*: Employees' thoughts and perceptions differ. Organisational members have their own personal values and beliefs. They may have different cultural backgrounds that may lead to differences in their attitudes, mindset, temperament and individual personality. The differences in organisational members' personality influence the prevailing culture in the organisation.
- *Leader–culture relationship*: Leadership and organisational culture are interrelated. Leadership affects the culture of the organisation. In the face of challenging situations such as an organisational crisis, leadership comes to play a role in ensuring stability within the organisation. Therefore, the enforcer of a new culture is the leader, who as a powerful agent can articulate a compelling vision of desired values (Liao & Chuang, 2007).
- *Organisational mission and vision*: The extent to which the culture is aligned with the organisation's strategic directions affects the organisational culture. Sometimes, organisations need to change their strategic direction and mission. For example, this might be introducing a new product, entering a new market, fundamental changes at the strategic level of an organisation (such as a new CEO or board members).
- *Organisational structure*: This includes how business is done within the organisation and how people are treated. Furthermore, organisational structure includes the

policies, practices and procedures of how business is done in the organisation as well as the management of employees' reward systems, the flow of information within the organisation, and the extent to which organisational members are brought into decision-making processes.

- *Communication*: Closely related to organisational culture is communication. Both formal and informal communication can have significant impacts on organisational culture, and there should be a balance between the emphasis that is put on either forms of communication. For example, while informal communication may significantly enhance and reinforce a new culture, over-emphasis on informal communication may damage transparency in the organisation. In contrast, in an organisation where informal communication is suppressed in favour of formal communication, developing and reinforcing shared values may become very challenging.

External factors

External influences on organisational culture include aspects that are mainly associated with the community within which the organisation operates. This may be the business community (organisations work in the same industry or along the supply chain, partnership) or society. Common external factors include economic, technological advancement, regulatory, social and legal issues. To assess the external factors, organisations may use analytical tools such as SWOT, PESTLE, environmental screening, and so forth.

- *Social factors*: New demands from customers and society may have significant impact on an organisation's culture. Expectations from the external stakeholders and societal expectations influence an organisation's culture. Demand from society for reduction in companies' carbon footprint on the environment is an example of social factors that affect organisational culture and may drive cultural change in the organisation.
- *Business stakeholders*: The business stakeholders include shareholders, vendors, customers and business partners. As an organisation is in continuous contact with the business stakeholders, the organisation's culture is profoundly affected by its business stakeholders. For instance, if the shareholders of a company put emphasis more on the company's contribution to address environmental issues, the company may incorporate into their mission and strategies the values that show the company's concerns for environmental issues. The values may then become part of the company's culture.
- *Technology*: Technological advances and complexity necessitate fundamental changes in the leadership task and the way that organisations operate. Leadership in a networked organisation is fundamentally different from leadership in a traditional hierarchy (Schneider, Ehrhart & Macey, 2011). The emergence of new forms of organisations such as virtual organisations requires leaders to take new approaches to identifying their organisational values and assumptions. Organisational members' perceptions, preferences

and behavioural patterns make organisational changes inevitable. For example, if an organisation operates in a business field where success requires constant implementation of new technologies (for example, in the telecommunication, or information technology industries), the organisational culture should support creativity and innovation.

To successfully change an organisation's culture it is highly important to ensure that both the internal and external factors are considered.

CASE STUDY 7.1

Reckitt Benckiser

In 1819, a mill was founded by Reckitt & Sons in England. In 1823, Johann A. Benckiser founded an industrial chemicals company in Germany. In 1999, these companies (then Reckitt & Colman plc and Benckiser NV) merged to form Reckitt Benckiser (RB). RB has many successful products, and many of their brands are household names in Australia: Mortein, Dettol, Air Wick, Finish, Veet, Bang, Nurofen, Strepsils, Vanish, Durex and Scholl. In the financial year ending 2015, RB's net revenue was more than A$14 billion. Of this net revenue, 30 per cent came from developing markets, including China, parts of Africa and the Middle East, Turkey and Latin America. Of their products, 74 per cent of their net revenue came from those classified as 'health and hygiene'.

Regarding its leadership model, RB suggested that its leaders should be participative and follow distributed leadership principles rather than strictly democratic or consensus-based leadership.

RB describes its culture as having four central values: achievement, ownership (taking responsibility, being proactive and valuing the organisation as if it were your own), entrepreneurship (including diversity) and partnership. RB holds policies to 'develop, attract, retain and engage talented women', including flexible working options and a worldwide maternity policy, and routinely offers staff international assignments to promote cross-cultural development. Since 2012, RB has run a health and safety improvement program for its staff and consumers, resulting in a 25 per cent reduction in 'lost work days' accident rates over this period.

However, the company is not without controversy or blemish. In 2012, it closed a factory in Sydney that produced pest-control products. One hundred and ninety staff lost their jobs with no recourse and, as a result, the public expressed anger about RB's pest-control products, there was a minor boycott and media coverage of the issue was negative. In 2016, RB admitted in an Australian court that their analgesic product line known as the Nurofen Specific Pain Range, which purported to deliver targeted pain relief to particular areas of the body (for example, the back and neck), had no such effect. It stated that it had engaged in 'deceptive and misleading' behaviour. The Australian Competition and Consumer Commission, which prosecuted RB, was seeking A$6 million in fines; media commentary had suggested that this amount was trivial for an organisation as large as RB, which is valued at more than A$80 billion.

In 2001, the South Korean branch of RB, known as Oxy Reckitt Benckiser, was part of a group of companies accused of producing toxic humidifier-disinfection products. In 2012, the South Korean government accused Oxy Reckitt Benckiser of causing 103 deaths, including those of many children, through lung disease associated with these products. Those affected waited five years to receive an official apology and begin discussions of compensation. It was discovered that the manufacturer of the products, which Oxy Reckitt Benckiser had acquired, had failed to conduct toxicity tests prior to the acquisition, despite its claims to the contrary.

Sources: AAP (2012); AFR (2012b); Bok-Hyeon (2016); Carter (2016); Cookson & Daneshku (2015); Da-sol (2016); Hyuk-Jin & Chung (2016); Reckitt Benckiser Group (RB) (2016a, 2016b)

Critical thinking questions
1. Identify four challenges that RB faces in seeking to change organisational culture across its organisation. How might RB deal with the challenges?
2. Describe the relationship between RB's stated cultural values and its business failures.
3. Identify three lessons that RB can learn from its failures. How might RB change its organisational culture by adopting these lessons?
4. Considering RB's behaviour in the context of Australian culture, what assumptions about RB's culture that Australian consumers might make? Explain your response.

THE PROCESS OF ORGANISATIONAL CULTURE CHANGE

Organisational culture change is a process. Organisational culture is not created overnight. More importantly, once a culture develops over time in an organisation and is internalised into the organisation's people and procedures, it is very difficult to change. More challenging would be sustaining cultural changes. Organisational cultural change begins with a critical evaluation of the existing culture, and continues with identifying the preferred values and beliefs, and encouraging and reinforcing the new culture. The process is recursive. That is, once the values and beliefs are encouraged in the organisation, they must be periodically re-evaluated for enhancement and, if required, further changes. However, it must be considered that continuous changes to an organisation's culture may confuse employees as to what values the organisation relies on over the long term. Unnecessary and continuous changes may turn the values promoted by the culture into words on paper, rather than deepening them as factors that can profoundly influence employees' behaviours.

Figure 7.2 illustrates the main phases of organisational culture change. Changing an organisation's culture engages four main phases: analysing the existing culture, defining the desired culture, making the cultural changes and sustaining the cultural changes. These phases will be discussed in the following sections.

Effective cultural change draws on an accurate understanding of the existing and desired cultures. Accordingly, before any culture change is initiated, it is important to decipher the culture that is dominant in the organisation as well as the culture that the organisation wants to

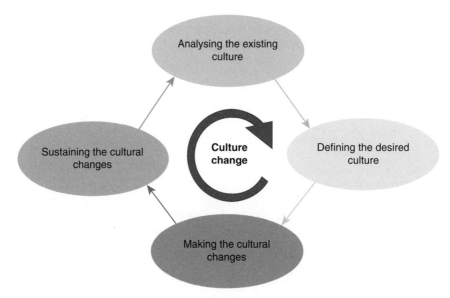

Figure 7.2 Organisational culture change model

adopt. Before the organisation gets involved in any changes, it is vital to clarify what change will mean to organisational members, including both employees and the leaders. The purpose of this step is to clarify the characteristics of the culture that need to be changed and the aspects of existing culture that can be preserved (Cameron, 2004; Cameron & Quinn, 2005). In this stage, shared values, beliefs and assumptions, and the way that organisational members express themselves, are identified. Moreover, the desired cultural attributes must be defined. Defining existing and new culture to be formed involves stakeholders' understanding of the aspect of the culture they must be committed to, and a realistic vision of what to strive for (Dawson, 2010).

Analysing an organisation's culture

A successful culture change requires an accurate understanding of the existing culture of the organisation. To gain a sound awareness of the current status of the organisational culture and create appropriate projection, it is very helpful to understand different types of cultures that identify an organisation. There are numerous classifications of organisational culture. In the following paragraphs some of the famous classifications of organisational culture, as well as the instruments that can be used to analyse an organisation's culture, are examined.

Hofstede's study of national cultures

A significant study of culture is the study conducted by Geert Hofstede (Hofstede, 1980, 1997, 2003; Hofstede, Hofstede & Minkov, 1991) that underlines the impact of national culture on organisational behaviour (see discussion in Chapter 6). Hofstede identifies five cultural dimensions that influence organisational culture:

- *Power distance*: This refers to the extent to which people in an organisation accept centralised power. If the power distance is high, employees believe that for the organisation to be successful, all the decisions must be made at the top of the organisation. In contrast, organisations with a low power distance benefit from employees' belief that they should have equal rights to participate in the decision-making process.
- *Masculinity versus femininity*: This factor is concerned with whether, and to what extent, gender diversity is valued in an organisation.
- *Individualism versus collectivism*: This cultural dimension refers to the extent to which a person identifies him or herself as an individual or a member of a group. People in an organisation with the individualist culture tend to work individually and are less willing to participate in teamwork.
- *Uncertainty avoidance*: In an uncertainty avoidance culture, risk taking is regarded as dangerous and therefore is discouraged. People are risk-averse and are disturbed by changes.
- *Long-term versus short-term orientation*: If the culture of an organisation is long-term oriented, planning is very important. This is because people in this culture believe that they have control over their future and they can shape their future.

Strong versus weak cultures

Deal and Kennedy (1982) argue that various organisational cultures can affect organisational effectiveness. They identify two specific types of organisational culture: strong and weak cultures. People in an organisation with a strongly articulated culture have a sense of direction and shared purpose. In contrast, in an organisation that suffers from a weak culture, employees lack coherence of thought and action. The strong culture can enhance an organisation's success.

In an organisation with a strong culture, the core values and beliefs are widely and intensely held by the organisational members. A strong culture can be defined as 'a set of norms and values that are widely shared and strongly held throughout the organisation' (O'Reilly & Chatman, 1996, p. 166). Organisations with strong cultures benefit from motivated employees who are highly committed to shared goals (Sørensen, 2002). In these organisations, individual and organisational performances are improved because of enhanced coordination, organisation-member goal alignment and increased employee effort (Sørensen, 2002). In contrast, weak cultures are characterised by inconsistency of values and beliefs within the organisation, lack of collaboration among the employees, as well as weak commitment to the organisational goals. Organisations with strong cultures demonstrate better performance than organisations with weak cultures.

Charles Handy's model of four cultures

Handy's (1993) approach to organisational culture has provoked many studies about the link between organisational culture and structure. Handy (1993) identifies four cultures:

- *Power culture*: In these organisations, power is centralised. Decisions are made by a few people and lack a rational basis. Multiplicity of views is not tolerated. Employees do not get involved in the decision-making process and do not have the liberty to express their perspectives. Employees are expected to strictly follow the instructions provided by those who have the power and make the decisions.

- *Task culture*: This culture is job-oriented and represents organisations where employees' work collaboration is encouraged. What brings team members together is their common interests and expertise. People are expected to contribute to the task at hand and help the team accomplish their assigned tasks.

- *Person culture*: Organisations with a person culture suffer from employees' lack of loyalty. Employees see themselves as much more important than the organisation. Employees do not have the feeling of attachment to the organisation, as due to their expertise the employees can often easily find other employment. The organisational hierarchy will be ineffective without mutual agreement and, as a result, influencing these employees is not easy.

- *Role culture*: In this culture, the organisation is clearly defined and employees have specific authorities and responsibilities based on their competence, qualifications and specialisation. Handy (1993) asserts that these organisations work based on rationality and logic and ensure that power comes with responsibility. People look for the ways that help them to use their capabilities to better perform their delegated roles.

Handy (1993) argues that employees who are effective in one culture may or may not be effective in another. Moreover, there is no priority among these cultures and different types of cultures may work in different organisations.

O'Reilly and Chatman and Jehn's dimensions of culture

O'Reilly et al. (1991) and Chatman and Jehn (1994) identify seven cultural dimensions that differentiate one organisation from another:

1. innovation; that is, the extent to which people in an organisation are encouraged to take risks and to be innovative in performing their tasks
2. stability; that is, how far people in the organisation avoid challenging the status quo
3. an orientation towards people
4. an orientation towards outcomes or results
5. an emphasis on being easy-going
6. attention to detail
7. a collaborative or team orientation.

Deciphering an organisation's culture

Several methods and instruments can be used to decipher organisational culture to understand the extent to which the organisation's core values are widely and strongly held throughout the organisation. The methods engage a diverse range of techniques including visiting and observing the organisational culture; examining artefacts and organisational structures and processes; surveying or interviewing organisational members, including asking why they do things the way they do them; and interviewing the leaders and top executives about the core values and assumptions underlying the organisation's identity (Cameron & Ettington, 1988; Cameron & Quinn, 2005; Jacobs, 2002; Jurkowski, 2013).

Examples of the assessment tools and methods to diagnose an organisation's culture are the Organisational Culture Assessment Instrument (OCAI) (Cameron & Quinn, 1999), Organisational Profile Questionnaire (OPQ) (Askansasy, Broadfoot & Falkus, 2000), Customer Orientation and Cultural Issues (PCOC) (Maull, Brown & Cliffe, 2001) and Cultural Assets Profiles (CAPS) (Glover, Shames & Friedman, 1994).

One of the widely and frequently used methods is the OCAI developed by Cameron and Quinn (1999). The instrument has been used by more than 15 000 organisations worldwide in diverse sectors including the private sector, the public sector, healthcare, NGOs and education (Cameron, 2004). In addition to its popularity as a validated method for assessing organisational culture, extensive and considerable research was involved in the development of the OCAI.

The Organisational Culture Assessment Instrument (OCAI) and Competing Value Framework (CVF)

The OCAI was developed based on a model of organisational core values, the Competing Values Framework (CVF), introduced by Quinn and Cameron (1983) and Cameron and Quinn (1999). The CVF draws on two dimensions that represent four competing organisational values: external focus and differentiation versus internal focus and integration, as well as flexibility/discretion versus stability/control (Cameron & Quinn, 1999; Quinn & Cameron, 1983). The conjunction of the two dimensions identifies four main characteristics of an organisation's cultures: mission, adaptation, involvement and consistency (Denison & Mishra, 1995).

Mission is a cultural characteristic that refers to the extent to which the organisation pursues a mission. Mission gives direction and meaning to the organisation and its members. Adaptation refers to an organisation's capacity to respond to dynamics in the external environment. Involvement is another cultural characteristic that represents the level of people's participation and involvement in the organisational decision making. Consistency is concerned with normative integration, or the degree to which an organisation has a consistent and collective definition of values and behaviours that enhances integration and coordination within the organisation.

While mission and adaptation are concerned with the external adaptation, involvement and consistency deal with the internal dynamics and integration of the organisation. Moreover, consistency and mission correspond to an organisation's ability to remain stable over time. Adaptation and involvement are associated with an organisation's capacity to change.

Based on the four characteristics, four major organisational cultures can be identified: (Cameron & Freeman, 1991; Cameron & Quinn, 2005; Denison & Spreitzer, 1991):

- market culture (rational)
- adhocracy culture (developmental)
- clan culture (group)
- hierarchical culture.

The market or rational culture is result-driven and concerned with organisational performance. In this culture, objectives are clearly defined and competition is encouraged. Effectiveness in this culture is measured by productivity and efficiency. Leaders are perceived as producers, competitors and hard drivers. The adhocracy or developmental culture represents a creative and dynamic working environment where employees take certain risks, and leaders are perceived as visionary, risk-takers and innovators. In the adhocracy culture the core value is the organisation's growth. Effectiveness is measured by the creation of new resources and successful competition with rivals in the market. The clan or group culture is concerned with people's relationships and their overall interests. The clan culture implies a friendly working environment where people have a lot in common and leaders are perceived as a facilitator and mentor. Under this culture, the core value that drives the organisation is trust. Effectiveness is measured by the level of communication, commitment and participation. The hierarchical culture is based on organisational structure and control, where guidance is informed by strict institutional procedures and rules. This culture tends to be conservative. Leaders are perceived as monitors and organisers. Effectiveness is measured by the level of control and stability. The leader's main responsibility is to ensure that processes are efficient, rules are strictly followed and standards are met.

There is no one ideal culture, and an organisation may have a mix of these four organisational cultures. Cameron and Quinn (2005) argue that an organisation's culture can be determined by using a valid survey. The OCAI employing the CVF is a predictive instrument that assesses six key dimensions of organisational culture based on the competing values addressed by the CVF (Cameron & Quinn, 2005):

1. *Dominant characteristics*: This dimension addresses aspects such as sense of belonging and teamwork, level of creativity, orientation towards goals and competition, level of reliance on systems and emphasis on efficiency.

2. *Organisational leadership*: This refers to the leadership style and approach that permeates the organisation. The leaders in the organisation may take up eight roles: mentor, facilitator, innovator, broker, producer, director, coordinator and monitor (Quinn & Rohrbaugh, 1981).

3. *Management of employees*: This dimension is concerned with aspects such as the way employees are treated, working environment, level of consultation, consensus and participation.

4. *Organisational glue*: This dimension refers to the extent to which the organisation is coherent, employees have commitment and loyalty, and teamwork is valued.

5. *Strategic emphasis*: This dimension deals with organisational features such as emphasis on organisational strategies, long-term planning and competitive advantages.

6. *Criteria for success*: The last dimension is concerned with the way success is defined and measured in the organisation.

These six dimensions address the three fundamental aspects of an organisation's culture: values and underlying assumptions (dominant characteristics, organisational glue), interaction patterns (leadership and management of employees) and organisational direction (strategic emphases and criteria for success) (Cameron & Quinn, 2005). To assess an organisation's culture, organisational members are asked to assess the present culture in their organisation by rating the six dimensions. Organisational members rate the six dimensions one more time and this time by thinking of their preferred organisational culture.

As with almost all other organisational culture assessment tools, the OCAI is not comprehensive (Cameron & Quinn, 2005). This, in fact, reflects the complexity of organisational culture. Because organisational culture is a complex and multidimensional phenomenon that develops through social interactions among an organisation's members, it is not easy to capture all the aspects of an organisation's culture. Accordingly, it must be noted that organisations may use a combination of culture assessment tools.

Defining the desired culture

Once the current organisational culture has been diagnosed, the leaders in the organisation need to articulate the reason for culture change and envision the desired culture. Three fundamental questions must be addressed: what should be preserved, what should be minimised or eliminated, and what is missing? Answers to the questions identify the depth and breadth of change. How profound must the changes be? And how widely are the changes expected to happen? Schein's (2010) three levels of organisational culture – artefacts, espoused beliefs and values and underlying assumptions – are very helpful in addressing the three questions. The level of changes could range from seemingly small changes in a single visible aspect of the organisation's culture (for instance, changing dress code, logos, offices layouts), to more drastic changes in the fundamental assumptions underlying the core values of the whole organisation. For example, moving to a rapidly changing industry such as the technology industry may require changes in employees' underlying values about the importance of creativity and innovation. It is worthwhile to mention that even seemingly small changes to the visible aspects of organisational culture may lead to more fundamental and deep values in the organisation.

This involves identifying the attitudes and activities that will have to stop, be improved, or when new ones need to start. In addition to values and activities, organisational procedures and processes may need to be amended to support and enhance the attitude and behavioural changes (Cameron & Quinn, 2005; Cummings, 2008). Envisaging the desired culture allows the organisational members to capture a sense of what the culture will be like once the changes are applied. Clarifying the changes also helps organisational members to handle the anxiety inherent in the changes.

At this stage, leaders may need to create a sense of urgency (Kotter, 2008). It is critically important that leaders define the need for culture change very clearly and create a motivating reason for changing comfortable and familiar behavioural patterns. Once the need for culture change is defined, the reason should be clearly articulated for and communicated with the organisational members (Dawson, 2010).

Making the cultural change

Once the organisation has assessed its current culture and defined its preferred values and beliefs, it is time to bring the needed cultural changes to the organisation. Since culture manifests in behavioural practices, procedures and rewards (who is rewarded and who is not), the role of a leader is significant in the process of creating and formulating a new culture for the organisation. Leaders need to be actively involved in the change process. They need to consider the uncertainty that is inherent in the change, and deal with the anxiety that is unleashed when those assumptions are challenged (Schein, 2010).

Changing an organisation's culture towards its desired culture is a process that involves numerous steps. The main steps that must be taken to ensure that the culture change is successfully implemented and sustained following the analysing the existing culture and defining the desired culture are discussed below (Beyer & Cameron, 1997; Cameron, 1985; Cameron & Ettington, 1988; Cameron & Whetten, 1981a, 1981b; Hooijberg & Petrock, 1993; Kotter, 1995; Schein, 1996; Schneider et al., 2013).

- *Getting support from the top management*: Management support is critical in developing a strong culture. Effecting a successful culture change is not only the leader's responsibility, but all organisational members including top management need to be on board and support the change throughout the change process. Top management support refers to the extent to which the senior executives in the organisation understand the importance of the cultural change and are involved in the change practices. It is very important that top management accepts the new culture as the desired culture and is committed to making the culture change happen.
- *Modelling the culture*: The change begins with the leader. Leaders are presumably expected to model changes in the organisation and carry on the organisational vision and culture in the future. Therefore, they are expected to be practical in leading the culture through their words and actions. If the leader fails to consistently model the behaviours of the desired values and beliefs in word and deed, it is unlikely that employees will enact the new culture (Dawson, 2010).

- *Facilitating people's development*: As adopting a new culture requires changes in attitudes and behavioural patterns, the organisational members may need to develop new skills and abilities. Cultural changes may lead to designing or redesigning the organisational processes. To perform organisational tasks through the new procedures may require new competencies. Moreover, changing values and beliefs often engages practices. Accordingly, providing appropriate trainings and learning activities to develop new skills and competencies in employees, senior executives and even the leader is vital.

Implementing cultural changes is easier when all the organisational members – both the leader and followers – are involved in defining and developing the desired culture. Organisational culture change will not be successful unless people's behaviours change, and this change can be sustained for as long as the organisation wishes.

Sustaining cultural change

Sustaining the organisational culture is a process through which shared values, beliefs and assumptions within the organisation endure for a period deemed appropriate by the organisations (Buchanan et al., 2005). The process of sustaining organisational culture change includes anchoring the change, institutionalising the change and sustaining best practices within the organisation.

- *Anchoring the culture change*: This involves consolidating improvements and producing more culture change and institutionalising new approaches (Kotter, 1995). According to Kotter (1995), there are two dimensions of institutionalising cultural change. The first is demonstrating a link between culture change in behaviours and attitudes and improvements in performance. The second dimension is management succession, which ensures that the effort of the current leader does not end at the end of his or her tenure. Thus, the new generation of leaders or management need to personify the new approach and initiatives of the new culture. In anchoring the culture change, the new leaders or managers need to champion the initiatives of their predecessors, without necessarily introducing their own ideas or initiative; the vision of the leader/manager should be clear; the guiding coalition should be powerful in maintaining the momentum; and time should be allowed for change to become part of the culture (Kotter, 1995).
- *Institutionalising the culture change*: Most culture change efforts lack persistence, and that accounts for why most culture change cannot be sustained (Jacobs, 2002). Jacobs (2002) defines institutionalising change as relative enduring and staying power over a length of time until the culture change becomes part of everyday activity within the organisation. Buchanan and co-authors (2005) believe that, to institutionalise culture change, there are a number of essential factors to put into consideration: training to establish competence and commitment, meeting the reward expectation of the organisational members, spread of new ideas and monitoring and controlling of the

entire process. If the institutionalisation is effectively done, then the desired goal of sustaining organisational culture can be achieved.

- *Sustaining best practices*: Sustaining the best practices in the organisation involves the support of the manager or the leader who is committed to effecting a culture change. There are a variety of ways that leaders can communicate organisational culture to employees. Schein (2010) identifies some of these ways: measuring, controlling, reacting to crisis situations, providing a personal role model, rewarding, selecting and promoting the employees. According to Schein (2010), all these practices inform organisational orientation in respect of strategic goals. The organisational culture is conveyed through what the leaders emphasise in their own actions, as well as the provision of encouragement and facilitation of enacting the new desired values and beliefs.

Implementing and sustaining a new culture is highly challenging. Successful changes result from shared values and commitment to the desired culture, which to a high degree relies on the relationship between the leader and other organisational members. The leader should be able to build trust and discretion in the organisation.

Organisational culture change is a continuous process. Given the never-ending and rapid changes in the economic, technological, social, political and environmental world, organisations' survival depends on their capacity to change. For this reason, once an organisation builds a new culture, changes in the culture must be constantly monitored and analysed to ensure that the desired values and beliefs are being maintained, and to identify what changes need to be implemented to improve future organisational performance.

CASE STUDY 7.2

Coates Hire

Coates Hire Limited was founded in 1885 as an engineering company in Melbourne, Australia and is presently operated as a construction hire company. In its 130 years of operation, it has grown into an international organisation with a strong history of innovation and development. It is the largest hire equipment business in Australia, and the fifth largest such business in the world. Some examples of its growth milestones include: in 1993, Coates Hire operated in Indonesia to support the growing mining and construction boom; in 2006, it supported the Commonwealth Games in Melbourne; it currently operates a highly profitable offshore air- and steam-generator leasing business; and the organisation has been publicly listed twice: first, between 1955 and 1972, and then between 1996 and 2008.

Coates Hire's second listing on the stock exchange brought increased challenges to deliver continuing performance improvements and profitability. Its leaders decided that the organisational culture was an important factor in this endeavour.

In 2004, Coates decided to use human resource management to propagate a strategy called 'The Coates Way': a culture-change program designed to communicate the company's values to all employees, along with practical steps to implement these values in their work. The Coates Way had four aspects: Purpose (why the business exists), Vision (goals for the business), Critical Success Factors (the conditions of reaching their goals) and Values (expected behaviours). These Critical Success Factors were: 'commit to our customers', 'develop our people', 'manage our fleet' and 'grow our company'.

The Human Resources Department at Coates championed The Coates Way throughout the organisation. Each unit of the organisation needed to develop its own implementation of the organisation's strategy. By influencing the organisation's culture, Coates sought to make the aspects of The Coates Way self-perpetuating. One means of influencing this culture was the institution of regular meetings in which staff would discuss ways of applying The Coates Way in their work and discuss any challenges that arose from this application. Performance standards and measures included the application of The Coates Way.

Sources: AFR (2012a); Coates Hire (2016)

Critical thinking questions

1. Can you find any similarities between The Coates Way (including its aspects) and the change process discussed in the chapter?
2. Can you think of three challenges that Coates Hire would have faced in operating an Australian business in Indonesia in 1993? How could the process of organisational culture change be used to face these challenges?
3. Can you think of three challenges that Coates Hire would have faced in supporting the 2006 Commonwealth Games? How could the process of organisational culture change be used to face these challenges?
4. What are some of the steps the Human Resources Department could have taken to support managers in their application of The Coates Way to their department?

SUMMARY

LEARNING OUTCOME 1: Describe organisational culture and explain how it is different
from organisational climate.

Culture is a complex phenomenon with competing views of the organisational culture. Generally, 'culture' refers to the collective values and beliefs of a group of people who have something in common, and interact socially as a result. Culture characterises an organisation, whereas climate defines the organisational atmosphere and environment. Unlike organisational culture that can outlast the organisation, organisational climate is individual-focused and is easier to assess and alter.

LEARNING OUTCOME 2: Identify the internal and external factors that affect
organisational culture.

Several factors affect an organisation's culture, and these can be described as internal and external. Internal factors include members' values, leader–culture relationship, organisational structure and communication. The external factors include the social factors, business stakeholders and technology.

LEARNING OUTCOME 3: Describe the process of organisational culture change.

Organisational culture change is a complex process that involves dealing with issues that are mostly difficult to identify and address. The change process has four major phases: analysing existing culture, defining the desired culture, and making and sustaining the culture change. Both leaders and followers all play a central role in dealing with organisational cultural change.

LEARNING OUTCOME 4: Analyse the existing culture of an organisation.

A successful culture change requires an accurate understanding of the existing culture of the organisation. There are a number organisational culture typologies that can help a leader to better understand their organisational culture. Leaders may use different methods and instruments to identify the culture that is prominent in their organisation. One of the most widely and frequently used methods is the OCAI.

LEARNING OUTCOME 5: Explain the process of defining the desired culture.

- -

Once leaders have identified the culture of their organisation, they need to articulate and communicate the reason for culture change. Three fundamental questions must be addressed: What should be preserved? What should be minimised or eliminated? And what is missing? Answers to these questions address the depth and breadth of the cultural change.

LEARNING OUTCOME 6: Explain the process of implementing and sustaining the
   organisational culture change.

- -

A real change is not achieved unless leaders' and followers' assumptions, attitudes and behaviours are changed. Accordingly, leaders need to ensure that a real change is made and the change is sustained for a period deemed appropriate by the organisations. To make real changes, the leaders need to gain top management support, model the desired culture and facilitate the organisational members' development.

   To sustain the cultural changes, the leaders need to anchor the culture change, institutionalise the culture change and sustain the best practices in the organisation.

REVIEW QUESTIONS

1. Think of the three levels of the organisational culture analysis suggested by Edgar Schein. How do you think the importance of each level may vary from one organisation to another?

2. Think of three successful Australian organisations, either in the public or private sectors. Visit the website of each organisation and investigate to see if you can identify the core values of each entity. List these and try to identify the symbols that the organisations use to promote their core values.

3. The chapter identifies some of the major internal and external factors that affect an organisation's culture. What other factors do you think may impact an organisation's culture?

4. Think of the process of culture change discussed in the chapter. Which phase of the process do you think is more important than the others? How do you think the significance of each phase varies in different industries (for example, the product or service industries)?

CASE STUDY 7.3

Fonterra

Fonterra is New Zealand's biggest employer, and is among the biggest organisations in the dairy industry in the globe. Fonterra produces about 16 billion litres of milk from farmers and collects 6 billion litres of milk from international suppliers every year. For more than 50 years, the cooperative has been at the forefront of New Zealand's global exports producing 25 per cent of New Zealand's exports. Fonterra is owned by more than 10 500 farmers and their families as shareholders, and the company operates in more than 100 countries and employs 22 000 people around the world.

The farmer-shareholders who supply Fonterra with milk are the company's top priority. The farmers benefit from the collective strength that the company, as a cooperative, offers (such as on-farm support from milk-quality specialists, sustainable dairying advisors, Shareholders' Councillors and combined purchasing power with the rural supplies network).

Fonterra's culture values a can-do attitude and a collaborative spirit, as well as product and production quality and innovation. Fonterra's business strategies are formulated based on the company's culture:

> Our purpose is to be the world's most trusted source of dairy nutrition. It defines why we are here and sits alongside our values at the heart of everything we do. Together our purpose and values drive our strategy, guide our actions and behaviours and bring focus to our business decisions (Champions Trophy, 2013).

Moreover, a high standard of leadership is central to the company's governance. This is reflected by Fonterra's governance statement: 'We're committed to the highest standard of corporate governance and leadership' (see www.fonterra.com). The company's governance focuses on, for example, promoting transparency, effectively managing risk, communicating with important stakeholders, promoting the interests of shareholders and creating a good balance between the roles and functions of the company's leadership team.

To promote this culture, Fonterra provides a working environment where people are supported and rewarded fairly. Employees and farmers are given many different experiences and opportunities to be able to enhance their professional, technical and leadership capabilities.

In 2006, Fonterra established a governance development program to help shareholders associated with the company address dairy industry and rural sector professional and succession needs. The program is aimed at developing future leaders from the farming community. Through the one-year program, the farmers develop the skills and abilities that they need to be able to govern Fonterra or rural organisations in the future. During the program, farmers enhance their leadership skills and competencies, gain a better understanding of their own personality styles, and explore how different styles can be used to effect change and increase their capability and capacity for reflective and critical thinking within a governance context.

Source: Stuff (2015); Champions Trophy (2013)

1. A can-do attitude and a collaborative spirit are at the core of Fonterra's culture. Given that the management team in an organisation may have a significant impact on organisational culture, how can Fonterra's leadership team promote these core values?
2. Considering the analytical levels of culture (as suggested by Schein, 2010) how would you describe the impact of the training program on the company's culture? Discuss how Fonterra might use its training programs to sustain, strengthen, and, if necessary, change its culture.
3. Identify three challenges that Fonterra may face if its strategies and culture were misaligned. How might the company address these challenges?
4. Fonterra is a cooperative. Examine key differences between the process of organisational culture change at a co-operative company and at a single-owner company.

REFERENCES

AAP (2012). *Reckitt Benckiser closes with 190 jobs.* AAP Bulletins, 1 February.

Askansasy, N.M., Broadfoot, L.E. & Falkus, S. (2000). Questionnaire measures of organisational culture. In N.M. Askansasy, L.E. Broadfoot & S. Falkus (eds), *Handbook of organisational culture and climate* (pp. 1–18). Thousand Oaks, CA: SAGE Publications.

Ashkanasy, N.M. & Härtel, C.E.J. (2014). Positive and negative affective climate and culture: The good, the bad and the ugly. *Oxford handbook of organizational climate and culture* (pp. 136–52). Oxford: Oxford University Press.

Australian Financial Review (AFR) (2012a). *Coates: Strategic human resources to achieve company goals AFR Business Case Studies,* 7th edn. Melbourne: Australian Business Case Studies.

—— (2012b). *Reckitt Benckiser: Strategy, leadership and company culture,* 7th edn. Melbourne: Australian Business Case Studies.

Beyer, J. & Cameron, K.S. (1997). *Organizational culture: Enhancing organizational performance.* Washington, DC: National Academies Press.

Bok-Hyeon, S. (2016). Oxy researchers are in hot water. *Korea JoongAng Daily.* 6 May.

Brown, A.D. (1995). *Organizational culture.* London: Pitman Publishing.

Buchanan, D. et al. (2005). No going back: A review of the literature on sustaining organizational change. *International Journal of Management Reviews,* 7(3), 189–205.

Burke, W.W. (2013). *Organization change: Theory and practice.* Thousand Oaks, CA: SAGE Publications.

Cameron, K.S. (1985). Cultural congruence, strength, and type: Relationships to effectiveness. Paper presented at ASHE Annual Meeting.

—— (2003). Ethics, virtuousness, and constant change. In *The ethical challenge: How to lead with unyielding integrity* (pp. 185–94). San Francisco, CA: Jossey-Bass.

—— (2004). A process for changing organizational culture. In T.G. Cummings (ed.), *Handbook of organization development* (pp. 429–45). Thousand Oaks, CA: SAGE Publications.

Cameron, K.S. & Ettington, D.R. (1988). The conceptual foundations of organizational culture. *Higher education: Handbook of theory and research*, 4, 429–47.

Cameron, K.S. & Freeman, S.J. (1991). Culture, congruence, strength and type: relationship to effectiveness. *Research in Organizational Change and Development*, 5, 23–58.

Cameron, K.S. & Quinn, R.E. (1999). *Diagnosing and changing organisational culture*. Reading: Addison-Wesley.

—— (2005). *Diagnosing and changing organizational culture: Based on the competing values framework*. San Francisco, CA: John Wiley & Sons.

Cameron, K.S. & Whetten, D.A. (1981a). Perceptions of organizational effectiveness across organizational life cycles. Paper presented at Academy of Management.

—— (1981b). Perceptions of organizational effectiveness over organizational life cycles. *Administrative Science Quarterly*, 26(4), 525–44.

Carter, L. (2016). Nurofen maker admits to court it engaged in 'deceptive and misleading' behaviour. *ABC News*, 14 April.

Catanzaro, D., Moore, H. & Marshall, T. R. (2010). The impact of organizational culture on attraction and recruitment of job applicants. *Journal of Business and Psychology*, 25(4), 649–62.

Champions Trophy (2013). Fonterra company overview. *Champions Trophy Case Competition 2013*, Case 4. Retrieved from: www.champions-trophy.co.nz/wp-content/uploads/2012/11/Fonterra-Company-Overview.pdf.

Chatman, J.A. & Jehn, K.A. (1994). Assessing the relationship between industry characteristics and organizational culture: How different can you be? *Academy of Management Journal*, 37(3), 522–33.

Coates Hire (2016). Coates hire: Our history, website, 16 June. Retrieved from: http://www.coateshire.com.au/About-Coates/our-history.

Collins, C.J. & Smith, K.G. (2006). Knowledge exchange and combination: The role of human resource practices in the performance of high-technology firms. *Academy of Management Journal*, 49, 544–60.

Cookson, R. & Daneshku, S. (2015). Nurofen maker Reckitt Benckiser suffers advertising headaches. *Financial Times*, 15 December.

Cummings, T.G. (2008). *Handbook of organization development*. Thousand Oaks, CA: University of Southern California.

Da-sol, K. (2016). Disinfectant maker under fire for allegedly skipping toxicity test. *Korea Herald*, 16 March.

Dawson, C.S. (2010). *Leading culture change: What every CEO needs to know*. Stanford, CA: Stanford University Press.

Deal, T.E. & Kennedy, A.A. (1982). *Corporate cultures*. Reading, MA: Addison-Wesley.

Denison, D.R. (1996). What is the difference between organizational culture and organizational climate? A native's point of view on a decade of paradigm wars. *Academy of Management Review*, 21, 619–54.

—— (2000). Organizational culture: Can it be a key driver for organisational change? In D.R. Denison (ed.), *The International Handbook of Organizational Culture and Climate* (pp. 317–372). London: John Wiley & Sons.

Denison, D.R. & Mishra, A.K. (1995). Toward a theory of organizational culture and effectiveness. *Organization Science*, 6, 204–23.

Denison, D.R. & Spreitzer, G.M. (1991). Organizational culture and organizational development: A competing values approach. *Research in Organizational Change and Development*, 5, 1–21.

Glover, J., Shames, G. & Friedman, H. (1994). *Developing cultural assets.* Cultural Assets Management Inc., HI.

Greenwood, R. & Hinings, C.R. (1996). Understanding radical organizational change: Bringing together the old and the new institutionalism. *Academy of Management Review*, 21, 1022–54.

Handy, C. (1993). *Understanding organizations*, 4th edn. London: Penguin Books.

Hempel, J. (2005). Why the boss really had to say goodbye. *Business Week*, 4 July.

Hofstede, G. (1980). *Culture's consequences: International differences in work-related values.* Beverly Hills, CA: SAGE Publications.

—— (1997). *Cultures and organizations: Software of the mind.* New York, NY: McGraw-Hill.

—— (2003). *Cultures and organisations: Intercultural cooperation and its importance for survival: Software of the mind.* London: Profile Books.

Hofstede, G., Hofstede, G.J. & Minkov, M. (1991). *Cultures and organizations: Software of the mind*, vol. 2. London: McGraw-Hill.

Hofstede, G., Neuijen, B., Ohayv, D.D. & Sanders, G. (1990). Measuring organizational cultures: A qualitative and quantitative study across twenty cases. *Administrative Science Quarterly*, 35(2), 286–316. doi:10.2307/2393392

Hooijberg, R. & Petrock, F. (1993). On cultural change: Using the competing values framework to help leaders execute a transformational strategy. *Human Resource Management*, 32(1), 29–50.

Hyuk-Jin, J. & Chung, E. (2016). Oxy probed over humidifier death disclosures. *Korea JoongAng Daily*, 20 April.

Intezari, A., Taskin, N. & Pauleen, D. (2017). Looking beyond knowledge sharing: An integrative approach to knowledge management culture. *Journal of Knowledge Management*, 21(2), 492–515.

Jacobs, R.L. (2002). Institutionalizing organizational change through cascade training. *Journal of European Industrial Training*, 26(2–4), 177–82.

Joyce, W. (1999). *Mega change: How today's leading companies have transformed their workforces.* New York, NY: Free Press.

Jurkowski, E.T. (2013). *Implementing culture change in long-term care: Benchmarks and strategies for management and practice*: New York, NY: Springer Publishing.

Kilman, R.H., Saxton, M.J. & Serpa, R. (1985). *Gaining control of the corporate culture*. San Francisco, CA: Jossey-Bass.

Kotter, J.P. (1995). Leading change: Why transformation efforts fail. *Harvard Business Review*, 73(2), 59–67.

—— (2008). *A sense of urgency*. Boston, MA: Harvard Business Press.

Liao, H. & Chuang, A. (2007). Transforming service employees and climate: A multilevel, multisource examination of transformational leadership in building long-term service relationships. *Journal of Applied Psychology*, 92(4), 1006–19.

Martin, J. (2002). *Organizational culture: Mapping the terrain*. Thousand Oaks, CA: SAGE Publications.

Martins, L.L. (2011). Organizational Change and Development. In S. Zedeck (ed.), *APA handbook of industrial and organizational psychology*, vol. 3 (pp. 691–728). Washington, DC: American Psychological Association.

Maull, R., Brown, P. & Cliffe, R. (2001). Organisational culture and quality improvement. *International Journal of Operations and Production Management*, 21(3), 302–26.

Naranjo-Valencia, J.C., Jimenez-Jimenez, D. & Sanz-Valle, R. (2011). Innovation or imitation? The role of organizational culture. *Management Decision*, 49(1), 55–72.

Needle, D. (2010). *Business in context: An introduction to business and its environment*: Hampshire, UK: South-Western Cengage Learning.

Nutt, P.C. & Backoff, R.W. (1997). Transforming organizations with second-order change. *Research in Organizational Change and Development*, 10, 229–74.

O'Reilly, C.A. (1989). Corporations, culture, and commitment: Motivation and social control in organizations. *California Management Review*, 31(4), 9–25. doi:10.2307/41166580

O'Reilly, C.A. & Chatman, J.A. (1996). Culture as social control: Corporations, cults, and commitment. *Research in Organizational Behavior*, 18, 157–200.

O'Reilly, C.A., Chatman, J.A. & Caldwell, D.F. (1991). People and organizational culture: A Q-sort approach to assessing person organization fit. *Academy of Management Journal*, 34, 487–516. doi:10.2307/256404

Ouchi, W.G. (1983). Theory Z: An elaboration of methodology and findings. *Journal of Contemporary Business*, 11, 27–41.

Pascale, R.T. & Athos, A.G. (1981). *The art of Japanese management: Applications for American executives*. New York, NY: Simon & Schuster.

Peters, T. & Waterman, R. (1982). *In search of excellence: Lessons from America's Best run companies*. New York, NY: Harper & Row.

Quinn, R.E. & Cameron, K.S. (1983). Organisational life cycles and some shifting criteria of effectiveness. *Management Science*, 29, 31–51.

Quinn, R.E. & Rohrbaugh, J. (1981). A competing values approach to organisational effectiveness. *Public Productivity Report,* June, 122–40.

Reckitt Benckiser Group plc (RB) (2016a). *2015 Annual Report and Financial Statements.* Retrieved from: www.rb.com/media/1598/rb-annual-report-2015_final.pdf.

—— (2016b). Reckitt Benckiser: About us. Retrieved from: www.rb.com/about-us.

Riggio, R. (2015). *Introduction to industrial and organizational psychology.* Milton Park, UK: Routledge.

Schein, E.H. (1985a). Defining organizational culture. In J.M. Shafritz & P.H. Whitbeck (eds), *Classics of Organization Theory*, vol. 3 (pp. 490–502). Oak Park, IL: Moore Publishing Company.

—— (1985b). *Organizational culture and leadership.* San Francisco, CA: Jossey-Bass.

—— (1992). *Organizational culture and leadership,* 2nd edn. San Francisco, CA: Jossey-Bass.

—— (1996). Culture: The missing concept in organization studies. *Administrative Science Quarterly,* 41(2), 229–40.

—— (2004). *Organizational culture and leadership,* 3rd edn. San Francisco, CA: Jossey-Bass.

—— (2010). *Organizational culture and leadership,* 4th edn. San Francisco, CA: Jossey-Bass.

Schneider, B. (2000). The psychological life of organizations. In N. Ashkanasy & M.F. Peterson (eds), *Handbook of organizational culture and climate* (pp. xvii–xxi). Thousand Oaks, CA: SAGE Publications.

Schneider, B., Brief, A.P. & Guzzo, R.A. (1996). Creating a climate and culture for sustainable organizational change. *Organizational Dynamics,* 24, 6–9.

Schneider, B., Erhart, M.G. & Macey, W.H. (2011). Perspectives on organizational climate and culture. In S. Zedeck (ed.), *APA handbook of industrial and organizational psychology,* vol. 1 (pp. 373–414). Washington, DC: American Psychological Association.

—— (2013). Organizational climate and culture. *Annual Review of Psychology,* 64, 361–88.

Schultz, M. (1995). *On studying organizational cultures: Diagnosis and understanding,* vol. 58. Berlin: Walter de Gruyter.

Sørensen, J.B. (2002). The strength of corporate culture and the reliability of firm performance. *Administrative Science Quarterly,* 47(1), 70–91.

Stuff (2015). Culture is king over strategy for Fonterra. *Stuff,* 1 March. Retrieved from: www.stuff.co.nz/business/opinion-analysis/66689313/culture-is-king-over-strategy-for-fonterra.

Weick, K.E. & Quinn, R.E. (1999). Organizational change and development. *Annual Review of Psychology,* 50(1), 361–86.

Williams, A., Dobson, P. & Walters, M. (1993). *Changing culture: New organizational approaches.* London: Institute of Personnel Management.

Yagil, D. (2014). Service quality. In B. Schneider & K.M. Barbera (eds), *Oxford handbook of organizational climate and culture* (pp. 297–316). Oxford: Oxford University Press.

8

POWER, POLITICS AND INFLUENCE

Bernard McKenna and Ali Intezari

LEARNING OUTCOMES

After reading this chapter, you should be able to:

1. define power and differentiate it from status

2. understand politics in relation to leadership and explain the four faces of power in organisations

3. identify the characteristics of toxic leadership and the profile of destructive leaders

4. identify the factors that create a labyrinth for women in their quest to obtain leadership positions.

INTRODUCTION

WHEN YOU THINK of powerful leaders, who comes to mind first? Significant historical figures such as Napoleon, Hitler or Churchill; major religious leaders or philosophers such as Jesus Christ, Prophet Mohammed or Confucius; or wealthy business entrepreneurs like Bill Gates or Mark Zuckerberg? Did you consider an outstanding scientist or a woman – someone like Angela Merkel, Gina Rinehart or Oprah Winfrey? It is worth asking what your automatic perceptions of powerful leaders indicate about your assumptions about leadership and power. For example, does it mean that powerful leaders need to use coercive force? Are they politicians? Are they likely to be women? Are they people who do good?

Political theory has produced hundreds of books defining power. However, this chapter is going to adopt a relatively simple understanding within an organisational context: 'Power is understood as the extent to which a person can influence or control other group members' (Frauendorfer et al., 2015, p. 392). Ultimately, power is concerned with achieving something. As Salancik and Pfeffer (1977, p. 14) propose, power is 'the ability to get things done the way one wants them to be done'. These definitions identify power in terms of outcomes. However, it is important to understand that the source of power is 'related to one's control over valued resources' (Magee & Galinsky, 2008, p. 351).

This chapter identifies the relationship between leadership and power, shows how power can be used to benefit organisations, how toxic leadership develops, and then considers two largely marginalised areas of leadership and power, namely whether it is possible for women to reach equity with men in leadership.

THE FOUNDATIONS OF LEADERSHIP POWER

To properly understand the role of **power** in leadership, we need to first understand what the words mean. This is because power manifests in different forms and the concept of leadership varies in different cultures and circumstances.

> **Power** – The extent to which a person can influence or control other group members; it is concerned with achieving something the way one wants it to be done.

Although first devised over 50 years ago, the definition of power in management provided by French and Raven (1962) defines power as the capacity or potential to influence and to affect others' beliefs, attitudes and actions. That is, those who have power possess the ability to control the actions of others and the outcomes in various circumstances. A leader is someone who can bring about a desired change in the behaviour of a group of people. It is important to distinguish between people who have power because of their position and those who have personal power (Bass, 1990). **Position power** is the result of having a position designated as a leadership role, such as an organisational manager. However, designated leadership positions with position power have often achieved this at least in part because of personal power. For example, an elected politician or a sports

> **Position power** – Power that is allocated to a designated organisational position.

team captain invariably also display personal power. Personal power may be the result of a person being regarded as likable, knowledgeable or competent.

Position power can emerge from four bases:

- Legitimate power: having the legitimate authority to administer an organisation or group in a way that people desire
- Reward power: the ability to control behaviour by providing rewards in the form of money, promotion, praise, and more fulfilling work assignments
- Coercive power: producing a form of follower behaviour by using punishment or threats. Although even 'soft' bureaucracies have some degree of underlying coercive power, excessive use of this sort of power produces negative feelings and outcomes. This is discussed more fully below
- Information power: based on having access to information and/or controlling the flow of information to others.

Personal power – Power derived from others' evaluation of a person being regarded as likable, knowledgeable or competent.

Personal power does not emerge from the person's position, but from referent and expert power, according to French and Raven (1962). Referent power develops when other people admire and respect a person, resulting in their willingness to become followers undertaking tasks rather than being required to do so. Expert power is exhibited when a leader is recognised for their knowledge and expertise in some required domain, although such leaders may not necessarily have the admiration or respect of their followers because of negative behaviour and values. It is likely that people who display emergent leadership – people who are seen by others as the most influential in a group or organisation, even if they are not formally identified as a leader – are likely to display referent or expert power.

Emergent leadership needs to be properly understood because it occurs more commonly in contemporary – so called 'post-bureaucratic' – organisations where hierarchy is flattened and teamwork is frequently used for projects. The claims that post-bureaucratic organisations are more democratic and participatory to some extent rest on ideological claims rather than the reality. That is, responsibilities may often devolve to people lower down in the hierarchy without adequate compensation or an organisation may be participatory only to the extent that 'democratic' and 'participative' decisions concur with management expectations. A major critic of these claims, Harold Leavitt (2005), asserts that organisations are still largely authoritarian power structures, but are 'cloaked in a veil of humanism' (p. x).

Hierarchies

Hierarchy – An unequal distribution of power, where senior positions have the authority to set tasks for people with less power to achieve a task.

Hierarchies form in groups and organisations when a certain level of complex activity is reached, requiring systems and job allocations to be arranged to solve a problem, produce a good or deliver a service. The essence of hierarchies is that power is unequally distributed so that those in more senior positions have the authority to set tasks for people with less power to complete. Those in more senior positions should have technical competence and high levels of knowledge, but are mostly selected to work at a more generalised level to design and implement strategies that provide overall coherence to the organisation's activities. The most senior people with most power also have responsibility for changing the organisation's mission and the strategies designed to meet that mission.

The two most important determinants of social hierarchy are **status** and power (Magee & Galinsky, 2008). Power needs to be distinguished from status, which can be defined as 'the respect one has in the eyes of others' (Magee & Galinsky, 2008, p. 351). Status often emerges from the social groups to which someone belongs. For example, a physician or an electrical engineer is likely to be accorded higher status than, say, a nurse or an electrical tradesman. Over time, social status can alter. For example, religious priests and ministers have almost always been considered to have relatively high status in Western countries. However, findings of an Australian Royal Commission on child sexual abuse (Royal Commission, 2017) and revelations in other countries have dramatically reduced the status of religious ministers and bishops when it was found that many church institutions not only provided the conditions for sexual predators to operate but also covered up wrongdoings. Many people now feel that the trust that accompanied the higher status was egregiously abused. Thus, it can be said that social status is not necessarily earned. This point is strongly supported by the fact that social status can be affected by ethnicity and gender. Status construction theory determines how these various factors combine to create high- and low-status groups over time. Dominant status beliefs are generally accepted by those who advantage from that status, and those who are disadvantaged accept these beliefs as 'a matter of social reality' (Ridgeway & Correll, 2006, p. 433). For example, an engineer on a mining site may exert his or her dominant status based on their university-based knowledge. The site workers may defer to this status in accepting instructions without question, thereby acknowledging their inferior status. As a result, their experience-based knowledge may be discounted in problem solving. However, site workers often refuse to acknowledge this status differential believing that the engineer's 'book knowledge' fails to take into account their 'common sense' knowledge gained from experience. As well, within such sites, Indigenous people are sometimes disadvantaged because of their allocated inferior status as a 'social reality'.

There are two major reasons why hierarchies will remain as a dominant organisational form. The first reason is that many hierarchies, despite the criticisms levelled at them, get the job done. While some hierarchies develop through differences in power (asymmetries in control over resources), through status (asymmetries in respect and admiration from others), and participation (asymmetries in how much group members contribute to group tasks and

Status – The respect one has in the eyes of others.

activities) (Halevy, Chou & Galinsky, 2011, p. 34), it has been established that hierarchies perform useful organisational functions. They:

- enhance coordination and cooperation among group members. As a result, because intragroup conflict is reduced, group performance is enhanced (Halevy et al., 2011)
- establish order which facilitates coordination; this helps to motivate organisational members (Magee & Galinsky, 2008)
- can also help to create a psychologically rewarding environment (Halevy et al., 2011).

Where an organisation has a division of labour (and any moderate to large organisation must have a division of labour to specialise in different tasks), hierarchies perform a useful role. A result of this coordinating role is that conflict is reduced and voluntary cooperation is enhanced (Halevy et al., 2011).

It is not commonly understood that when groups are newly formed, hierarchies form automatically and quite rapidly. That is, a leader emerges when power is dispersed in groups with a task. The leader who emerges most commonly is the person who displays the greatest level of competence in helping a group to complete the task. Research appears to confirm that a more hierarchical power structure enhances group performance (Greer & Van Kleef, 2010). This was also shown to be the case for group performance in a context of emergent hierarchies in peer groups (Frauendorfer et al., 2015). However, an important – and surprising – qualification needs to be acknowledged. It was found that 'the degree to which the power hierarchy is based on the task-competence hierarchy within a group does not affect overall group performance' (Frauendorfer et al., 2015, p. 395). In other words, although a hierarchy naturally emerges in a dispersed-power group, and the leader who is chosen is most commonly selected for competence, the leader's competence does not affect the group's effectiveness in achieving its task. This need for some level of hierarchy may have implications for cultures that have low scores for Hofstede's dimension of power distance (PD), which is the extent or degree to which members of an organisation or society expect and agree that power should be stratified (Hofstede, 1984). Australia and New Zealand are such cultures.

Formal and informal hierarchies

Groups and organisational hierarchies may be either formal or informal. Formal hierarchies develop when organisations become more complex, involving separate divisions with specified roles, proper accounting and responsibility, and reporting internally and externally. Those with higher formal rank have greater control over resources and expect deference and compliance from their subordinates to complete specified tasks. Highly ranked people derive their legitimacy from possessing the skills, knowledge and ability to make decisions and perform higher-order tasks.

Informal hierarchies do not emerge from formally designated positions. As stated above, informal hierarchies form quite rapidly. This is because people can form accurate assessments of others on thin 'slices' of information. This is largely due to observing non-verbal cues that influence people's judgements about some personality attributes. Non-verbal cues include arm position; gazing down; frowning; fidgeting with hands or with an object; nodding or shaking one's head; laughing; leaning forward; sitting; smiling; and touching one's head (Kendon, Sebeok & Umiker-Sebeok, 1981). Notably, physical attractiveness does not strongly affect these judgements. The attributes that people predicted to varying degrees from non-verbal cues included accepting, active, attentive, competent, confident, dominant, empathic, enthusiastic, honest, likable, (not) anxious, optimistic, professional, supportive and warm. Research by Ambady and Rosenthal (1993) showed that people could accurately rate attributes from the non-verbal cues of complete strangers based on thin slices of non-verbal behaviour (video clips of between 2 and 10 seconds).

When set with a task, members of an informal group will determine the characteristic that they believe is most important in a given circumstance. This can be explained by **social identity theory**. When group members judge one dimension or characteristic to be the most important for their group or organisation, the group 'will naturally and spontaneously differentiate hierarchically along that dimension', according to social identity theorist Michael Hogg (2001, p. 184). Those members perceived as strong in that dimension will represent the prototypical features of that group. Other research has shown that conscientiousness is a better predictor of hierarchical rank than extraversion when an organisation is task-oriented while extraversion is a better predictor of rank in socially oriented organisations (Magee & Galinsky, 2008).

> **Social identity theory** – A theory that explains how groups naturally and spontaneously form hierarchies based on a dimension or characteristic judged to be the most important for their group or organisation.

Self-reinforcing nature of hierarchies

Hierarchies are relatively steadfast, and so do not change quickly or significantly. Several organisational and psychological processes 'conspire' to create provide different degrees of opportunity to gain and maintain power, according to Magee and Galinsky (2008). This means that even though low-ranking members are disadvantaged relative to high-ranking members, certain hierarchical functions provide low-ranking members with the motivation to invest in its continuation. A major factor is people's individual needs for order and stability. Apart from this fundamental need, our psychological state alters according to whether we have high or low levels of power, and these psychological states help to reinforce the power structures. One of the earliest researchers in this area, David Kipnis (1976), an expert in the field of organisational psychology, reached the pessimistic conclusion that people who hold power are able to use a variety of influence strategies to maintain their dominance over others, and also use 'strong tactics' or directive strategies, more frequently than those with less power. He called this the 'metamorphic effect of power', which he claimed helped to explain the corrupting effect of authoritarian leadership.

Later research by Keltner, Gruenfeld and Anderson (2003) provided support for Kipnis's findings. Their research provided a model of power that identified:

- determinants of power:
  - individual variables such as personality traits and physical characteristics
  - dyadic variables such as interest in relationships and relative commitment
  - within-group variables such as role authority and status
  - between-group variables such as ethnicity, gender, class, ideology, numerical majority or minority
- social power (high and low) according to resources and freedom
- social consequences:
  - approach (attention to rewards; positive emotion; automatic cognition; disinhibited state or trait-driven behaviour)
  - inhibition (attention to threats; negative emotion; systematic or controlled cognition; inhibited, situationally constrained behaviour).

So, high or low social power is determined by four factors (individual variables, dyadic variables, within-group variables and between-group variables). The social consequences of high or low power, in terms of approach and inhibition, serve to maintain rather than change the relations of power within a group or organisation. There are five psychological reasons why high-power people maintain their power:

1. Those with high power generally have positive affect.

2. Once such people obtain power, they can reinforce their power. For example, they may become more attentive to rewards and how to obtain them, which can produce raised dopamine levels in the brain and create dopamine neural pathways that promote reward-motivated behaviour.

3. High-power people are more likely to be extraverted and impulsive, which can sometimes border on psychopathy. Thus, high-power people are usually better at detecting opportunities for rewards, and become increasingly willing to take risks.

4. High-power people are relatively inconsiderate to other people. They are more likely to consider other people instrumentally in terms of how they can be used by the power holder to satisfy their goals and desires. Because high-power individuals tend to construe social events in a more automatic fashion than low-power individuals, they are less likely to consider the consequences of their actions for other people. Further, they are more likely to draw on stereotypes rather than using cognitive complex processes to understand other people. As a result, high-power individuals are less attentive to information about the other person, and so are likely to form a rather shallow understanding of other people and their needs.

5. High-power people – that is, high in personality dominance – are much more likely to express their true attitudes and opinions openly than low-power people (Anderson & Berdahl, 2002). Consequently, it is more likely that their opinions will override the often-unexpressed opinions of those with less power.

In terms of factors inhibiting low-power people from gaining more power, it is well established from research in a range of domains that low-power people (and these are invariably people with low socioeconomic status) experience more negative moods, which in turn inhibit behaviours that could alter their position. Typical of this is the lower turnout among Afro-American voters as compared to white voters in most US elections because many believe – and probably with some justification – that things will not change. As well, low-power people are likely to have an anxious disposition, and such people are more likely to focus on punishment and threats. To sum up, there is a complementarity of the characteristics of high and low power that continuously reinforces and maintains power asymmetries. Thus, people in higher positions within social hierarchies can create situational pressures on behaviour, because they can set agendas, norms for discussion, rules for behaviour, and standards for thought and opinion, all of which constrain the psychological freedom experienced by individuals lower in the hierarchy and help maintain the current power hierarchy (Magee & Galinsky, 2008, p. 367).

CASE STUDY 8.1

Studies of Japanese organisational power

Theories about how power operates in an organisation and how it impacts performance are hard to operationalise and measure empirically. However, a study by Greve and Mitsuhashi (2007) provided an elaborate study of organisational power.

Nineteen Japanese firms were studied: 10 in the shipbuilding industry and nine firms in the robotics industry. It was a longitudinal study from 1975 to 1996 of the role of the upper levels of the firms' hierarchies. The researchers wanted to consider how concentrated power at the CEO or the top management team (TMT) level was exercised in leading the firms to a high rate of strategic change. Thus, the main dependent variable was the amount of change that occurred in the firms' product line diversification. The reason for this was that, when power is concentrated at the TMT level, strategic change occurs, causing a break in organisational momentum.

The research examined both formal and informal power sources. Because the CEO's formal power is considered as a constant (which was determined by the hierarchical distance between a leader and other organisational members), they focused their research on the CEO's informal power. The major source of informal power is social capital. Leaders at CEO or TMT level can build social capital among less senior organisational members by doing things for which others feel obliged to act favourably to the leader. This might include assisting with an internal promotion, making some allowance for personal issues or providing opportunities. Thus, less senior organisational members reciprocate by responding favourably when called upon by the leader to do something or to display support. Because social capital is built up over time, the level of social capital was determined by the CEO's or TMT's length of tenure in the organisation. However, this accumulation of social capital doesn't just provide an arithmetic increase in the amount of power that a leader can wield. After a certain level has been reached, repeated exercise of power will create a reputation for being powerful. This reputation has the added impact of reducing resistance by lower-power people to future actions because these people become reluctant to challenge or resist the powerful executive.

Greve and Mitsuhashi's (2007) major findings
- The CEO's tenure had a positive and significant effect on the level of organisational change. From this they inferred that higher levels of social capital enhanced the CEO's power to make changes in diversification.
- Informal power arising from tenure differences leads to momentum-breaking change, that is, significant change.
- CEOs with long tenure (i.e., higher social capital) are more likely to reverse a diversification strategy.
- The proportion of TMT members appointed during the CEO's tenure, which could enhance CEO power, had no discernible effect on levels of diversification, suggesting that leaders building social capital among TMTs did not produce greater compliance among them.
- TMTs with more concentrated formal power made more extensive change in diversification.
- TMTs with more concentrated informal power also made more extensive changes in diversification.
- The proportion of executives appointed during the CEO's tenure had no measurable effect.

Critical thinking questions
Having read the case study, respond to these questions:
1. Identify and discuss the aspects of hierarchical power that Greve and Mitsuhashi's (2007) study examined.
2. Greve and Mitsuhashi's study showed that 'concentrated power results in strategic change' (2007, p. 1214). Address the implications of this finding in terms of the viability of dispersed power in hierarchies.

Rejecting the 'great man' view of leadership

Management and leadership theory for many years was dominated by the 'great man' theory of leadership. The iconic example of this is Henry Ford at the turn of the twentieth century; and by the 1980s, some CEOs became celebrities because of their apparently heroic achievements. One of these was Lee Iacocca, who took over as Chrysler Corporation's CEO when it was near bankruptcy. Several years later, Chrysler returned a record $2.4 billion profit. He wrote two best-selling books that contributed to his heroic status. Admittedly this was an impressive achievement; however, it would not have been possible without a $1.5 billion federal loan guarantee, a fact that was not always made evident in the 'great man' stories about him. Another celebrity CEO of the 1980s was Jack Welch, who was chairman and CEO of General Electric (GE) between 1981 and 2001. Again, his tenure as CEO produced outstanding results that repositioned GE, which had been a giant of the old economy, as an adept performer in the new economy. It was Welch's manner that produced this larger-than-life persona. He would make surprise visits to GE sites. He applied a ruthless 'rank and yank' policy which meant that the bottom 10 per cent of managers were fired, even if they were performing well, and rewarded the top 20 per cent with bonuses. He would sometimes helicopter in to meetings in the New York office, and earned the nickname of 'Neutron Jack' (a reference to the neutron bomb) for getting rid of employees while the buildings remained intact. The problem with the great man view is that it erases the efforts of the others who work in the organisation: their loyalty, their commitment and their sacrifices which are never rewarded at the same level of the CEO (Welch received over $400 million when he left GE).

A major reason for the abandonment of the great man leadership approach is the disillusionment many now feel about apparent heroic corporate leaders who have been revealed as frauds; this is particularly so since the global financial crisis of 2007–09. This will be covered later in the section dealing with toxic leadership. Another reason for the decline of this model is the feminist critique of masculinist and patriarchal values and traits that this model implies. Furthermore, the transformation of industry into the knowledge economy also mitigates against the single strong leader approach. That is, the knowledge domains needed for contemporary organisations require people with high-level knowledge and skills who are less likely to accept hierarchical relations of power. As well, the hierarchical model is not always the most effective model for responding to an information-based society where fast action and responses are crucial. Thus, it is important to understand that the most appropriate sort of leadership for contemporary organisations with relatively flat structures (i.e. few hierarchical layers), where workers with different skills can more effectively cooperate, and where mistakes are tolerated when the organisation needs to experiment, may not be the great man type. Such organisations adopt an open culture where degrees of autonomy are encouraged. This has been called distributed leadership (Bennett et al., 2003), where leadership responsibility does not necessarily align with the organisational hierarchy. The boundaries of leadership are relatively flexible; and leadership is likely to emerge because the properties of a group or network are highly valued.

Prior to these economic changes occurring and contemporaneous with corporate heroes like Iacocca and Welch, leadership theorists were imagining a type of leadership other than the 'great man'. One of the earliest of these management leadership theorists, James M. Burns (1978), conceived of leadership as a leader directing followers' behaviour to satisfy the collective needs not just of the leader, but also follower and the organisation. Another early leadership theorist, Ralph Stodgill, described a leader as one who initiates and maintains structures of expectation and interaction.

Authenticity as a source of power

What was emerging in these theories rejecting the heroic model of leadership was an understanding that the most desirable source of power for leaders is when followers choose to be led by someone whom they believe to be authentic. This is usually understood as someone who

> **Authenticity** – Being true to oneself by maintaining coherence between what you say or do and what you feel, based on values. The experience of understanding the oneness and connectedness of humankind.

cares about other people and who 'walks the talk'. Although most people believe that they can identify **authenticity** in others, the reality is that psychopaths can mimic desirable behaviours. Another potential trap in becoming a follower of an authentic leader is the context (Klenke, 2005). For example, we are seeing the rise of the 'anti-politician politician' in response to the apparent inability of traditional parties in democracies to deal with intractable problems such as growing unemployment, debt levels and related social problems. The most obvious example of this anti-politician is the Republican Party's choice of Donald Trump to run in the 2016 presidential election. His willingness to say outrageous things was seen by many of his supporters as being authentic because he said things that other politicians were 'too afraid' to say. To say that Trump is being 'true to himself' clearly does not designate authenticity. Whether his campaign was truly authentic is unclear, but the perception of authenticity contributed to his election win.

Being eccentric, flouting social and moral norms and speaking and behaving according to one's own culture and upbringing are not necessarily the same thing. For example, Richard Branson, the founder of the Virgin group of companies, does not conform to the usual suit-wearing apparel of other CEOs, has made several attempts to break records for the fastest Atlantic Ocean crossing, circumnavigating the globe by balloon and other feats of daring, and is prepared to make public statements that are not devised by a PR machine. He may be considered as eccentric. Nonetheless, he has amassed enormous wealth by creating a range of disparate companies that are considered good places to work in and is a significant philanthropist. He appears to have remained true to his original values throughout his life. By contrast, one could not say that the 'authenticity' of the Kardashians is virtuous. They flaunt their wealth and revel in narcissism. Philosopher Charles Guignon calls this Rousseauian 'sincere spontaneous self-expression' (Guignon, 2004, p. 152). Herminia Ibarra, a professor of leadership, identifies three components of authenticity: being true to yourself, maintaining a strict coherence between what you say and what you feel; and making values-based choices. However, this definition still falls short of being authentic as a leader.

The essence of authenticity, says Guignon, is the dual notion of oneness and connectedness. While we celebrate our uniqueness and individualism, what separates the authentic person is an understanding that 'all things are connected by an underlying life force or principle of being' (Guignon, 2004, p. 17). The authentic self needs to experience a 'strong sense of belongingness' or being part of the larger whole (p. 18). Implied in this belongingness is a moral code that considers the rights and welfare of others. When a truly authentic leader exercises power, they need to keep this vital element of humanity central to their behaviour and decision making. Their moral principles must be based on the rights and welfare of others (Klenke, 2005). Although an authentic leader displays confidence and optimism, their self-efficacy needs to be calibrated by feedback from subordinates, peers, supervisors, mentors, family and friends. Doing this does not diminish a leader's power; rather it should provide greater confidence in their ability to make the right call while building the support of their followers who feel that their opinions, interests and concerns are being considered by their leader.

Authentic leadership is now well established theoretically. One of its foundational theorists, Bill Gardner, was motivated by profound concerns about the unethical conduct of corporate and government leaders and the greed that underpinned much of this malfeasance. The etymology of the word *authenticity* in its original ancient Greek philosophical injunction to 'Know Thyself' originates in the Greek word *authento*, 'to have full power' (Gardner et al., 2011). However, this power rests in one's own self; to have power over oneself particularly in an ethical sense. Feeling a sense of autonomy and self-worth, authentic leaders do not feel the need to control, to micro-manage or to claim credit in dubious circumstances. In fact, authentic leaders feel confident in 'letting go' (Ladkin & Spiller, 2013, p. 7). This is particularly important in high-tech, creative and professional industries to allow creative and skilled followers to work unimpeded. To be truly authentic, there must be 'congruence between values and self-identities', which is achieved when a coherent set of values and follower self-identities is activated. (Gardner et al., 2005, p. 361). In this way, authentic leaders transfer power to their followers by meeting their needs for competence and autonomy as they 'discover their talents, develop them into strengths' and by 'empowering them to do tasks for which they have the capacity to excel' (Gardner et al., 2005, p. 364).

A good example of a person establishing power by values-based authenticity is Edward 'Weary' Dunlop. Before enlisting as an officer in the Australian Army Medical Corps at the outbreak of the European war in 1939, Dunlop won a scholarship to study medicine at Melbourne University. Although an outstanding athlete in several sports – he represented Australia in rugby union – he graduated in medicine with first-class honours. After serving in the Middle East, he was transferred to Java as Lieutenant Colonel, but became a prisoner of war when the Japanese overran Australian and British forces in Java. The Japanese army was notoriously cruel to its prisoners during this war. In the most primitive of jungle conditions working on the Burma-Thailand railway, Dunlop improvised surgical implements and medicines and worked endless hours to save the wounded and sick prisoners who were also severely malnourished. As well, Dunlop risked his own life by challenging the Japanese captors. He used his imposing physical presence – he was two metres tall – to literally stand up to his captors. Despite the circumstances he kept medical notes on his men and a diary of events. The men with whom he served revered him, and for many years after the war he mentored and privately helped hundreds of former prisoners of war. After the war, despite the appalling treatment he had suffered, Dunlop supported efforts to rebuild relations with Japan. Although he resumed work as a surgeon, much of his time was spent advocating for his former colleagues to ensure that they were cared for by the government. The Weary Dunlop story is a good example of how value-based authenticity provided a source of power for him to promote the many concerns he supported. Governments listened to him because they knew that his many supporters were immensely loyal to Dunlop.

Nonetheless, a leader who acts in a way that is true to him or herself needs to be aware that expressing one's true self can result in severe social sanctions (Ilies, Morgeson & Nahrgang, 2005). This is because acting contrary to social norms can lead to public criticism and ostracism. Building leadership through true authenticity is more appropriate for our contemporary times and enhances the quality of followership by its inclusiveness. In this way, leaders can build an effective and more resilient leadership.

Why people become leaders

To become a successful leader in the longer term one needs a mixture of intrapersonal and interpersonal factors, motivation and the right circumstances. Initially people must possess certain attributes if they are to be successful leaders (Day et al., 2014). These include **intrapersonsal skills** such as:

> **Intrapersonal skills –**
> Attributes that successful leaders have developed, including experience and learning, problem solving, planning and implementation skills, metacognition and strategic and business skills.
> **Interpersonal skills –**
> Attributes such as a leader's social awareness, political awareness, empathy, team orientation and conflict management, which help to build social capital in an organisation.

- experience and learning
- the ability to solve problems
- the ability to plan and implement
- metacognitive processing skill (understanding one's cognitive processes)
- strategic and business skills.

It is also known that the personality trait of conscientiousness can significantly predict leader performance.

Another skills set is **interpersonal skills**. The most important outcome of high-quality interpersonal skills is to build social capital. Social capital is distinct from a human capital approach to leadership, which focuses on individual characteristics of leaders (Burt, 1997). Skilful leaders embed their personal qualities in the context of the organisation in which they are located. That is, social capital is a quality 'created between people' (Burt, 1997, p. 339). Social capital enables human capital to be built in an organisation. Research shows that it is 'an important viable antecedent for a large range of organisational activities, including inter-unit exchanges and collaboration activities, such as cross-collaboration activities' (Bilhuber Galli & Müller-Stewens, 2012, p. 178). This social capital capability emerges from a leader's social awareness, political awareness, empathy, team orientation and conflict management. These are socially oriented capabilities. Using this capability, an effective leader builds and develops networks of relationships that lead to greater cooperation and exchange of resources (Bilhuber Galli & Müller-Stewens, 2012). All organisations will have 'structural holes' in their networks. These are 'gaps between non-redundant contacts' that act like a buffer or insulator in an electric circuit (Burt, 1997,

p. 341). This happens when clusters in a network are unaware of each other because they are too focused on their own activities. Thus, a leader with social capital acts like an internal entrepreneur who can (re-)connect groups on either side of the hole. Ultimately, such a capability builds the power of a leader with social capital because they earn a reputation for creating rewarding opportunities, they understand the information flows and can use information faster than other organisational members (Burt, 1997).

But why do people decide to strive to become leaders? The vital element is to possess the implicit motive. Although not conscious, implicit motives help us to orient, make selections and direct our behaviours towards career success or well-being. More specifically, however, the leader motive pattern identifies three variables that are evident in effective leaders:

- a high implicit need for power
- a low implicit need for affiliation
- a high level of activity inhibition (that is, a 'stable tendency to refine and modulate the behavioral expression of motives') (Steinmann et al., 2014, p. 168).

Implied in this finding is the potential for bad leadership lacking in empathy and human concern because of the need for power. However, this research also showed that attaining team goals and achieving desired income are most likely to occur when there is a high implicit need for power, a high implicit need for affiliation and a high level of activity inhibition. Thus, while a need for power is important for those seeking leadership, the most successful leaders are more likely to display humane characteristics.

POWER AND POLITICS IN ORGANISATIONS

Often, when people feel overwhelmed by an organisation or observe someone of mediocre talent being promoted above them they will explain it in terms of an organisation being 'political'. The truth is that all organisations are political if we understand politics to mean the way that power is accorded to people (e.g. democratic elections, merit), how that power is used (e.g. inclusive, authoritarian) and to what ends (e.g. the good of all or a few). Power in organisations manifests as struggles within its formal boundaries to either maintain or change hierarchies and norms that govern its operation.

The four faces of power

A comprehensive overview of politics in organisations is provided by Fleming and Spicer (2014) who identify four 'faces' of power in organisational politics.

Coercion

The first face, coercion, is an overt display of power to achieve a particular end. Coercive leaders use their power to induce another person to do something they would prefer not to do. While coercive power is most obviously revealed in threat and reward structures, more recent studies have identified a subtler form of coercive power, control of resources. Of note in these studies, it was found that to obtain more resources, an organisational unit first needed to be well resourced so that it could claim its past success as an indicator of future success. As a result, strong organisational sections got stronger while those in need of resources went without.

Manipulation

The second face, manipulation, occurs when 'actors seek to either limit the issues that are discussed or to fit issues within (what are perceived to be) acceptable boundaries' (Fleming & Spicer, 2014, p. 4): it can be understood as agenda setting. Manipulation occurs in three ways. The first is the use of social networks. Within the formal structures of an organisation, the more central networks are usually the most successful because they have access to resources. However, second, informal networks are also important, particularly in hiring decisions. Informal cooperative ties can be useful in bypassing resource dependency within the formal structure that can weaken actors seeking these resources through normal channels. In such instances, boundary spanners – organisational actors who have strong networks in more than one organisational area or externally – can become quite powerful. The third form of manipulation is to use cultural resources such as stories, rituals and narratives to frame decision making. For example, an organisational narrative of being lean and agile might be used to justify sacking staff or closing a section.

Domination

The third face, domination, is an insidious exercise in which organisational actors influence outcomes by constructing ideological values that become hegemonic organisational values. In this way little coercion is needed because appropriate preferences, attitudes and political outlooks are predetermined. If a leader can establish cultural norms of behaviour that fulfil a desired outcome, then their task is considerably easier. The leader helps to socially construct the desired reality of normative behavior so that subordinates will accept the conditions of their own subordination. This is known as 'hegemonic' control, a notion devised by the neo-Marxist Gramsci, who stated:

> The spontaneous consent given by the great masses of the population to the general direction imposed by the dominant fundamental group; this consent is 'historically' caused by the prestige (and consequent confidence) which the dominant group enjoys because of its position and function in the world of production (Mumby, 1997, p. 348).

An example of this is provided by Contu and Willmott's (2003) critique of the well-accepted concept of 'communities of practice'. They point out that workers become part of a community of practice 'by observing "old-timers" and experts doing their job, and by interacting physically and verbally with them'. In other words, organisational learning really becomes 'the process of being socialised or enculturated into a community of practice … acquiring that particular community's subjective viewpoint and learn[ing] to speak its language' (p. 288).

Subjectification

The fourth face, subjectification, which draws on Foucauldian theory, is even more subtle because it achieves the desired end by influencing an actor's sense of self, including their emotions and identity. Although it is similar to ideological domination in some ways, it goes more deeply into the organisational members' sense of organisational identity. When organisational identity is linked with a preferred personal identity, it becomes naturalised. Foucault's concept of disciplinary power explains that through self-regulation actors 'embody' the routines, norms and often tacit directives of the organisation. They do this by incorporating the organisational subject position into their own to shape an identity. The neo-Foucauldian scholar Nikolas Rose (1992, p. 154) has described the reconceptualisation of the modern worker and workplace as a realm in which productivity is to be enhanced, quality ensured and innovations fostered through 'the active engagement of the self-fulfilling impulses of the employee, through aligning the objectives of the organisation with the desires of the self' (p. 154). In other words, the boundary between the work self and private self dissolve such that the worker or citizen builds his or her identity in relation to their work performance above all else.

McCabe's (2004) study of a UK bank that was reengineering to change the organisational culture provides an example. The new management claimed that they were working as a 'team', that workers were being empowered and that hierarchies were being delayered. The past structure was discredited as an old-fashioned, inefficient bureaucracy that was no longer appropriate. Of course, this meant that the bank workers now had to reconstruct their previous subject position and identity that had been built around the previous organisational structure and norms. Given that the management had retrenched a significant number of workers, there was an unspoken incentive for workers to adopt their new roles with its strong emotional and psychodynamic implications.

Being political: *Mētis* vs Machiavellianism

Clearly, then, being political is inevitable when one works in an organisation. Even a person who chooses to simply turn up on time, do their job and conform to the social norms of an organisation is being political because they contribute to the status quo and reinforce the authority structure within the organisation. For those who seek to be organisational leaders, it is vital that they develop political skills to achieve power and to use that power well. To know how to do this, the ancient Greek philosophical notion of *mētis* is useful. *Mētis* is an important consideration in effectively and ethically leading organisations;

> *Mētis* – Living by one's wits in an organisation when devising a positive outcome that negotiates power relationships, regulations and organisational mores; cunning intelligence; the ability to deal with difficult and unexpected situations not simply by applying rules or procedures.

however, it involves a capacity that might be considered to border on being sly, cunning, perhaps even Machiavellian.

Niccolò Machiavelli was a statesman in sixteenth-century Florence. He outlined a set of principles in a book called *The Prince* to guide Lorenzo de' Medici, the ruler of Florence, to maintain power. He made no excuses about the pragmatism and brutality of his advice. For example, he advocated a rule based on fear: 'If an injury has to be done to a man it should be so severe that his vengeance need not be feared.' Lying and deceit were condoned so long as it achieved the desired end: 'Never attempt to win by force what can be won by deception.' The twentieth-century Machiavellian administrator can be defined as a leader who employs aggressive, manipulative, exploitative and devious moves to achieve personal and organisational objectives. These moves are undertaken when they are perceived to be feasible in a given situation. Little or no consideration is given to the feelings, needs and/or 'rights' of others. Machiavellianism exists in today's corporate leadership. However, quite apart from its unethical nature, Machiavellian leadership produces performance that is equal to or worse than average performance (Gable & Topol, 1991). The major negative impacts are organisational cynicism and emotional burnout (McHoskey & Hicks, 1999; O'Boyle et al., 2012).

In contrast, the concept of *mētis* comes from Greek philosophy. *Mētis* means living by one's wits when trying to devise a positive outcome that negotiates power relationships, regulations and organisational mores. It is well established in ancient Greek history where it was understood as cunning intelligence. It was 'brought into play in large sectors of their [Greek] social and spiritual life [and] valued highly within their religious system' according to Detienne and Vernant (1991, p. 1). This notion of *mētis* does not encourage leaders to be sly and devious; rather it refers to how a leader can use their practical intelligence to know which laws to apply to a given situation; where one rule rather than another should be considered; and when to forgo the rules altogether and shift to other goals. It is most appropriate in fluid situations where variables and the environment are constantly changing. In this way, *mētis* can deal with the unexpected and with those situations where the attempt to simply apply rules or procedures does not bring about an effective outcome.

What separates the wise person's application of *mētis* from the clever opportunist, the sly Machiavellian or the outright criminal is that a wise person uses *mētis* to bring about a greater good and is directed by noble virtues. A wise person is therefore able to be timely, anticipatory and a contributor to the social good. Invariably *mētis* depends not just on cunning, but on experience and the perception to know how things really happen rather than how they are supposed to happen.

To sum up, a leader can use power to achieve positive ends by knowing the official and unofficial rules of the game. They don't break the rules technically, but devise alternative routes or find other relevant rules to justify a certain action. For example, in human resources there are many rules that can lead to potentially time-consuming negotiation and arbitration processes. A successful leader tries to achieve a just end without necessarily jumping straight into the legalistic route which is far less flexible. This might mean making a concession even when it is not legally required to reduce the volatility of a situation, which in turn might convince a potential complainant to withdraw their complaint. A successful leader anticipates situations, sounds out possibilities and caucuses effectively before meetings by identifying potential allies and opponents and preparing responses to likely challenges.

The idea of caucusing is well understood in parliamentary politics. Within each individual party there are inevitably factions that might be ideological (e.g. conservative or progressive; left wing or right wing) or sectional (e.g. urban or rural). Because it is rare for a faction to control more than 50 per cent of a party, politicians within that party would be unwise to propose a policy within their party room meeting without first having 'run it past' their colleagues. By talking with one's party colleagues to gain support for a proposal – the act of caucusing – a skilful politician can not only identify allies, but also find out about potential objections. With this knowledge, the politician can modify their proposal to reduce opposition on certain grounds, but they can also 'cut a deal' where they obtain factional support for the proposal provided they support another proposal by the other faction. This might be labelled pejoratively as 'back room deals' and regarded as somehow morally shameful. However, one might argue to the contrary that this is how politics should work. Not everyone will get exactly what they want – nor should they. By caucusing, a politician engages in dialogue that requires them to listen to the concerns of the person whose support is sought. Provided that each negotiator feels that they are not contravening their fundamental values, then there seems to be little reason to criticise such 'wheeling and dealing' provided people's needs are met to an acceptable degree and people's personal values are maintained.

TOXIC LEADERSHIP

Leadership has a potential dark side, which is destructive. Destructive leadership occurs when:

- coercion and control rather than persuasion and commitment are used to obtain compliance
- the leader is more concerned with selfish interests rather than the interests of the organisation
- the effect on susceptible followers and conducive environments is negative (Padilla, Hogan & Kaiser, 2007, p. 179).

At first, **toxic** leaders can have positive effects in an organisation. For example, they may provide a new sense of purpose and energy, they may scrap inefficient practices and perhaps even force some non-performers to leave the organisation. However, this benefit, if it occurs, is short-lived because in the medium to longer term such leaders impact badly on the organisation. For example, a poorly performing organisation may need to shed some sections or some levels of management that refuse to conform to reasonable expectations such as treating

> **Toxic leadership** – Use of coercion and control rather than persuasion and commitment to obtain compliance; when the leader is more concerned with selfish interests; result is a negative effect on followers and the organisational environment.

the clients respectfully or observing proper safety standards. A toxic leader who gets pleasure from hurting others may do that job of shedding with little concern for people's welfare. While this may bring about a short-term gain, maintaining that toxicity in the medium to longer term will damage people and the organisation. When a toxic triangle exists, according to Padilla and co-authors (2007), bad outcomes will ensue for organisational members and the organisation. The toxic triangle comprises destructive leaders, susceptible followers and conducive environments.

Destructive leaders

A destructive leader will display several of the following five characteristics, according to Padilla and co-authors (2007):

- *Charisma:* Charisma can be a positive force. However, destructive charismatic leaders use their power for self-serving ends. They take the credit for achievements to which others may have contributed, but cover up or blame others when mistakes occur. In terms of power, they are more concerned to build support for themselves through favours or nepotistic appointments than to contribute to power being shared.
- *Need for power:* Destructive leaders see power as a form of self-aggrandisement rather than as the basis for serving others.
- *Narcissism:* Narcissism is a natural corollary of the previous two factors. Psychologists identify the characteristics of narcissism as dominance, grandiosity, arrogance, entitlement and the selfish pursuit of pleasure. Such leaders are self-absorbed, seek attention and care little for others' viewpoints or welfare. Because of a sense of entitlement, they usually adopt an autocratic style.
- *Negative life themes:* Destructive leaders quite often provide a life narrative that is negative. Commonly this includes abusive or discordant parents, fathers with criminal records, mothers with psychiatric disorders, child abuse and low socio-economic status. There is good psychological evidence that traumatic childhoods can lead to destructive leadership.
- *Ideology of hate:* The rhetoric and world view of destructive leaders are hateful. This is seen in creating despised enemies who must be destroyed and a need to destroy rather than create.

Susceptible followers

Leaders need followers. Followers who are most susceptible to destructive leaders will have several of the following characteristics:

- *Unmet basic needs:* People who have physical or psychological needs that they feel others can provide for.
- *Negative core self-evaluations:* People who lack self-esteem, self-efficacy or feel that they lack control over their fate.

- *Low maturity*: Maturity can be usefully gauged by using
  - Erikson's psycho-social virtues (trust, autonomy, initiative, industry, ego-identity, intimacy, generativity, ego integrity)
  - Kohlberg's stages of moral development (obedience, self-interest, conformity, social accord, social contract and universal principles)
  - Piaget's stages of intellectual development (sensorimotor; pre-operational; concrete operational; and formal operations).

  People who have low levels of virtue such as trust or ego integrity, low levels of moral development (for example, they comply with rules to avoid punishment or simply to conform) and have limited cognitive capacity to think conceptually or to imagine different possibilities would be extremely vulnerable to destructive charismatic leaders.
- *Ambition*: Ambitious people will follow destructive leaders if they feel that their own personal ambitions will be advanced or met.
- *Congruent values and beliefs*: If people share the leader's values and beliefs then they are more likely feel committed to the cause being espoused. Thus, if a leader believes that women should perform menial roles or that certain ethnic groups lack a work ethic, then they are likely to attract people who have similar narrow views.
- *Unsocialised values*: If people espouse unsocialised values such as greed and selfishness, then they are more likely to follow destructive leaders.

Conducive environments

Four environmental characteristics that are likely to assist destructive leaders are:
- instability
- a perceived external threat
- cultures that avoid uncertainty, are collectivist and have high power distance
- when institutional checks and balances are limited.

A classic example of this would be leaders who emerge in a turbulent era claiming that the organisation (or country) faces an external threat such as a takeover and that they need more power to deal with this threat on behalf of the organisation.

WOMEN AND POWER

Statistics consistently show that women are underrepresented in upper-level management positions. Women hold only:
- 29 (5.8 per cent) of CEO positions at the S&P top 500 companies (Catalyst, 2018)
- less than 20 per cent of the seats in the US Congress (83 out 435 in the House of Representatives and 21 out of 100 in the Senate) (CAWP, 2017)
- 7.1 per cent of high-ranking positions (e.g. generals and admirals) in the US military.

While these numbers are low, the situation has been improving. For example, in Australia 17 per cent of CEOs are women (ABS, 2015), three of the seven High Court of Australia judges are women and 40 per cent of Australian senators are women. In the state of Queensland, women were elected in 2015 and again in 2017, both as Premier and Deputy Premier.

Despite these improvements, equal power between men and women has yet to be achieved. The term 'glass ceiling' has been in use for over 30 years. However, feminist organisational scholars Alice Eagly and Linda Carli (2007) prefer the term **labyrinth** because it better represents the continuous obstacles faced by women in reaching the top. The three components of the labyrinth that withhold women are the arguments about human capital and gender differences, which are subtle, as well as prejudice, which is overt.

> **Labyrinth** – Three components withhold women from leadership: human capital, gender differences and prejudice.

Human capital differences

Human capital differences refer to the justifications frequently used to explain why women are not better represented at the top. The first, the Pipeline Problem, claims that women have less education, training and work experience than men, resulting in a dearth of qualified women. The claim about training is clearly wrong as women are graduating from universities throughout the world at a faster rate than men, and the university enrolment ratio for women exceeds that for men in two thirds of countries. In Poland, Sweden and Brazil, women represent more than 60 per cent of graduates (Chamie, 2014).

However, a subtle latent factor may be the type of degree. That is, women have far lower graduation rates in science, technology, engineering and maths ('STEM') disciplines and far higher rates in what are sometimes called the soft disciplines of health professions, public administration, education and communication. These soft disciplines rarely provide a path to senior levels in highly paid industries. In Australia, women make up 28 per cent of the employed STEM-qualified Australian workforce aged 15 years and over, compared to 55 per cent for all fields in the tertiary qualified population. In engineering, 14 per cent are women, rising to 25 per cent in information technology. The least disparity in STEM-based employment was in the natural and physical sciences, where women are 47 per cent of the workforce (Professionals Australia, 2011).

Another claim put forward under the human capital justification is that women have not been in managerial positions long enough to progress their career organically. Again, this is a claim with little empirical support. Of course, if women are not given the opportunity to display their aptitude by being given middle management positions then the claim becomes a self-fulfilling prophecy. However, the evidence shows that women are making it to middle management levels in good numbers. An International Labour Organization report shows that in 2012, some 30.8 per cent of Australian senior and middle-level managers were women (ILO, 2015, p. 21). Thus, there is a systemic failure for women reaching the highest level of management and leadership in similar numbers. The third claim, the impact of parenting on career progression, has some veracity simply because it is women who bear children and, in many instances, care for children in early infancy. Nonetheless, it is a problem that, with the support of an organisation, can largely be overcome. For example, as far back as 1983, Ros Kelly became the first Australian federal member of parliament to give birth while in office and four years later, she became the first female Labor minister from the House of Representatives. In 2018, the recently elected New Zealand prime minister Jacinda Ardern announced that she would remain in her post after giving birth to her first child. Further, this problem can be considerably reduced if legislation requires employers to provide more flexible work hours and parental leave for men and women as well as high-quality childcare.

Gender differences in leadership styles and commitment

A range of explanations for women not achieving as well as men is attributed to gender differences in leadership styles and the effectiveness of those styles. However, the issue of gender and leadership is far too complex to offer simple explanations. In the first place, post-feminist theory now accounts for multiple forms of femininity, the incorporation of an individualist ethic, widened choices and renegotiated forms of sexuality among other things (Lewis, 2014, p. 1851). Second, in the light of this multiplicity of the 'feminine', it is inappropriate to claim that women will bring certain feminine attributes to their leadership role. Two experimental studies (Vinkenburg et al., 2011) that considered men and women's transformational, transactional and laissez-faire leadership styles found that:

- participants accurately believe that women display more transformational and contingent reward behaviours and fewer management-by-exception and laissez-faire behaviours than men
- leadership style affects the promotion of women and men to different levels in organisations; that is, inspirational motivation is perceived as more important for men than women, and as especially important for promotion to CEO
- individualised consideration (one of the characteristics of authentic leadership) is perceived as more important for women than men and especially important for promotion to senior management.

So, how do women perform as leaders? The research shows that men and women are equally effective, but both men and women are more effective when leading in roles that are congruent with traditional notions of gender (for example, male-dominated industries such as mining, and female-dominated ones such as education and social services). Consequently, acceptance depends heavily on followers' perceptions of gender. In other words, if followers believe that mining or trade work is a 'man's job', then they are less likely to accept women leaders. However, in terms of motivation to lead, women are less likely to promote themselves for leadership positions and they are likely to be group facilitators rather than group leaders. Beyond the issue of gender, there is evidence that shows that workplace diversity in general benefits organisational performance (Ellemers et al., 2012, p. 167).

Prejudice

In terms of prejudice, a lot of social change is needed. Because prejudice against women in leadership pervades social norms, it takes considerable time to change. This is primarily because prejudice occurs when prejudicial social norms are internalised. Social norms form when groups develop (families, communities, religions, associations such as sport and nations in particular). To be a member of a group one needs to abide by the norms: in this way, individual perceptions and judgement are predominantly formed in relation to group norms (Crandall, Eshleman & O'Brien, 2002). Thus, eliminating prejudice is best done in society at large, rather than at the individual level.

Women leaders and legitimacy

Underlying these social norms is perceived legitimacy, according to Vial, Napier and Brescoll (2016). That is, women in powerful positions often do not elicit the same level of respect and admiration from subordinates as men do. This reduces the amount of cooperation and compliance while also sometimes triggering negative responses by female leaders towards their subordinates. This then feeds back into a negative loop that confirms subordinates' negative expectations of female leaders, which in turn undermines the woman's authority.

Legitimacy is the belief that 'rules and regulations are entitled to be obeyed by virtue of who made the decision or how it was made' (Levi, Sacks & Tyler, 2009, p. 354). In government, the evidence shows that when those who are governed believe that a government is legitimate, 'they are more likely to defer to political authorities and uphold laws', and there is an 'increased likelihood of compliance with governmental rules and regulations' (p. 354). Little coercion is needed. But when people see the leader as illegitimate, their compliance will decline, and some may openly defy the expected behaviour. Legitimacy in turn is determined by a leader's status, which is determined by the subordinate, and therein lies the problem. If subordinates hold highly gendered understandings of what is normative, then their response to women leaders will be a sense of a 'lack of fit'. Thus, leadership traits such as agency, assertiveness, decisiveness and confidence might be seen as inappropriate feminine traits. Those with such perceptions often penalise the 'gender-deviant' female leader.

The underlying principles of gendered social norms are well known. Women's socially prescriptive personality traits are warmth, social sensitivity and other-centeredness while for men they are dominance, competence and agency (Williams & Tiedens, 2016). A meta-analysis of 63 studies provides quite conclusive evidence that women are penalised more than are men for expressing identical dominance behaviours and that 'the tendency for dominance to be liked less in women than in men emerged only for explicit, direct forms of dominance, and not for implicit forms' (Williams & Tiedens, 2016, p. 178). The 'penalty' for women displaying dominance was reduced likability and poorer instrumental outcomes such as being hired, although women were not perceived as less competent. As a result, women suffer a 'backlash' (Rudman, 1998), as others may prefer to have a male over a female boss; may have lower intentions to hire or promote a woman when a male candidate is available; and may offer lower salaries for female leaders. The link between this backlash and lower numbers of female leaders is clear.

Faced with this diminished legitimacy, uncooperativeness and resistance, women leaders can then be psychologically affected. Given the reality of such behaviours towards them, women leaders can become apprehensive and lower their expectations of control or influence. To avoid backlash, women may reduce their assertiveness and goal-focused behaviour, or try to pre-empt negative reactions by adopting more masculine traits, including aggression, as they seek to assimilate with dominant masculine cultures.

Clearly there is much to do in improving the potential for women to become leaders.

CASE STUDY 8.2

Christine Nixon – Police Commissioner

When Christine Nixon was appointed Victorian Police Commissioner in 2001, she was the first woman in Australia to be appointed to this level. She was responsible for about 13 000 personnel in a state of 4.6 million people. She had joined the New South Wales Police in 1972 against the wishes of her father, who was also a police officer. Very few options were available to women officers in those times; however, after reading the feminist book *The Female Eunuch*, she set about educating herself, beginning first with technical college and then university, including Harvard. Her mother had also been a role model as she worked at a time when this was not the norm. At 21, Nixon was elected President of the Women's Branch of the Police Association. Although she reached the level of Assistant Commissioner after 20 years in the force, it was in human resources, which some may have considered a 'soft' role appropriate for a woman. However, she took a relieving role in operations command of Sydney's western suburbs, a difficult policing region. She then took responsibility for another local area command in another part of Sydney. Using her position as operations commander she emphasised a philosophy of problem-oriented policing; that is, looking at crime within a broader social context. She also identified the police under her command as a 'service' not a 'force', particularly in domestic violence and child abuse situations. She respected people's right to protest in a democratic society. She also sponsored restorative justice for youth offenders. She emphasised good management over lazy practice; she also realised the usefulness of involving the community in solving social problems.

When Nixon took command of the Victorian Police Force in 2001, morale was low after the previous government had reduced police numbers and resources. The police union was hot-tempered, causing many conflicts with management. Prisoners were being kept in police cells for far too long. For quite some time, the Victorian police had developed a bad reputation for their 'cowboy' behaviour, involving police shootings, extreme sex discrimination and rough handling in public-order policing and raids. They were increasingly being successfully sued for abuses of power.

On taking power, Nixon began a series of substantive and symbolic steps. Substantively, she outlined her changes and told officers to 'change from today' because 'we are doing things differently in the future'. Officers had the opportunity to start afresh. She explained to police and community, particularly in problem locations, what she considered important and stated that there would be fair process in everything the police did. Rather than taking an agenda to them, she asked these communities what they wanted fixed. She also made herself accessible to all police officers who could email her. This irked senior officers around her because she could obtain on-the-ground information rather than relying on what her senior management told her. During her time, she also set up the Purana Task Force, which had considerable success in cleaning out and jailing Melbourne's crime gangs. She overtly made a point of talking with all ranks of police, not just the senior officers. For example, after an official police ceremony, she stayed behind to speak with police there, asking them about their lives and experiences. They were shocked because this had not ever happened before. On another occasion, after finding out that four police officers who had been shot in Bendigo a few years prior had not received medals, Nixon created a major ceremony, with the whole community invited, which allowed a healing process to occur. The police returned to work and were paid compensation that had not been paid. She also participated in an LBGTI parade, although she is not gay, and allowed the police pipe band to take part too.

When she retired in 2009, she was highly regarded in the community, and the police service's practices had been vastly improved.

Source: Information from Prenzler (n.d.)

Critical thinking questions
1. From your knowledge of attributes of successful leaders, how many attributes can you determine from this brief biography of Christine Nixon?
2. From your knowledge of successfully using power in hierarchies, what lessons can you learn from Nixon's achievement as a police commissioner?
3. Given the obstacles for women to gain power outlined above, how might you account for the success of this woman in a male-dominant domain?

SUMMARY

LEARNING OUTCOME 1: Define power and differentiate it from status.

Power is the capacity or potential to influence and to affect others' beliefs, attitudes and actions in various circumstances. Position power is the result of being designated as a leader, while personal power emerges from the person's position, and from referent and expert power.

LEARNING OUTCOME 2: Understand politics in relation to leadership and explain the four faces of power in organisations.

Hierarchies form in groups and organisations when a certain level of complex activity is reached, requiring systems and job allocations to be arranged to solve a problem, produce a good or deliver a service. Formal hierarchies develop when organisations become more complex. Informal hierarchies emerge quite rapidly because people can form accurate assessments of others on thin 'slices' of information. Hierarchies tend to be self-reinforcing, and do not change quickly or significantly, mostly because of various psychological processes that create a 'metamorphic effect of power'. Management and leadership theory is no longer dominated by the 'great man' theory of leadership. Instead, authentic leaders 'walk the talk', and understand the dual notion of oneness and connectedness. People become successful leaders by possessing a mixture of intrapersonal and interpersonal factors, motivation and the right circumstances. Fleming and Spicer (2014) identify four 'faces' of power in organisational politics: coercion, manipulation, domination and subjectification. Leaders who use *mētis* can devise positive outcomes by knowing how to negotiate power relationships, regulations and organisational mores.

LEARNING OUTCOME 3: Identify the characteristics of toxic leadership and the profile of destructive leaders.

Destructive leadership occurs when coercion is used to obtain compliance; the leader is more concerned with selfish interests; and the effect on the organisation and susceptible followers is negative. A destructive leader will display several of five characteristics: charisma; need for power; narcissism; negative life themes; ideology of hate. Destructive leaders need susceptible followers who display several of the following characteristics: unmet basic needs; negative core self-evaluations; low maturity; ambition; congruent values and beliefs and; unsocialised values. Conducive environments often display: instability; a perceived external threat; cultures that avoid uncertainty, are collectivist and have high power distance; limited institutional checks and balances.

LEARNING OUTCOME 4: Identify the factors that create a labyrinth for women in their quest to obtain leadership positions.

Women are underrepresented in upper-level management positions. The term 'glass ceiling' has been has been challenged by Eagly and Carli's (2007) 'labyrinth' to explain the continuous obstacles faced by women. The labyrinth has three components: human capital, gender differences and prejudice. Claims of human capital differences include claims of less education and work experience. Claims of gender differences in leadership style may be true, but this may make women more suited to transformational leadership. Although women are equally effective leaders as men, gendered forms of perception by followers limit their acceptance. Prejudice is founded on internalised social norms that are difficult to change. These social norms affect perceived legitimacy. As a result, 'gender-deviant' female leaders are punished.

REVIEW QUESTIONS

1. After graduation, you may need to gain several years of experience before taking on a leadership role in an organisation. From what you have read about power, how will you develop your own personal characteristics to be an effective leader who uses power for the benefit of the organisation and society?

2. Proponents of the post-bureaucratic organisation assert that hierarchies have been flattened in most contemporary organisations. Do you agree?

3. Identify the mixture of interpersonal and intrapersonal characteristics that are needed in a good leader.

4. How can one distinguish between a Machiavellian leader and a leader who uses *mētis*?

5. What are the signs that a leader is toxic?

6. How can Eagly and Carli's research help women to achieve power in organisations?

CASE STUDY 8.3

Al 'Chainsaw' Dunlap

Al 'Chainsaw' Dunlap gained notoriety as a charismatic tough man as CEO of several companies such as Scott Paper and Sunbeam. He not only aggressively reduced staff numbers, but seemed to revel in doing so. His hubristically titled book *Mean business: How I save bad companies and make good companies great* stated that success requires ruthless competition. At Scott Paper in the early 1990s, Dunlap made almost a third of the workforce redundant, and stockholder value increased substantially. When he left the organisation, he received a 'golden parachute' of more than $120 million. He repeated this as CEO of Sunbeam in 1996. However, in 1998 Dunlap was identified as a fraud using illegal accounting practices. He was fired, and Sunbeam filed for bankruptcy in 2002 (Nirenberg, 2001).

The features of psychopathy

Robert Hare, Emeritus Professor of Psychology at the University of British Columbia, is one of the best-known researchers of psychopathy. Much of his work is based in prisons, through which he has learned that highly psychopathic people can dupe other people into believing that they are well intentioned. His checklist of psychopathic traits is available online (see www.sociopathicstyle.com/psychopathic-traits). Some of the characteristics Hare identifies are:

- *Superficial charm:* A psychopath can be engaging, charming and verbally facile. Lacking self-consciousness, they are never afraid to say anything.
- *Grandiosity:* A grossly inflated view of one's abilities and self-worth; self-assured, opinionated and cocky. They believe they are superior human beings.
- *Need for stimulation:* They continually need stimulation and enjoy doing risky things. Because they often have low self-discipline they get bored easily. They hate routine.
- *Pathological lying:* Because they are cunning and sly, they will lie whenever they need to.
- *Manipulative:* They deceive and cheat others for personal gain.
- *Lack of remorse or guilt:* They lack any feelings for their victims' suffering because they lack empathy.
- *Poor behavioural controls:* They are quick to express annoyance and impatience, and to threaten with physical and verbal abuse.
- *Impulsivity:* They find it hard to resist temptation and urges. They do not consider the consequences of their actions.

Critical thinking question

Consider Al 'Chainsaw' Dunlap's leadership style, as described in the case study, and use the information about psychopathy provided to assess his approach. What aspects of psychopathy, if any, do you see in Dunlap's behaviour as a leader?

REFERENCES

Ambady, N. & Rosenthal, R. (1993). Half a minute: Predicting teacher evaluations from thin slices of nonverbal behavior and physical attractiveness. *Journal of Personality and Social Psychology*, 64(3), 431–41.

Anderson, C. & Berdahl, J.L. (2002). The experience of power: Examining the effects of power on approach and inhibition tendencies. *Journal of Personality and Social Psychology*, 83(6), 1362–77.

Australian Bureau of Statistics (ABS) (2015). Still fewer women in positions of leadership. Media release, 25 August. Retrieved from: www.abs.gov.au/ausstats/abs@.nsf/Lookup/by per cent20Subject/4125.0~Aug per cent202015~Media per cent20Release~Still per cent20fewer per cent20women per cent20in per cent20positions per cent20of per cent20leadership per cent20(Media per cent20Release)~10011.

Bass, B.M. (1990). *A handbook of leadership: Theory, research, and managerial implications*, 3rd edn. New York, NY: Free Press.

Bennett, N., Wise, C., Woods, P. & Harvey, J.A. (2003). *Distributed leadership*. Nottingham: NCSL.

Bilhuber Galli, E. & Müller-Stewens, G. (2012). How to build social capital with leadership development: Lessons from an explorative case study of a multibusiness firm. *The Leadership Quarterly*, 23(1), 176–201.

Burns, J.M. (1978). *Leadership*. New York, NY: Harper Torchbooks.

Burt, R.S. (1997). The contingent value of social capital. *Administrative Science Quarterly*, 42(2), 339–65.

Catalyst (2018). Women CEOs of the S&P 500. Retrieved from: www.catalyst.org/knowledge/women-ceos-sp-500.

Center for American Women and Politics (CAWP) (2017). Women in US Congress, 2017. CAWP, Rutgers University. Retrieved from: www.cawp.rutgers.edu/women-us-congress-2017.

Chamie, J. (2014). Women more educated than men but still paid less. YaleGlobal Online, Yale University, 6 March. Retrieved from: https://yaleglobal.yale.edu/content/women-more-educated-men-still-paid-less.

Contu, A. & Willmott, H. (2003). Re-embedding situatedness: The importance of power relations in learning theory. *Organization Science*, 14(3), 283–96.

Crandall, C.S., Eshleman, A. & O'Brien, L. (2002). Social norms and the expression and suppression of prejudice: The struggle for internalization. *Journal of Personality and Social Psychology*, 82(3), 359–78.

Day, D.V., Fleenor, J.W., Atwater, L.E., Sturm, R.E. & McKee, R.A. (2014). Advances in leader and leadership development: A review of 25 years of research and theory. *Leadership Quarterly*, 25(1), 63–82.

Detienne, M. & Vernant, J-P. (1991). *Cunning Intelligence in Greek culture and society* (trans. J. Lloyd). Chicago: University of Chicago Press.

Eagly, A.H. & Carli, L.L. (2007). *Through the labyrinth: The truth about how women become leaders*: Boston: Harvard Business School Press.

Ellemers, N., Rink, F., Derks, B. & Ryan, M.K. (2012). Women in high places: When and why promoting women into top positions can harm them individually or as a group (and how to prevent this). *Research in Organizational Behavior*, 32, 163–87.

Fleming, P. & Spicer, A. (2014). Power in management and organization science. *Academy of Management Annals*, 8(1), 237–98.

Frauendorfer, D., Schmid Mast, M., Sanchez-Cortes, D. & Gatica-Perez, D. (2015). Emergent power hierarchies and group performance. *International Journal of Psychology*, 50(5), 392–96.

French, J.R.P., Jr & Raven, B. (1962). The bases of social power. In D. Cartwright (ed.), *Group dynamics: Research and theory* (pp. 259–69). New York, NY: Harper & Row.

Gable, M. & Topol, M.T. (1991). Machiavellian managers: Do they perform better? *Journal of Business and Psychology*, 5(3), 355–65.

Gardner, W.L., Avolio, B.J., Luthans, F., May, D.R. & Walumbwa, F.O. (2005). 'Can you see the real me?' A self-based model of authentic leader and follower development. *Leadership Quarterly*, 16(3), 343–72.

Gardner, W.L., Cogliser, C.C., Davis, K.M. & Dickens, M.P. (2011). Authentic leadership: A review of the literature and research agenda. *Leadership Quarterly*, 22(6), 1120–45.

Greer, L.L. & Van Kleef, G.A. (2010). Equality versus differentiation: The effects of power dispersion on group interaction. *Journal of Applied Psychology*, 95(6), 1032–44.

Greve, H.R. & Mitsuhashi, H. (2007). Power and glory: Concentrated power in top management teams. *Organization Studies*, 28(8), 1197–221.

Guignon, C. (2004). *On being authentic*. London: Routledge.

Halevy, N., Chou, E.Y. & Galinsky, A.D. (2011). A functional model of hierarchy: Why, how, and when vertical differentiation enhances group performance. *Organizational Psychology Review*, 1(1), 32–52.

Hofstede, G. (1984). *Culture's consequences: International differences in work-related values*, abridged edn. Beverly Hills, CA: SAGE Publications.

Hogg, M.A. (2001). A social identity theory of leadership. *Personality and Social Psychology Review*, 5(3), 184–200.

Ilies, R., Morgeson, F.P. & Nahrgang, J.D. (2005). Authentic leadership and eudaemonic well-being: Understanding leader-follower outcomes. *Leadership Quarterly*, 16(3), 373–94.

International Labour Organization (ILO). (2015). *Women in business and management: Gaining momentum*. Geneva: International Labour Organization.

Keltner, D., Gruenfeld, D.H. & Anderson, C. (2003). Power, approach, and inhibition. *Psychological Review*, 110(2), 265–84.

Kendon, A., Sebeok, T.A. & Umiker-Sebeok, J. (eds). (1981). *Nonverbal communication, interaction, and gesture: Selections from Semiotica*, vol. 41. The Hague: Mouton.

Kipnis, D. (1976). *The powerholders*. Chicago: University of Chicago Press.

Klenke, K. (2005). The internal theater of the authentic leader: Integrating cognitive, affective, conative and spiritual facets of authentic leadership. In W.L. Gardner, B.J. Avolio & F.O. Walumbwa (eds), *Authentic leadership and practice: origins, effects and development*. Amsterdam: Elsevier BV.

Ladkin, D. & Spiller, C. (eds). (2013). *Authentic leadership: Clashes, convergences and coalescences*. Cheltenham, UK: Edward Elgar Publishing. Retrieved from: www.elgaronline .com /9781781006375.00007.xml.

Leavitt, H.J. (2005). *Top down: Why hierarchies are here to stay and how to manage them more effectively*. Boston, MA: Harvard Business School Press.

Levi, M., Sacks, A. & Tyler, T. (2009). Conceptualizing legitimacy, measuring legitimating beliefs. *American Behavioral Scientist*, 53(3), 354–75.

Lewis, P. (2014). Postfeminism, femininities and organization studies: Exploring a new agenda. *Organization Studies*, 335(12), 1845–66.

Magee, J.C. & Galinsky, A.D. (2008). Social hierarchy – the self-reinforcing nature of power and status. *Academy of Management Annals*, 2(1), 351–98.

McCabe, D. (2004). 'A land of milk and honey'? Reengineering the 'past' and 'present' in a call centre. *Journal of Management Studies*, 41(5), 827–56.

McHoskey, J.W. & Hicks, B. (1999). Machiavellianism, adjustment, and ethics. *Psychological Reports*, 85(1), 138–42.

Mumby, D.K. (1997). The problem of hegemony: Rereading Gramsci for organizational communication studies. *Western Journal of Communication (includes Communication Reports)*, 61(4), 343–75.

Nirenberg, J. (2001). Leadership: a practitioner's perspective on the literature. *Singapore Management Review*, 23(1), 1–34.

O'Boyle, E.H., Jr, Donelson, R.F., Banks, G.C. & McDaniel, M.A. (2012). A meta-analysis of the dark triad and work behavior: A social exchange perspective. *Journal of Applied Psychology*, 97(3), 557–79.

Padilla, A., Hogan, R. & Kaiser, R.B. (2007). The toxic triangle: Destructive leaders, susceptible followers, and conducive environments. *Leadership Quarterly*, 18(3), 176–94.

Prenzler, T. (n.d.). Interview with Chief Commissioner Christine Nixon: Australia's first female police chief. Interview, School of Criminology and Criminal Justice, Griffith University. Retrieved from: www98.griffith.edu.au/dspace/downloaduriredirect?itemId=5010&bitstre am=201.

Professionals Australia. (2011). Women in STEM in Australia. Position paper. Retrieved from: www.professionalsaustralia.org.au/professional-women.

Ridgeway, C.L. & Correll, S.J. (2006). Consensus and the creation of status beliefs. *Social Forces*, 85(1), 431–53.

Rose, N. (1992). Governing the enterprising self. In P. Heelas & P. Morris (eds), *The values of the enterprise culture: The moral debate* (pp. 141–64). London: Routledge.

Royal Commission (2017). *Royal Commission into institutional responses to child sexual abuse: Final report*. Retrieved from: www.childabuseroyalcommission.gov.au/final-report.

Rudman, L.A. (1998). Self-promotion as a risk factor for women: The costs and benefits of counterstereotypical impression management. *Journal of Personality and Social Psychology*, 74(3), 629.

Salancik, G.R. & Pfeffer, J. (1977). Who gets power and how they hold on to it: A strategic contingency model of power. *Organizational Dynamics*, 5(1), 3–21.

Steinmann, B., Dörr, S. L., Schultheiss, O.C. & Maier, G.W. (2014). Implicit motives and leadership performance revisited: What constitutes the leadership motive pattern? *Motivation and Emotion*, 39(2), 167–174. doi:10.1007/s11031-014-9458-6

Vial, A.C., Napier, J.L. & Brescoll, V.L. (2016). A bed of thorns: Female leaders and the self-reinforcing cycle of illegitimacy. *The Leadership Quarterly*, 27(3), 400–14.

Vinkenburg, C.J., Van Engen, M.L., Eagly, A.H. & Johannesen-Schmidt, M.C. (2011). An exploration of stereotypical beliefs about leadership styles: Is transformational leadership a route to women's promotion? *Leadership Quarterly*, 22(1), 10–21.

Williams, M.J. & Tiedens, L.Z. (2016). The subtle suspension of backlash: A meta-analysis of penalties for women's implicit and explicit dominance behavior. *Psychological Bulletin*, 142(2), 165–197.

9

COMMUNICATION AND CONFLICT RESOLUTION

Sarah Bankins and Jennifer Waterhouse

LEARNING OUTCOMES

After reading this chapter, you should be able to:

1. identify and explain the elements of the transactional model of communication, including the roles of communicators, noise, channels and context in the communication process

2. explain how differences in leadership style and social and emotional skills will influence leaders' communication

3. recognise that conflict may be inevitable and can be either dysfunctional or functional

4. differentiate between various conflict resolution approaches of leaders.

INTRODUCTION

THIS CHAPTER BEGINS by outlining one of the seminal models of communication: the transactional model. This framework explains communication as an ongoing and dynamic process between communicators located in specific contexts. It also highlights different factors that can impede communication. This model is then applied to explore how different leadership styles can result in different approaches to communication. How both emotional and social skills (verbal and non-verbal) link to effective leadership is then outlined.

The second part of this chapter deals with an important, but often ignored, aspect of communication: conflict and its resolution. Reasons are put forward as to why conflict might not always be recognised, including that conflict is often seen as undesirable or dysfunctional. This section proposes that conflict does not need to be seen in such a negative way and that leaders who effectively resolve conflict may help achieve positive organisational outcomes. Leaders' different approaches to conflict are explored.

UNDERSTANDING COMMUNICATION

Communication is vital in organisations. Many seminal authors in leadership and management (e.g., Mintzberg, Kotter and Blanchard) have identified how important communication is when managing others. Previous chapters have shown how leaders must articulate a vision for their organisations and must motivate, influence, guide and inspire their employees to reach the goals they've set. This can only happen through effective, accurate and timely communication.

> **Communication** – 'A transactional process of exchanging messages and negotiating meaning to establish and maintain relationships' (Steinberg, 1995, p. 13).

Communication can be defined as 'a transactional process of exchanging messages and negotiating meaning to establish and maintain relationships' (Steinberg, 1995, p. 13). The way in which leaders communicate – how they develop their messages, the mediums they use to send them and the style and **context** in which they are delivered – has an important bearing on how effective they are in their role. While communicating may seem like a straightforward activity (we do it all the time), it is a process that involves many elements and there are many opportunities for it to go wrong. Because effective communication is a critical part of leadership, various models have been developed to help leaders better understand the process, their role in it and the influence of context.

> **Context in communication** – The environment in which communication occurs; can be categorised as interpersonal (between people) and intrapersonal (within people).

Evolving models of communication

Our understanding of communication has evolved over time. Early linear (or transmission) models were relatively static and focused largely upon a person (the sender) transmitting a message via a channel (such as speaking) to another person (the receiver) (West & Turner, 2017). Shannon and Weaver's (1948) work studying the transmission of messages across new (at the time) communication technologies such as telegraph and radio generated the earliest linear models of communication, while also introducing terms such as '**noise**' to identify factors interfering with message transmission. While important for building our understanding of the elements of communication, these early models were critiqued for being overly simplistic by viewing communication as uni-directional and not recognising the reciprocal interaction between senders and receivers (Wood, 2013).

Other models have developed since this foundational work to try to capture the complexity and context-dependent nature of communication. For example, contemporary models have increasingly focused on: how communicators are engaged in ongoing processes of sending, receiving and clarifying messages through repeated feedback loops; integrating the role of context; and exploring how individuals co-generate meaning through their ongoing interactions. The first half of this chapter focuses on one of the best-known and often-applied models of communication: the transactional model.

The transactional model of communication

Transactional model of communication – A model of communication that acknowledges that communication is ongoing, reciprocal and dynamic and that the creation of shared meaning develops through the interactions of the communicators. It includes the elements of encoding, decoding, channels, noise and context.

An overview of the **transactional model of communication** is provided in Figure 9.1. This model acknowledges that communication is ongoing, reciprocal and dynamic and that the creation of shared meaning develops through the interactions of the communicators over time (Steinberg, 1995). In this model there is a sender and a receiver, termed Communicator A and Communicator B (Wood, 2013). Some variations of this model maintain the terms 'sender' and 'receiver'; however, because the model incorporates cycles of feedback as individuals clarify each other's meaning, the 'sender' can also become the 'receiver' and vice versa.

Any communication then begins with a person wanting to convey something to another. In this model, messages first need to be encoded (or 'produced') by a communicator (let's say Communicator A instigates the interaction). This means moving from thinking about the message to be communicated to converting it into a format that is meaningful and understandable for the other person. This usually involves using words, as well as the tone, inflections, gestures and other cues we use to convey them, but can include a range of other sounds, symbols and gestures.

Once the message is encoded the sender then needs to 'package' it and send it to Communicator B, using one or more channels. A channel is a medium through which people communicate and these have changed significantly over time. Whereas 'snail mail' (posted letters) was once a commonplace medium of correspondence, we now have a vast array of **communication channels** at our fingertips. These include organisation-specific channels (email, intranet, video-conferencing, Skype, Yammer) and social media (Twitter, Facebook, Instagram).

Communication channels – A channel is a medium through which people communicate, such as speaking or email.

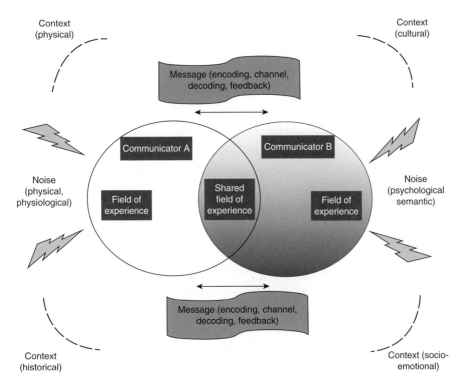

Figure 9.1 The transactional model of communication
Source: Adapted from West & Turner (2008); Wood (2013)

Once the message has been sent, Communicator B needs to receive and decode (or interpret) it. This involves firstly taking delivery of the message (e.g. was it heard (if face-to-face)? Or was it read (if via email)?) and then making sense of what Communicator A is trying to convey. Given there are many areas where possible miscommunication can occur, the process of **decoding** is aided by seeking feedback. For example, to assess how effective the decoding has been, Communicator A may look for feedback from Communicator B in the form of words (e.g. 'Yes I understand') or expressions and gestures (e.g. smiling and nodding).

Communication is dynamic, and its effectiveness depends on a range of almost-simultaneous processes such as **encoding**, channelling, decoding and feeding back between communicators, the broad context, and each individual's background and field of experience. The transactional model also identifies that noise can interfere with the process by distorting the messages being conveyed. We now expand on some of these components of the transactional model.

> **Decoding** – The process of interpreting, or making sense of, a message sent by another person.
> **Encoding** – The process of producing or constructing a message and converting it into a format that is meaningful and understandable for the other person.

Channels

As identified earlier, a channel is the medium through which a communicator chooses to send his or her message.

What is heard and what is seen: Verbal and non-verbal communication

Verbal communication – The act of conveying meaning through the spoken word.

A common distinction in communication theory is between verbal and non-verbal communication behaviour. **Verbal communication** refers to what we say, whereas non-verbal communication 'encompasses all behaviours – other than spoken words – that communicate messages' (West & Turner, 2017, p. 93). Although we may think verbal communication is paramount in getting a message across, non-verbal communication can be just as important to confirm the words spoken or to seek further meaning when what is said is unclear. Darioly and Mast (2014) further break down **non-verbal communication** into speech-related (tone and speed of voice, modulation, duration of speech, etc.) and speech-unrelated (eye contact, gestures, facial expressions, etc.) non-verbal behaviour.

Non-verbal communication – The act of conveying meaning through all behaviours other than spoken words.

Leaders need to be mindful of how their non-verbal and verbal behaviour interact when communicating. To illustrate the power of non-verbal communication, consider the following example. A manager is meeting with a team member to discuss opportunities for promotion. As a topic of importance, and some sensitivity for the team member, the manager has scheduled an hour for the meeting. Now, while the manager may say 'this meeting is important' and 'I want to spend a lot of time with you discussing this' (verbal communication), she may be continually looking at her watch and looking stressed (speech-unrelated non-verbal behaviour) and speaking very quickly (speech-related non-verbal behaviour). Here, the non-verbal behaviours do not align with the words spoken, sending a conflicting message to the team member.

The degree of control: Formal and informal communication

Formal communication – Communication that leaders have some control over, and which is explicitly recognised as a legitimate part of the communication 'infrastructure' of an organisation.

Informal communication – Communication that develops through employees' discussions outside of formal channels, either inside or outside of the workplace. A well-known example of this is the office 'grapevine'.

Within organisations communications may not always flow through channels that are under the control of leaders. **Formal communication** channels are those that leaders have some control over and are explicitly recognised as a legitimate part of the communication 'infrastructure' of an organisation. For example, formal channels include briefing notes, memos, emailed newsletters and intranet updates, or regular meetings and video conferences. **Informal communication** channels are those which leaders have far less control over. These channels develop through the discussions of employees 'outside' of the formal channels and may occur inside or outside of the workplace. A well-known example of this is the office 'grapevine' or 'water cooler talk'. The 'grapevine' (often composed of rumours) constitutes a 'rapid form of communication' and is 'entwined throughout the organisation with branches going in all directions' (Crampton, Hodge & Mishra, 1998, p. 569). While often not under the control of leaders it can operate as a powerful channel for conveying messages, in some instances more so than formal communication channels.

For example, leaders in an organisation may be implementing a timesheet policy and use formal channels such as emailed newsletters and staff briefings to communicate the change. However, employees may start discussing this change among themselves through more informal channels, such as the 'grapevine', or in extra-organisational settings such as over lunch or a coffee. These informal channels may offer employees the opportunity to jointly 'decode' the formal messages sent by the organisation's leadership (for example, by comparing leaders' verbal and non-verbal behaviour), but may also generate rumour, gossip and innuendo if leaders aren't offering clear, consistent and precise messages.

The direction: Downward, upward and horizontal communication

It is important to recognise that information flows in various directions, largely according to the organisational structure (Goldhaber, 1989). **Downward communication** refers to messages sent from higher levels of the organisation to lower levels, such as a CEO sending a memo to a line manager. **Upward communication** refers to messages sent from lower levels of the organisation to higher levels, such as an employee sending a briefing note to a manager to seek approval for a policy change. **Horizontal communication** involves messages sent across the organisation through peers, or individuals at the same hierarchical level, and includes communication within and across teams and workgroups.

> **Downward communication** – Messages sent from higher levels of the organisation to lower levels.
>
> **Upward communication** – Messages sent from lower levels of the organisation to higher levels.
>
> **Horizontal communication** – Messages sent across the organisation through peers, or individuals at the same hierarchical level.

Noise

Communication isn't always straightforward. What the sender intends to convey and what the recipient understands the message to mean don't always align. As leaders seek to influence individuals towards achieving a common purpose, it's important to understand what factors can distort the meaning of their messages. 'Noise' refers to the range of physical, psychological (or cognitive) and language-based factors that can result in a message not being effectively or accurately encoded and/or decoded, thus interfering with the communication process. West and Turner (2017) categorise 'noise' in four ways:

*   *Physical (external)*: This refers to those factors external to the communicators, namely their physical environment, that can distract them from the communication process or make it difficult for them to engage in it (Priest & Gass, 2005). For example, ambient noise from construction work in an adjoining room could distract people trying to talk and make it difficult for them to hear each other's messages.
*   *Physiological (internal)*: This refers to a communicator's physical abilities to encode and decode messages (De Vito, 2007). Physiological noise can manifest in an individual's impaired ability to hear, see and speak. For example, if someone has extremely poor vision this will make it difficult to pick up subtle, non-verbal communication such as facial expressions.

- *Psychological (internal)*: This refers to 'a communicator's biases, prejudices, and feelings toward a person or a message' (West & Turner, 2017, p. 8). A wide range of cognitive and perceptual errors partly constitute this form of noise. Internal noise can also result from individuals being overloaded with information and constrained by time (Priest & Gass, 2005). Researchers (McShane, Olekalns & Travaglione, 2013; Shriberg & Shriberg, 2010) have offered many examples of errors associated with psychological noise:
  - *selective attention* (we focus on some information and screen out other information)
  - *false-consensus effect* (we overestimate the extent to which our beliefs are also held by others)
  - *recency effect* (when the most recent information we have received dominates our perception of a situation/person)
  - *'sender' filtering* (manipulating information to make it more palatable to the receiver)
  - *confirmation bias* (we focus on information that confirms our beliefs and ignore contrary information)
- *Semantic (language-based)*: This refers to the different ways in which individuals use, define and understand words (Priest & Gass, 2005). The most familiar forms of this type of noise in organisations are when occupation-specific technical language or 'jargon' is used. For example, if an IT officer is speaking to a HR manager about a network problem and is using terms like 'default gateway', 'VPN' and 'bandwidth', the HR manager may be unfamiliar with some of this jargon. This means that if one party can't understand the language being used by the other, both encoding and decoding problems ensue.

Context and fields of experience

Communication doesn't occur in a vacuum. An understanding of how context impacts upon the way in which messages are developed and delivered is important for leaders. Context can be understood as the environment in which communication occurs (West & Turner, 2008). At a broad level, context is represented in Figure 9.1 as the dashed curves 'sitting around' the model and is termed the interpersonal (between people) context. At a more micro level, the fields of experience circles illustrate context at the intrapersonal (within person) level. We will now discuss these two levels of context in more detail.

Interpersonal (between people) context

West and Turner (2017) discuss the role of context through four categories. First, the physical context refers to the environment that you can hear, see, touch and feel. For example, this can be as simple as a meeting room. Depending on how the furniture is arranged (are the communicators sitting close together or far apart?), whether other people can see into the room (are there transparent glass walls or opaque ones?) and how much ambient noise is present (can you easily hear people talking outside?), the physical environment can influence the level of 'noise' or message distortion and, subsequently, how effectively a message can be sent, decoded and feedback offered.

Second, the cultural context refers to the 'rules, roles, norms and patterns of communication that are unique to particular cultures' (West & Turner, 2008, p. 9). In Chapter 6, the concept of cross-cultural leadership was explored, and it was argued that it is critical for leaders to understand cultural diversity within and outside their organisations. One reason for this is because it can influence the communication process. Examples of the cultural context include the languages communicators use (the same or different?), the appropriateness of using particular non-verbal cues (such as shaking hands or eye contact) and whether the use of jargon or slang is appropriate (will someone from another culture understand colloquial terms?). Cultural context can particularly influence the degree of overlap between communicators' fields of experience as well as the processes of encoding, decoding and feeding back messages.

Third, the socio-emotional context focuses on the type of relationship, or connection, between the communicators. Some individuals will have a very friendly, open and close relationship and this will likely impact upon their communication through the channels they use (probably more informal) and if their fields of experience overlap significantly they may be well versed in decoding each other's messages (making the need for feedback unnecessary). This context may also influence the interactions between strangers. For example, during a meeting non-verbal cues such as shaking hands, smiling, laughing and nodding in appreciation may make the other person feel more comfortable and supported, creating a positive and warm socio-emotional context in which the rest of the communication takes place.

Finally, historical context refers to the 'history' of the relationship between the communicators and the content and form of the messages that have been sent in the past. Like the socio-emotional context, history can directly inform the degree of overlap that exists between two communicators and their fields of experience, as well as their level of comfort with each other. Historical context can also help someone identify when feedback is required when communicating. For example, a leader and employee (who know each other very well and have worked together for many years) are speaking and the employee is exhibiting body language (non-verbal communication) that indicates sadness and anxiety. If this person is generally bubbly and outgoing the historical context between the two would indicate that the leader needs to instigate a feedback process to better understand the state of mind of the employee.

Intrapersonal (within person) context and fields of experience

More specifically, each communicator has a **field of experience** that includes 'a person's culture, past experiences, personal history, and heredity' (West & Turner, 2008, p. 18). A person's field of experience can also be informed by the broader dimensions of context discussed above. Fields of experience will influence how

Field of experience – Part of an individual's context, including their culture, past experiences, personal history and heredity.

a person approaches the communication process. For example, in an individual's family he or she may have been taught to always address strangers with a title (such as 'Sir').

Further, the degree to which individuals' fields of experience overlap (reflecting the level of common experiences and understanding) then has a bearing on how effectively they communicate. Generally, greater overlap will result in more effective communication. Individuals' first interactions begin the process of determining this degree of 'field' overlap, with more interactions and more common experiences created and shared then likely resulting in increased overlap (West & Turner, 2008).

Individuals' fields of experience obviously change over time, as their experiences change. The degree of overlap between two communicators' fields of experience can also change, perhaps as they get to know each other better as their working relationship grows (more overlap) or as they spend less time together as their changing work roles mean they no longer work in the same part of the organisation (less overlap).

CASE STUDY 9.1

When a tattoo 'conveys a thousand words'

Nanaia Mahuta is a politician and Labour MP who, in 2016 and after 20 years in politics, became the first New Zealand member of parliament to wear the chin tattoo of Māori women, or *moko kauae*. In receiving her tattoo, Mahuta has been variously hailed by other members of parliament as a leader for Māori people, and particularly for Māori women, and as a role model for reinforcing the importance of identification with one's cultural heritage.

To understand the impact of Mahuta's tattoo, and what it communicates, requires understanding some historical and cultural context. While it may look like 'just a tattoo', this facial marking is richly imbued with history and meaning derived from Māori culture. As Mahuta explained in an interview with *The Guardian* newspaper: '*Moko* is a statement of identity, like a passport' (Roy, 2016). This extends to the design of the tattoo itself and in another interview with an online news service in New Zealand, Mahuta explained the meaning behind its design and its link to her tribal heritage:

> The design is taken from the ridgepole of our ancestral meeting house … there are *kowhaiwhai* designs there that each artist has personalised to each of the 14 women (who received tattoos at the same time as Mahuta) (Price, 2016).

Mahuta's tattoo also speaks to the intersection between New Zealand's Māori and colonial histories. In the same interview for *The Guardian* (Roy, 2016), the co-leader of the Māori Party, Marama Fox, discussed the broader meaning of Mahuta's tattoo in this way:

> I'm proud as a Māori woman to sit alongside her in parliament restoring to our political landscape a symbolic gesture of rangatiratanga [self-determination] previously dissuaded during our colonial struggle to give vote to Māori women in their land of inheritance (Roy, 2016).

Mahuta also believes that as a prominent public figure who has proudly received a facial *moko*, she is helping to destigmatise the wearing of facial tattoos which have, in the past, been associated with gang and criminal activity. Overall, this overt and public proclamation by Mahuta of her pride in her Māori heritage has also encouraged more public conversations about the role of traditional Māori culture in contemporary New Zealand society (Roy, 2016).

Critical thinking questions
1. What sorts of messages do you think Nanaia Mahuta is seeking to convey? Do you think the message/s are conveyed more powerfully through verbal or non-verbal communication? Why?
2. What sort of 'noise' do you think could distort the messages that Nanaia Mahuta is communicating through her tattoo?
3. Do you think the interpersonal and/or intrapersonal context affects the process of communication here? If so, how?

LEADERSHIP AND COMMUNICATION
Leadership styles and communication

Recall that Chapter 3 introduced a range of leadership styles. In Table 9.1, Hackman and Johnson's (2013) work helps us to link three key leadership styles to communication behaviours: autocratic (also termed *authoritarian*); participative (also termed *democratic*); and delegative (also termed *laissez-faire*). Each style reflects how a leader approaches their role and has implications for how he or she interacts and communicates with employees.

Communication and autocratic leadership

An autocratic leader typically uses high levels of control. This type of leader makes decisions with little, or often no, input from others; does not seek opinions, counsel or feedback from others; sets very clear and specific directions for employees to obey; and creates a very clear hierarchical separation between him or herself and followers.

Drawing on Hackman and Johnson's (2013) work in Table 9.1 and the transactional model of communication discussed earlier, the communication style of autocratic leaders can be characterised in the following ways:

- *They will often engage in only 'one-way' communication (from the leader to another person/group of people) and are not likely to allow much, if any, opportunity for feedback.* If the leader is clear and explicit and the communication is unambiguous this may be fine, but if there is noise in the communication process employees may be unclear on the meaning of the message and what is expected of them (problems with decoding). Given this, more informal communication channels between employees may be utilised (the 'grapevine') and potentially distort the leader's intended message.
- *They are likely to utilise more formal and downward communication channels.* As decision making under this style of leadership largely rests on the knowledge and expertise of the

Table 9.1 Styles of leadership communication

Democratic	Authoritarian	Laissez-faire
Involves followers in setting circles	Sets goals individually	Allows followers free rein to set their own goals
Engages in two-way, open communication	Engages primarily in one-way, downward communication	Engages in noncommittal, superficial communication
Facilitates discussion with followers	Controls discussion with followers	Avoids discussion with followers
Solicits input regarding determination of policy and procedures	Sets policy and procedures unilaterally	Allows followers to set policy and procedures
Focuses interaction	Dominates interaction	Avoids interaction
Provides suggestions and alternatives for the completion of tasks	Personally directs the completion of tasks	Provides suggestions and alternatives for the completion of tasks only when asked to do so by followers
Provides frequent positive feedback	Provides infrequent positive feedback	Provides infrequent feedback of any kind
Rewards good work and uses punishment only as a last resort	Rewards obedience and punishes mistakes	Avoids offering rewards or punishments
Exhibits effective listening skills	Exhibits poor listening skills	May exhibit either poor or effective listening skills
Mediates conflict for group gain	Uses conflict for personal gain	Avoids conflict

Source: Hackman & Johnson (2013, p. 41), reproduced with permission

leader, it generally doesn't allow for a wide range of opinions and ideas to be gathered from others in the organisation. Therefore, upward communication will be minimal and while horizontal communication may occur between employees, it is unlikely to then be directed upward. Both verbal ('I am the one solely making this decision') and non-verbal (speaking quickly in meetings, arms crossed, no eye contact) behaviour may also reinforce the focus on downward communication.

- *Interpersonal context may also reinforce this leader's communication style.* For example, physical context (leader in a separate office, door closed), socio-emotional context (does the leader seem distant and impersonal?) and historical context (is this how the leader has always communicated?) all shape other elements within the transactional model for this type of leader.

Communication and participative leadership

A participative leader typically devolves some control to others. This type of leader makes decisions with the participation and input of their followers; will actively seek the involvement of others in the process of leading, including eliciting views, opinions and feedback from others; and, while promoting inclusivity, will maintain responsibility and accountability for the decisions made and the outcomes achieved within the organisation.

Drawing on Hackman and Johnson's (2013) work in Table 9.1 and the transactional model of communication discussed earlier, the communication style of participative leaders can be characterised in the following ways:

- *They focus on 'two-way' communication (from leaders to other people and back again) to gather multiple viewpoints and ideas from anywhere, and at any level, in the organisation to inform decision making.* This allows for ongoing feedback between leaders and their followers to clarify messages, share ideas and discuss dissenting opinions (facilitating accurate decoding and minimising the impact of noise).
- *They are usually more attuned to, and involved in, the organisation's informal communication channels, while using formal channels to gather information across the organisation (e.g., online discussion forums, idea competitions).* Because these leaders seek a high level of staff involvement and actively seek their feedback, they may participate in more informal conversations with employees to discuss their ideas while minimising the need for 'grapevine' communication to occur. Both verbal ('I value your thoughts on this') and non-verbal (actively listening in meetings, not directing, nodding, eye contact) behaviour should also reflect the inclusive nature of this style of leadership.
- *Their highly accessible style is apparent in the interpersonal context through, for example, an 'open-door' policy (physical context) and an open and inclusive demeanour (socio-emotional context).* The latter may also result in greater overlap between leaders' and employees' fields of experience, through the time spent together in discussions and jointly participating in decision making.
- *They need to be mindful that their style could promote psychological (internal) noise in the communication process.* For example, if too many opinions and viewpoints are elicited this could result in information overload, potentially distorting communications by generating confusion and uncertainty.

Communication and delegative leadership

A delegative leader typically exerts very low levels of control. This type of leader delegates a large proportion of their decision-making power to their followers, leaving it to them to identify appropriate courses of action; offers minimal guidance or direction; views their role as focused on ensuring appropriate resources are provided to allow organisational members to do their jobs; will recognise that responsibility and accountability for decisions and outcomes still resides with them, but how decisions and outcomes are reached rests almost solely with their followers.

Drawing on Hackman and Johnson's (2013) work in Table 9.1 and the transactional model of communication discussed earlier, the communication style of delegative leaders can be characterised in the following ways:

- *The type of communication used within this style can be difficult to identify.* At times it may be one-way or two-way, but at its extreme it could be termed 'no-way'. Because this type of leader leaves so much to the discretion of their employees, communication with them can be minimal.
- *'Delegative leaders can practice "guided freedom", where the leader takes a role in decision-making when requested by followers or when absolutely required to get a task completed'* (Hackman & Johnson, 2013, p. 40). This type of action may manifest in communicative behaviour focused on observation of group members and intervening when asked or when the leader believes it is required (Hackman & Johnson, 2013). Here, the non-verbal behaviour of the leader may be particularly important; for example, their posture, eye contact, facial expressions and general demeanour in meetings may indicate to employees the leader's support, or otherwise, for their decisions.
- *The 'hands-off' approach of this type of leader will also shape the interpersonal context of any messages sent.* For example, a delegative leader may have only a very distant relationship with staff (socio-emotional context), leading to quite separate fields of experience. Taken together, this may impede the quality of the communication that does occur.

Leaders' social and emotional skills for communication

Communication is an inherently social process, as it involves interpersonal communication occurring between people. The concept of emotional intelligence has been used throughout this book; it is 'the capacity of an individual to recognise and manage emotions in themselves and in others' (see Chapter 1). We have also discussed in this chapter the importance of both verbal and non-verbal behaviour in the communication process and the role of inter- and intrapersonal context in shaping how people communicate. Riggio's (2014) **social skills model** for leader communication draws together the emotional and social skill dimensions of leadership to demonstrate how they influence relationship development between leaders and their followers. For our purposes, this offers important insights into how and why various forms of communication lie at the heart of effective leadership.

Social skills model – A model of leadership communication where communication is viewed as an inherently social process, emphasising the importance of strong relationships a leader builds through social (verbal) and emotional (non-verbal) skills, such as expressiveness, sensitivity and control.

As shown in Table 9.2, Riggio's (2014) model is made up of 'two halves' and draws together the emotional (non-verbal) and social (verbal) domains to explain effective leader communication. Three key skills are identified within each domain: expressiveness (the ability to effectively encode messages); sensitivity (the ability to effectively decode messages); and control (the ability to exercise emotional/social skills appropriately).

Table 9.2 Emotional/non-verbal skills and social/verbal skills

Emotional/non-verbal skills	
Emotional expressiveness	Skill in sending (encoding) non-verbal and emotional messages. Persons high in EE are spontaneously expressive, animated, and often referred to as charismatic.
Emotional sensitivity	Skills in receiving (decoding) emotional and non-verbal messages. Persons high in ES are emotionally empathic, observant, and responsive to others' feelings, but may be susceptible to 'emotional contagion'.
Emotional control	Skill in regulating and controlling the expression of emotional messages. Persons high in EC seem emotionally distant, but are able to mask felt emotional states with a different emotional expression.
Social/verbal skills	
Social expressiveness	Verbal speaking skill and the ability to engage others in conversation. SE is related to, but distinct from, being outgoing and extraverted.
Social sensitivity	Verbal decoding skill (listening ability), but also involves one's knowledge of social rules and conventions. In extremes, SS can lead to social anxiety and withdrawal.
Social control	Sophisticated social role-playing skill. SC is related to being tactful and socially competent.

Source: Riggio (2014, p. 33), reproduced with permission

Riggio (2014) argues that an emotional (non-verbal) skills set allows leaders to inspire and motivate others (emotional expressiveness) and to develop close connections and relationships with others and be attentive to the socio-emotional context of the communication process (emotional sensitivity). However, leaders must deploy their emotional skills in ways that are appropriate to the situation (emotional control). Social skills are viewed as particularly important, as they include 'complex abilities to read social situations, understand subtle social norms, respond to social cues, adhere to social scripts, and regulate one's own social behaviour' (Riggio, 2014, p. 35). A social skills set allows leaders to verbally utilise different communication channels to engage others (social expressiveness), be mindful of the interpersonal context between communicators (social sensitivity) and then deploy these skills appropriately (social control). Taken together, these skills become particularly important for leaders when they are involved in another key function of managing people: managing conflict. It is to this area that we will shortly turn our attention.

Leaders as spokespeople: External communication

In this chapter we have so far focused on interpersonal communication and communication within organisations. However, leaders' communications are not always focused *internally* to the organisation. As one of the seminal authors in the management field, Mintzberg (1989) identified that leaders may also take on what he termed informational and interpersonal roles, that of 'spokesperson' and 'figurehead'. This means that leaders also face *externally* to the organisation and can be responsible for communicating with various stakeholders and managing a company's reputation. So, the relationship between leadership communication within and outside the organisation is important.

Barrett (2006, p. 386) has developed a spiral model that identifies different types of communications and how these unfold as leaders gather power and become more senior in the organisational hierarchy. She describes leadership communication as being comprised of three 'rings' (see Figure 9.2): core, managerial and corporate. Barrett's (2006) model suggests that all effective communication begins with those skills at the centre of her spiral (the inner ring). The individual-level, core skills of speaking, writing and strategically crafting messages for different audiences (Barrett, 2006) are foundational and relate to communication elements already discussed in this chapter, such as encoding, decoding and selecting appropriate message channels. The middle ring depicts managerial communication, where leaders must interact with individuals and teams within the organisation and links to other skills discussed in this chapter, such as emotional intelligence (as in Riggio's social skills model [2014]), cultural literacy (interpersonal context), coaching/mentoring and listening (intrapersonal context, fields of experience and noise) (Barrett, 2006).

Figure 9.2 Barrett's leadership communication framework
Source: Barrett (2006, p. 387)

However, it is the outer layer of Barrett's (2006) spiral (corporate communication) that positions leaders as external communicators. As leaders become more prominent and senior in an organisation they must communicate with both internal and external stakeholders. In Barrett's (2006) model, corporate communication refers to activities such as media relations, crisis communications and image/reputation management, and we discuss each of these below. Walker (2015, p. 316) subsumes these areas under the term 'external strategic communications' and further defines these activities as 'management's public relations and issues management efforts designed to influence consumers, communities, special interest groups, voters, regulators, legislators and others outside the organisation'. While these activities may be coordinated through public relations areas within companies, leaders are still the individuals required to face the public and communicate on behalf of the organisation.

Media relations refers to interactions with traditional outlets such as newspapers, trade publications, radio and television, but increasingly includes communicating through social media channels such as Twitter and Facebook and via webcasts, podcasts and YouTube channels. Here, leaders engage in 'public communication' or the process of 'one communicating with many' (Walker, 2015, p. 316). Leaders also play a key role in communicating externally in times of crisis. Ulmer, Sellnow and Seeger (2015, p. 8) define a crisis as a 'specific, unexpected and nonroutine event or series of events that create high levels of uncertainty', including natural and industrial disasters. At such times, the role of leaders becomes particularly critical, with a heightened need to communicate with internal and external stakeholders, plan, control and organise, comfort and reassure, communicate information and updates and assert a vision for recovery (Ulmer et al., 2015). As Ulmer and co-authors (2015, p. 151) identify, and in line with Riggio's (2014) social skills model, during a crisis leaders need to be 'visible, open and honest' in their communication and 'work to build a reservoir of goodwill' with stakeholders. Finally, image and reputation management are also important 'external-facing' communication activities. Forman and Argenti (2005, p. 248) describe this as 'managing communications to mould the interpretations and perceptions of constituents'. A company's reputation is based on the perceptions of these multiple stakeholders, such as investors, community members, customers and employees. Here, leaders must employ the diversity of communication skills discussed in this chapter so far, and as outlined in Barrett's (2006) spiral model, to tailor their communications effectively for each of these groups. It is also important to note that it is not just what leaders say that is critical for their external communications (verbal), but also what they do through their behaviours (non-verbal), as we have shown that the latter can also convey powerful messages regarding what a company stands for and what its values are (Hackman & Johnson, 2013).

CASE STUDY 9.2

Leading with the 'human touch'

Gail Kelly is one of the most successful and well-known businesspeople in Australia. Born in South Africa, she moved to Australia with her family in the late 1990s. Her career in Australia has spanned several of the country's largest banks. After an initial tenure of five years at the Commonwealth Bank, Kelly became CEO of St George Bank, where she built a reputation as a highly effective and successful leader. In 2008, she became CEO of Westpac. In assuming these roles, Kelly became the first female chief executive of a major Australian bank.

But there is more to Kelly's accomplishments than overseeing profit growth and expansion of market share. Her leadership style is considered one of the key drivers of her success and is noted as being unique in the financial sector. She has been described as a 'banking CEO with a human touch', a leader who stresses the importance of work–life balance and leading a 'whole life', of loving what you do and empowering staff to shape their own work lives (Murphy, 2005). In an interview with *The Australian*, she discussed how generosity of spirit informs her leadership style:

> generosity of spirit at its very heart goes to a fundamental belief in the power of people to make a difference, respect for individuals, respect for difference. At its core is the philosophy of saying 'I want the very best for you', of creating an environment where each individual can thrive and prosper at every level of an organisation (Legge, 2015).

In that same interview, Kelly reflected on the role of self-awareness, and by extension emotional intelligence, in the practice of leadership. In her own words:

> I'm amazed at how many leaders I see who seem so unaware of their impact. They will walk through an open corridor or their lift well or foyer and they are just tunnel vision. You need to be aware that there is a whole group of people observing you. You need to be aware of that, you need to look at people, smile at people, acknowledge people everywhere you go. You'll notice I do that all the time (Legge, 2015).

Critical thinking questions

1. What style of leadership do you think best reflects Gail Kelly's approach?
2. Thinking about the social skills model of communication, can you identify any emotional (non-verbal) and social (verbal) skills that Gail Kelly uses when communicating as a leader?
3. What type of corporate image or reputation do you think Gail Kelly conveys to external stakeholders through her communications?

THE NATURE OF CONFLICT

Conflict – Active disagreement between people that is accompanied by a belief that each person cannot simultaneously achieve their goals.

Interdependence – A relationship in which people depend on each other for the achievement of their goals.

Conflict is generally understood as an active disagreement between people that is accompanied by a belief that each person cannot achieve their goals simultaneously (Pruitt & Rubin, 1986). It is possible to be in conflict with yourself, but conflict usually occurs between people or groups of people because of the nature of their mutual relationship. The nature of that relationship is one of **interdependence** where each individual or group is reliant on another individual or group to achieve their goals or satisfy their interests. Where goals can be achieved without the assistance or intervention of others, then conflict does not arise. It is only when there is dependence on another person to achieve goals or outcomes that the potential for conflict arises because that other person may not be willing to provide what is wanted or needed.

Dysfunctional conflict – A view of conflict as an aberration that leads to negative consequences.

For many, conflict is considered in a very negative light. Its poor reputation has developed because of a view that conflict only arises because something is wrong. Translating this view to the workplace, conflict is often seen as being caused by either poor management practices or failures in communication. In addition, conflict is often thought to have negative consequences and is **dysfunctional** because:

- one party will win and the other must lose
- the other person is not being fair in what they are asking for
- people might get emotional
- communication decreases in an effort to avoid conflict
- things begin to look overly complex. It appears more difficult to achieve our goals when another person is demanding something different
- people hold tight to what they want and will not listen to reason
- it results in an 'us and them' mentality where people only see the differences, not the similarities
- the conflict might escalate to the point that it will destroy any future opportunity to resolve it and will therefore destroy relationships (Lewicki, Saunders & Barry, 2015).

A very different way to consider conflict is that it is largely inevitable and can, in fact, be **functional**. In this view, conflict arises naturally, not because something is wrong. In the workplace, for example, conflict is inevitable because of the natural tension between an employer's need for profitability and an employee's need to earn a decent wage. When considered as functional and positive, conflict can provide an opportunity to detect potentially serious workplace

> **Functional conflict** – A view of conflict as being largely inevitable and, if addressed well, can lead to positive consequences.

issues and respond appropriately to issues before they escalate and cause harm. Functional views of conflict see it as providing opportunities for people to: better deal with problems; spur organisational change; help strengthen relationships; improve self-development; and, for some, can be stimulating and fun (Lewicki et al., 2015).

Conflict is generally understood to occur on four levels:

- intrapersonal (with oneself)
- interpersonal (between individual people)
- intragroup (between members of the same group, e.g. an executive committee)
- intergroup (between groups within an organisation, e.g. Sales and Accounts; or between organisations, e.g. two competing companies).

Leaders therefore deal with conflict both within their organisations and across organisational boundaries. Disgruntled employees, unhappy customers, poor performing suppliers and ruthless competitors are all sources of conflict for leaders. Leaders who can identify and effectively resolve conflict at all levels can avert the potentially serious consequences of unresolved conflict, including lost productivity, industrial action and lawsuits causing both reputational and financial damage to individuals and/or their organisations.

Interpersonal power and influence

There are various forms of power, and Chapter 8 introduced some of these. To truly understand conflict there is a need to understand power. On the surface, conflict is about satisfying people's goals, but underpinning the substantive issues in conflict is also what Kolb (1999) describes as a 'shadow negotiation' for power. Leaders are involved in and need to address conflict, and so leaders also exercise power.

Interpersonal power – Having the ability to persuade or influence others to do what they would otherwise not have done.

Interpersonal power is a power that is used to influence others to adopt a particular view or position. Interpersonal power provides its possessor with the ability to influence others' decisions. Those who possess interpersonal power can persuade others to do what they would not otherwise do (Dahl, 1957). Lewicki et al. (2015) identify several sources of interpersonal power including:

- *information and expert power*
- *resource control*
- *legitimate power:* authority, reputation, performance
- *location in structure:* centrality, criticality, flexibility, visibility
- *personal power:* friendliness, integrity, patience, tenacity, emotion.

Many of these sources of power will seem familiar to you from previous chapters. Chapter 3 introduced different styles of leadership. Applying these styles of leadership to power and influence, it can be seen how authoritarian leaders may use the legitimate power of their position or their location within the structure of an organisation to influence the decisions of others. Charismatic leaders, on the other hand, may use personal power to influence decisions while transactional leaders may use their control of resources (such as money) to achieve influence.

RESOLVING CONFLICT
Conflict resolution strategies

Conflict resolution spans a continuum, from negotiation (where two parties seek to resolve their own conflict) to mediation (in which an independent third party is engaged to resolve a dispute), and ultimately to arbitration (where a dispute is resolved in a court of law). At its most basic and common form, conflict resolution is about negotiation. To be effective at resolving conflict a leader needs to be a good negotiator. There has been much written on the characteristics that make someone a good negotiator. Many of these are the characteristics that also make a good leader. For example, Raiffa (1982) describes a good negotiator as someone who:

- is well prepared
- possesses knowledge of the subject matter
- thinks clearly and quickly
- is articulate
- has good listening skills
- is intelligent
- has integrity
- is persuasive
- has patience
- is decisive.

Two other characteristics or skills can be added to this list: versatility and reflective practice (Waterhouse, Keast & Brown, 2011). The business environment is not stable; it is changing at an exponential rate. Under these conditions those people that can effectively resolve conflict need to be versatile. Leaders cannot therefore be confined to any single conflict resolution approach. They must continuously monitor the operating environment and be prepared to adjust accordingly. A balance between observation and action is required to successfully resolve conflict. Leaders need to develop proficiency in operating in situations of significant change and learn to navigate this environment.

Negotiators also need to monitor and reflect on their own behaviour and styles. In essence, reflective negotiation practitioners are always examining their practice and its impact. A questioning of their knowledge and skills base and its application to context is central to this process. Moon (1999, p. 63) describes reflective practice as 'a set of abilities and skills, to indicate the taking of a critical stance, an orientation to problem solving or state of mind'. In this way, reflective practice is grounded in self-understanding and critical thinking skills.

Two main strategies

Two main negotiation strategies are identified: **distributive** (competitive) and **integrative** (cooperative) (Walton & McKersie, 1965; Fells, 2016). A distributive strategy assumes that conflict and its resolution is a fixed-sum, competitive game. That is, conflict is approached as a win–lose situation where the main 'game' is to win the conflict at all costs and make the other party lose. In these scenarios, conflict is approached as a fixed pie with the aim of winning as much of the pie as possible (see Figure 9.3).

> **Distributive negotiation** – An approach to conflict resolution that views resources as fixed and scarce. Conflict is therefore viewed as a competition for those scarce resources.
> **Integrative negotiation** – A problem-solving approach to conflict resolution that holds that conflict can be an opportunity to add value.

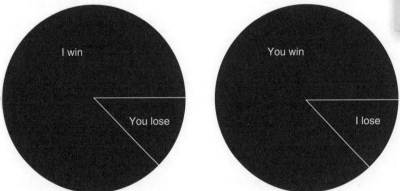

Figure 9.3 The 'fixed pie' distributive approach to conflict resolution

The problem with a distributive approach, however, is that the tactics employed are designed to take advantage of the other party. These tactics may include intimidation, exaggeration and deceit. The use of such tactics, in combination with a dissatisfied loser, means that the relationship between the people in conflict may well be damaged or destroyed. Furthermore, where neither side will back down, the strategy could result in the cost of agreement becoming so high that both parties effectively lose. A distributive approach is therefore only appropriate where the ongoing relationship between the parties is not important, but where the need to win (or at least not to lose) is paramount.

In contrast, an integrative or cooperative strategy is one that seeks to achieve a win–win resolution. Based on the early twentieth-century work of Mary Parker Follett, conflict is reframed as either a problem to be solved or an opportunity for mutual gain. In contrasting a distributive approach to an integrative one, Follett (1924) asks:

> Is there then any other method of ending conflict? There is a way beginning now to be recognized at least, and even occasionally followed: when two desires are *integrated*, that means that a solution has been found in which both desires have found a place, that neither side has had to sacrifice anything.

An integrative strategy therefore relies on the open sharing of information about the conflict and exploring genuine interests. Such an approach results in a mutually agreeable solution. The use of integrative strategies therefore tends to result in greater satisfaction and increased ownership of the solution because it is jointly created. An additional advantage is that the relationship is not damaged and, in many cases, can be improved.

Various adaptations of Follett's work have resulted in a plethora of models on how to achieve integrative solutions to conflict. These models often depict conflict resolution in stages or phases such as the following.

Stage 1: Defining the conflict or problem

Coming to an understanding about the nature of the conflict or issue seems, on the surface, very easy. Often those in conflict do not know themselves what the nature of the problem really is. The first stage in resolving conflict is therefore one of the most challenging: defining the conflict or problem.

In this first phase of conflict resolution, an understanding of the difference between positions and interests is paramount. *Positions* are the stances that people take when they are in conflict. For example, a supplier of equipment may take a position that they will only sell their equipment at a certain price, while the purchaser takes a position that they will only pay an amount somewhere below what the supplier is demanding. Understanding the supplier's and purchaser's *interests* is to explore and understand what motivates the positions they adopt. The most obvious is that both the supplier and purchaser need to make a profit. There may, however, be further interests to be explored such as the purchaser needing to transport the equipment to a distant site that adds to their costs or the supplier having issues with the timing of the order.

Care also needs to be taken as to how the problem is defined. Oversimplification of the problem may result in a feeling that the problem is not being taken seriously. Furthermore, if all issues are not identified, the solution search (next stage) may not explore sufficient possibilities to genuinely and comprehensively address the problems (Lewicki et al., 2015). Fisher, Ury and Patton (1991) identify the importance too of 'separating the people from the problem'. Assigning blame and personalising the problem may result in people not wanting to engage in the search for a solution.

Stage 2: Undertaking a solution search

This stage of the conflict resolution process is the problem-solving phase. Proposing solutions too early may result in issues not being fully explored and developed. It is therefore important that the solution search be kept separate from the first stage of problem definition (Lewicki et al., 2015). The solution search is a creative phase where the parties in conflict brainstorm possible solutions. The main aim of this phase is to generate as many alternatives as possible. This may involve:

- considering what each party considers more and less important, to help identify what each may be willing to concede
- adding new ideas or resources onto the list of possible solutions
- inventing creative options that suit everyone's needs.

The solution search is often considered an integrative phase in resolving conflict because people share ideas, put proposals forward and seek to 'expand the pie'. At the end of this stage, there should be a comprehensive list of possible solutions that have the potential to address the problem or problems identified.

Stage 3: Selecting a solution

Having identified several possible solutions, it is now time to decide on the action that is going to be taken. This process can sometimes become competitive as each person may try to impose their own preferred solutions. To reduce the risk of coming to a poor choice among the possible options, it is advisable to set some objectives by which the outcome will be measured. Here, Lewicki et al. (2015) identify that it is important to achieve both objective outcomes (such as cost, productivity, monetary benefit) as well as subjective outcomes (how satisfied people are about the decision). In integrative negotiations it is arguably more important to focus on the subjective outcomes because of the benefit these have for the long-term relationship between the parties involved in the conflict.

THE ROLE OF LEADERSHIP IN CONFLICT RESOLUTION

Leaders play two distinct roles in conflict resolution: they may negotiate by acting for themselves in a conflict; or they may act as a mediator between other people who are in conflict. Because of their position in the organisation, leaders can more readily exercise legitimate power to bring about a resolution to conflict. They can, in effect, exercise 'power over' and order disputing parties to accept a resolution. But this is not always ideal nor is it how many leaders choose to resolve conflict.

Mediating conflict

In mediating conflict between people, experts increasingly recognise the benefits of a facilitative, interest-based approach (Fells, 2016). Several mediation bodies have adopted this approach, including the Resolution Institute in Australia. This approach to mediation is facilitative because the mediator encourages individuals in conflict to resolve their conflict through exploring and creating their own solutions rather than having a solution imposed upon them. It is interest-based because it encourages an exploration of the real interests of people in conflict to ensure that the solution or solutions agreed to address the underlying cause of the conflict and/or the real problem an individual is experiencing.

Facilitative mediation – An approach to conflict resolution where a third party assists people with the processes to resolve their conflict.
Evaluative mediation – An approach to conflict resolution where a third party assists people to resolve their conflict through providing expert advice and potential solutions.

In contrast to **facilitative mediation**, **evaluative mediation** utilises the expert knowledge of a mediator to persuade the parties in conflict to a solution based on the recommendations of the mediator. The two approaches are somewhat blurred so when observing mediation, mediators can be seen to propose both solutions and provide disputing parties with skills to resolve their own conflict.

In addressing conflict, leaders can draw on several approaches, including the facilitative and evaluative mediation approaches described above. A leader's choice of approach, just as with their approach to communication in general, depends on several factors pertinent to the situation and influenced by their own personal style.

Leadership styles for conflict resolution

As noted earlier, conflict can be considered as either an aberration or as largely inevitable. How leaders think and feel about conflict influences how they then respond to it and how they seek to resolve it. Such responses are highly varied. In attempting to explain these variances, in 1964 Blake and Mouton developed a five-mode model that classifies the ways in which individuals deal with conflict (see Figure 9.4). These five modes are:

- competing
- collaborating
- compromising
- avoiding
- accommodating.

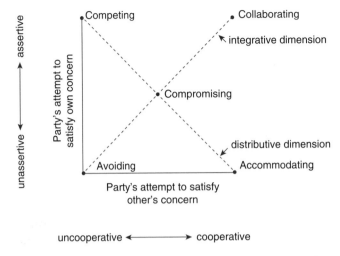

Figure 9.4 Conflict-handling modes across cooperative/assertive and integrative/distributive dimensions

Source: Kilmann & Thomas (1975, p. 972), reproduced with permission

Subsequent development of this model (Thomas, 1976; Kilmann & Thomas, 1975) has laid the foundation for assessing an individual's behaviour in conflict situations that remains valid and widely used to the current date. Kilmann and Thomas (1975) noted two further insights. First, that the five identifiable conflict responses are underpinned by two main dimensions: the extent of assertiveness (interest in achieving one's own goals); and cooperativeness (interest in achieving the other person's goals). The model was then overlaid to show how such preferences lead to the selection of either a distributive or integrative strategy.

To help explain this further, a description of the five modes follows.

Competing

Competing appears in the model as a preference to satisfy one's own concerns or interests (assertive) combined with little or no desire to satisfy the other person's concerns. Competing is therefore an assertive, uncooperative and power-oriented approach to conflict resolution where the primary aim of resolving the conflict is to win and, in doing so, make the other person lose. It is a distributive orientation in that the matter in dispute is viewed as a fixed pie to be divided (refer to Figure 9.3). Conflict is approached as a need to exercise power over others, persuading and influencing them to accept a preferred action or position.

Collaborating

Collaborating is illustrated as being both assertive and cooperative – that is, individuals who approach conflict with this mode have concern for both their own outcomes, but also concern for the other person's outcomes. This approach to conflict resolution therefore involves uncovering the real issues associated with the conflict and developing creative solutions that meet the concerns of all involved. Unlike competing, where the outcome of the dispute is a fixed pie, approaches that involve collaboration see the outcome as an expandable pie whose limits are not initially known.

Collaborating is therefore associated with integrative approaches to conflict resolution. In collaborative approaches to conflict resolution, power is shared, and each person involved in the conflict combines their power and influence to develop and implement innovative and novel solutions.

Compromising

Compromising is often the only solution that most people see when they address conflict, yet compromising is not necessarily the most beneficial way to resolve conflict. When compromising, no one involved in the conflict achieves the best solution because parties find an expedient, mutually acceptable outcome that only partially satisfies their needs. Therefore, while compromising addresses and acknowledges conflict in a more direct way than avoidance, this approach does not allow for the exploration of creative solutions that can be found through collaboration. Power is seen as divided between the parties and therefore concessions to that divided power must be made if conflict is to be resolved.

Avoiding

Avoiding is both unassertive and uncooperative, which results in an individual not addressing either their own concerns or those of the other person. The result of avoidance is that dealing with conflict may be either temporarily or permanently delayed. Avoidance denies issues of power and denies also the existence, or legitimacy, of conflict.

Accommodating

Accommodating is an approach that is unassertive but cooperative. Individuals who accommodate place greater importance on the other person's outcomes and little to none on their own. In effect, this is a self-sacrificing mode of conflict resolution because a person sacrifices their own interests for the benefit of another's. Often this approach is wrongly identified as an integrative form of negotiation. Accommodating is the mirror image of competing. Instead of trying to win as much of the 'pie' as possible, the person purposefully gives away most of the pie to preserve the relationship, resulting in the 'you win, I lose' scenario in Figure 9.3. The other party is seen as possessing more power and is permitted to exercise that power. Concessions are made without compensation.

CASE STUDY 9.3

Not calm waters – conflict over the Murray–Darling Basin Plan

Water is a valuable and scarce resource in Australia. It is therefore not surprising that leading up to the final approval of the Murray–Darling River Plan in November 2012, there had been little consensus between Australian states, the large number of community groups with their various interests in water usage, political parties and even members of the same political party. Despite years of negotiation, the agreement remains contentious with various groups still dissatisfied.

Under the approved plan, the Murray–Darling Water Authority (the Authority) is responsible for the process of returning 2750 gigalitres (GL) of water to the river. The authority initially proposed as much as 7600 GL be returned to the river each year because this was the level it believed would make the river environmentally sustainable. But even at the much lower amount agreed, farmers along the river predict an end to their livelihoods.

On the way to finalising the agreement there was considerable conflict between members of the South Australian branch of the Liberal Party and their federal colleagues. Jamie Brown, a South Australian Liberal MP, stated on the ABC's *7.30 Report* in 2012 that:

> I certainly have views about where it [the then proposed agreement] can be improved, however, ultimately I want an independent authority making this decision for a plan for the future based on science and not based on petty, parochial state politics which has damaged the Basin for so long (Cooper, 2012).

In response, the federal representative for the Coalition at the time, Senator Barnaby Joyce, stated: 'We are not going to approve a plan that basically pulls the economic rug out from 2.1 million people who live in the Basin'.

Critical thinking questions

1. The plan signed in November 2012 agreed to the return of 2750 GL of water to the river, a long way off the 7600 GL earlier proposed by the Authority. How did the leaders in this story approach the issue of water conservation? What conflict resolution styles are evident?

2. Do you think there was a better way to resolve this conflict? If so, how and why?

SUMMARY

LEARNING OUTCOME 1: Identify and explain the elements of the transactional model of communication, including the roles of communicators, noise, channels and context in the communication process.

The transactional model recognises that communication is an ongoing and reciprocal process. It involves communicators (in this model usually two), a cycle of developing and encoding messages, sending them through a specific channel (verbal and non-verbal behaviours, formal and informal means and the direction of the message), receiving and decoding them and then engaging in reciprocal and ongoing feedback to demonstrate understanding of (and if necessary clarify) the message. This occurs while seeking to avoid message distortions through various forms of 'noise'. Communicators also interact in specific contexts, with both interpersonal (physical, cultural, socio-emotional, historical) and intrapersonal (fields of experience) shaping how the communication takes place and its effectiveness.

LEARNING OUTCOME 2: Explain how differences in leadership style and social and emotional skills will influence leaders' communication.

Different leadership styles result in different approaches to communication. Autocratic leaders will generally engage in more 'one-way', downward and formal communication, given their almost sole control of decision-making processes. Participative leaders will likely use more 'two-way' communication, focused in many directions (upward, downward, horizontally), and may make use of both formal and informal channels. Delegative leaders may not initiate much communication at all with their employees, given the high level of control they delegate to others. However, they may engage in more observation of groups, meaning their non-verbal behaviour can be important. For all leadership styles, both inter- and intrapersonal context will play a role in influencing how communications unfold. More generally, as leadership is an inherently social process where the strength of the relationships built with employees is important for a leader's effectiveness, various social (verbal) and emotional (non-verbal) skills such as expressiveness, sensitivity and control are important for leaders to hone.

LEARNING OUTCOME 3: Recognise that conflict may be inevitable and can be either dysfunctional or functional.

Conflict occurs where two people with apparent differences seek to resolve those differences to achieve their aims. It is often considered that conflict is not normal and is a sign that something is wrong. A different way of thinking about conflict is that it is inevitable and occurs because individuals can have fundamentally opposing needs. When viewed as inevitable, rather than an aberration, conflict can be thought of as functional because it airs those differences. Positive and innovative outcomes can be achieved where conflict is constructively and creatively resolved.

LEARNING OUTCOME 4: Differentiate between various conflict resolution approaches of leaders.

The conflict resolution styles of leaders are influenced by how they understand and relate to the nature of conflict and power. Conflict resolution styles include competing, collaborating, accommodating, avoiding and compromising.

REVIEW QUESTIONS

1. What is the transactional model of communication? Explain its components and discuss its usefulness in understanding leader communications.

2. Explain how an individual's leadership style influences how they communicate with their staff. Use examples to illustrate your points.

3. Discuss the importance of social and emotional skills when communicating. Also draw on your understanding of verbal and non-verbal communication channels in your response.

4. Describe how conflict can be functional.

5. Describe the five different conflict resolution styles as they relate to cooperativeness and competitiveness.

CASE STUDY 9.4

Leading and managing conflict 'under fire'

Major General John Patrick Cantwell (AO, DSC) is a retired Australian Army officer. Starting as a regular soldier with the rank of Private in the Australian Army in 1974, Cantwell's illustrious 38-year career with the Australian Army resulted in him rising through the ranks of the Australian Army and receiving various accolades. In 1990–91, as an exchange officer with the British Armed Services, the then Major Cantwell commanded a British tank squadron during Operation Desert Storm in Saudi Arabia, Iraq and Kuwait. Fifteen years later, in 2006, while on operation in Iraq Cantwell was promoted to the rank of Major General by General George Casey and Major General David Fastabend of the United States Army. At the same time, the United States recognised his services with the award of Officer of the Legion of Merit. He has also received the Distinguished Service Cross (DSC) for his work in leading troops in Afghanistan and is an Officer of the Order of Australia (AO). However, General Cantwell's story reflects the reality that many service men and women have faced upon their return from conflict and the horrors of war. In his book *Exit Wounds* (Cantwell & Bearup, 2012), he recounts his experiences of dealing with post-traumatic stress disorder and depression and he is now an advocate for raising awareness of mental health issues in the defence forces.

Given this background, it's perhaps not surprising that Major General Cantwell is much sought after to share his experiences of leadership in the battle field. He has spoken about his own views of leadership and has reflected on the need for leaders to remember that leading is not just about them. In an interview with Rob Blackmore and John Coghill on 90.3 ABC Sunshine Coast, he elaborated:

> They (leaders) get in their head that 'I'm the leader, I'm the decision-maker, I'm entitled to respect, I'm entitled to a helicopter ride when I could drive a car … Stop using the word 'I'; stop thinking about 'me' (Blackmore & Coghill, 2015).

In the same interview he went on to describe how the notion of leadership as service, or servant leadership, informs his leadership practice:

> you're there to make them (your followers) successful. You're there to encourage, inspire and lead them. To inform them and to pick them up when they fall down.

In this way, he stated, leaders are there to 'serve your people, your company, or your nation depending on where you fit'. In his book, and in an interview with Leigh Sales on the ABC's *7.30 Report* (Sales, 2015), Major General Cantwell recounted an experience he had as a 34-year-old major in command of a British tank squadron in the Middle East in 1990–91. In his interview he describes how, as a middle-ranking officer, he was in charge of two young British soldiers. The three of them had been under heavy fire for two days, trapped in a tank like a 'metal box'. External communications had been knocked out. Cantwell advised the two young soldiers that, to fix communications, they had to get outside to put up a larger antenna. One soldier responded with 'Get stuffed. That's stupid. We'll get killed' and the other didn't respond at all. In his interview Cantwell noted that 'It's not like in the movies where, you know, Clint Eastwood says, "Follow me, men" and they all go. It's not like that'. He recounted how he needed to overcome his own fear and just 'lead, lead'. Cantwell went on to describe how he gave the two soldiers 'a little pep talk', which he described as 'crappy … but it got the message across'. He explained why the replacing of the antenna was important, what was expected of them and how proud he was of them for what they had done. In essence, Cantwell showed both soldiers their mutual interest in replacing the antenna. The result was that both soldiers followed him outside and successfully accomplished a dangerous job.

When asked how he had built such a relationship with those two soldiers, such that they were willing to listen to him and follow him into such a dangerous situation, Major General Cantwell explained:

> well, I try to be a real human being. You know, I'm the officer, they were the soldiers. But you can communicate and relate to people in ways that show you have some humanity. You're not just some mandarin who issues orders (Sales, 2015).

It can be easy to stereotype leadership in the defence forces as authoritarian, but Major General Cantwell's view is that while being a disciplinarian 'might get compliance', it 'won't get loyalty'. He suggests that to get loyalty, a leader needs to 'show people that you care about them, (that) you genuinely care about them as people, not just as some commodity'. And how does he describe receiving loyalty back from those he is leading? 'It's gold!' (Sales, 2015).

Source: Blackmore & Coghill (2015); Cantwell & Bearup (2012); Sales (2015)

Critical thinking questions
1. Thinking about the transactional model of communication, how did context and noise impact upon the communication process in the examples Major General Cantwell discusses?
2. Thinking about styles of leadership and the social skills model, what elements of these frameworks can describe the type of leadership Major General Cantwell practises? In the context of being in a theatre of war, do you think this style of leadership is effective?
3. It is rare that dissent and conflict occurs in organisations under such life-threatening conditions as those described above. Sometimes, however, conflict needs to be resolved very quickly. In addition, it is often thought that in a 'command and control' organisation such as the army, this type of intragroup conflict does not occur, yet clearly it does. What do you think you would have done if you needed to resolve a conflict like the one between Major Cantwell and the two soldiers quickly? Why?

REFERENCES

Barrett, D. (2006). Strong communication skills a must for today's leaders. *Handbook of Business Strategy*, 7(1), 385–90.

Blake, R.R. & Mouton, J.S. (1964). *The managerial grid*. Houston, TX: Gulf Publications.

Blackmore, R. & Coghill, J. (2015). Leadership laid bare by former army boss John Cantwell. Broadcast, Australian Broadcasting Corporation, 19 August.

Cantwell, J. & Bearup, G. (2012). *Exit wounds: One Australian's war on terror*. Carlton, Vic.: Melbourne University Press.

Cooper, H. (2012). South Australian Liberals at odds with Abbott over Murray–Darling plan. Broadcast, Australian Broadcasting Corporation, 11 January.

Crampton, S., Hodge, J. & Mishra, J. (1998). The informal communication network: Factors influencing grapevine activity. *Public Personnel Management*, 27(4), 569–84.

Dahl, R. (1957). The concept of power. *Systems Research and Behavioral Science*, 2(3), 201–15.

Darioly, A. & Mast, M.S. (2014). The role of nonverbal behavior in leadership: An integrative review. In R. Riggio & S.J. Tan (eds), *Leader interpersonal and influence skills: The soft skills of leadership*. (pp. 73–100). New York, NY: Routledge.

De Vito, J.A. (2007). *The interpersonal communication book*. Boston, MA: Allyn & Bacon.

Fells, R. (2016). *Effective negotiation: From research to results*, 3rd edn. Port Melbourne, Vic: Cambridge University Press.

Fisher, R., Ury, W. & Patton, B. (1991). *Getting to yes: Negotiating agreement without giving in*, 2nd edn. New York, NY: Penguin.

Follett, M.P. (1924) *Creative experience*. New York, NY: Longman Green & Co (repr. Peter Owen, London, 1951).

Forman, J. & Argenti, P. (2005). How corporate communication influences strategy implementation, reputation and the corporate brand: An exploratory qualitative study. *Corporate Reputation Review*, 8(3), 245.

Goldhaber, G.M. (1989). *Organizational communication*, 5th edn. Boston: McGraw-Hill Higher Education.

Hackman, M. & Johnson, C. (2013). *Leadership: A communication perspective*, 6th edn. Long Grove, IL: Waveland Press.

Kilmann, R.H. & Thomas, K.W. (1975). Interpersonal conflict-handling behavior as reflections of Jungian personality dimensions. *Psychological Reports*, 37, 971–80.

Kolb D. (1999). *The Kolb Learning Style Inventory, Version 3*. Boston: Hay Group.

Legge, K. (2015). Gail Kelly explains true leadership. *The Australian*, 1 August. Retrieved from: www.theaustralian.com.au/business/gail-kelly-explains-true-leadership/news-story/e8ae0 6ea4125f99b3a2c019b21d5ccd7.

Lewicki, R.J., Saunders, D.M. & Barry, B. (2015). *Negotiation*, 7th edn. New York, NY: McGraw-Hill Education.

McShane, S., Olekalns, M. & Travaglione, T. (2013). *Organizational behaviour: Emerging knowledge, global insights*. North Ryde, NSW: McGraw-Hill.

Mintzberg, H. (1989). *Mintzberg on management: Inside our strange world of organizations*. New York, NY: Free Press.

Moon, J. (1999). *Learning journals: A handbook for academics, students and professional development*. London: Kogan Page.

Murphy, D. (2005). CEO who gave birth to triplets. *The Age*, 3 July. Retrieved from: www.theage.com.au/news/business/ceo-who-gave-birth-to-triple ts/2005/07/02/1119724845747.html.

Price, R. (2016). 'It's a beautiful thing': Nanaia Mahuta encourages Maori to wear moko with pride. *Stuff*, 17 August. Retrieved from: www.stuff.co.nz/national/politics/83252777/Its-a-beautiful-thing-Nanaia-Mahuta-encourages-Maori-to-wear-moko-with-pride.

Priest, S. & Gass, M.A. (2005). *Effective leadership in adventure programming*. Champaign, IL: Human Kinetics.

Pruitt, D. & Rubin, J. (1986). *Social conflict escalation, stalemate, and settlement*. New York, NY: Random House.

Raiffa, H. (1982). *The art and science of negotiation*. Cambridge, MASS: Harvard University Press.

Riggio, R. (2014). A social skills model for understanding the foundations of leader communication. In R. Riggio & S.J. Tan (eds), *Leader interpersonal and influence skills: The soft skills of leadership*. (pp. 31–50). New York, NY: Routledge.

Roy, E. (2016). 'This is who I am', says first female MP to wear Māori facial tattoo in NZ parliament. *The Guardian*, 11 August. Retrieved from: www.theguardian.com/world/2016/aug/11/first-woman-mp-maori-facial-tattoo-nz-parliament-moko-kauae.

Sales, L. (2015). Leadership lessons from Australia's top military commander. Broadcast, Australian Broadcasting Corporation, 26 August.

Shannon, C. & Weaver, W. (1948). A mathematical theory of communication. *Bell System Technical Journal*, 27, 379–423.

Shriberg, D. & Shriberg, A. (2010). *Practicing leadership principles and applications*, 4th edn. Chichester, UK: John Wiley & Sons.

Steinberg, S. (1995). *Introduction to communication course book 1: The basics*. Cape Town, South Africa: Juta & Co.

Thomas, K. (1976). Conflict and conflict management. In M.D. Dunnette (ed.), *Handbook of industrial and organizational psychology* (pp. 889–935). Chicago: Rand-McNally.

Ulmer, R., Sellnow, T. & Seeger, M. (2015). *Effective crisis communication: Moving from crisis to opportunity*. Thousand Oaks, CA: SAGE Publications.

Walker, R. (2015). *Strategic management communication for leaders*, 3rd edn. Stamford, CT: Cengage.

Walton, R. & McKersie, R. (1965). *A behavioral theory of labor negotiations*. Ithaca, NY: ILR Press.

Waterhouse J., Keast R. & Brown K. (2011). *Negotiating the business environment: Theory and practice for all governance styles*. Prahran, Vic.: Tilde University Press.

West, R. & Turner, L.H. (2008). *Understanding interpersonal communication: Making choices in changing times*. Boston: Cengage Learning.

—— (2017). *IPC (Interpersonal Communication)*, 3rd edn. Boston: Cengage Learning.

Wood, J.T. (2013). *Communication mosaics: An introduction to the field of communication*. Belmont, CA: Thomson Wadsworth.

10

LEADING TEAMS, COACHING AND MENTORING

Nuttawuth Muenjohn and Adela McMurray

LEARNING OUTCOMES

After reading this chapter, you should be able to:

1. identify the general stages of team development and types of effective teams

2. illustrate the characteristics of effective teams

3. explain the role of the leader in effective teams

4. explain the leader–member exchange (LMX) leadership model and its development

5. understand how to apply coaching models, skills and techniques to build and develop effective teams.

INTRODUCTION

THIS CHAPTER DISCUSSES teams and teamwork from three perspectives. First, it focuses on what makes an effective team. It defines work groups and work teams, and explains Tuchman's four stages of team development (forming, storming, norming and performing). In addition, the types and characteristics of an effective team are outlined.

Second, the chapter discusses the role of the leader and team members in team effectiveness. The four-stage development of the leader–member exchange (LMX) model of leadership is explained, highlighting that leadership is a multifaceted construct built on the dyadic relationship between the leader and the follower.

Third, this chapter explains the relationship between coaching and leadership. Coaching skills, techniques and models are discussed to help effect successful coaching practices. By illustrating the key differences between coaching and mentoring, we show that coaching and mentoring are not distinct practices, but rather can be constructed as a continuum of practice. Both coaching and mentoring aim to help people to develop skills, improve performance and reach their potential, achieving a sense of meaning from their work and performance.

UNDERSTANDING TEAMWORK
Work groups and teams

Work groups comprise three or more people who have a certain degree of similarity (Annett & Stanton, 2000), share a common frame of reference and perform a common task by interacting regularly. They may work together and have other common ties, but they may also have different work goals, which they pursue either collaboratively or in competition. Their behaviours and outcomes are interdependent, which means that they may have common work outcomes (Levine & Moreland, 1991), but how they achieve these may vary. A work group is likely to have group members who focus on their individual contributions to the task (Koch, 2015). The group composition can be highly varied even though people tend to seek predictability when choosing work group members (Hinds et al., 2000). Differences between group members may affect a team's performance, although this depends on many factors (Knippenberg & Schippers, 2007), including the diversity of the group, the cultural and work norms of the group members and the extent of cultural differences between them (Thomas 1999). Managing tensions related to diverse group membership, so that all group members function well, requires all group members to feel respected and valued, at a minimum (Ely & Thomas 2001).

> **Work groups** – Three or more people who have a certain degree of similarity, share a common frame of reference, and perform a common task by interacting regularly.

Work systems are often designed with teams of people working together. A **team** can also be a group, but not all groups are teams (Annett & Stanton, 2000). This is because a team is specifically defined as 'two or more individuals who share common task objectives, perform interdependent tasks, and are

> **Team** – Two or more individuals who share common task objectives, perform interdependent tasks, and are mutually accountable for collective task outcomes.

mutually accountable for collective task outcomes' (Chen et al., 2007, p. 331). The characteristic that makes a group into a team is that the members share a common goal or target that is collectively and collaboratively pursued (Annett & Stanton, 2000; Koch, 2015). In pursuing a shared purpose and common goals, the team share their skills in cooperation with each other (National Council for Voluntary Organisations, 2014). A team's members share in the success or failure of their team, and there is now great interest in how teams with shared goals can be developed so that they work together effectively and cohesively. Generally, teams are comprised of specialised individuals who contribute to achieving the team's goal. The question of how each individual contributes to the team performance and towards meeting the outcomes is complex because the success of the team is rarely down to the isolated effort of one person. Many factors influence team effectiveness, including the political skill of individual team members, trust between team members, and their awareness of time and deadlines (Lvina et al., 2016; Gersick, 1988). Analysis of team dynamics, team tasks and team performance is fundamental to understanding how to design organisations for team effectiveness.

Strengths and weaknesses of work teams

In successful teams, all team members are developed so that they can focus on and achieve shared outcomes, and yet even teams that do so are not guaranteed to succeed. Notable weaknesses include a narrowing of options for work process, as team preferences come to replace individual ways of working. Internal conflicts may arise and team communication may become difficult, as different perspectives need to be accommodated into team goals and targets. This may cause resentment for team members who do not have responsibility for setting team goals. Teams bring together a range of different people, talents and skills, but without skilful alignment of the team these differences can be sources of ongoing tensions in the workplace. Another source of weakness of teams is the risk that team members may make unequal contribution to work, leading to issues when those who contributed less receive the same rewards as those who contributed more. Some teams, left unchecked, can develop their own sub-culture which can create divisions within the organisation (Koch, 2015). Not all teams are successful and produce gains for the organisation, but a team's strength depends on effective management of a range of issues such as these, requiring ongoing and systematic development.

Stages of team development

Teams can be formed in several different ways, depending on the context, tasks and team members. While there are general stages of team development, not all complexities associated with working in a team can be explained as a sequence. Some teams may never reach the norm of performance and may never progress through the stages of development (Rickards & Moger, 2000). Team members need to bond and gradually mature into working together effectively, at which point they are more likely to be able to focus on achieving their shared goals.

The formation of teams can be messy and complex, and each team has its own way of building habits of collaboration (Mohr & Dichter, 1996). The most widely recognised way of forming teams draws on the work of Tuckman and co-authors (Tuckman, 1965; Tuckman & Jensen, 1977), who identified that small teams go through four distinct stages of team development. In Tuckman's studies, a group tested their dependence on each other as they became oriented to their task. Team members tended to respond emotionally to the demands of their tasks, and some experienced intra-group conflict (see Chapter 9). Through open discussion of what has caused the conflict, the members can begin to engage in resolution through communication, working together towards greater mutual engagement and ultimately to reach a solution. At the final stage, the team moves towards functional roles. Tuckman presented these four stages as 'forming', 'storming', 'norming' and 'performing' (Tuckman, 1965; Tuckman & Jensen, 1977).

Forming a team: The development stage

The forming stage brings together individuals responding to identified issues, problems or scenarios. To form a team, several organisational and team development activities need to occur for the team to become functional and effective in responding to the initial call for the team to develop, notably:

- building collective knowledge about team members
- common goals: shared mission or vision
- decision-making methods
- group limits to the work
- capacity and priorities (Mohr & Dichter, 1996).

Storming: The conflict stage

The second phase of team development, the storming phase, focuses on the team learning to work together to achieve the desired goals or outcomes. This stage requires specific team learning and the building of trust between team members as people have differences and must learn how best to deal with them. This stage of team development is often mired in conflict.

This is a valuable and natural stage of team development because a group without conflict may experience difficulties where points of view are suppressed and inhibited, thereby obstructing opportunities to engage in solutions (Miles, 1971). The essential part of the conflict stage is to develop a strategy for dealing with conflict; for example, warning the group that conflict will arise and that it is part of team development can lessen anxiety when it happens. The conflict stage is when team members learn about and acquire skills for negotiating, mediating and resolving intra-team conflict (Mohr & Dichter, 1996). Team leaders and members may be tempted to ignore conflict, but this can lead to further issues in the development of the team, such as resentment that influences the quality of team performance. The role of the team leader is critical in this conflict phase because he or she requires the courage to identify, expose and confront difficult issues. For example, issues that arise from team differences in race, gender, class and so forth may call on a team leader's most advanced skills in conflict resolution. It may be tempting, too, for team members to rely on the team leader to resolve conflict on behalf of the team, but the value from the conflict stage of team development is that the team learns to manage their own conflicts (Schwarz, 2000).

Norming: The messy stage

When the team starts to gel and establishes a set of ground rules for team behaviour and team norms, team members' desire to live up to team norms becomes more influential than management directives (Mackey, 1999).

Sometimes, a team falls into the trap of 'process worship' (Mohr & Dichter, 1996, p. 7), where they follow process and procedures to achieve set goal and outcomes, without question. The issue here is that the team may rely on rote ways of working, rather than continuously using their judgement to gauge their progress towards goals, or learning to work effectively with ambiguity in decision making. This stage of team development requires multiple forms of communication that enable strong collaboration and collective responsibility. The team needs to develop a system of communication that will allow differences to emerge yet also enable real solutions to be developed:

> It is important that the group build an accountability system that ensures its work is based on substantive information and data and not solely on the opinions and preferences of its members. Accountability is built on the lateral flow of information sharing and on the group's ability to critique itself. It is in this stage that the group begins to see itself as a professional learning community rather than merely a decision-making group (Mohr & Dichter, 1996, p. 10).

Performing: The mature stage

When the team matures and is performing its functional tasks well, the challenge for the team leader is to enable the team to operate sustainably at this level. The characteristics of a team in the performing stage include:

- high levels of motivation
- creativity
- a clear focus on results
- confident team members
- continuous learning
- functional relationships (Koch, 2015).

Maintaining a sense of purpose and focus during this stage is critical, as the context for the team's work and the projects they work on change over time. Dealing with conflict needs to occur early so that divisions do not develop between team members. While few interventions need to happen at this phase, team meetings and workshops can help to steer team progress and team strategy. Team-building activities such as regular workshops may be used to foster ideas for improvement in a team's work practices (Koch, 2015).

Team types

Teams are created for different purposes. There are at least six types of teams.

Strategic teams

Strategic teams are part of the leadership of an organisation focused on setting organisational goals. They monitor the external environment to determine the organisation's direction by setting key objectives, developing strategic plans and monitoring progress of the organisation. Strategic teams are important in providing organisational leadership.

Management teams

Management teams are responsible for setting out more detailed organisational development strategies that focus on the day-to-day organisational operations. They devise detailed objectives, plan operations, allocate resources and organise the work. Management teams provide leadership in the day-to-day running of the organisation and its people.

Project teams

As projects and tasks arise, temporary teams are formed to respond as required. The make-up of the project team depends on the requirements of the tasks and potential team members with the necessary skills. Team members usually come from different departments and bring together a range of expertise focused on having a specific result as a target (for example, developing a new product, a marketing campaign, or beginning a new project). The project team usually has clear guidelines about its role and objectives and is associated with a budget, timeline, and resources available to achieve targets. Once the team has delivered the project, the team is dissolved (Koch, 2015).

Operational teams

Operational teams are more likely to work directly with people, providing goods and services as required. They are the front line of the organisation and perform the key tasks, implement policies, and perform their work in accordance to established standards and benchmarks. Operational teams are often the 'face' of the organisation (National Council for Voluntary Organisations, 2014).

Support teams

Support teams enable others to do their job by providing backup and support so the work is done effectively and efficiently. The support team may provide technical support, such as IT services, or financial or human resource support. Support teams work in the background and their work can be less visible; however, without effective support teams, organisational goals cannot be efficiently achieved.

Virtual teams

A virtual team is comprised of geographically dispersed members who use technological communications to enable teamwork towards shared outcomes. They rarely meet in person and tend not to travel routinely to each other's work sites. Virtual teams collaborate onscreen (Sarker & Sahay, 2003, p. 2) via computers, tablets and mobile phones, and use enabling technologies such as Skype, Google Hangouts, email, online collaboration platforms and other electronic work tools.

Characteristics of teams

To create an effective team requires development of individuals' capabilities in the core skills and tools required to complete core work (Clark & Wheelwright, 1992); that is, teams need to have skills for both task work and teamwork, to be effective (Salas et al., 1992). While there are several different ways to develop teams, depending on the work and the tasks, several common characteristics shape effective teams.

1. *Clear goals*: Team goals should have meaning and resonate with each team member. Developing goals using SMART criteria can help clarify the targets for the team, and through understanding of the goals each team member can build their engagement and commitment to the team targets (Zaccaro et al., 2002).

2. *Aligned roles*: Having clearly defined roles and responsibilities means that each team member understands their contribution to the team tasks. This requires team members that are competent and are a good fit for the team dynamics. In fulfilling their role, the team member can demonstrate their talents and skills and their commitment to the team and team success.

3. *Effective processes*: This includes effective planning, follow up and control procedures. The way that the team works together is coordinated, allowing the team to bond and coordinate their work to be both efficient and effective. An effective way of working together creates high-performing team norms and the high standards shape the team culture and practices of team members (Warrick, 2016).

4. *Effective communication*: Ensuring that the team can utilise multiple communication methods and channels allows them to mutually construct shared meaning (Warrick, 2016).

5. *Appropriate leadership*: Leadership is a key factor in team effectiveness (Yoo & Alavi, 2004). Participative leadership uses a democratic leadership style to involve and engage team members. The role of the leader changes as the team members mature and become more successful. The leader needs to foster self-management, especially in problem solving, so the team can continue to perform in a range of environments. The leader's role is to enable teams to become self-managers (Bell & Kozlowski, 2002).

6. *Support, trust and openness*: Several components contribute to this team characteristic. In a team of this sort, team members trust each other and have a sense of their team's trustworthiness as an entity. An open team deals with conflicts openly and transparently and does not allow grudges to fester and damage team morale. This type of team values team diversity, recognising, acknowledging and valuing the diversity of team members' experience and backgrounds, and contributing to various viewpoints. This tends to lead to better decision making and solutions (National Council for Voluntary Organisations, 2014).

7. *Development of team members*: The team can only achieve outcomes when its members have the required competencies for both task work and teamwork. Effective team development includes the professional development of individual team members to ensure that all member strengths are used. By encouraging ongoing professional development, the team can also develop independently and bring new skills and thinking into the team (Warrick, 2016). By encouraging team-planning activities and the metacognitive processes that should follow team performance, leaders can facilitate team learning in discrete performance episodes (Zaccaro et al., 2002).

8. *Team relations*: The team should maintain a positive and flexible working relationship to ensure that it can respond to changes and demand. Team culture requires to be open and positive (Warrick, 2016); it needs to be future focused to be able to continue to evolve and maintain positive atmosphere (National Council for Voluntary Organisations, 2014).

CASE STUDY 10.1

Thankyou

Thankyou is a social enterprise that exists to help end global poverty by committing 100 per cent of the profit from their water, personal care and baby products to fund sustainable development work around the world. In 2008, 19-year-old Daniel Flynn, Thankyou's Co-founder and Managing Director, discovered that 900 million people worldwide didn't have access to safe drinking water, yet the Australian bottled water industry was selling $600 million worth of bottled water per year. Inspired to do something, Daniel enlisted his best friend Jarryd Burns and then girlfriend, now wife, Justine Flynn, and together they came up with the idea to launch a bottled water that would fund safe water projects around the world.

The group, while working part-time jobs and juggling university degrees, volunteered their time over three and a half years to make the dream a reality. The team was told they faced over $250 000 of start-up expenses, not to mention the millions of dollars they would need to market the brand; they now often joke they had a combined net worth of about $1000 at the time. Despite the lack of cash flow, they set up meetings with bottling factories until finally they secured their first production of Thankyou water, minus any upfront costs.

After initial success and a lot of excitement, the team experienced a series of setbacks including two recalls, trouble with bottlers and distribution deals with several major retailers falling through. Finally, in 2011, they took a big leap forward and landed a huge deal with 7-Eleven Australia thanks to their social media campaign that asked fans to back them.

By 2013, Thankyou water was available to purchase in over 3000 retail outlets, but the major supermarkets still refused to stock Thankyou products. The team decided to launch another disruptive social media campaign, calling on the support of their Facebook fans to get their products into Coles and Woolworths. Thousands of Thankyou supporters across Australia answered the call, and by the end of the year Thankyou products started rolling out in supermarkets around the country.

In 2016, Thankyou launched a book written by Daniel Flynn called Chapter One. It tells the story of Thankyou's start-up journey and is sold at a pay-what-you-want price to help fund the future of Thankyou. The book campaign aimed to raise $1.2 million in four weeks to fund the Thankyou baby range and the launch of Thankyou New Zealand. In what became a record-breaking four weeks, Thankyou raised $1.45 million and sold 55 000 books, making it a bestseller.

To date, Thankyou has funded life-changing projects for over 785 000 people in need around the world.

Source: Thankyou, reproduced with permission

Critical thinking question
After reading this case study, what do you think are the keys to the success of Thankyou?

TEAM STRUCTURE: ALIGNING STRENGTHS AND WEAKNESSES OF TEAM MEMBERS

Team roles summarise the way we tend to behave, contribute and interrelate to the team over a period of time, often develop informally and may go unacknowledged.

The leader's role in an effective team

In today's organisational landscape, where teams drive productivity and achievement of work goals, traditional definitions of leadership as a positional construct have given way to relational and interpersonal definitions of leadership (Seers et al., 2003). As team types and compositions vary, team leadership also varies, in the interests of alignment with the team, its goals and challenges.

Most common in current definitions of leadership is the social influence role of leaders. Regarding team leadership, there are two distinct ways to characterise the role of the leader. Leaders of teams may shape and impact team processes and outcomes, but there is also team leadership, that is, leadership that develops within teams responsive to the set tasks and targets (Day et al., 2006). Both types of leadership influence effective teams.

Most of the research on team leadership has focused on a formally appointed leader who can provide the necessary resources for the team to complete responsibilities, activities and work. This can be considered a top-down approach to team leadership (Day et al., 2006). The effectiveness and quality of the team leader depends on their capacity to shape the processes and performance of the team. Some argue that being able to effectively shape processes is the most significant factor in enabling teams to achieve successfully (Zaccaro et al., 2002). The leader requires skills that guide and structure the team experiences, creates team coherence and ensures the adaptive capacity of the team is progressing and achieving their goals and tasks (Kozlowski et al., 1996).

To facilitate team effectiveness (Hackman, 2002), the leader needs to ensure that the team is real; that is, highly functional and stable, working on a clear task with well-defined boundaries, and holding enough capacity to manage work expectations. The team must have clear direction and purpose in a context that enables the team to work. An enabling context is created in the way the work is designed, conducted and organised. In addition to creating enabling conditions for the team to achieve set tasks, leaders can provide support by creating rewards systems and providing training opportunities.

The function of the team leader to enable the effectiveness of the team has been described as an ongoing process of social problem solving relative to four areas: information and data gathering, information implementation towards solving problems, management and supervision of team members, and managing resources (Burke et al., 2006). While leading through these four areas it has been argued that leaders take on different roles such as facilitator, instructor, mentor and coach (Kozlowski et al., 1996). A leader is effective when he or she has ensured that all functions essential to the team's task are completed to a determined standard.

When the team is mature and becomes a highly performing team, the role of the appointed leader may change and be less influential in setting the team's direction and goals. In this case, the team's collective capacity for self-direction may reduce the need for formal leadership interventions (Kozlowski et al., 1996), enabling the leader to step back from directing teamwork and managing team performance (Zaccaro et al., 2002).

The leader–member exchange (LMX) leadership model

The leader–member exchange (LMX) model was first theorised in the late 1990s as an alternative to leadership theories and practices that focused solely on the role of the leader without much information about the role of the follower in the leadership dynamics (Graen & Uhl-Bien, 1995). It has been defined as 'the quality of the social exchange between leaders and followers, characterised by mutual trust, respect, and obligation' (Chen et al., 2007, p. 333). Underlying the development of the LMX model is conceptualising leadership as involving three domains: the leader, the follower and the relationship. Studies of leadership may focus on each domain independently, such as trait or behavioural theories of leadership, or in combinations, for example, situational approaches to leadership. The LMX model of leadership emphasises the three domains of leadership, consolidating the idea that leadership is a multifaceted construct built on the dyadic relationship between the leader and the follower. There have been four stages in the evolution of the LMX concept, each of which reflects the multifaceted development of leadership and the processes leadership uses.

Stage 1

Studies on socialisation in the early 1970s showed that, contrary to popular leadership theories that focused on the effective leadership as behavioural actions, the success of managerial processes were social and dyadic. To achieve desired outcomes managers were developing differentiated relationships with their direct reports (Graen & Uhl-Bien, 1995). It became evident that differentiated leader and member relationships were important to achieving outcomes. The research showed that when members were asked to describe their leader, they gave strongly divergent descriptions of the same person. When analysing the quality of the leadership exchanges, some members reported high mutual trust, respect and reciprocal obligations between themselves and the leader. Another group of members reported almost the opposite. This led the researchers to conclude that the high-quality exchanges between leader and follower cemented a relationship where the follower was like a 'trusted assistant'; while in the low-quality exchanges the follower was like a 'hired hand' (Zalesny, 1987). The discovery of these differentiated dyads defines the first stage in the evolution of LMX leadership. This relationship between the leader and the follower became known as the 'vertical dyad linkage' (VDL).

Stage 2

The second stage of the development of LMX leadership focused closely on the quality of leader–member exchanges. The extensive research unpacking the context and the process of exchange ranged from macro factors such as organisational climate, cross-cultural issue and workplace performance, detailing a broad range of contextual conditions that influence the quality of leader–member exchanges. The research investigated the quality of the relationship from the intra-connections between leader and member. For example, these are the role of communication frequency, the patterns of communication, the patterns of interaction, the construction of roles, and the strategies and tactics in the interactions patterns. These extensive interrogations of the relationship between leaders and members further evidenced how the differentiated relationships developed and functioned. Their findings supported the contention that positive relationship that created high-quality exchange produced desired outcomes. This stage outlined a set of characteristics of LMX relationships and the implications for organisations and leadership (Graen & Uhl-Bien, 1995).

Stage 3

The third stage provided the groundwork for an understanding of how high-quality relationships may be achieved, offering explanations for how LMX relationships develop, showing likely consequences for organisations, and articulating how effective leaders can develop and maintain high-quality LMX. The focus is on how managers can work with each member and develop a unique relationship. The key is to move away from thinking about the work member as a subordinate towards developing a working partnership among all the members of the work group. Rather than thinking about leadership as a superior position, leadership is a way to form extensive partnerships. A key development of this stage of the evolution of LMX is the notion of **leadership making**, whereby leaders were trained to offer high-quality relationships with all the members of their group. The results showed that members who accepted the offer by the leader to form a partnership also experienced improvement in their performance. Overall, the results showed that performance and productivity gains were enhanced by increasing the number of high-quality LMX relationships (Graen & Uhl-Bien, 1995).

> **Leadership making** – In the LMX model, a cycle in which a leader's maturity in building relationships is developed. Leaders are trained to build high-quality partnerships with followers, resulting in performance and productivity gains.

Leadership making is described as a cycle in which the maturity of leaders as relationship-builders is developed (Graen & Uhl-Bien, 1995). It begins with the introduction of the leader and the follower as strangers, where the exchanges are formal and contractual based on work obligations. Leaders provide their followers with what they need to get the job done and the followers do as is required. This phase is improved through some career-oriented social exchange offer that is made by the leader and accepted by the follower. The leader and follower, initially unfamiliar with each other, become acquaintances. Increased social exchanges between the leader and the follower are not all based on contractual obligations; rather, there is a greater sharing of information and resources both at the work and more personal levels. These exchanges test the relationship.

A mature partnership between the leader and follower develops when exchanges are in kind; that is, reciprocal and maintained over a longer time span. The leader and follower can count on each other for support and show loyalty to the relationship. The influence of the leader has been described as the core ingredient of leadership (Yukl, 2013) and in this context, as the relationship matures, this influence plays a crucial role in shaping the quality of the exchange. more emotional and involved, leading to the development of mutual trust and respect between leader and follower. This stage of partnership development, drawing on a solid foundation of trust and loyalty between the leader and follower, can lead to marked increases in performance and pay offs in productivity. Leaders can count on their followers to engage in challenging targets and goals, providing partnership assistance when needed. Similarly, the follower can take on challenges without feeling overwhelmed and unsupported. The mature partnership acts to empower and motivate both leader and follower to perform beyond their contract and formalised roles. Members move from working for self-interest towards larger mutual interests.

Effective leadership using the LMX model fosters high-quality partnership relationship building between the leader and his or her followers, and does away with notions of the 'in' and 'out' groups in the interests of fostering consistently high-quality exchanges across the team.

A leader who has advanced to Stage 3 of the LMX model is more equitable, and makes offers of partnership to all group members.

Stage 4

The fourth stage of the LMX model sees the leader expanding partnerships to a wider range of groups, teams and networks in the organisation. A systems perspective aims to bring together the differentiated dyadic relationships to form a larger assembly of teams and networks (Graen & Uhl-Bien, 1995). What emerges from the aggregation of the differentiated dyadic relationship is a structure of leadership. **Leadership structure** is defined as:

Leadership structure – The pattern of leadership relationships among individuals throughout the organisation.

> the pattern of leadership relationships among individuals throughout the organisation. This structure includes but is not limited to the work unit. Rather, the relationships that make up the leadership structure cut across work unit, functional, divisional, and even organizational boundaries (Graen & Uhl-Bien, 1995, p. 234).

The structure of LMX-based leadership emerges from how leadership is practised, which reveals how the work is done and completed. In other words, the structure of leadership is revealed though patterns of relationship forming through work on a task, and how differentiated relationships among the members facilitate the completion of tasks. A key focus for leaders is to understand how to enact positive relationships that influence the interplay both between individuals within the team and with the team as an entity (Chen et al., 2007). The leader cannot assume that, having formed differentiated relationships with each individual team member, he or she will automatically have the same level of influence with the team as a whole.

Developing commitment and motivation among team members

Achieving and reaching team goals requires that team members are committed to the task and that this commitment is shared by all members of the group (Zaccaro et al., 2002). **Motivation** refers to behaviours that increase team members' efforts to achieve success. Motivational behaviours are positive affirmations and do not involve any coercion-based influence. Behaviours that are associated with motivation include: reward and recognition of performance, provision of support and the affirmation of needs and values of team members.

Motivation – Behaviours that increase team members' efforts to achieve success. Motivational behaviours are positive affirmations and do not involve any coercive influences.

Examples of motivational behaviours may include public statements affirming encouragement of team activities and positive comments regarding team capabilities. Motivation of teams is critical as it can influence the amount and duration of effort that individuals contribute to a task. As tasks become more complex and require adaptive changes, the extra effort required to manage and coordinate work requires added motivation (Burke et al., 2006). The quality of team cohesion and collective identity and efficacy affects levels of motivation (Zaccaro et al., 2002). The effectiveness of the team rests on members being motivated to work on behalf of the team. The team leader carries critical responsibility for team motivation and may use overt motivational strategies such as agreeing to development support for team members and providing quality feedback.

Virtual, self-managed and international teams

Increasingly, organisations are using self-managing or self-directing work teams in lieu of formalised management and supervision (Seers et al., 2003). Virtual teams – also known as 'distributed' or 'remote' teams – face particular challenges due to the various gaps between team members, for example, different geographical locations, cultural contexts, time zones, languages, company expectations and even management structures (Griesinger & Schmitt, 2016). Creating an effective virtual team means being able to rapidly reduce such gaps between members, so that the team can rapidly and effectively establish collaborative relationships and work towards early achievement of shared goals (Sarker & Sahay, 2003).

Despite the increasing demand for virtual teams, understanding how these teams develop is a complex process because of the different processes and contexts that are part of team collaboration. Establishing a set of process standards and expectations that team members can readily understand helps to create the positive conditions for effective virtual collaboration (Delery & Shaw, 2001).

Team members need a shared understanding of their common mission and purpose, and each individual needs to feel clear on how they will contribute towards achievement of the team's goals. The team should have common markers for success, and be agreed on the milestones that they will meet as they progress towards the desired outcomes. Having understood the task and the processes involved in achieving those outcomes, each team member is responsible for managing their own performance to achieve the same standards as other team members (Eubanks et al., 2016).

Effective leadership of virtual teams may require leaders to have specific skills in logistical coordination and organisation, beyond the more traditional leadership skill of providing expert guidance to team members. The virtual team is more likely to operate in a form of distributed leadership in which the expertise is distributed among the team members. Virtual team members adopt a range of leadership and management roles as needed. Some of the key functions that the team needs to adopt include individual team performance management, problem solving, identifying shared values, setting safety standards and maintaining inventory. The leader traditionally performs these tasks, but in the case of the virtual team individual team members with specific skills may be responsible for specific leadership tasks (Liff & Gustavson, 2016).

COACHING, MENTORING AND LEADERSHIP

As a team matures, it becomes better able to self-manage, allowing leaders to focus on building the capacity of the team by enabling relationship building and team learning. The leader thus has the opportunity to develop the team and individual team members through coaching.

While there are different forms of coaching, in the context of building and developing effective teams coaching is a way to empower teams and enable team relationships, making it easier for teams to reach functional competency and to embrace learning (Ellinger & Bostrom, 1999). Generally, coaching is a short-term intervention that targets learning to improve some aspect of performance (Deans et al., 2006). Coaching aims to improve competencies and enhance professional judgement, in the interests of driving performance improvement.

Coaching, like leadership, can take on many forms, depending on the situation, the coach and the relationship. In some cases, as with authoritarian leadership, coaching can be based on directive, prescriptive and controlling behaviour. The most effective coaching associated with team development, however, is coaching that empowers team members by encouraging and motivating them to continue to learn and improve their work, relationships and knowledge. Learning, collaboration and discovery are the priorities here (Ellinger & Bostrom, 1999). Coaching aims to improve the performance and skill level of each team member and endeavours to strengthen the relationship between the team member and the coach to develop inner factors that lead team members to success (Popper & Lipshitz, 1992). The quality of the relationship between the team member and the coach has been identified as an important factor in successful coaching (Boyce et al., 2010).

Coaching

Leaders can adopt a range of coaching skills and techniques, depending on the situation and the task at hand. However, there are some guidelines about what successful coaching should do. First, there is the need to identify, and define, what the coach intends to do and how to define successful team or organisational outcomes. Second, the coach needs to create the structure for success by identifying situations that may be used as learning events and have the potential to apply skills and knowledge to succeed. These two factors draw on the coach's capacity to think ahead and plan the process of learning and the potential episodes for success. Third, the coach needs to identify and understand the factors that will lead to success, for example, situational and contextual factors influencing a team member's performance. Fourth, the coach needs to identify and understand the inner sources of success, for example, what drives staff motivation and commitment (Popper & Lipshitz, 1992). These last two factors relate to the concept of reflexive learning, in which an individual engages in self-reflection and reviews the quality of their actions, to deepen his or her understanding of where and how to bring through improvements (Popper & Lipshitz, 1992).

Developing a coaching relationship can be achieved by following these general guidelines that help shape the coaching practice:

- establishing and managing the relationship, which includes getting to know each other, outlining the grounds for the relationship and setting mutual goals and expectations

- setting goals, focusing especially on performance gaps and outcomes
- understanding context so that components of context and situation that may influence goals are understood both intellectually and emotionally
- understanding self-behaviour and the behaviour of others
- dealing with obstacles and being creative in problem solving
- creating action plans
- building networks and alliances (Garvey et al., 2014; Megginson & Clutterbuck, 2005).

The quality of feedback the coach gives is critical to the development and improvement of team performance. Traditionally, interactive feedback between the coach and team member is one in which the coach listens and observes, gives feedback and then clarifies how this feedback can shape the performance of the team member. However, there are multiple ways to provide feedback to team members, such as observational, reflective and third party (Ellinger & Bostrom, 1999).

Coaching models and characteristics

The STEER model

This five-step approach suits coaching for specific tasks and can help structure a formal on-the-job coaching interaction. The coaching helps the individual spot new opportunities for coaching and proceed to tailoring the coaching experience for the individual. The coach needs to explain the purpose of the coaching session and check that there is mutual understanding of the purpose. Once the actions are underway, the role of the coach is to encourage the individual as they make progress through constructive feedback and praise. A progress review is negotiated at specified intervals to keep the learning on track and to monitor the achievement towards specified goals (Paul et al., 2012).

The GROW model

In this four-step coaching model (see Figure 10.1), the coach adopts a Socratic learning approach by using open questions to help the individual move through the four steps (Passmore, 2007).

The OSKAR model

The OSKAR model (Outcome, Scaling, Know-how and Resources, Affirm and Action, and Review) focuses on solutions and replication of good practices to ensure the solution can be repeated (McKergow, 2012). This model aims to envisage a desired future and then the coach moves the individual towards achieving that future. Rather than focus on problem analysis, this model heads straight for solutions (Waldman, 2010).

> **The GROW Model of Coaching**
>
> **G – Goal.** The person's goal should be as specific and measurable as possible, enabling the coach to ask:
> - How will you know that you have achieved that goal?
> - What are the expectations of others?
> - Who else needs to know about the plan? How will you inform them?
>
> **R – Reality.** The current situation the person is experiencing needs careful analysis. Sometimes, simply by seeing the situation clearly (rather than what was imagined), the resolution becomes obvious. Coaches can ask:
> - What has been stopping you reaching your goal?
> - Do you know anyone who has achieved that goal?
> - What can you learn from them?
>
> **O – Options.** Once you know where you are and where you want to go, the next step is to explore the options you have for getting there. Coaches can ask:
> - What could you do as a first step?
> - What else could you do?
> - What would happen if you did nothing?
>
> **W – Will.** To change and improve performance, motivation is necessary. The desired outcome from this stage is a commitment to action. The following questions can guide coaches:
> - Where does this goal fit in with your personal priorities at the moment?
> - What obstacles do you expect to meet? How will you overcome them?
> - How committed are you to this goal?
> - What steps do you need to take to achieve this?

Figure 10.1 The GROW model

Source: Deans et al. (2006, p. 9), reproduced with the permission of INTRAC, Oxbridge Court, Osney Mead, Oxford, OX2 0ES, UK, www.intrac.org

Mentoring

Mentoring – Helping to support people to manage their own learning to maximise their potential, develop their skills, improve their performance and become the person they want to be.

Mentoring can be defined as helping to 'support people to manage their own learning in order to maximise their potential, develop their skills, improve their performance and become the person they want to be' (Murray, 1998). Mentoring can take many forms depending on the identified need, the context and resources available. The mentoring program or scheme is as varied as the people involved and continues to evolve over time. For example, it may occur in teams or as individuals, it may be formal or informal, ad hoc or formally organised. All mentoring schemes require finance, time, people and commitment and effort. Mentoring may focus on a skills approach where the individual is helped to improve their skills and performance. The mentoring may be formal or informal. Mentoring can also occur informally when an individual seeks out a peer or a more skilled colleague, and engages with them to learn from their experience and approaches (Clutterbuck & Ragins, 2002).

The mentoring and coaching debate

At the centre of debate about coaching and mentoring is how 'help' is defined and enacted (Garvey, 2004). Both coaching and mentoring are popular capacity-building tools

(Deans et al., 2006) that help a person to improve their performance. Both involve a direct relationship between two individuals. However, while there is much overlap between the role of a coach and that of a mentor (Garvey, 2004), coaching is more likely to focus on performance in the current role or job and is more task-oriented and skills-focused. Mentoring is more concerned with long-term development goals and is an open-ended process focused on personal development (Deans et al., 2006). The distinction between coaching and mentoring is becoming less important and in practice there is increasing overlap between them. For example, both involve:

- setting expectations for learning and improvement
- building trust through open and honest conversations
- focusing on empowerment of the individual learner
- adapting to context
- relying on effective communication
- encouraging new behaviours (Deans et al., 2006).

Table 10.1 represents the key differences between coaching and mentoring.

Table 10.1 Differences between coaching and mentoring

Coaching	Mentoring
Concerned with task	Concerned with implications beyond the task
Focuses on skills and performance	Focuses on capability and potential
Primarily line manager role	Works best offline
Agenda set by or with coach	Agenda set by learner
Emphasises feedback to the learner	Emphasises feedback and reflection by the learner
Typically addresses a short-term need	Typically a longer relationship, often 'for life'
Feedback and discussion primarily explicit	Feedback and discussion primarily about implicit, intuitive issues and behaviours

Source: Deans et al. (2006, p. 6), reproduced with the permission of INTRAC, Oxbridge Court, Osney Mead, Oxford, OX2 0ES, UK, www.intrac.org

Rather than seeing coaching and mentoring as distinct practices, they can be constructed as a continuum of practices (see Figure 10.2).

Coaching and mentoring aim to assist people in developing their skills, improving their performance and reaching their potential to achieve a sense of meaning from their work and performance.

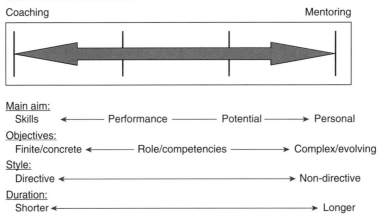

Coach–Mentor Continuum

Coaching   Mentoring

Main aim:
  Skills ←——— Performance ——— Potential ——→ Personal

Objectives:
  Finite/concrete ←——— Role/competencies ——→ Complex/evolving

Style:
  Directive ←————————————————→ Non-directive

Duration:
  Shorter ←————————————————→ Longer

Figure 10.2 The coaching–mentoring continuum

Source: Deans et al. (2006, p. 7). Reproduced with the permission of INTRAC, Oxbridge Court, Osney Mead, Oxford, OX2 0ES, UK, www.intrac.org

CASE STUDY 10.2

David Gonski

David Gonski is the best-connected business professional in Australia. He's the most powerful of the big bank chairs, chairing the ANZ Banking Group and Coca-Cola Amatil, and Chancellor of the University of New South Wales, as well as President of the Art Gallery of New South Wales Trust. He has mentored many leaders in corporate Australia and has helped women break into the 'blokey' directors' club, becoming the go-to person for senior professionals aiming to obtain board and executive roles.

Given this background, Gonski has spoken about his views on mentoring. In an interview, Gonski indicated that he was helped in two ways by mentors. The first of these ways was the advice provided by a past mentor, a NSW Supreme Court Judge, Kim Santow, who gave him the strength to take up an opportunity. The second way in which David indicated that a mentor had provided value was by that person providing knowledge that was based on experience where, as an older person, he had encountered situations that as a young person he found unfamiliar. However, Gonski says that he is not convinced that a supervisor or manager can be an effective mentor, because of the risk that they may have a conflict of interest. If such a conflict arose, the supervisor or mentor might be focused on achieving value for themselves rather than supporting the mentee.

Gonski shows his skill as a mentor in three ways. He always finds time to help, so that in his words, 'you send him a text, he will always make himself available'. He makes useful suggestions, going 'out of his way to know you, your aspirations and background', which means that any advice is specific to the circumstance. Finally, he promotes the interests of anyone that he mentors.

Source: Adapted from Durkin (2015)

Critical thinking question

Think about the qualities of an effective mentor. Who might help you to further your career by providing the inputs identified in the case study?

SUMMARY

LEARNING OUTCOME 1: Identify the general stages of team development and types of effective teams.

Teams can be formed in several different ways, depending on the context, tasks and team members. While there are general stages of team development not all team complexities can be explained be a sequence. The formation of teams can be messy and complex and each team has its own way of building habits of collaboration. The most widely recognised way of forming teams draws on the work of Tuckman, who identified that small teams go through four distinct stages of team development. The forming stage brings together individuals responding to identified issues, problems or scenarios. The second phase of team development, storming, focuses on the team learning to work together to achieve the desired goals or outcomes. This stage of team development is often mired in conflict. When the team starts to gel and it establishes a set of ground rules for team behaviour and team norms, the pressure of measuring up to team norms replaces management directives for team performance. The norming stage requires effective and multiple forms of communication that enable strong collaboration and collective responsibility. When the team matures and is highly functional, the focus is to keep the team operating at that level. This is the performing stage. Some teams may never reach the norm of performance and may never progress through the stages of development.

LEARNING OUTCOME 2: Illustrate the characteristics of effective teams.

While there are several different ways to develop teams, depending on the work and the tasks, there are common characteristics that shape effective teams. Team goals should have meaning and resonate with each team member. Teams need to have clearly defined roles and responsibility that each team member understands their contribution to the team tasks. An effective way of working together is another key characteristic of effective teams, which creates the high-performing team norms and standards that shape the team culture and practices of team members. Effective teams also need to embrace effective and clear communication and to develop mutual trust and support. Leadership is a key factor in team effectiveness. Further, when a leader encourages ongoing professional development, team members can develop independently and bring new skills and thinking back into the team as they acquire them. Finally, the team needs to maintain a positive and flexible working relationship to ensure that it can respond to changes in tasks and context.

LEARNING OUTCOME 3: Explain the role of the leader in effective teams.

Team roles often develop informally over time and may go unacknowledged. Regarding team leadership, there are two distinct ways to characterise the role of the leader. Leaders of teams may shape and impact team processes and outcomes, but there is also team leadership, that is, leadership that develops within teams responsive to the set tasks and targets. Both types of leadership are influential in leading effective teams. The function of the team leader to enable the effectiveness of the team has been described as an ongoing process of social problem solving relative to four areas: information and data gathering, information implementation towards solving problems, managing and supervision of team members, and managing resources. While leading through these four areas, leaders may take on different roles, such as facilitator, instructor, mentor or coach. When a team is mature and high-performing, the role of the leader may change and the need for him or her to influence and set the team's direction and goals may reduce.

LEARNING OUTCOME 4: Explain the leader–member exchange (LMX) leadership model and its development.

Leader–member exchange (LMX) was first theorised in the late 1990s as an alternative to leadership theories and practices that focused solely on the role of the leader without much consideration of the role of the follower. It has been defined as the quality of social exchange between leaders and followers, characterised by mutual trust, respect and obligation. Underlying the development of LMX-based leadership is conceptualising leadership as involving three domains: the leader, the follower and the relationship. The LMX model emphasises three domains of leadership, consolidating the idea that leadership is a multifaceted construct built on the dyadic relationship between the leader and the follower. The LMX model has been developed through four stages, each of which reflects the multifaceted development of leadership and leadership processes. The first stage of the development of LMX leadership occurred in the early 1970s, when the success of managerial processes was shown to be social and dyadic. The second stage of development focused closely on the quality of leader–member exchanges. The third stage of research provided the groundwork for understanding how high-quality relationships can be achieved, and showed how managers can work with each member to develop a unique relationship. Finally, the fourth stage showed how leader–follower partnerships can be expanded to broader groups, teams and networks.

LEARNING OUTCOME 5: Understand how to apply coaching models, skills and techniques to build and develop effective teams.

As teams become self-managed, leaders can take on the role of building relationships and enabling team learning in building the capacity of their teams. Leadership may involve coaching of the team and team members. While there are different forms of coaching, in the context of building and developing effective teams coaching is a way of empowering teams and enabling team relationships so it is easier for teams to function and to learn. Coaching aims at improving competencies and judgements that lead to performance improvement. Generally, coaching is a short-term intervention that targets learning aimed at improving various aspects of performance. There are a range of coaching skills and techniques, depending on the situation and the tasks. However, there are guidelines about what successful coaching should do, such as the need to identify and define what the coaching intends to do and how to define successful outcomes; to create the structure for success by identifying situations that may be used as learning events and that these have the potential to apply skills and knowledge to succeed; and to identify and understand the factors that lead to success. The STEER model (Spot, Tailor, Explain, Encourage and Review), the GROW model (Goal, Reality, Options and Will) and the OSKAR model (Outcome, Scaling, Know-how and Resources, Affirm and Action, and Review) are the three commonly used coaching models.

REVIEW QUESTIONS

1. What are the similarities and differences between work groups and work teams?

2. What are the main stages of developing a team?

3. What are the characteristics of effective teams?

4. Use the leader–member exchange (LMX) model to explain relationships between the leader and the follower.

5. How can coaching and mentoring contribute to leadership development?

CASE STUDY 10.3

Australian call centres – Servo and Tellcorp

Broek and co-authors (2004) interviewed 55 employees from two Australia-based call centres, Servo and Tellcorp, and found that teamworking did not exist in the call centres, even though teams exist based largely on their normative benefits to management. Interviews with Servo and Tellcorp staff offer perspectives on teams and teamwork:

TEAM MEMBER 1: I don't know why they put us in teams, but it's easier if you've one person to refer to, your team leader, and not chasing about. They know your stats and what you're capable of … I do believe that the team leader if they are leading their team, can encourage their people working on an individual job to work together. That to me is the difference between a sweatshop and between a customer service centre. In a sweatshop you'd expect everyone to be individuals and the team leaders are controllers. We like team leaders to be controllers definitely because that's why call centres have been built, but also to lead that team of individuals and treat them as people.

TEAM MEMBER 2: It can be a really lonely job because you're on the phone all the time. We try, we have competitions for one team to beat another, stats and that sort of things … They've got something just now with weekend and evening teams and you get a shield! Wow!! Why bother? They have to have someone watching you, a team leader, so I suppose they have to put you in teams.

TEAM MEMBER 3: Some [staff] are very positive and others can't be bothered. It's the same people that do things all the time. Arrange nights out. Our manager had this thing where if you arranged a night out he would give £10 to the person who arranged it. That was a wee bit of motivation … Morale is a big thing in here, they try to build morale. We actually have quite low morale in our team at the moment… You'll see they've decorated, a lot of bright coloured walls, this is all psychology. Once you've been here a long time it's basically bollocks. You come in and do your job. You don't really feel part of a team. In a sense it's a big team, but you're in 12 segments.

Critical thinking questions
1. Why do teams exist when there is apparently little teamwork in the call centres?
2. What are the strength and weakness of teams in the context of a call centre?
3. What are the characteristics of effective teamwork? Give an example from an industry or organisation that you are familiar with.

REFERENCES

Annett, J. & Stanton, N.A. (2000). Team work: A problem for ergonomics? *Ergonomics*, 43(8), 1045–51.

Bell, B.S. & Kozlowski, S.W. (2002). A typology of virtual teams: Implications for effective leadership. *Group & Organization Management*, 27(1), 14–49.

Boyce, L.A., Jeffrey Jackson, R. & Neal, L.J. (2010). Building successful leadership coaching relationships: Examining impact of matching criteria in a leadership coaching program. *Journal of Management Development*, 29(10), 914–31.

Broek, D.V.D., Callaghan, G. & Thompson, P. (2004). Teams without teamwork? Explaining the call centre paradox. *Economic and Industrial Democracy*, 25(2), 197–218. doi:10.1177/0143831x04042500

Burke, C.S., Stagl, K.C., Klein, C., Goodwin, G.F., Salas E. & Halpin, S.M. (2006). What type of leadership behaviors are functional in teams? A meta-analysis. *Leadership Quarterly*, 17(3), 288–307.

Chen, G., Kirkman, B.L., Kanfer, R., Allen, D. & Rosen, B. (2007). A multilevel study of leadership, empowerment, and performance in teams. *Journal of Applied Psychology*, 92(2), 331.

Clark, K.B. & Wheelwright, S.C. (1992). Organizing and leading 'heavyweight' development teams. *California Management Review*, 34(3), 9–28.

Clutterbuck, D. & Ragins, B.R. (2002). *Mentoring and diversity: An international perspective*. Oxford: Butterworth-Heinemann.

Day, D.V., Gronn, P. & Salas E. (2006). Leadership in team-based organizations: On the threshold of a new era. *Leadership Quarterly*, 17(3), 211–16.

Deans, F., Oakley, L., James, R. & Wrigley, R. (2006). Coaching and mentoring for leadership development in civil society. *Praxis Paper*, 14, 1-37.

Delery, J.E. & Shaw, J.D. (2001), The strategic management of people in work organizations: Review, synthesis, and extension. *Research in Personnel and Human Resources Management*, 20, 165–97.

Durkin, P. (2015). David Gonski's tips for getting ahead, *Australian Financial Review*, 12 February. Retrieved from: www.afr.com/brand/boss/david-gonskis-tips-for-getting-ahead-20150212-13cqn3.

Ellinger, A.D. & Bostrom, R.P. (1999). Managerial coaching behaviors in learning organizations. *Journal of Management Development*, 18(9), 752–71.

Ely, R.J. & Thomas D.A. (2001). Cultural diversity at work: The effects of diversity perspectives on work group processes and outcomes. *Administrative Science Quarterly*, 46(2), 229–73.

Eubanks, D.L., Palanski, M., Olabisi, J., Joinson, A. & Dove, J. (2016). Team dynamics in virtual, partially distributed teams: Optimal role fulfillment. *Computers in Human Behavior*, 61, 556–68.

Garvey, B. (2004). The mentoring/counseling/coaching debate: Call a rose by any other name and perhaps it's a bramble? *Development and Learning in Organizations: An International Journal*, 18(2), 6–8.

Garvey, B., Stokes, P. & Megginson, D. (2014). *Coaching and mentoring: Theory and practice*: Thousand Oaks, CA: SAGE Publications.

Gersick, C.J. (1988). Time and transition in work teams: Toward a new model of group development. *Academy of Management journal*, 31(1), 9–41.

Graen, G.B. & Uhl-Bien, M. (1995). Relationship-based approach to leadership: Development of leader–member exchange (LMX) theory of leadership over 25 years: Applying a multi-level multi-domain perspective. *Leadership Quarterly*, 6(2), 219–47.

Griesinger, A. & Schmitt, T. (2016). Training and qualification: Recommendations for virtual team development. In M. Zeuch (ed.), *Handbook of human resources management* (pp. 395–404). Frankfurt: Springer Berlin Heidelberg.

Hackman, J.R. (2002). *Leading teams: Setting the stage for great performances*. Boston: Harvard Business School Press.

Hinds, P. J., Carley, K.M., Krackhardt, D. & Wholey, D. (2000). Choosing work group members: Balancing similarity, competence, and familiarity. *Organizational behavior and human decision processes*, 81(2), 226–51.

Knippenberg, D.V. & Schippers, M.C. (2007). Work group diversity. *Annual Review of Psychology*, 58, 515–41.

Koch, K. (2015). Training and qualification: Essentials of team development. In M. Zeuch (ed.), *Handbook of human resources management* (pp. 1–24). Frankfurt: Springer Berlin Heidelberg.

Kozlowski, S.W., Gully, S.M., Salas E. & Cannon-Bowers, J.A. (1996). Team leadership and development: Theory, principles, and guidelines for training leaders and teams. In M.M. Beyerlein, D.A. Johnson & S.T. Beyerlein (eds), *Advances in interdisciplinary studies of work teams: Team leadership*, vol. 3 (pp. 253–91). Greenwich, CT: Elsevier Science/JAI Press.

Levine, J.M. & Moreland, R.L. (1991). Culture and socialization in work groups. In L.B. Resnick, J.M. Levine & S.D. Teasley (eds), *Perspectives on socially shared cognition* (pp. 257–79). Washington, DC: American Psychological Association.

Liff, S. & Gustavson, P. (2016). Designed for success: How building a team of leaders transformed a company. *Global Business and Organizational Excellence*, 35(4), 17–27.

Lvina, E., Maher, L.P. & Harris, J.N. (2016). Political skill, trust, and efficacy in teams. *Journal of Leadership & Organizational Studies*, 24(1), 95–105.

Mackey, K. (1999). Stages of team development. *IEEE Software*, 16(4), 90–1.

McKergow, M. (2012). Solution-focused approaches in management. In C. Franklin, T.S. Trepper, W.J. Gingerich & E.E. McCollum (eds), *Solution-focused brief therapy: A handbook of evidence-based practice* (pp. 327–41). New York, NY: Oxford University Press.

Megginson, D. & Clutterbuck, D. (2005). *Techniques for coaching and mentoring*. Burlington, MA: Elsevier Butterworth Heinemann.

Miles, M. (1971). Book review section: *Learning to work in groups*. Book review, *Small Group Research*, 2(1), 85–9.

Mohr, N. & Dichter, A. (1996). *Stages of team development: Lessons from the struggles of site-based management*. Providence, RI: Annenberg Institute for School Reform.

Murray, B. (1998). Psychologist takes a Taoist approach to mentoring. *APA Monitor*, 29(11).

National Council for Voluntary Organisations. (2014). Effective teams. 30 June. Retrieved from: https://knowhownonprofit.org/people/teams/effectiveteam/developing.

Passmore, J. (2007). An integrative model for executive coaching. *Consulting Psychology Journal: Practice and Research*, 59(1), 68.

Paul, D., Thomas P. & Cadle, J. (2012). *The human touch: Personal skills for professional success*. Swindon: BCS Learning and Development Ltd, The Chartered Institute for IT.

Popper, M. & Lipshitz, R. (1992). Coaching on leadership. *Leadership and Organization Development Journal*, 13(7), 15–18.

Rickards, T. & Moger, S. (2000). Creative leadership processes in project team development: An alternative to Tuckman's stage model. *British Journal of Management*, 11(4), 273–83.

Salas E., Dickinson T.L. & Converse, S.A. (1992) Toward an understanding of team performance and training. In R.W. Swezey & E. Salas (eds), *Teams: Their training and performance* (pp. 3–29). Norwood, NJ: Ablex.

Sarker, S. & Sahay, S. (2003). Understanding virtual team development: An interpretive study. *Journal of the Association for Information Systems*, 4(1), 1.

Schwarz, R.M. (2000). *The skilled facilitator: A comprehensive resource for consultants, facilitators, managers, trainers, and coaches*, revised edn. San Francisco, CA: Jossey-Bass.

Seers, A., Keller, T. & Wikerson, J.M. (2003). Can team members share leadership? In C.L. Pearce & J.A. Conger (eds), *Shared leadership: Reframing the hows and whys of leadership* (pp. 77–102). Thousand Oaks, CA: SAGE Publications.

Thomas, D.C. (1999). Cultural diversity and work group effectiveness an experimental study. *Journal of Cross-Cultural Psychology*, 30(2), 242–63.

Tuckman, B.W. (1965). Developmental sequence in small groups. *Psychological Bulletin*, 63(6), 384–99.

Tuckman, B.W. & Jensen, M.A.C. (1977). Stages of small-group development revisited. *Group and Organization Management*, 2(4), 419–27.

Waldman, J. (2010). Creating a coaching culture one conversation at a time: Solutions-focused coaching at John Laing Integrated Services. Retrieved from: www.thesolutionsfocus.co.uk/creating-a-coaching-culture-john-laing-case-study.html.

Warrick, D. (2016). What leaders can learn about teamwork and developing high performance teams from organization development practitioners. *Performance Improvement*, 55(3), 13–21.

Yoo, Y. & Alavi, M. (2004). Emergent leadership in virtual teams: What do emergent leaders do? *Information and Organization*, 14(1), 27–58.

Yukl, G.A. (2013). *Leadership in organizations*, 8th edn. Boston: Pearson Education.

Zaccaro, S.J., Rittman, A.L. & Marks, M.A. (2002). Team leadership. *Leadership Quarterly*, 12(4), 451–83.

Zalesny, M.D. & Graen, G.B. (1987). Exchange theory in leadership research. In G.R.A. Kieser & R. Wanderer (eds), *Handbook of leadership* (pp. 714–27). Stuttgart: C.E. Paeschel Verlag.

11

LEADING CHANGE

Mario Fernando

LEARNING OUTCOMES

After reading this chapter, you should be able to:

1. explain the need for change in organisations

2. discuss the factors that influence leading change

3. explain the leader's role in managing change

4. demonstrate an awareness of key theories in change management

5. identify and explain challenges of leading change.

INTRODUCTION

THIS CHAPTER WILL explore how leaders can identify the need to change and how they can use change to generate effective leadership outcomes. One of the most critical and difficult leadership responsibilities is leading change. Whether the change is short term or long term, the role of the leader is key. Leaders need to develop a clear and compelling vision to guide organisations through changing times. In the leadership process, change can be described as various shifting scenarios that play out in the particular context of the organisation. The other variables in the process – the leader, follower and goals – can be influenced by how change occurs in the context or situation, and how leaders and followers adapt and maximise the opportunities that change offers. Change is perhaps the most – some would say the only – constant feature in organisations. Organisational leaders face change every day and need to be adequately equipped to overcome the challenges it generates. Although not all information will be available at a given time, leaders need to make realistic assumptions so that the change process can begin. It is important that leaders are able to optimise the opportunities and manage the challenges that change presents. Change management has been studied for some time, and several theories have emerged that attempt to explain it. In this chapter, the focus is on leading change, addressing how leaders can make change their ally and use it to generate effective leadership outcomes.

THE NEED FOR CHANGE IN ORGANISATIONS

Change is essential to contemporary organisations. The nature of the organisational landscape is forever changing and organisations must continually adapt to ensure their ability to meet the needs of a dynamic market. Many scholars argue that the pace of change has never been so rapid, and that the management of change has become a key leadership task (D'Ortenzio, 2012; Dawson, 1994; Kanter et al., 1992; Wilson, 1992). The need for change is often unpredictable, making responses reactive and ad hoc. This makes it even more crucial for organisational leaders to develop the skills and perspectives that help them ensure their organisations' long-term viability in an organisational environment that makes comprehensive planning covering all contingencies virtually impossible. Although some changes may be reactionary, others may be proactive and planned in readiness for the changing environment. For example, organisations such as Apple set and lead the environment by pre-empting or even disrupting the status quo through innovation – these firms do not just follow and make changes to follow competitors. It is critical for leaders to develop skills, perspectives and processes to ensure short-, medium- and long-term organisational viability. Thus, organisations must change to keep ahead of the competition, respond to market demands and take advantage of new opportunities. The need for change may be triggered both internally and externally to the organisation.

Internal change

Catalysts for internal change include the arrival of a new leader, organisational growth and change in the availability of organisational resources. New leaders often bring about significant change within an organisation. A new CEO will often make changes to the organisation that reflect their own leadership style, drawing on their perceptions, experience and knowledge about what needs to change within the organisation to make it more successful, or if changing the way things are done is an implied or explicit part of their appointment to their leadership position. An example of another internally triggered change might be the automation of a factory plant, which can create complex issues in dealing with human resource management. Some employees may have to be retrained, some retrenched and others transferred to different units. While automation may bring about efficient outcomes in terms of productivity and quality, a leader will need a strategy to address human resource management during the implementation of that change. It is essential that, where change is needed, the change and its rationale are clearly communicated throughout the organisation.

External change

The need for change may be triggered externally to the organisation. Events in the external environment that drive organisational change may occur because of various drivers outside the boundaries of the organisation, including changes in the laws and regulations relevant to an industry, a corporation's client base and broader community, economic cycles, such as periods of boom and depression, or politics and social values. For instance, a mining company may need to undergo change if new environmental laws prohibiting fracking are passed that make certain parts of its operations illegal. All organisations operate within a context; therefore, they must be responsive to and develop and nurture appropriate relationships within their environment if they are to remain viable. According to Dawson (1994), the major components of an organisation are not static. Over the organisation's life cycle, the interests and intentions of other organisational players may alter, thereby altering the direction, scope of operations or other strategic decisions pertinent to the organisation's continued viability. For example, during an organisation's growth phase, leaders may be interested in capturing market share and perhaps poaching suppliers from their competitors. Yet such intentions may change when growth plateaus and market share is lost. The patterns of interaction between constituent parts of interacting organisations may vary. These constituent parts refer to elements such as communication, competition and cooperation between organisations. For instance, in the supermarket business, when Aldi entered the Australian market organisations such as Coles and Woolworths encountered enhanced competition and changed as a result. The amount of power and influence an organisation can wield over the external environment can bring about change to its own constituent parts and those of other organisations. For example, large multinationals are commonly perceived to have the capacity to wield significant amounts of power over governments. A growing organisation with increasing economic power may respond to this change by adopting a more aggressive strategy in its interactions with the governments of the countries in which it operates.

Organisational growth is often accompanied by a need to change. For instance, when Apple entered the MP3 market with the iPod, the company experienced high growth, which led to the renaming of Apple Computers as Apple Inc. The company's growth triggered a change in its corporate strategy, with a greater focus on telecommunications and less on computing. When companies grow – or decline, for that matter – changes may be necessary to company hierarchy and organisational structure. For example, a company losing market share may need to cut costs, and may do that by reducing the number of middle managers, flattening the organisational hierarchy. A company experiencing growth (or even in decline) may respond by hiring new people and introducing new leaders. Whatever the change, it is imperative that all employees understand why the change is needed and feel a part of the change process.

FACTORS INFLUENCING CHANGE LEADERSHIP

Many factors influence the need for organisations to change. In fact, any one change may be influenced by a range of factors. For example, a company deciding to invest in renewable energies may be influenced by technological advancements and social and environmental concerns. We have seen that internal organisational pressures can bring about change, such as a desire to expand goals, or from external forces, such as government regulations and advances in technology. Two factors commonly necessitate change: competition and growth.

Competition

Competition is classified as an external force. The entrance of new market competitors, for example, can trigger a change of strategy, the need for an expanded product range or further research and development. As an illustration, when the camera brand GoPro entered the market it gained significant popularity through offering a product highly differentiated from the standard Panasonic or Kodak market offerings. The increased competition caused other camera companies to change their products to reflect the market demand for active cameras.

Growth

Change may be a result of actual organisational growth or an organisation's desire to grow. An organisation may have experienced an increase in sales volume and therefore might need to change premises or hire new staff to keep up with demand. Similarly, a growing firm might decide to sell its product or service overseas to satisfy new markets. Alternatively, an organisation may attempt to grow in terms of advertising and staffing to give the impression of success, as a strategy to expand the organisation in terms of revenue and assets. A great example of this is Subway. The initial launch of Subway was rather uncertain. It first started as 'Pete's Super Submarines' in the 1960s. It then changed its name and opened new stores to create the impression that the restaurant was more popular than it was. Subway's strategy was successful.

PESTLE

The common external drivers of change in organisations can be described using the acronym **PESTLE,** which covers political, economic, social, technological, legal and environmental factors. Changes in any of these areas of an organisation's external environment can influence the need for organisational change.

Political

Changes in the political sphere can cause change within an organisation. A major change to the political environment has been the blurring of the public and private sectors as governments move to privatise areas of service delivery. For example, the New South Wales government has looked at privatising the energy sector. A decline in the power of the sovereign nation-state has also catalysed change in the organisational environment, where companies can now assert more economic and financial pressure on governments. Of the top 100 governments and corporations by annual revenue in 2014, some 63 were corporations, and only 37 were national governments (Freudenberg, 2015). That is, most corporations have annual sales more than the annual gross domestic product of nations. For instance, Walmart's 2014 annual sales in US dollars were greater than the annual gross domestic product of Russia.

Economic

Economies like that of Australia are shifting from manufacturing to knowledge-based economies. You may be aware of the relocation of the Australian manufacturing operations of Holden and Qantas to overseas sites. Due to the Australian manufacturing sector's lack of competitiveness, Ford has stopped manufacturing cars in Australia as well. The plateauing of the mining sector has also affected the Australian economy and forced a change of focus onto the services sector. Another significant issue constraining how organisations do business is the rise of film and music piracy and counterfeiting. The pirating of music and films has led to the rise of alternate providers, such as Spotify and Netflix, that reduce the consumers' cost of viewing and listening to media. Economic cycles such as the global financial crisis of 2007–09 have also caused major changes. Many companies have had to downsize and change their operations to avoid going out of business. On the other hand, the rise of what is known as the BRIC countries (Brazil, Russia, India and China) presents a significant opportunity for companies due to the size of these markets and the influential middle class within them.

Social

Potentially the biggest social change phenomenon to affect organisations and force them to change is the rise in importance of **corporate social responsibility (CSR)**. CSR refers to the push for companies to carry out their operations in an ethical and responsible manner. Managers can lead change within their organisations by introducing CSR initiatives such as environmental awareness programs and ethical sourcing of supplies. Young people are increasingly socially aware, and they expect that the products and services they use are produced through responsible practices. For example, when one compares the tobacco industry and fast food chains like McDonald's, why is the latter still operating but the former continues to lose its consumer base? McDonald's has responded to increasing consumer awareness of health-conscious eating by taking steps to reduce the unhealthy ingredients in its menus. Tobacco companies, on the other hand, failed to respond to consumer concerns of harm to health. If the tobacco industry had been as responsive to the consumer as McDonald's has been by offering less harmful products, it would still be a thriving market.

> **Corporate social responsibility (CSR) –** Organisational practices that are carried out in an ethical and responsible manner.

Technological

Innovation drives change (Dawson & Andriopoulos, 2009). Keeping up with new technologies is integral to market success. An organisation may seek to continually change and update its products in line with technological advancements. In contrast, a business may attempt to remain at the forefront of technological innovation and hire teams to create innovation and drive technological advancements. For example, Facebook employs teams of people to solve problems and change the nature of online communication. Facebook CEO Mark Zuckerberg launched the initiative internet.org, with its Connectivity Lab, to drive communication technology at a reduced cost for the four billion people in the world who do not have online access.

Legal

Changes to the legal system in a state or national context can mean changes to organisations. For example, each time the minimum wage level in Australia is increased, organisations need to account for this increase in the annual salary bill of their budget. A legal requirement on increasing safety at the workplace would mean changes to the way operations are conducted with necessary training of relevant staff. Leaders would need to be aware of impending legal changes that may affect their organisations significantly.

Environmental

For the past few years, and into the foreseeable future, the single most important factor in the external environment that has affected (and will continue to affect) organisations are changes associated with climate change. Whether complying with carbon emissions taxes, making technological changes to reduce emission levels, or complying with legal requirements to meet new emissions targets, organisations have had to change in drastic ways to respond to the ongoing climate change debate taking place globally at the national, organisational and social levels. Climate change has triggered the growth of renewable energies and caused companies to reconsider the effect that their operations have on the environment.

THE LEADER'S ROLE IN MANAGING CHANGE

Leaders have a difficult job when it comes to managing change. Change is essential in organisations. Therefore, leaders must possess the skills to make change happen. These skills range from addressing the budget and time frames, known as **hard management skills**, to communicating the change and engaging employees, known as **soft management skills**. Not only do leaders need to ensure that the proposed change is delivered on time and on budget, but they also need to garner the support of their employees to ensure that the change is effective. Leaders that are more transactional, and focused on budgets, processes and efficiencies might not be effective at the beginning of a change process. A more transformational leadership style is more appropriate at the beginning of a change process, when developing a new strategic plan, communicating, encouraging, supporting and motivating employees. Yet transactional leadership is important during the short and middle term of a change process. Thus, application of different styles of leadership (depending on the context) would be useful at different times in the change process.

> **Hard management skills –**
> Skills that will help to assign large allocations of resources, and meet targets and deadlines.
> **Soft management skills –**
> Skills that are useful to valuing employees as human assets.

Hard management skills

It is critical that leaders possess hard management skills when managing change. Most major changes require a large allocation of resources, incur significant costs and must meet a deadline. These duties of leaders must always be set against the need for them to coach their employees or subordinates through the change process to reduce the impact of employee resistance. To keep the change program on track and on time, leaders must set measurable goals and achievable targets. Setting up a timeline that allows employees to have small successes throughout the change program not only ensures that momentum is kept up but also helps to encourage staff to stay motivated throughout the change process.

Soft management skills

As opposed to hard management skills, soft management skills value employees as human assets. They are considered a key source of competitive advantage. There are several ways in which soft management skills can be implemented in organisations. One way is by having employees involved in decision making and promoting employee voice as valuable. Another way is by engaging in a high level of transparency and communication to generate employee commitment. As a human asset, soft management skills promote the idea of training employees and developing them to meet changing environmental conditions.

Communicating change

It is also important that the leader, when managing change, communicates both the content of the change and its rationale to employees. The leader must facilitate conversations with and among employees to discover any potential reasons for resistance and identify those who are likely to strongly resist or encourage others to do so. Leaders may do this by scheduling meetings to outline the nature of the change and what the change will entail. The leader should seek to appease employee concerns and ensure that the employees do not feel threatened by the proposed changes. Further, the employees must understand their role and how they fit into the change process. By engaging employees, the leader can help ensure a smoother transition during the change.

Appointing change agents

During the change, leaders may take on a guiding role by appointing **change agents**, or by acting as change agents themselves. A change agent is a person, either internal or external to the organisation, who helps to facilitate the change process. A manager as a change agent helps to communicate the vision of the change, motivate others and ensure that the nature of the change is understood.

Change agent – A person, either internal or external to the organisation, who helps to facilitate the change process.

Stakeholder mapping

During times of major organisational change, a leader may need to manage not only interests internal to the organisation but also those of external stakeholders such as customers, government, lobby groups, board members and trade unions. Radical changes may mean that there is strong opposition to a change from outside the organisation. For example, recently BP sought to expand its drilling operations into the Great Australian Bight. This proposed change to the business's operation was met with substantial resistance from activist groups. Resistance was based on the perceived threat of the drilling venture to the environment. When companies make major organisational changes they need to manage not only internal but external resistance to ensure the success of a change program. To help to manage the change and balance the needs of various groups who have a stake in the change, the leader can do what is called **stakeholder mapping**: identifying key groups and individuals who have a stake in the change process or who will be affected by it, and who will wish to have a say in the change. This process requires the leader to be highly aware of the different motivations of each group and to understand their ability to derail the change process.

Stakeholder mapping – A method to identify key groups and individuals who have a stake in the change process or who will be affected by it, and who will wish to have a say in the change.

Transparency

The role of the leader in managing change is diverse, from managing a budget to balancing competing stakeholder concerns and motivating employees to accept and engage with the change. The leader will often be a central figure during the change process, dealing with the internal and external reactions to the proposed change. It is important that during change, leaders are open and transparent and that they encourage their subordinates to buy into the change process.

CASE STUDY 11.1

Not leading change at Kodak

Not long ago, the Kodak company was a popular American company dealing in photographic films and cameras. According to Sparkes (2012), in 1994, Apple launched one of the first consumer digital cameras which was designed by Kodak. In 2004, due to the heavy demand of digital cameras, Kodak stopped selling film cameras. Although in 2005 Kodak was the largest seller of digital cameras in the United States, by 2010 it had fallen to seventh place. In 2009, Kodak produced its last 35mm colour film, having manufactured the product for some 74 years (Sparkes, 2012). The company went bankrupt in 2012, and later emerged as a smaller company in 2013. Many consider the failure to capture the right moment to exploit the digital photography market led to the downfall of the company. During the time, former Kodak CEO Antonio Perez referred to digital cameras a 'crappy business' (Weissmann, 2012). Since its fall, the company has a market value of only about US$1 billion (Anthony, 2016). There was a time that the 'Kodak moment' was etched in in the public's minds. Through a powerful advertising campaign, the company was positioned as the leading company dealing with retaining memories. With the advent of the digital camera, the need for films declined drastically; once every mobile phone had a camera feature, the company's sales dropped catastrophically. Further, photos are now mostly shared and stored online and in other digital formats, rather than printed.

How could such a large and successful company not be sensitive to the changes occurring in the external environment? Why couldn't Kodak move into the digital photography market at the right time? The company was in a prime position to exploit the rising digital market but was unable to take advantage of it.

Critical thinking questions

1. If you had been the leader at Kodak during the rise of the digital photography market, how would you have responded?
2. What challenges would you expect to face in leading change at Kodak to take advantage of the rising digital photography market?
3. Identify and explain three factors that leaders need to focus on to ensure that they take advantage of opportunities occurring in the external environment.

THEORY AND PRACTICE IN CHANGE MANAGEMENT

Organisational performance may not be improved when the organisation is in a state of change (Burnes, 2004). Employees need work to a routine to be effective and to facilitate improved performance. It is now understood that an ability to undergo change is highly important to organisational success. Change may be classified as either incremental or discontinuous. **Incremental change** refers to the often step-by-step or small changes made to improve the organisation. **Discontinuous change**s, on the other hand, are major changes such as an overhauled company strategy.

The type of change has implications for how it is to be best managed. Change can also be categorised by how it comes about, as either planned or emergent. **Planned change** is self-explanatory; **emergent change** is characterised as unpredictable, and responses to it will be reactive. But before developing change responses, it is critical to develop a proper assessment of organisational processes and diagnose what needs to be done to improve these processes. An accurate assessment and diagnosis exercise is vital to lead and feed the change process. In this chapter, we will examine four change models; Kurt Lewin's change model, Kotter's eight-step emergent approach model, the organisational development model and the appreciative inquiry (AI) model.

> **Incremental change** – Minor changes that are introduced step by step, with a focus on improvement.
> **Discontinuous change** – Major changes that are made to an organisation, such as the creation of a new company strategy.
> **Planned change** – Change that is documented and to which resources are allocated
> **Emergent change** – Unpredictable change, to which responses are necessarily reactive (as opposed to proactive)

Kurt Lewin's model of a planned approach to organisational change

Planned change is associated with Kurt Lewin's (1951) unfreeze, change, refreeze process. When a company decides that change is necessary, it follows that the change will be planned and the process managed. Lewin's (1951) model states that when an organisation decides to make a change it must first unfreeze the way that things are done, make the changes required and then refreeze so that the change remains.

Unfreeze

During the unfreezing phase, managers must create awareness of how the status quo will be changed and prepare employees by effectively communicating the need for change. In this stage, followers are expected to break away from the traditional mould and work towards a different set of work goals. This stage might be uncomfortable, as followers are expected to move away from their comfort zones to embrace a new way doing things. Leaders during this stage will typically try to motivate followers to embrace a new and compelling vision, to change their habits of working and to shift their goals (Cooke & Burnes, 2013). In return, the leader can grant more resources and time to employees and develop a more facilitating environment in which to work (Harper, 2001). This stage is typically fraught with challenges relating to followers' anxiety due to risks that they are expected to take before they can really see the benefits of actual change (Argyris, 1993). So, leaders' focus during this stage should be to win over followers and make them believe in a future that is more beneficial for them.

Change

During the change phase, the organisation or work unit will transition to a new state, learning new behaviours and processes. The actual change action will take place during this stage and followers will be expected to implement the new change plan through taking part in the day-to-day tasks that will unfold the change process. Leaders will be required to engage all followers in a bottom-up decision-making process. Under this process, all followers as stakeholders will be consulted about and engaged in the final decisions. The commitment generated through such a process will ensure higher levels of participation (Harper, 2001).

Refreeze

Finally, during the refreezing stage the new behaviours or processes will be reinforced and solidified. In this stage, leaders' focus will be on reinforcing the change that has taken place so that it is made permanent. Followers can be continuously rewarded for adopting change, helping the new behaviour pattern to become habitual practice. Appropriate recognition to followers for adopting the new change will ensure that they follow the new practice in the long term without shifting back to former practice (Cooke & Burnes, 2013).

Leaders may use Lewin's model to accomplish change in three ways. The first is by changing their followers' skills, values, attitudes and behaviour, thus instrumentally achieving overall organisational change. The goal should be to achieve the ultimate objectives of the change process. The second way leaders can use this model is by changing the structures, systems and processes in the organisation. These changes can help leaders implement the change process more effectively. The changes to organisational structures, systems and processes can facilitate an organisational environment that makes the change process central to the day-to-day operations of the organisation. The final way that leaders can use Kurt Lewin's model is by changing the way followers interact with each other in the organisation. By focusing on the organisational climate, leaders can use this model to achieve organisational change outcomes by shaping how followers deal with interpersonal conflict during difficult organisational decision-making situations.

Several criticisms have been aimed at this model. One of the key objections is that the model is too simplistic and mechanistic. Lewin's model seems to be too straightforward to cater for today's complex organisational environment, where organisational change is continuous and open-ended (Van, 2015; D'Ortenzio, 2012; Dawson, 1994; Stacey, 1993). While the model may be relevant for discrete projects, it is unlikely to be useful for complex and long-term transformational projects (D'Ortenzio, 2012; Dunphy & Stace, 1992, 1993;

Miller & Friesen, 1984). Another criticism is that this model ignores the underlying power relationships and politics that can either promote or hinder the change process, especially in the second stage, when the change actually takes place (Hatch, 1997; Pettigrew, 1990a; Pfeffer, 1992; Wilson, 1992). In terms of the direction of change, critics point out that this model advocates a primarily top-down management approach, where the top management directs communication and instructions to the bottom levels without much consultation or participation (Van, 2015; D'Ortenzio, 2012; Pettigrew, 1990b; Kanter et al., 1992; Wilson, 1992).

In summary, Lewin's model offers a basic understanding of a simplistic, three-stage change process. The model has been applied in many contexts within and outside of organisations. It is one of the most popular change models because of its easy application and understanding.

Kotter's eight-step model of emergent organisational change

Kotter's (1996) model seeks to address the key challenges faced when managing a change program. This model is also called the continuous improvement model or the organisational learning model. Kotter's emergent model of change was developed to address some of the criticisms of Lewin's model. The key difference of this model is that change is driven from the bottom up by fully engaging the followers with, and committing them to, the change process. Change is also considered to be continuous. Thus, planning for change becomes difficult with a planned approach such as that advocated by Lewin. In Kotter's change model, the change process is considered as open-ended (Wilson, 1992).

However, planning for change in open-ended situations is difficult, as change needs to be addressed as an ongoing process (Burnes, 1996). Kotter's model also underscores the importance that change should not be considered as linear. According to Burnes (1996), the emergent approach promotes 'extensive and in-depth understanding of strategy, structure, systems, people, style and culture, and how these can function either as sources of inertia that can block change, or alternatively, as levers to encourage an effective change process' (p. 14). Rather than planned change, this model recommends readiness to address change on a continuous basis. Kotter's model introduces eight critical steps in leading change (1996, pp. 133–45):

1. create a sense of urgency
2. form a guiding coalition
3. create a vision
4. communicate the vision
5. empower others to act on the vision
6. create quick wins
7. build on the change
8. institutionalise the change.

The model describes the change process as a sequence. First, managers need to explain why the change is needed and describe the dangers ahead if the need for change is ignored. Forming a guiding coalition refers to establishing a group of people who will act as change agents and drive the change. Key people should be brought in from all levels of the organisation, given adequate resources, and fully supported by senior management. These staff bring their expertise, relationships and reputation to bear on their roles, and as such they enjoy an appropriate title and position. It is then critical for the vision of the change to be communicated through all the organisation's levels. Then, others in the organisation need to be empowered to buy in and take up the challenge of implementing the organisation's change vision. Creating quick wins – small successes that can be celebrated – is important to continue the momentum of the change and encourage employees' continued support. Finally, change is to be built upon and institutionalised so that it becomes an entrenched part of the organisation. An important point to remember is that this model was presented by Kotter not as a checklist but as a series of steps to be followed.

As with any model, Kotter's also has attracted several criticisms. It must be followed in sequence from end to end, otherwise the change program is likely to collapse. Before undertaking a new step, the previous stage's outcomes must be reinforced. Implementing all eight steps in the change process also is a very time-consuming task (Rose, 2002). It requires a significant amount of organisational resources, a dedicated team of change champions and the willingness and commitment of the followers to accept and believe in the vision the leader has created.

That said, compared to other organisational models this model has fewer disadvantages. Most organisations have embraced this model to effect medium- to long-term organisational changes. From a leader's perspective, the most difficult task is to prepare the organisation to accept the change process. In this regard, leaders must have excellent communication channels for the change process that the organisational members accept and follow. Examples are monthly email updates that include what the leader's thoughts are about what's happening in the organisational environment, personal social media updates, and periodic virtual or face-to-face meetings with key personnel.

CASE STUDY 11.2

Change at Global IT

Michael Hanley is the CEO of Global IT, which is active in Australia, India, Ireland, New Zealand and Hong Kong. The company provides IT solutions to organisations across the world with the CEO operating from the head office, based in Sydney. Due to the nature of the project-based work environment, Michael's staff needs to travel to Global IT's affiliated offices to work on projects. Some specialists would physically be at other locations for over six months. Under these circumstances, the human resource management of the company has pointed out that due to different workplace routines and policies in each of the affiliate companies, the staff who are posted overseas on assignments are observing that local staff are treated differently to staff at their own home offices. For example, on a recent visit to the Irish subsidiary, a Sydney-based software specialist noted that many staff were taking long lunch breaks. After returning to her local office in Sydney, she asked Michael's HR manager why she and her colleagues in Sydney couldn't have such long lunch breaks. This was discussed at the recent senior management meeting.

At the meeting, some managers pointed out that the local rules should apply to any visiting staff member. This was not taken favourably by those staff who would lose some privileges that they are used to in their local offices. Others suggested a universal human resource system where all offices implement the same rules. This would mean that some office privileges would have to be sacrificed because Global IT was a small company just beginning to enjoy increasing market share and couldn't afford to introduce the more relaxed and extravagant privileges of some locations into all its offices. Michael wanted to address this issue before it became too serious.

He appointed a team to consider what needed to be done. A staff member from each of the subsidiary organisations was invited to join the team. After looking at the issue, the team recommended that a global human resource system that is applicable to all staff, regardless of location, be implemented. Michael thinks that this is a major undertaking, and that the changes to all company human resource systems should be introduced with care. He has decided to hire you as the organisational consultant to design and implement the change at Global IT.

Critical thinking questions

1. Using Kotter's approach to emergent organisational change, explain how leaders can use each stage of the model to effectively implement Global IT's change management process.
2. Explain briefly the nature and types of resistance to change you might expect in introducing the global human resource system across Global IT.
3. What course of action would you recommend to Michael to overcome the resistance to change? Why?

Organisational development model

The change model of **organisational development** (Waddell et al., 2017; Cummings & Worley, 1997) is a highly popular approach in change management that has been developed over many years. It is built on the principle that organisational structures and processes influence employee behaviour. It involves a process of capacity-building in an organisation to manage future change. It involves four steps:

1. continuous diagnosis
2. action planning
3. intervention
4. evaluation.

> **Organisational development –** A change model based on the principle that organisational structures and processes influence employee behaviour, and focused on building an organisation's capacity for future change.

In the first step, leaders' focus should be on developing ways to diagnose the problems in the organisation that may hamper an effective response to change. Most organisations hire organisational change consultants to carry out the diagnosis process (Cummings & Worley, 1997). Such consultants would typically look at the high-level strategy and policies, including the mission, vision, goals, structures and processes, the organisational climate, the capacity of employees to respond to change, organisational culture and environmental factors. While various approaches can be used to diagnose and to collect information, formal and informal interviews, statistics and questionnaires are essential tools and processes for diagnosing and evaluating change processes.

The second stage involves action planning. This process determines the who, how and when of actions to take place. A typical action plan will explain the resources devoted to an action, including the employees in charge, and the time and place at which the actions will take place. It comprehensively explains how the problems found through the earlier diagnosing stage can be addressed. Leaders can find this stage very useful, as it enables them to design a road map for addressing problems found within the organisation.

The third stage involves the actual implementation of the intervention, which is detailed in a step-by-step guide, including what likely consequences may follow, and how these can be addressed. Leaders usually delegate this process to change agents or the change team. Change agents develop when employees either volunteer or are appointed to positions of influence that are critical for making change happen.

The final stage involves evaluation. After the implementation of the change action, leaders need to monitor the impact it has on the organisation and its employees. This is an important process, as it involves documenting for future reference any feedback on the process followed. The goal of this stage is to develop the knowledge and skills of the employees to manage change better.

Leaders may use this approach to encourage their followers to accept change as a constant in business and face changes as they occur on a continuous basis. This valuable approach facilitates collaboration and engagement in effecting change. Organisational development is a planned approach, where the emphasis is on dealing with the human element of change, specifically employees' reactions to change programs. Rooted in humane values such as openness and honesty, an organisational development program usually takes up to two years to implement.

Appreciative inquiry (AI) – A change model based on the principle that in every organisation there is something that is working right, and which asks leaders to value their organisation's strengths and connect these to the desired change.

Appreciative inquiry model

Another model of change management is **appreciative inquiry (AI)**. David Cooperrider and colleagues developed this model in the 1980s. His model stands out because of its focus on the positive aspects of change management. All the other change management models try to identify what is wrong with the system and what is broken; they are problem-based models. In contrast, the AI model asks leaders to value what is working in their organisations. It works on the assumption that in all organisations some things are going well:

…things that give life when it is most alive, effective, successful, and connected in healthy ways to its stakeholders and communities. AI begins by identifying what is positive and connecting to it in ways that heighten energy, vision, and action for change (Cooperrider et al., 2005, xv).

Instead of the emphasis on the negative and the problematic, the AI method looks for the 'positive core': the key aspects of the organisation that tell a positive story. The positive core can be identified by examining aspects such as achievements, strategic opportunities, product strengths, assets, innovations, best business practices, suppliers and partners (Cooperrider et al., 2005).

Based on the positive core, the change agenda is prepared using the collective input of all staff. This is a planned change process where change is led from the top down, meaning that the senior managers institute the change on the assumption of employees' full participation and engagement. Appreciative inquiry (AI) makes use of groups, often large, to encourage enthusiasm for change using storytelling and envisioning the future (see Figure 11.1).

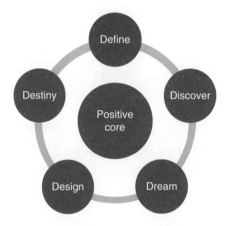

Figure 11.1   The appreciative inquiry model

As a change process, AI has five phases:

1. *Define*: In this stage the goals and project management structure are set, and the approach to enabling change is decided. The approach may be based on available resources, and the appropriate timing is based on the operations of the organisation.

2. *Discover*: Change participants think about the times when the organisation is at its best. The goal is for the group and individuals to think about and understand what they value about themselves and their work. It involves crafting interview questions and the approach to interviewing participants. Input from all stakeholders is sought. The interview questions are designed with the positive core in mind, and aim to elicit positive stories about what the best has been and is in the organisation. In a powerful way, stories and images of the organisation from a collective perspective will be used to develop the questions that will be used in the next step.

3. *Dream*: This is the stage where change participants envision the future, inspired by the questions from the previous step. Participants think about the best elements of the past and can break any rules needed to create the new, desired future. This stage calls on the change participants to focus on the future, what might be and what employees hope for in terms of working for the organisation, and to develop and nurture relationships at work. This stage invites all participants to think innovatively and from a global perspective, and to see how the organisation can contribute in a positive way and achieve its change goals. Leaders may use this stage to get followers to blossom into their full potential.

4. *Design*: This stage translates the dreams to reality by considering what organisational elements need to be changed. It calls on the participants to think how the dreams can be made real within the organisational context. It compels them to develop, create and recreate processes, structures and systems so that the past, present and future of the organisation are appropriately aligned.

5. *Destiny*: In this stage, actual implementation of the plans take place. The destiny of the organisation will depend on how inspired the employees are when they execute the plans. Change is expected to occur throughout the organisation, and all stakeholders are expected to participate in the change process. This is an important aspect of appreciative inquiry, because only then will there be widespread buy-in and acceptance of the changes.

Phases 2 through 5 are worked through by the group at a workshop, usually lasting around three days; the group focuses on the positive so that there will be little resistance for change from the rest of the organisation. Negativity, finger pointing and problem identification processes are not the focus.

CHALLENGES IN LEADING CHANGE

It is rare for an organisational change to occur without some level of internal resistance from employees who do not want the status quo to shift (Kotter, 1996). Leading change in an organisation can be an incredibly difficult task for leaders, and resistance to change is a major factor obstructing the success of a change program. An employee may act based on their feelings of uncertainty and fear, if a leader does not communicate about the change and its rationale clearly. Employees resisting change may openly defy the wishes of management or reduce their work effort to try and prevent change (Weick & Quinn, 1999).

Types of resistance to change

According to Kotter and Schlesinger (1979), there are four main types of resistance. The first is known as parochial self-interest, when people resist because they are focused on their own needs and not the needs of the organisation. The second emerges from a misunderstanding surrounding the change or a mistrust of what is to happen. Therefore, it is important that managers establish a level of trust with their employees, during the period leading up to the change. It is also important that leaders communicate the need for change and be open and honest with their employees so that they feel secure.

The third reason for resistance is that some employees have a low tolerance for change, which causes them to feel stressed and anxious about the change program. An employee may feel insecure and scared about the changes to their job role or the need to learn new skills. For example, changes in technology that lead to a change in work processes might mean that someone over the age of 60 needs to learn new skills. This person may feel that they are at the end of their career and not want to invest time and energy into learning something new, or they may feel insecure about their ability to do their job now that the role has changed.

The final reason for resistance is referred to as 'different assessments'. This means that people interpret data differently to the way the change leaders intend. If the data is misinterpreted, employees may perceive that there are fewer benefits available for them during the change, and therefore start to resist it.

Two other types of resistance that challenge the change process are targeted and diffused. Targeted resistance focuses on a perceived threat. For example, in supermarkets the introduction of self-serve checkouts may have been met with resistance by employees, who might show targeted resistance by refusing the training needed to learn to operate the new self-service machines. Diffused resistance, on the other hand, is more general, not targeted towards anything. This type of resistance tends to be covert and passive.

Many challenges associated with change relate to the effect that change has on the human element of an organisation (Peters, 2012). During the initiating phase of change, leaders must invest time and resources to guide employees through the process. Such costs must be prepared for so that the cost and time frame of the change are sufficient, and thus do not pose additional threats to the change process. This leads to another major challenge when leading change: time.

Change can be a very time-consuming task, so it is important that there is a structure and method behind the change. Leaders can reduce the challenge of finding enough time by setting small and achievable goals so that the change program does not lose momentum, and by setting milestones so that the process stays on track. If time is too pressured, employees' trust in the change may deteriorate because they feel that they are being rushed and don't have enough time to make sense of and adjust to the change. For example, when the health insurance entity Medibank was privatised in 2014, this required radical change, which employees met with strong initial resistance because they feared for their jobs. Medibank's leaders responded by setting goals for the change process and by constantly communicating about progress towards those goals in the organisation's newsletter.

There will often be many challenges faced when leading change. In major change projects, some challenges may be minor and easily overcome, such as reassuring an employee that their job is not under threat; others may present more difficulties, such as curbing strong resistance from internal and external stakeholder groups. Communication and trust are key to combatting many of the challenges a leader may face in making change successful.

CASE STUDY 11.3

Appreciative inquiry (AI) at British Airways

AI was used at British Airways to address a bad experience in the history of the airline. It was not always able to deliver baggage on the same flight as the passenger, and the airline was consequently gaining a bad reputation and incurring unnecessary costs. The organisation used AI to manage change. AI was used to identify the positive core, and, based on the results, to determine that staff should be focusing on passengers' arrival experience. The entire AI process was focused on 'what makes an exceptional arrival experience'. A key question in the staff interview process was to 'describe times when customers had an exceptional arrival experience'. After analysing the responses, staff identified the elements of an 'exceptional arrival experience' and developed a plan to deliver that experience to customers. Several best practices were developed.

Source: Adapted from Thomas (n.d.)

Critical thinking questions
1. If you were the organisational consultant hired to conduct the AI at British Airways, describe the steps you would follow. Explain your response.
2. Outline the challenges involved in focusing on the positive while addressing the problem with BA's handling of passengers' baggage.
3. Explain the strategies you would use to address any resistance to change.

SUMMARY

LEARNING OUTCOME 1: Explain the need for change in organisations.

Change is a constant in organisations. Leaders, whether they like it or not, must deal with change daily. Changing as the internal and external environments demand can make the difference between bankruptcy and survival. As the Kodak case study demonstrates, change may offer significant opportunities to extend the life cycle of the organisation to another generation. It should not be viewed in a negative light.

LEARNING OUTCOME 2: Discuss the factors that influence leading change.

Several factors may influence change in organisations. At different times, various factors can force an organisation to change. These factors may be in the internal or external environment. The PESTLE framework is useful to identify typical external factors that may force change in organisations.

LEARNING OUTCOME 3: Explain the leader's role in managing change.

The leader is responsible for the ultimate survival and performance of the organisation. The leader must be ready to address change when it happens. Not to do so may bring drastic consequences to the organisation and the followers. Leaders need to have a compelling vision and excellent communication skills to deliver change across their organisation. Their role is central to the success of the change process.

LEARNING OUTCOME 4: Demonstrate an awareness of key theories in change management.

There are several theories of change management. While most address problems as the focal point in implementing change, AI emphasises the positive aspects of the organisation in the change process.

LEARNING OUTCOME 5: Identify and explain challenges of leading change.

Leading change involves several challenges. One of the most critical is to manage resistance to change. Resistance to change can occur for several reasons, most of which relate to humans' fundamental preference for stability and the known, as opposed to instability and the unknown.

REVIEW QUESTIONS

1. Why is change necessary in contemporary organisations?

2. Explain three ways leaders can make change their ally in organisational survival and growth.

3. Describe Kurt Lewin's model of a planned approach to organisational change and explain three strengths and three weaknesses of the model.

4. Compare and contrast Kotter's eight-step approach to emergent organisational change with the appreciative inquiry model. If you were an organisational leader, which model would you use to implement change processes in your organisation?

5. Leading change is an incredibly difficult task. Identify the challenges an organisational leader in the energy industry faces from the external environment. Describe how these can force change in the organisation.

CASE STUDY 11.4

Alan Joyce – the turnaround king

Alan Joyce is the CEO of Qantas, the national airline carrier of Australia. In 2014, due to heavy losses, he had to let go 5000 of his staff, the share price fell below A\$1 and the airline posted a huge loss (Smith, 2016). Joyce was expected to resign after trade unions, media and the federal government made known their displeasure at his performance. However, in 2016, Qantas shares hit the A\$4 mark, and the airline is now expected to post record pre-tax earnings.

Qantas achieved a significant turnaround in profitability: from a loss before tax of A\$646 million in 2013–14 to an underlying profit before tax of A\$975 million in 2014–15 (O'Halloran, 2016; Qantas, 2016). The airline was proclaimed the international turnaround airline of the year in 2015. Joyce's turnaround cause was helped by events in the external environment, particularly falling oil prices. The company's low-cost carrier Jetstar contributed by posting a A\$262 million profit. During this period, Jetstar generated more money in a six-month period than in any previous 12-month period (O'Halloran, 2016; Deloitte Access Economics, 2016).

How did Joyce change a loss-making company into a very profitable company?

Born in Ireland, Joyce holds a Master's degree in Operations Research from Trinity College in Dublin (O'Halloran, 2016). He got a taste for the airline business after working for the Irish national carrier, Aer Lingus. He moved to Australia in 1996 and became the CEO of Jetstar, the low-cost airline branch of the Qantas Group, after working as a network and schedule planner. In 2008, he took the helm at Qantas as the CEO. During his successful reign at Qantas and Jetstar, both airlines gained market leadership in their respective markets. He developed a new strategic direction for Qantas, aligning with major airlines and focusing more on the Asian market. More than anything else, he will be remembered for his signature transformation program for Qantas, the company's largest since its privatisation in 1995. Joyce served as Chairman of the International Air Transport Association between July 2012 and June 2013. In 2015, he was named Airline CEO of the Year by the CAPA Centre for Aviation, an aviation industry research firm. He was also identified as the world's second most influential gay business leader by *Financial Times* list of Top 100 Leading LGBT Executives.

During the period of the transformation, the Qantas Group has taken delivery of more than 150 new aircraft – increasing the size of its fleet by a third – and invested in infrastructure, technology and training to achieve record customer satisfaction.

Joyce is well known in the industry for having a thick skin. As the CEO of Qantas during its darkest days, he maintained a steadfast commitment to the organisation and its employees, refusing to resign. He was determined to turn the company around. He retrenched 5000 staff and received heavy criticism for the state of the company. He faced public backlash for grounding Qantas planes in response to union strike action. At the time it looked like a public relations disaster for Qantas, but the company quickly resolved the union action. After three years, various stakeholders, including the unions, media and politicians, called for him to resign. Anticipation of his fall was so widespread that John Addis from the Intelligent Investor eventually had to apologise in the *Sydney Morning Herald* for wrongly predicting that Qantas would sack its CEO (O'Halloran, 2016).

Scholars like Peter Gahan (2014) claim that Joyce faced the perfect storm at the worst possible time, and that blaming Joyce for Qantas's disastrous run was uncalled for. For example, Gahan claims that in the international market, low-cost airlines have eaten away at Qantas's traditional income routes as a full-service operator. Qantas has not been alone in losing once profitable routes to low-cost airlines. Gahan points out that Joyce faced particularly difficult challenges in Asia and the Middle East, where most airlines operate as fully or partially state-owned businesses, or benefit from subsidies and tax concessions.

After directly dealing with the unions, Joyce requested the support of the federal government to help him to revamp the company. He looked to the external environment and identified that the legal framework relating to foreign ownership of Qantas was a limiting factor in attracting significant investment funds to the company. His competitors, on the other hand, enjoyed more relaxed regulations on attracting foreign funds. The government supported him, and allowed Qantas to attract foreign investments. This was a substantial boost to Joyce's turnaround plans.

Throughout the turnaround period, Joyce says that he never wanted to compromise on the level of customer satisfaction. He was determined that none of his cost-cutting measures would lower customer satisfaction. He later expressed gratitude for the 30 000 staff who stuck by him and pulled together one of the most miraculous corporate recoveries in Australian corporate history (B & T, 2016).

As the national carrier of Australia, the Qantas Group plays a significant role in marketing Australian tourism. According to O'Halloran (2016), 32 airlines fly the 'kangaroo route' from Australia to Britain. The Asian routes are similarly competitive. Emirates, Etihad and Qatar Airlines have recently joined Singapore and Cathay Pacific Airlines in competing along these routes. Joyce has ambitious plans for Qantas, including the purchase of the new Boeing 777 8X in 2021. He has plans to fly to Ireland and other European destinations from Australia.

Addressing Qantas's 2016 Annual General Meeting, Joyce said:

> For 95 years, Qantas has always looked ahead to the next wave of change. And when we look ahead today, we see many opportunities in the rapid global changes taking place around us. The ongoing rise of Asia and its aviation market – which is already home to 50 per cent of the Qantas Group's international network. The digital and big data revolution, which is so important to how we engage our customers – and how they engage us. The changing expectations of new generations of potential customers and employees. And the need to respond to climate change with new technologies and approaches. We believe we have the knowledge and skills to turn these global forces into competitive advantages for our business. Unique experiences for our customers. And great jobs for our people. So Qantas will always keep evolving (Qantas, 2016).

The *Australian Financial Review* reports that Joyce is now seen as a role model in corporate turnarounds. He has even been dubbed the 'turnaround king' (Smith, 2016) and is considered a leader not only in the aviation industry but also in the gay community and among activists promoting research into the issue of prostate cancer, with which he was recently diagnosed. His corporate and personal profiles are very impressive, with multiple non-executive board positions, roles in mentoring innovators and contributions to global economic forums.

Critical thinking questions

1. Explain the internal and external factors that led to the radical change process at Qantas.
2. Why did Qantas employees resist to change?
3. Why is Alan Joyce considered a 'turnaround king'?
4. If you were leading Qantas at the time, how differently would you have led the change process?

REFERENCES

Anthony, S. (2016). Kodak's downfall wasn't about technology. *Harvard Business Review*, 15 July. Retrieved from: https://hbr.org/2016/07/kodaks-downfall-wasnt-about-technology.

Argyris, C. (1993). *On organizational learning*. Cambridge: Blackwell Business.

B & T (2016). Alan Joyce on the turnaround At Qantas. *B and T*, 6 April. Retrieved from: http://www.bandt.com.au/media/alan-joyce-turnaround-qantas.

Burnes, B. (1996). No such thing as… a 'one best way' to manage organizational change. *Management Decision*, 34(10), 11–18.

—— (2004). *Managing change*. 4th edn. London: FT Prentice Hall.

Cooke, B. & Burnes, B. (2013). Kurt Lewin's field theory: A review and re-evaluation. *International Journal of Management Reviews*, 15, 408–25.

Cooperrider, D., Whitney, D. & Stavros, J. (2005). *Appreciative inquiry handbook*. San Francisco, CA: Berrett-Koehler.

Cummings, T.G. & Worley, C.G. (1997). *Organisation development and change*, 6th edn. Cincinnati, OH: South-Western College Publishing.

Dawson, P. (1994). *Organisational change: A processual approach*. London: Paul Chapman Publishing.

Dawson, P.M.B. & Andriopoulos, C. (2009). *Managing change, creativity and innovation*. London: SAGE Publications.

Deloitte Access Economics (2016). *The economic contribution of Qantas Group to Australia*. Report. Retrieved from: www.qantas.com.au/infodetail/about/company/DAE-final-report .pdf.

D'Ortenzio, Carlo (2012). *Understanding change and change management processes: A case study*. Unpublished PhD thesis, University of Canberra.

Dunphy, D.C. & Stace, D.A. (1992). *Under new management: Australian organizations in transition*. Sydney: McGraw-Hill.

Freudenberg, Nicholas (2015). The 100 largest governments and corporations by revenue. *Corporations and Health Watch*. Retrieved from: www.corporationsandhealth .org/2015/08/27/the-100-largest-governments-and-corporations-by-revenue.

Gahan, P. (2014). Qantas turn-around: is Alan Joyce the right leader for the job? *The Conversation*. Retrieved from: https://theconversation.com/qantas-turn-around-is-alan-joyce-the-right-leader-for-the-job–31051.

Harper, S.C. (2001). *The forward-focused organization*. New York, NY: American Management Association.

Hatch, M.J. (1997). *Organization theory: Modern, symbolic and postmodern perspectives*. Oxford: Oxford University Press.

Kanter, R.M., Stein, B.A. & Jick, T.D. (1992). *The challenges of organizational change: How companies experience it and how leaders guide it*. New York, NY: Free Press.

Kotter, J. (1996). *Leading change*. Boston, MA: Harvard Business School Press.

Kotter, J. & Schlesinger, L. (1979). Choosing strategies for change. *Harvard Business Review*, 57(2), 106–14.

Lewin, K. (1951). Field theory in social science. In D. Cartwright (ed.), *Selected Theoretical Papers*. New York, NY: Harper & Row.

Miller, D. & Friesen, P.H. (1984). *Organizations: A quantum view*. Englewood Cliffs, NJ: Prentice Hall.

O'Halloran, B. (2016). Interview: Alan Joyce on the turnaround at Qantas. *Irish Times*, 2 April. Retrieved from: https://www.irishtimes.com/business/transport-and-tourism/interview-alan-joyce-on-the-turnaround-at-qantas-1.2595650.

Peters, L. (2012). The rhythm of leading change: Living with paradox. *Journal of Management Inquiry*, 21(4), 405–11.

Pettigrew, A.M. (1980). The politics of organizational change. In N.B. Anderson (ed.), *The human side of information processing* (pp. 45–51). Amsterdam: North Holland.

—— (1990a). Longitudinal field research on change: Theory and practice. *Organizational Science*, 3(1), 267–92.

—— (1990b). Studying strategic choice and strategic change. *Organizational Studies*, 11(1), 6–11.

Pfeffer, J. (1992). *Managing with power: Politics and influence in organizations*. Boston, MA: Harvard Business School Press.

Qantas (2016). CEO's address to Qantas 2016 Annual General Meeting. Retrieved from: www .qantasnewsroom.com.au/speeches/ceos-address-to-qantas-2016-annual-general-meeting.

Rose, K.H. (2002). Leading change: A model by John Kotter. Vanguard Ministries. Retrieved from: https://vanguardministries.org/wp-content/uploads/2017/06/Leading-Change-KottersModel_Rose.pdf

Smith, M. (2016). True leaders 2016: How Qantas CEO Alan Joyce became the turnaround king. *Australian Financial Review*, 9 August. Retrieved from: www.afr.com/brand/boss/true-leaders-2016-alan-joyce-qantas-ceo-20160711-gq37e9#ixzz4j6SaWCob.

Sparkes, M. (2012). Kodak: 130 years of history. *The Telegraph*, 19 January. Retrieved from: www.telegraph.co.uk/finance/newsbysector/retailandconsumer/9024539/Kod ak-130-years-of-history.html..

Stacey, R.D. (1993). *Strategic management and organisational dynamics*. London: Pitman.

Thomas, E.C. (n.d.). Appreciative inquiry: A positive approach to change. Institute for Public Service and Policy Research, University of South Carolina. Retrieved from: http://apiahf-c4h-wp-uploads.s3.amazonaws.com/wp-content/uploads/2016/03/Appreciative-Inquiry-Fact-Sheet.pdf.

Van, D.V., Kuipers, B. & Groeneveld, S. (2015). Held back and pushed forward: Leading change in a complex public sector environment. *Journal of Organizational Change Management*, 28(2), 290–300.

Waddell, D., Creed, A., Cummings, T. & Worley, C. (2017). *Organisation development and change*, 6th edn. Melbourne: Cengage Learning.

Weick, K.E. & Quinn, R.E. (1999). Organizational change and development. *Annual Review of Psychology*, 50, 361–86.

Weissmann, J. (2012). What killed Kodak? *The Atlantic*, 5 January. Retrieved from: www .theatlantic.com/business/archive/2012/01/what-killed-kodak/250925.

Wilson, D.C. (1992). *A strategy of change*. London: Routledge.

12

STRATEGIC LEADERSHIP AND SUCCESSION PLANNING

Nuttawuth Muenjohn and Adela McMurray

LEARNING OUTCOMES

After reading this chapter, you should be able to:

1. define a strategic plan and understand how it is developed
2. understand the critical role of strategic leadership and decision making in setting the direction and ensuring the success of organisations
3. understand the conceptual link between innovation, creativity and leadership
4. recognise the importance of succession planning in ensuring continuously effective leadership in organisations.

INTRODUCTION

THIS CHAPTER BEGINS by outlining the three main areas of activity involved in strategic management and five important stages of developing a strategic plan. The importance of communicating an organisational vision and enhancing employee motivation and commitment throughout the organisation is addressed. The critical role of strategic leadership in the success of the organisation and differences between strategic leadership and organisational leadership are then discussed. This chapter finishes by highlighting the importance of succession planning and the need to deal with employee needs and expectations regarding status and promotion within the organisation.

THE STRATEGIC MANAGEMENT PROCESS

Strategic management aims to strengthen the effectiveness of an organisation by providing an organised, coherent and systematic approach to achieving strategic objectives. It focuses attention on common goals, processes and operational decisions on longer-term objectives and is essential for maintaining strong links between the organisation and its stakeholders (Poister & Streib, 1999). **Strategy** refers to the processes by which managers translate and implement organisational policy so that distinct patterns emerge that inform and establish the organisation's intention (Mintzberg, 1981). The process of designing and implementing strategy is complex, involving many participants within a context of continually changing information that impacts on strategy (Kaplan & Norton, 2001). The process needs to be adaptive, repetitive and cyclic so that organisational strategic patterns can emerge (Thomas, 1984).

Strategy – The processes by which managers translate and implement organisational policy so that distinct patterns emerge that inform and establish the organisation's intentions.

Strategic management can be divided into three main areas of activity: strategic formulation, implementation, and evaluation (Pollard & Hotho, 2006).

At the core of strategic management is strategic formulation through the vision statement, which includes the organisation's mission, values, goals, objectives and assessment of the external context relevant to the organisation. Strategic choices are made based on what is most desirable for the organisation. The next stage of management is to implement effective change measures to successfully implement the desired strategy. The third aspect of strategic management is the evaluation of strategy. This is concerned with performance management and measures to ensure that the chosen strategy was successful or may require adjustments in the light of the context and changing conditions. Strategy is a continual process of strategic formulation and implementation and not a single event (Pollard & Hotho, 2006). Strategic management drives a continual strategic process made up of strategic planning, finances including budgeting activities, performance management, and organisational management (Poister & Streib, 1999).

Researchers have criticised the linear and rational model of managing strategic processes because it leaves little room for innovation and creativity (Stacey, 2003). They argue this model relies too heavily on measures, predictability and controlling the organisation rather than being more generative and expansive, especially in an era of rapid change. However, others argue that managing the strategic process may appear narrow and linear, yet the step-by-step process creates the foundation for effective design and implementation of strategy (Pollard & Hotho, 2006).

Developing the strategic plan

Strategy is a way to set yourself apart from others and from your competition. It represents an organisation's unique purpose and identity (Porter, 1996). According to Hamel and Prahalad (cited in Maltz et al., 2003), strategy is viewed in these terms: 'Competition for the future is competition to create and dominate emerging opportunities – to stake out new competitive space'. Strategy relies on the communication of an organisational vision that sets it apart from other similar organisations and other competitors. Strategic planning is a formal and systematic process of creating strategy (Vecchiato, 2015). A **strategic plan** is a set of concepts and processes that shape, design and accomplish the task of formulating and implementing organisational vision (Schraeder, 2002). It guides an organisation in decisions and actions that enable it to meet challenges and manage change in a deliberate way (Bryson, 2011). Strategic planning encapsulates how an organisation acts and engages in macro thinking and engages in micro perspectives, implementing specific actions, proactivity and flexibility including decision making.

> **Strategic plan** – A set of concepts and processes that shape, design and accomplish the task of formulating and implementing the organisational vision.

Key reasons for engaging in strategic planning are to improve organisational performance (Hahn & Powers, 1999; Shrader et al., 1984) and provide the operational framework that organises how key strategies will be implemented to enhance competitive advantage and improve organisational performance (Porter, 1997). It can help build focus and momentum for change while enhancing teamwork as part of the planning process. However, not all strategic plans have a positive outcome; for example, the costs of the planning process inclusive of time and resources should not override the benefits. It requires a talented team that is committed to change and improvement because a poor strategic plan can produce a strategic wrong turn and create a strategic faux pas. Too much planning can hinder innovation and flexibility (Barry, 1998), which in turn may impact on the innovation processes that occur between employees and the innovation outcomes such as products and services (Muenjohn & McMurray, 2017).

The outcomes of the strategic plan depend on what aspects of the organisation's operations are the focus for improvement and increasing performance. For example, some organisations may focus on cutting back expenditure and reorganising and redistributing existing resources, while another may focus on improving its products and services (Byrne, 1996). Strategic plans may be used to inform staff and stakeholders with organisational information about its future direction and expectations, thereby aiming to elicit a buy-in from internal and external key stakeholders (Stahl, 1998). Strategic plans provide opportunity to inform and appease different interests within the organisation and enhance organisational coherence. Forming a favourable impression of the organisation to appease shareholders or financial institutions is a function of the strategic plan (Schraeder, 2002).

As a set of concepts and processes, the strategic plan progresses through a set of stages before completion (Barry, 1998). These are described below.

Stage 1

Organising the team, resources and current state of the organisation comprises Stage 1. A thorough analysis of the organisation's current vision and mission statements provides a focal point for what is working or not working and the foundation for further planning (Schraeder, 2002). The activity of developing a new mission statement or evaluating the effectiveness of the current statement can be a focal exercise for drawing attention to the current mission of the organisation (Schraeder, 2002).

Stage 2

At this stage, the key activity is assessing the strategic personality of the organisation (Sherman et al., 2007). The aim is to create a profile of the organisation that takes context into account, particularly positioning against competitors. This stage is focused on evaluating the internal and external environment by assessing organisational structure and culture and the effectiveness of these current frameworks and processes in meeting new strategic challenges.

> **Organisational structure –** The formalised way in which the main activities of the organisation are coordinated.

The **organisational structure** is defined as the formalised way in which the main activities of the organisation are coordinated (Sherman et al., 2007). These may differ across organisations depending on the size, strategy, purpose, technology and products and services in the market. Traditional structures are usually centralised and have a formal chain of command and control. Lesser traditional structures are more decentralised and may rely more on sharing power and control with informal channels for communication and authority Traditional structures tend to be less flexible in nature and can be effective in stable markets. On the other hand, in changing market conditions, a flexible and adaptable structure enables quicker responses to market conditions as not all of the organisation has to be involved in making quick decisions (Kukalis, 1989).

> **Organisational culture –** A framework of values, rules, symbols and rituals that have evolved over time in how things are done within an organisation.

The **organisational culture** is an organising framework of values, rules, symbols and rituals that have evolved over time in how things are done within an organisation. Those working within the organisation share common ways of doing work although the degree to which the common cultural values and rules are shared by organisational members can vary. Cultures can be integrated, differentiated or fragmented (Sherman et al., 2007). An integrated culture is characterised as consistent across the organisation. Members demonstrate clarity and consistency in reacting to change and act in a homogeneous way; that is, as a single unit. A culture that is differentiated is made up of different sub-cultures that may have differing perceptions of change and how to achieve this. In a differentiated culture, there may be groups that are more dominant and powerful in shaping change and this may cause conflict between groups. When faced with organisational change, the company reacts inconsistently, with some groups embracing it, others resisting the change and others seeing it as presenting an opportunity for a different, unrelated change. However, while change may be messy and create conflict, the firm can reach a form of internal consensus. A fragmented culture is one in which there is much discord and ambiguity, so that members are disconnected from core values and behaviours, which makes distinct workplace culture unclear. This is the most unstable environment, and consensus is difficult to achieve in this setting (Sherman et al., 2007).

Assessing the structure and culture of an organisation is a fundamental step in building a strategic profile because part of strategic planning may involve changing the structure and culture of the organisation in response to growth, change and market competitiveness. A shared culture drives the expected behaviours of those working within the organisation and shapes the interactions between people and the environment.

To assess the strength of the organisation's current strategy and the effectiveness of its market approach it is essential to conduct an assessment. For example, in terms of the effectiveness of the organisation's competitive strategy, a determination is needed about the purpose of the organisation. Is it a 'low-cost provider' that can provide cheaper services and costs than its competition? Is the organisation a differentiator because of its unique products and services? Does the organisation have focus on a specific part of the market? Does the organisation provide goods and services for specific markets? These are examples of ways to identify the organisation's strategic personality (Porter, 1980).

The assessment of the strategic personality can be coupled with the assessment of the organisation's market approach. For example, is the organisation a prospector, which means that it creates new products and services and opens new markets by responding quickly to changing conditions and new opportunities? If not, the organisation may be a defender that maintains its current products and services through improvements in processes and production. The organisation may be an analyser, which means its approach is to wait for others to create the markets, and only then seeks to enter the market by making improvements to products that compete with the existing products or services. The reactor approach, as the name suggests, has a limited strategic approach, and those using this approach only change when they are forced to. The adaptor approach, by contrast, seeks to constantly adapt strategy to fit the industry and in line with the changing life cycle of products and services (Sherman et al., 2007).

There are many tools that can be used to evaluate and assess current strategic personality and analyse organisational structure and culture. The most common tool is a SWOT analysis that frames a way to make strategic choices (Houben et al., 1999). By analysing the strengths, weaknesses, opportunities and threats, the strategic plan begins a process of mapping and identifying the driving influences and forces that decision makers need to be aware of in making decisions about the future direction of the organisations. Once these four aspects of the analysis have been identified then specific strategies can be formulated to address the priorities and timelines can be drawn up to achieve any desired outcomes (Schraeder, 2002).

Stage 3

Setting the direction of change and strategy formulation is the next stage in the strategic planning process. Making decisions about the future strategy requires that multiple stakeholders have a voice in the planning process. Having an effective strategy means that different voices within the organisation can be represented in the planning processes. Having a diversity of interests in the strategic plan improves the quality of the strategy because it allows different individuals and/or groups to participate in the decision making and future orientation of the organisation. Participation in strategic planning has shown to have ancillary benefits such as improved job engagement and job satisfaction (Daniels & Bailey, 1999) and lessened job anxiety regarding security and change (Stahl, 1998). Broad employee involvement in strategic planning does not diminish the involvement of senior management; instead it provides the opportunity for senior management to be facilitators of change, to work with a range of information, create a knowledge base from the organisation and use this to create an overall strategic planning process representative of the various stakeholders in the organisation (Schraeder, 2002). The strategic plan levels can vary; for example, there are the functional or operational-level strategies, business-level strategies, corporate-level strategies and global strategies. Various strategic tools, such as scenario planning, can be used to enhance the sense making of the strategy for inter- and intra-organisational strategising (Bowman, 2016).

Stage 4

Organisational strategic objectives and alternatives are identified and the focus is on refining the plans against key performance measures (Fletcher & Smith, 2004).

Stage 5

The final stage is to implement the plan (Barry, 1998).

Developing and communicating organisational vision

A vision is like an 'enduring promise' (Lipton, 1996, p. 85) which does not fluctuate from year to year. It creates an image of the organisation in the future but is communicated in the present to create momentum for change. A vision is made up of three parts working together to create a total picture of the organisation and its purpose and goals. A vision should inspire, clarify and focus the work of the organisation (Cartwright & Baldwin, 2007). An effective vision communicates an accessible future that is achievable and realistic. It should be compelling and inspiring to create personal connection and motivate people to action. It needs to be clear in its purpose and be flexible enough to adapt and develop to the changing context (Cartwright & Baldwin, 2007).

The mission is the first part of the vision statement and communicates why the organisation exists, who the stakeholders are and what they can expect from the organisation. The mission must appeal widely to the range of diverse stakeholders and not be relevant only to a select group or to specific interests within the organisation. The mission should help build a common understanding of the organisation and garner commitment from all stakeholders. The second part of a vision is the strategy that gives 'operational logic' (Lipton, 1996, p. 87) to the mission. The strategy explains how the mission will be achieved and the underlying principles of action in a competitive context. The third element of the vision pertains to culture. Organisational values drive many of the job-related behaviours and when they understand the values that support the mission and strategy they know what is expected of them within the context of the organisation. Shared values affect personal relations and organisational relations and provide a clear, consistent message about culture that helps create the basis for a better working environment and increased job satisfaction (Lipton, 1996).

CEOs have identified having a strong organisational vision as a key leadership trait, which includes having the knowledge and skills to convey the vision (Lipton, 1996); the leader can effectively communicate the vision so as to create significant organisational impact (Baum et al., 1998). According to Lipton (1996), a strong vision can be used to influence the organisation in the following five key ways:

1. It enhances a range of performance measures because it identifies and clarifies what is important and communicates this to internal and external stakeholders.
2. It creates a roadmap for change and can be used as a management tool to keep transformation and change on track. The vision sees the need for change and moves the organisation towards the future state.
3. It forms the basis of the strategic plan.
4. It motivates employees and gives them a common understanding of their role and career. It can also form the basis of hiring new talent and acquiring skills needed to move towards the vision goals.
5. It gives context to decisions and decision making as these are made in relation with short-term and long-term goals.

Effective communication 'synchronises the words and actions' (Knorr, 1993, p. 19) of the vision by creating an understanding about the organisation and its future direction. Communication of change is critical to the success of the organisation moving forward and much emphasis through repetition and through actions should be the basis of effective communication. For example, senior managers can effectively and consistently communicate the vision though their language, to support change. In addition, actions of senior managers, such as making regular team updates and communiques about the change, keep discussions embedded as part of the organisation's working culture (Pollack & Pollack, 2015).

Effective communication can allay much fear and distrust in employees, who may fear the worse when faced with change (Knorr, 1993). Creating a compelling message about the vision means that it is essential to show personal commitment to move the organisation in the direction of change. Leaders need to be passionate about the vision and communicate their own commitment to the future direction of the organisation. They need to be dynamic in how they communicate their future vision promises (Cartwright & Baldwin, 2007).

CASE STUDY 12.1

The Chia Co

A decade ago, chia seeds were virtually unheard of globally, but now the Aussie-grown chia is taking over the world. In 2001, while travelling the world on a Nuffield Scholarship that recognises excellence in farming, John Foss, a farmer raised in Western Australia, discovered chia seeds. With the vision to 'make a positive contribution to health and wellness globally' (Chia Co, 2017), Foss partnered with farmers who shared his vision and established the world's largest scale sustainable chia farms in the Kimberley region of Western Australia in 2003. Foss aims to make the omega-3, fiber- and protein-packed chia seeds 'available to everyone, everyday' (Crawford, 2015). The Chia Co started as a supplier for manufacturers in Asia and the USA before it expanded into the retail industry with its own brand. The Chia Co now works directly with food companies and retailers to market a farm-to-consumer product through the entire supply chain. The Chia Co has won the NAB Agribusiness Award for innovation in a new and emerging industry and the Westpac food industry association award for innovation with a new product. The Chia Co is now the world's largest producer of raw chia seeds.

Critical thinking questions
1. What is The Chia Co's vision?
2. How does The Chia Co's vision contribute to its success?

Developing motivation and commitment throughout the organisation

Commitment – A stabilising or obligation force that binds a person to a course of action in relation to their work or to the organisation.

Commitment can take many forms within and outside the organisation. The definitions of commitment generally refer to it as a stabilising or obligation force that binds a person to a course of action in relation to their work or to the organisation. These two factors, commitment as a stabilising force and one that directs behaviour, are common to most forms of commitment (Meyer, 2015).

While not all forms of commitment are beneficial (Meyer, 2015), the reduced likelihood of employee turnover with higher commitment to the organisation is a good reason to focus on enhancing commitment. It cannot be assumed that employee commitment will develop overnight; rather, the behaviours and attitudes of a committed employee develop incrementally and deeply depend on the organisation's culture and management systems. Management, as a series of symbolic actions, can clarify and interpret reasons for working in the organisation, identify behavioural cues from other employees to help shape attitudes and behaviours, and highlight the systems that recognise and support positive workplace expectations (O'Reilly, 1989).

Commitment is distinguished as affective, continuance and normative commitment. Each of these types of commitment refers to a different mindset, also referred to as a psychological bond, in how the employee is obligated to the organisation and their resultant behaviours (Meyer & Herscovitch, 2001). Developing organisational commitment is a lengthy process in which different aspects of the work and the relationships in the workplace need to be addressed.

A five-step model to develop organisational commitment based on meeting workplace needs (Stum, 2001) demonstrates the range of influences on behaviour and how employees determine if they stay or if they leave. First is the sense of well-being, both psychological and physical, as being critical to ensure that the employee works in an environment that is free from intimidation and behaviour that may be interpreted as threatening. An organisation's commitment to workplace safety and health and employee well-being enables the foundations of a relationship to form. Second, work compensations, benefits and rewards shape the relationship between the employee and their work. Seeing these workplace benefits as part of organisational culture fosters commitment as opposed to perceiving them as motivating rewards. Commitment is influenced by a sense of belonging – that is, individuals being part of a team and part of a larger vision. This means that the employee is not merely a worker, but is involved in organisational vision and ongoing development of the organisation. Open communication and transparency, which are drivers of a strong organisational culture, have been identified as ways to enhance belonging and affiliation. Leaders able to communicate a strong vision and strategy to their employees have the capacity to positively influence commitment to the organisation (Andrew & Kent, 2007).

Commitment to the organisation is enhanced when employees have opportunities for growth and development in their work. This includes opportunities to change their work, learn and develop from new experiences and have opportunities for personal growth. Work teams can influence commitment, especially when they have opportunities to develop work practices and improve efficiencies, productivity and quality. The opportunity for growth builds an obligation to stay in the organisation and continue to thrive as a result. Finally, the growing importance of work–life balance among today's employees means that the work needs to be in harmony with the life the employee has chosen. Support for employees in how their work is performed and managed needs to be matched with support for the home, family and personal interests of the employee. Recognising the importance of work and life balance enables the employee to create a lifestyle in which work and life are in harmony (Stum, 2001).

Workplace **motivation** refers to 'forces that initiate and influence an individual's work-related behaviour in terms of its form, direction, intensity and duration' (Pinder, 1998, p. 11). It refers to forces that initiate, start, energise and continue the application of our experience and expertise. These forces can come from within the individual and outside the individual, creating a process for how the individual works within their environment and the quality of the interactions.

> **Motivation** – Forces that initiate and influence an individual's work-related behaviour in terms of its form, direction, intensity and duration.

Generally, three theories dominate the explanation of how motivation is constructed. First, motivation is constructed as a form of goal setting in which the individual strives to achieve determined goals. Second, motivation can be explained as a social cognitive force in which the individual comes to realise their needs and how these can be attained or met through interactions. Finally, motivation can be enhanced by notions of organisational justice in which the distribution of rewards creates fair and equitable systems that provide individuals with what they value (Latham & Pinder, 2005). What these theoretical conceptualisations of motivation have in common is that they are a psychological process which shapes how an individual interacts with their environment. Several variables influence work motivation, such as job meaning and motivation, advancement opportunities, role clarity, job routineness, and group culture (Moynihan & Pandey, 2007).

The common typologies of motivation take two forms. *Intrinsic motivation* arises from the value of the work and the meaning it has for the individual, while *extrinsic motivation* arises from the desire to achieve outcomes that may be outside the work itself (Chalofsky & Krishna, 2009). Motivation gaps exist when individuals resist doing their work, avoid starting something new, stop doing something important or switch to doing something of lesser importance.

Drawing on Herzberg (1968), the following seven strategies enhance intrinsic and extrinsic motivation within the organisation:

1. Avoid even the appearance of dishonesty, hypocrisy, and unfairness.
2. Discourage vague, impossible and constantly changing performance goals.
3. Eliminate unnecessary rules, policy and work barriers.
4. Discourage constant competition with everyone.
5. Replace negative and/or prejudicial feedback with gap-focused feedback.
6. Help people develop self-confidence in their work skills.
7. Create a positive emotional environment at work.

To Herzberg's (1968) seven strategies above, we add an eighth strategy drawn from Clark (2003):

8. Support the development of strong personal values for performance goals.

STRATEGIC LEADERSHIP

Strategic leadership has the capacity to determine where an organisation is heading and putting in place all the necessary planning strategies to get there. In a competitive and changing organisational context, strategic leadership is needed to improve the organisation's capability and resources inclusive of building the capabilities of human resources within the organisation. Building the capability of the people ensures that the repository for important knowledge and skills is developed and grows with the organisation as it moves towards a future direction. Developing a skilled workforce is a key advantage in today's knowledge-driven economy. How leaders manage the company's resources, create value and increase capabilities requires strategic thinking, planning, implementing and evaluating (Finkelstein et al., 2009; Hitt & Duane, 2002).

Strategic leaders have the overall responsibility for the direction and success of the organisation and are ultimately held accountable for strategic decisions that influence the organisation (Annett & Stanton, 2000). Determining an organisation's direction mainly engages leaders and senior management, who are responsible for company strategy and are focused on long-range planning (Cheng, 2000, p 17).

There are numerous organisational strategic approaches, including processes, and the talent of an effective strategic leader is to make decisions about which approaches and strategies will achieve the best organisational goals (Davies, 2008). One way to differentiate strategic leadership from organisational leadership is that most leadership focuses on leading in the organisation, while strategic leadership is concerned with the leading of organisations (Boal & Hooijberg, 2001). Four characteristics are common to strategic leaders: focus on aligning the internal and external goals of the organisation; dealing with complexity, ambiguity and an overload of data and information; multitasking; and reliance on effective teams and advisors to achieve outcomes (Simsek et al., 2015).

Strategic leadership is not a one-off event; rather, it is a deliberate practice of strategic intent that also builds sustained practices (Finkelstein et al., 2009). It involves analysing, planning, implementing, monitoring and evaluating processes that influence the future of the organisation. Skills identified as critical to strategic leadership, and which enable leaders to engage their strategic thinking, include: the ability to anticipate trends, challenge convention and the status quo; the ability to interpret information and data, align policy and processes; and an open mind to learning opportunities (Schoemaker et al., 2013).

More specific understanding of strategic leadership, as distinct from leadership, can be discerned by seven specific principles that shape the role of the strategic leader. First, the strategic leader is always looking towards the future and is future oriented so that strategic planning is a future-looking strategy. The second principle is that determining the future direction requires that the strategic leader is led by good research and an evidence base for their decisions. They are held accountable for decisions and research-led and evidence-based decisions provide the necessary information to inform decision making. Strategic leaders are action oriented and focus on creating change within the organisation and being ahead of the competition. Another principle of strategic leaders is that they are open to new ideas and new ways of doing things and can evaluate new horizons for the organisation. For this reason, strategic leaders not only do the right thing but know the next right thing to do. Their strategic mindset makes them fit to lead because they understand the responsibilities and accountability of strategic leadership. Finally, a strategic leader is only as good as their team. Strategic leaders are therefore good team members, who inspire and motivate their team to create and enable the complex process of strategy (Quong & Walker, 2010).

INNOVATION, CREATIVITY AND LEADERSHIP

A range of factors have been identified as influencing organisational innovation. One of the key determinants is the style of leadership (Jung et al., 2003). Leadership that is transformational is foundational to an organisation because it has a positive influence in fostering creativity at the individual level through empowerment. At the organisational level, transformational leadership creates an innovative and supportive organisational climate (Gumusluoglu & Ilsev, 2009). Transformational leadership is an approach to leadership that creates change in individuals and the organisation with the end goal of developing engaged and empowered individuals (Bass, 1985). Transformational approaches to leadership enable creativity through the empowerment of the individual to be more autonomous in the workplace and have a greater voice in workplace processes and decision making. Fostering an individual's creativity may not be a direct result of leadership, though it may more likely be due to the autonomous nature of creative people within organisational practices and culture, influenced by the style of leadership (Mumford & Licuanan, 2004). Solving problems at the workplace level engages individuals' creativity and knowledge about the work and how it is achieved. By enabling individuals to have greater autonomy, they can define problems as they experience them, draw on relevant information, and generate a different set of possible solutions. At the heart of these activities are creativity and creative outcomes, which cannot be realised without support from leadership, who are responsible for showing that employee creative capacity is valued, and that they understand how to leverage creative values in workplace problem solving (Reiter-Palmon & Illies, 2004).

To facilitate creativity and innovation, leaders need to possess specific characteristics to lead creative efforts. For example, the leader should be a technical and professional expert in their work and have attuned creative thinking skills, so that they can contribute to development of creative and innovative suggestions and solutions. They must be able to make a discernible choice about which propositions are better suited to the situation and organisation. The leader may be called upon to influence the direction of the creativity and innovation by making a significant creative contribution to the workplace. One of the key constraints on leaders being more creative and contributing to workplace innovation is the demand on their time to meet the multifunctional role of leadership (Mintzberg, 1975). Without making time for creative thought they can only contribute in a moderate way. However, the main task of a leader who encourages creativity and innovation and has substantial expertise in their field is that they can discern between ideas and recognise value including the value proposition.

To lead creativity and innovation within an organisation requires that the leader is motivated to innovate and implement strategic choices that favour innovation (Mumford & Licuanan, 2004). The ability to communicate and motivate individuals has a positive influence on the leader's ability to create the conditions for change and innovation (Gilley et al., 2008). The leader's perception about the risks and opportunities that innovation affords is a key leadership skill for innovative organisations. Favouring innovation means that the leader does not always follow convention but seeks ways to break the rules and pursue goals that may be more broadly defined so that the unexpected can be pursued. The leader needs to have a repertoire of management strategies that enable ideas to be generated and processes that enable ideas to be implemented and trialled. The leader may or may not contribute to creativity and idea generation, but what is critical is how the creativity is managed. A leader's skills and knowledge enable them to structure for creativity at the individual and organisational levels, and direct the work around creativity. A leader needs to consider how creativity and innovation are evaluated and rewarded to build a sustainable culture of innovation (Mumford & Licuanan, 2004).

CASE STUDY 12.2

Planet Innovation

In 2016, Planet Innovation (PI) was voted Australia's Most Innovative Company for the third time in four years, among more than 1000 competitors (Langsdon, 2016). PI also won Best Innovation Culture, Best Innovation Program and Most Consistently Innovative Company. The company's innovation program includes specialised innovation training for all staff, and dedicated funding that ensures all staff can contribute to both commercial and technical ventures. Based in Melbourne, PI was founded in 2009 by four globally experienced biomedical executives (Langsdon, 2016). The following is part of a speech on innovation made by Stuart Elliott, the CEO of PI, at the 2016 CEO Institute Summit in Sydney. Read the extract and discuss what leadership styles and characteristics discussed above are reflected in Stuart's leadership style and organisational success.

> Innovation happens at the interface of different ways of thinking. It is critical to bring together people with different backgrounds, disciplines and world views to create an innovative environment. Paying attention to the floor plan so we don't have groups of people isolated from others is a simple but key step, in my view, for ensuring engineers are talking with scientists, who are talking with designers, who are talking with sales and marketing people. We currently have a team dedicated to a successful business venture that grew out of a simple conversation between one of our designers and one of our physicists over lunch. It was their different ways of thinking about the same challenge that provided the spark for what is now a product being sold around the world. Too often we see companies close the door to innovative opportunities by isolating all their staff by division. I have walked through the doors of large companies that actually put their R&D staff, manufacturing, marketing, finance and sales teams all

in separate buildings and in some cases separate cities. I often think to myself that it is as if they are deliberately trying to stifle innovation.

Getting your own people talking to each other is a big step. The next step is to stimulate innovative thinking by getting your staff out of the office, and out of their comfort, and engaging with customers. In our case, as developers of medical products, this is often engineers engaging with medical professionals, doctors, scientist, patients and sales people to better understand the true needs of the customer. Most companies I meet leave customer engagement to only a very small number of their staff. I recommend exposing as many of your team as possible to customers, partners and opinion leaders outside your four walls. This has a dramatic impact on the quality of the ideas your team can produce (Elliott, 2016).'

Reproduced with permission of Planet Innovation

Critical thinking question
Could the leadership style and characteristics that are illustrated in the above extract be applied to another business such as an iron ore mining company?

SUCCESSION PLANNING AND DEVELOPING FUTURE TALENT

As organisations continue to change and innovate, the need for talented individuals to maintain programs of change and contribute to the ongoing success of the organisation will increase (Leibman et al., 1996). While the search for and acquisition of talent is a globally competitive endeavour, effective succession planning within the organisation can ensure that the flow of talent continues. Succession planning is a necessity for most organisations to consider, especially as the demographic trends in most countries clearly show that with many baby boomers hitting retirement age there is a need to supplement their numbers with the next generation of workers. It cannot be taken for granted that the new generation of workers have the same values and requirements as previous generations. Many studies (Eisner, 2005; Nicholas, 2009) have shown that younger employees have different values and attitudes towards their work, organisation and careers. For example, the younger generation of workers desire a greater work–life balance, want work that is interesting and has meaning, and tend to be more independent than workers of previous generations (Nicholas, 2009). To attract and retain younger workers there is a need to nurture and develop talent within the organisation.

Retaining talent

Retaining talent ensures that there is capacity for knowledge transfer from senior employees to up-and-coming employees because building organisational knowledge can be a key competitive advantage in building and developing organisational continuity and know-how (Rothwell, 2002). This is especially valuable when considering expected workforce changes such as retirement, mid-career moves, company restructures and greater movement of workers between organisations and types and duration of work. A focus on succession building means that despite change, the organisation does not decrease its capacity in productivity, innovation and continued growth.

Succession planning for leadership ensures that the organisation continues to develop, especially in the face of leadership shortages at the senior levels. According to Bernthal and Wellins (2006), the organisation has three choices in response to leadership and succession building. These are to recruit highly priced external talent; develop internal talent; or simply do nothing and experience organisational decline.

Succession building is important to ensure a continuation of effective leadership within the organisation (Rothwell, 2002). Most organisations take the development and succession building of their leaders seriously. They integrate leadership development and succession planning as part of good governance expectations. While the increase of globalisation means that there is a greater supply of global leaders, great care needs to be taken when appointing an outsider. The incoming leader needs to share common organisational values and assumptions with the outgoing leader, holding many of the same qualities.

Succession planning utilises current managerial and leadership personnel to develop the next generation of leaders through mentor networks, targeted project-based learning and facilitated workshops as examples of succession planning activities (Groves, 2007). The lack of development and growth within organisations is regularly cited as a key reason for employee turnover. When the development needs of employees are addressed through effective succession management programs, employees are encouraged to stay within the organisation and apply their talent (Bernthal & Wellins, 2006).

As the organisational context continues to experience accelerated change in technologies, markets and customer demand, succession building provides the mechanism through which organisations can manage the risks resulting from workforce movement and prevent knowledge transfer loss that may result in loss of continuity and development. By building strong career paths for employees, avenues for continued staff growth and development remain open, and the organisation can more readily maintain and develop its competitive outlook and positioning (Barnett & Davis, 2008).

Succession planning requires the implementation of the following steps in a succession planning process, to ensure high impact.

Step 1. Effective succession planning requires preliminary planning that begins with support from the executive team to endorse the program. The executive team ensures that succession planning is part of the strategic vision and organisational plan, including hiring, developing and coaching employees (Cadmus, 2006). The full value of the leadership development strategy can be appreciated when senior executives take program ownership (Conner, 2000). This stage requires that succession planning tools be developed as part of the training – for example, mentor networks, project-based learning, manager-facilitated workshops, organisation-wide forums and establishing a supportive culture. To help shape the program, specific questions can form the basis of the program design: (1) What are the experiences that can best prepare people for senior management positions? (2) What skills and behaviours are needed to succeed in a global company? (3) Is the current practice of leadership development working well, and (4) how can it be modified to make it more effective? (Conner, 2000)

Step 2. Succession planning is not only to replace personnel but serves more to build and develop talent to continue and improve the organisation's performance. Communication of the program and making it transparent ensures that potential individuals are aware of the program. The program needs to have effective evaluation and a method of data collection to assess the process and the outcomes. The identification of participants can occur once the evaluation details have been confirmed.

Step 3. Review the participants and purpose for succession planning. Identify key positions within the organisation that will require new talent (Conger & Fulmer, 2003). Key tasks include identification of experiences that prepare individuals for senior management, identification of behaviours needed in the organisation and understanding of current leadership practices that work well within the organisation (Conner, 2000).

Step 4. Provide individual action plans and feedback to participants. This step may be lengthy and depends on the initial program design.

Step 5. At this stage a final evaluation of the participants is given. In the evaluation focus should be on the satisfaction rating of the program and its effectiveness as an experience by both participants and others integral to the program. From the program feedback process improvements can be implemented for the next iteration (Barnett & Davis, 2008; Hills, 2009).

CASE STUDY 12.3

Sean Cortis – CEO and Principal, Chapman Eastway

Here we present an overview of an interview with Sean Cortis, CEO and Principal of Chapman Eastway. The interview addresses Australian farm succession planning and the findings of a new report entitled *Australian farming families: Succession and inheritance* (Falkiner & Steen, 2016).

In Sean Cortis's opinion, there have been major changes in farming procedures that have taken place over the last 20 years. This is attributable to new models of business ownership being adopted by younger farmers, who have also been more willing to use business planning methods, to discuss their activities and to consult and implement professional advice. Because of changes in family structures that might, for example, be brought on by divorce, there is a greater interest in using company structures, trusts or leasing arrangements and a turning away from rigid ownership structures to newer formats that can be used as platforms for investment and capital growth and thereby provide a fairer treatment of children.

Because Australian farms are usually not large enough to sustain more than one family there has been an increasing tendency for farmers to take on additional off-farm work and the report found that two-thirds of inherited farms require the inheritors to work additional jobs off site from their farms to obtain a satisfactory income.

With the ageing of the farmer population such that more than half of Australian farmers are reported to be over 55 years of age, and with a majority indicating that they expect to retire in the next 15 years, there are looming issues for government policy and the future for agricultural productivity in Australia unless arrangements are made for successful succession planning. However, since only 54 per cent of surveyed farmers have a succession plan in place, the potential for retirement will become difficult. It was found that farmers do not understand the potential difficulty in their being able to access sufficient funds for retirement and that they have an inadequate understanding of the legal, financial and taxation implications for the transfer of assets. As a result, they are likely to have to rely on the sale of farm assets to fund their retirement and are likely to encounter family conflict because of misunderstandings and unsatisfied expectations.

Source: Adapted from Queensland Country Life (2016)

Critical thinking questions

1. Why it is crucial for Australian farmers to develop succession plans?
2. In your opinion, what are the major challenges for Australian farmers in developing succession plans?
3. What key factors do Australian farmers need to consider when developing a succession plan?

Dealing with employee needs and expectations regarding career progression

In accepting a position within the organisation, an employee enters into a psychological contract in which they have certain career expectations from their contract of employment, including entitlements as part of employer–employee obligations. A psychological contract refers to beliefs about the employment conditions and terms and how these can be met by the individual's commitment and the organisation's commitment to the employee (Turnley & Feldman, 2000). In this relationship exchange, there is an expectancy about rewards and benefits for the employee in exchange for performance. For example, workplace opportunities such as career planning and development, job security and prospects of internal mobility are related to strengthening the psychological commitment and are part of work expectations leading to job satisfaction (Gaertner & Nollen, 1989). Without organisational practices related to career planning and development and the lack of opportunities to take on new roles, perceptions of career plateauing are accentuated, leading to lower job satisfaction in employees and a break in the psychological contract.

Promotion systems are used by organisations to identify and control the mobility of individuals within the organisation (Ferris et al., 1992). However, the promotion system needs to be perceived as fair and equitable in the way that decisions are made and how the rewards, such as promotion, are distributed. Research shows that positive perceptions between organisational commitment and procedural processes that are deemed fair and just enhance organisation commitment (Lemons & Jones, 2001). This means that employees have faith in the processes of promotion and in the belief that entitlements will be fairly fulfilled by the organisation.

When entitlements are not fulfilled this may result in a belief about a breach of the psychological contract between the individual and the employer. The result may lead to behaviour that is counterproductive in terms of organisational goals and performance expectations (Paul et al., 2000) and leads to greater employee turnover (Cotton & Tuttle, 1986). Managing the career and promotion expectations of the employee is as critical as providing opportunities for career advancement and professional development.

Promotions are often based on numerous and ambiguous criteria that involved some subjective judgement. How promotions are managed reflects equal opportunity, organisational effectiveness and career development and planning. Promotion processes can vary across industry and organisation but they generally occur in five stages: strategy and policy formulation, search for candidates, information gathering and managing, evaluation and choice, and implementation. An effective promotion process needs to define appropriate criteria for promotion and suitable measures for meeting promotion standards. Effective organisational promotion measures also need to consider future performance, potential and promotability in addition to the broader success of the team in which the incumbent is working (Stumpf & London, 1981).

Different workers exhibit different strengths in playing out their own psychological contract. There are negligible differences in job satisfaction and effective commitment when comparing full-time and part-time employees. Work status does not affect how employees respond to their expectations and seems to have limited influence on their psychological contract (Conway & Briner, 2002).

SUMMARY

LEARNING OUTCOME 1: Define a strategic plan and understand how it is developed.

A strategic plan is a set of concepts and processes that shape, design and accomplish the task of formulating and implementing organisational vision. It guides an organisation in decisions and actions that enable it to meet challenges and manage change in a deliberate way. Strategic planning encapsulates how an organisation acts and thinks. It is both big picture and specific in its actions, is proactive and flexible, and is a guide for decision making. Key reasons for strategic planning are to improve organisational performance and provide the operational framework that organises how key strategies will be implemented to enhance competitive advantage and improve organisational performance.

As a set of concepts and processes, the strategic plan progresses through distinct stages before completion: (1) organising the team, resources and current state of the organisation; (2) assessing the strategic personality of the organisation; (3) setting the direction of change and strategy formulation; (4) identifying strategic objectives and alternatives; and (5) implementing the plan.

LEARNING OUTCOME 2: Understand the critical role of strategic leadership and decision making in setting the direction and ensuring the success of organisations.

In a competitive and changing organisational context strategic leadership is needed to increase the organisation's capability and resources, including building the human resource capabilities within the organisation. Strategic leaders have the overall responsibility for the direction and success of the organisation and are ultimately held accountable for strategic decisions that influence the organisation. Strategic leadership is not a one-off event; rather, it is a deliberate practice of strategic intent that also builds sustained practices. It involves analysing, planning, implementing, monitoring and evaluating processes that influence the future of the organisation.

LEARNING OUTCOME 3: Understand the conceptual link between innovation, creativity and leadership.

One of the key determinants that influences organisational innovation is leadership style. Leadership that is transformational is foundational. It has a positive influence in fostering creativity at the individual level via empowerment and at organisational levels through an innovative supportive organisational climate. Fostering individual creativity may not be a direct result of leadership; more likely the autonomous nature of creative people is recognised within organisational practices and culture, which are influenced by the style of leadership. By enabling individuals to have greater autonomy, leaders can help employees to define problems as they experience them, draw on relevant information and generate a different set of possible solutions. To enable creativity and innovation, leaders require specific characteristics to lead creative efforts, such as being a technical and professional expert, and being creative. Furthermore, leaders must be motivated to innovate and implement strategic choices that favour innovation.

LEARNING OUTCOME 4: Recognise the importance of succession planning in ensuring continuously effective leadership in organisations.

Succession planning is a necessity for most organisations to consider, especially as the demographic trends in most countries clearly show that with many baby boomers hitting retirement age, there is a need to supplement their numbers with the next generation of workers. It cannot be taken for granted that the new generation of workers have the same values and requirements as the previous generations. While the search for and acquisition of talent is a globally competitive endeavour, effective succession planning within the organisation can ensure that the flow of talent continues. Retaining talent also ensures that there is capacity for the transfer of knowledge from senior to up-and-coming employees. Building on organisational knowledge can be a key competitive advantage in building and developing continuity of the know-how of the organisation. Succession building is important to ensure a continuation of effective leadership within the organisation. As the organisational context continues to experience accelerated change in technologies, markets, and customers' demands, succession building provides the mechanism through which organisations can manage the risks resulting from workforce movement and prevent knowledge transfer loss that may result in loss of continuity and development.

REVIEW QUESTIONS

1. What are the processes of developing a strategic plan?

2. How to communicate organisational vision to employees?

3. What are the most effective ways for a strategic leader to motivate staff?

4. Why is succession planning for leadership important? Please use an Australian example to illustrate.

5. How does the style of leadership contribute to an organisation's innovation and creativity capabilities?

CASE STUDY 12.4

Australian Pork Strategic Plan

The following is an extract from Australian Pork's Strategic Plan for 2015–20.

The Australian pork industry has made great progress in the 2010–2015 period. Pig producer balance sheets have been rebuilt after the profitability crisis of 2007–2008. We've seen the proactive and progressive change on the voluntary removal of sow stalls, the acceptance and adoption of a world class industry quality assurance system and our recognition as leaders in Australian rural research, development and extension strategies. This is being done in a way that results in more predictable returns and outcomes to pig producers and Australian society more broadly. As a consequence of this progress, our vision has evolved to:

'Australian Pork – A uniquely contemporary part of our food industry'

The central tenet of this 2015–2020 Strategic Plan is anticipating and responding to emerging consumer opportunities and community expectations while significantly contributing to the improvement and certainty of pig producer revenues. The content and direction of this Plan have been prepared following significant consultation with producers, processors, retailers, governments – both state and federal, as well as aligned key industry stakeholders. I would like to especially thank the Australian Pork Limited Delegates, who formed the Delegates Reference Group during the consultation process.

This plan has as a core strategic focus the goal of maintaining the momentum of profitable and sustainable growth in existing markets. An additional area of focus is building robust foundations to expand new business opportunities in new markets, both internationally and domestically.

There are five Strategic Objectives underpinning the achievement of this growth and expansion.

- Growing Consumer Appeal aims to improve consumer experiences with Australian pork and its image and popularity through better understanding of how to prepare it and what makes it different.
- Building Markets focuses on converting that consumer appeal into better value for producers and other participants in the value chain through a deep understanding of customer needs in chosen segments.
- Driving Value Chain Integrity refers to building on Australia's clean and safe image both at home and abroad while strengthening the already high degree of trust for Australian pork through industry integrity systems.
- Leading Sustainability highlights our priorities to be proactive as an industry in fostering the delivery of viable and sustainable farming practices and a healthy and profitable industry.
- Improving Capability continues the focus on rapid and complete uptake and adoption of information and technologies that will improve the productivity and reputation of the total pork value chain. It also looks to optimise operational effectiveness to maximise the return on producer levies and Federal Government funding.

As one of our most important investors the Australian taxpayer, as represented by the Federal Government, should feel comfort in the knowledge that this Strategic Plan represents positive benefits for not only our industry but for the community at large. Australians can feel proud of their pork industry as one which operates responsibly and ethically in the production of nutritious and affordable food.

One demonstration of the clarity and focus of this Strategic Plan is that the major objectives, programs, outcomes and key results measures have been refined to such an extent that they can be articulated in two tables included later in this document.

The next five years are devoted to accelerating the current momentum in existing markets and developing new and exciting market prospects for the future. We look forward to the implementation of this Strategic Plan as providing a uniting and catalytic influence on the Australian pork industry.

Source: Australian Pork (2015), reproduced with permission

Critical thinking questions
1. What is Australian Pork Limited's 2015–20 vision?
2. What are Australian Pork Limited's strategic objectives?
3. How do Australian Pork Limited's 2015–20 vision, strategic objectives and strategic plan serve the market needs?
4. What drawbacks from the organisation's strategic plan do you perceive from the CEO's statement? Justify your answer.

REFERENCES

Andrew, D.P. & Kent, A. (2007). The impact of perceived leadership behaviors on satisfaction, commitment, and motivation. *International Journal of Coaching Science*, 1(1), 37–58.

Annett, J. & Stanton, N.A. (2000). Team work: A problem for ergonomics? *Ergonomics*, 43(8), 1045–51.

Australian Pork (2015). *Australian Pork Limited: Strategic plan, 2015–2020*. Barton, ACT: A. P. Limited.

Barnett, R. & Davis, S. (2008). Creating greater success in succession planning. *Advances in Developing Human Resources*, 10(5), 721–39.

Barry, B.W. (1998). A beginner's guide to strategic planning. *The Futurist*, 32(3), 33.

Bass, B.M. (1985). *Leadership and performance beyond expectations*. New York, NY: Free Press.

Baum, J.R., Locke, E.A. & Kirkpatrick, S.A. (1998). A longitudinal study of the relation of vision and vision communication to venture growth in entrepreneurial firms. *Journal of Applied Psychology*, 83(1), 43–54.

Bernthal, P. & Wellins, R. (2006). Trends in leader development and succession. *People and Strategy*, 29(2), 31.

Boal, K.B. & Hooijberg, R. (2001). Strategic leadership research: Moving on. *Leadership Quarterly*, 11(4), 515–49.

Bowman, G. (2016). The practice of scenario planning: An analysis of inter- and intra-organizational strategizing. *British Journal of Management*, 27(1), 77–96.

Bryson, J.M. (2011). *Strategic planning for public and nonprofit organizations: A guide to strengthening and sustaining organizational achievement*, 4th edn. New York, NY: John Wiley & Sons.

Byrne, J.A. (1996). Strategic planing: It's back. *Business Week*, 26 August, 46–52.

Cadmus, E. (2006). Succession planning: Multilevel organizational strategies for the new workforce. *Journal of Nursing Administration*, 36(6), 298–303.

Cartwright, T. & Baldwin, D. (2007). *Communicating your vision*. Greensboro, NC: Center for Creative Leadership.

Chalofsky, N. & Krishna, V. (2009). Meaningfulness, commitment, and engagement: The intersection of a deeper level of intrinsic motivation. *Advances in Developing Human Resources*, 11(2), 189–203.

Cheng, Y.C. (2000). Strategic leadership for educational transformation in the new millennium, *Chulalongkorn Educational Review*, 6(2), 15–32.

Chia Company (2017). Our story. Retrieved from https://thechiaco.com/au/our-story.

Clark, R.E. (2003). Fostering the work motivation of individuals and teams. *Performance Improvement*, 42(3), 21–9.

Conger, J.A. & Fulmer, R.M. (2003). Developing your leadership pipeline. *Harvard Business Review*, 81(12), 76–85.

Conner, J. (2000). Developing the global leaders of tomorrow. *Human Resource Management*, 39(2–3), 147–157.

Conway, N. & Briner, R.B. (2002). Full-time versus part-time employees: Understanding the links between work status, the psychological contract, and attitudes. *Journal of Vocational Behavior*, 61(2), 279–301.

Cotton, J.L. & Tuttle, J.M. (1986). Employee turnover: A meta-analysis and review with implications for research. *Academy of Management Review*, 11(1), 55–70.

Crawford, E. (2015). Chia is here to stay, thanks to long-term planning by the Chia Co. Food Navigator, 9 January. Retrieved from: www.foodnavigator-usa.com/Article/2015/01/09/Chia-is-here-to-stay-thanks-to-long-term-planning-by-The-Chia-Co.

Daniels, K. & Bailey, A. (1999). Strategy development processes and participation in decision making: Predictors of role stressors and job satisfaction. *Journal of Applied Management Studies*, 8(1), 27.

Davies, P.L. (2008). *Gower and Davies: The principles of modern company law*, 8th edn. London: Sweet & Maxwell.

Eisner, S.P. (2005). Managing generation Y. *SAM Advanced Management Journal*, 70(4), 4.

Elliott, S. (2016). Two ways every CEO can increase innovation. *Planet Innovation*. Retrieved from: https://planetinnovation.com.au/two-ways-every-ceo-can-increase-innovation.

Falkiner, O. & Steen, A. (2016). *Australian farming families: Succession and inheritance*. Report. Sydney: Chapman Eastway and Charles Sturt University. Retrieved from: www.chapmaneastway.com.au/sites/default/files/CE_Succession Report.pdf.

Ferris, G.R., Buckley, M.R. & Allen, G.M. (1992). Promotion systems in organizations. *People and Strategy*, 15(3), 47–68.

Finkelstein, S., Hambrick, D.C. & Cannella, A.A. (2009). *Strategic leadership: Theory and research on executives, top management teams, and boards*. Oxford: Oxford University Press.

Fletcher, H.D. & Smith, D.B. (2004). Managing for value: Developing a performance measurement system integrating economic value added and the balanced scorecard in strategic planning. *Journal of Business Strategies*, 21(1), 1–17.

Gaertner, K.N. & Nollen, S.D. (1989). Career experiences, perceptions of employment practices, and psychological commitment to the organization. *Human Relations*, 42(11), 975–91.

Gilley, A., Dixon, P. & Gilley, J.W. (2008). Characteristics of leadership effectiveness: Implementing change and driving innovation in organizations. *Human Resource Development Quarterly*, 19(2), 153–69.

Groves, K.S. (2007). Integrating leadership development and succession planning best practices. *Journal of Management Development*, 26(3), 239–60.

Gumusluoglu, L. & Ilsev, A. (2009). Transformational leadership, creativity, and organizational innovation. *Journal of Business Research*, 62(4), 461–73.

Hahn, W. & Powers, T. (1999). The impact of planning sophistication and implementation on firm performance. *Journal of Business and Economic Studies*, 5(2), 19–35.

Herzberg, F. (1968*)*. One more time: How do you motivate employees?, *Harvard Business Review*, 46(1), 53–62.

Hills, A. (2009). Succession planning – or smart talent management? *Industrial and Commercial Training*, 41(1), 3–8.

Hitt, M.A. & Duane, R. (2002). The essence of strategic leadership: Managing human and social capital. *Journal of Leadership & Organizational Studies*, 9(1), 3–14.

Houben, G., Lenie, K. & Vanhoof, K. (1999). A knowledge-based SWOT-analysis system as an instrument for strategic planning in small and medium sized enterprises. *Decision Support Systems*, 26(2), 125–35.

Jung, D.I., Chow, C. & Wu, A. (2003). The role of transformational leadership in enhancing organizational innovation: Hypotheses and some preliminary findings. *Leadership Quarterly*, 14(4), 525–44.

Kaplan, R.S. & Norton, D.P. (2001). The strategy-focused organization. *Strategy and Leadership*, 29(3), 41–2.

Knorr, R.O. (1993). Leadership: A strategy for communicating change. *Journal of Business Strategy*, 14(4), 18–20.

Kukalis, S. (1989). The relationship among firm characteristics and design of strategic planning systems in large organizations. *Journal of Management*, 15(4), 565–79.

Langsdon, R. (2016). PI wins Australia's most innovative company award for the third time. *Planet Innovation*. Retrieved from: https://planetinnovation.com.au/pi-wins-australias-innovative-company-award-third-time.

Latham, G.P. & Pinder, C.C. (2005). Work motivation theory and research at the dawn of the twenty-first century. *Annual Review of Psychology*, 56, 485–516.

Leibman, M., Bruer, R.A. & Maki, B.R. (1996). Succession management: The next generation of succession planning. *People and Strategy*, 19(3), 16–29.

Lemons, M.A. & Jones, C.A. (2001). Procedural justice in promotion decisions: Using perceptions of fairness to build employee commitment. *Journal of Managerial Psychology*, 16(4), 268–81.

Lipton, M. (1996). Demystifying the development of an organizational vision. *MIT Sloan Management Review*, 37(4), 83.

Maltz, A.C., Shenhar, A.J. & Reilly, R.R. (2003). Beyond the balanced scorecard: Refining the search for organizational success measures. *Long Range Planning*, 36(2), 187–204.

Meyer, J.P. (2015). Organizational commitment. In C.L. Cooper (ed.),*Wiley Encyclopedia of Management*, vol. 5 (pp. 1–3). New York, NY: John Wiley & Sons.

Meyer, J.P. & Herscovitch, L. (2001). Commitment in the workplace: Toward a general model. *Human Resource Management Review*, 11(3), 299–326.

Mintzberg, H. (1975). *Impediments to the use of managment information: A Study*. New York, NY: National Association of Accountants.

—— (1981). Research notes and communications what is planning anyway? *Strategic Management Journal*, 2(3), 319–24.

Moynihan, D.P. & Pandey, S.K. (2007). The role of organizations in fostering public service motivation. *Public Administration Review*, 67(1), 40–53.

Muenjohn, N. & McMurray, A. (2017). Design leadership, work values ethic and workplace innovation: An investigation of SMEs in Thailand and Vietnam. *Asia Pacific Business Research: Special Issue: Human Capital in Asia*, 23(2), 192–204.

Mumford, M.D. & Licuanan, B. (2004). Leading for innovation: Conclusions, issues, and directions. *The leadership quarterly*, 15(1), 163–71.

Nicholas, A. (2009). Generational perceptions: Workers and consumers. *Journal of Business and Economics Research*, 7(10), 47–52.

O'Reilly, C. (1989). Corporations, culture, and commitment: Motivation and social control in organizations. *California Management Review*, 31(4), 9–25.

Paul, R.J., Niehoff, B.P. & Turnley, W.H. (2000). Empowerment, expectations, and the psychological contract – managing the dilemmas and gaining the advantages. *Journal of Socio-Economics*, 29(5), 471–85.

Pinder, C.C. (1998). *Work motivation in organizational behavior*. New Jersey: Prentice Hall.

Poister, T.H. & Streib, G.D. (1999). Strategic management in the public sector: Concepts, models, and processes. *Public Productivity and Management Review*, 308–25.

Pollack, J. & Pollack, R. (2015). Using Kotter's eight stage process to manage an organisational change program: Presentation and practice. *Systemic Practice and Action Research*, 28(1), 51–66.

Pollard, D. & Hotho, S. (2006). Crises, scenarios and the strategic management process. *Management Decision*, 44(6), 721–36.

Porter, M.E. (1980). *Competitive strategy: Techniques for analyzing industries and competitors*. New York, NY: Free Press.

—— (1996). What is strategy? *Harvard Business Review*, 74(6), 61–78.

—— (1997). Competitive strategy. *Measuring Business Excellence*, 1(2), 12–17.

Queensland Country Life (2016). Succession planning failure continues to limit retirement, ownership options. Retrieved from: www.queenslandcountrylife.com.au/story/4143291/succession-planning-failure-continues-to-hamper-farm-families.

Quong, T. & Walker, A. (2010). Seven principles of strategic leadership. *International Studies in Educational Administration*, 38(1), 22–34.

Reiter-Palmon, R. & Illies, J.J. (2004). Leadership and creativity: Understanding leadership from a creative problem-solving perspective. *Leadership Quarterly*, 15(1), 55–77.

Rothwell, W.J. (2002). Putting success into your succession planning. *Journal of Business Strategy*, 23(3), 32–7.

Schoemaker, P.J., Krupp, S. & Howland, S. (2013). Strategic leadership: The essential skills. *Harvard Business Review*, 91(1), 131–4.

Schraeder, M. (2002). A simplified approach to strategic planning: practical considerations and an illustrated example. *Business Process Management Journal*, 8(1), 8–18.

Sherman, H., Rowley, D.J. & Armandi, B.R. (2007). Developing a strategic profile: The pre-planning phase of strategic management. *Business Strategy Series*, 8(3), 162–71.

Shrader, C.B., Taylor, L. & Dalton, D.R. (1984). Strategic planning and organizational performance: a critical appraisal. *Journal of Management*, 10(2), 149–71.

Simsek, Z., Jansen, J.J., Minichilli, A. & Escriba-Esteve, A. (2015). Strategic leadership and leaders in entrepreneurial contexts: A nexus for innovation and impact missed? *Journal of Management Studies*, 52(4), 463–78.

Stacey, R. (2003). *Strategic management and organizational dynamics*. London: Pittman.

Stahl, D.A. (1988). Leadership in these changing times. *Nursing Management*, 29(4), 16–8.

Stum, D.L. (2001). Maslow revisited: Building the employee commitment pyramid. *Strategy and Leadership*, 29(4), 4–9.

Stumpf, S.A. & London, M. (1981). Management promotions: Individual and organizational factors influencing the decision process. *Academy of Management Review*, 6(4), 539–49.

Thomas, H. (1984). Strategic decision analysis: applied decision analysis and its role in the strategic management process. *Strategic Management Journal*, 5(2), 139–56.

Turnley, W.H. & Feldman, D.C. (2000). Re-examining the effects of psychological contract violations: unmet expectations and job dissatisfaction as mediators. *Journal of Organizational Behavior*, 21(1), 25–42.

Vecchiato, R. (2015). Strategic planning and organizational flexibility in turbulent environments. *Foresight*, 17(3), 257–73.

13

EVALUATING LEADERSHIP PERFORMANCE AND LEADERSHIP DEVELOPMENT

Nuttawuth Muenjohn and Adela McMurray

LEARNING OUTCOMES

After reading this chapter, you should be able to:

1. explain the five widely used leadership inventories

2. identify and describe the differences between leader development and leadership development

3. explain why feedback is important for evaluating leadership performance

4. apply the key models and types of feedback, in particular the 360-degree model

5. understand virtual leadership.

INTRODUCTION

THIS CHAPTER INCORPORATES three main parts. The first part starts with an explanation of the relationship between effective leadership and organisational performance, a challenging situation in the current competitive business context. Organisational leadership inventories and indicators are further discussed. These include the Leadership Practices Inventory, Inventory of Leadership Styles, Multifactor Leadership Questionnaire, Global Executive Leadership Inventory, and the Leadership Effectiveness and Adaptability Description inventory.

The second part of this chapter discusses the importance of evaluating leadership performance. Key models and different types of feedback are presented, with a focus on the 360-degree model. This 360-degree feedback approach can offer the recipient unique and important information about their performance from various perspectives.

This chapter concludes with a description and summary of key qualitative and quantitative instruments in leadership evaluation, after which there is an in-depth discussion addressing virtual leadership of teams.

LEADERSHIP EFFECTIVENESS
Evaluating leadership performance

Current research focuses on the links between effective leadership and organisational effectiveness (Bass, 1985; Yukl, 2013). Leaders are instrumental in shaping organisational norms and can help shape how employees work within their environments. Aspects of leadership, such as leadership style, skills and competences, can be seen as assets that shape and influence how organisations work with their people and processes to generate performance. However, measuring a leader's performance is complicated because, while there may be a link between the leadership and organisational performance, the link can be indirect, which can make measures difficult to identify and specify (de Hoogh et al., 2004).

The relationship between performance and effectiveness is especially strong in the current competitive business context where specific leadership behaviours can enhance the overall organisational performance. For example, effective transactional leaders can ensure that organisations meet their goals and objectives by their capacity to use rewards that enhance job performance and ensure necessary resources are available to employees. Visionary leadership can build strategy towards a future state and draw on skills to build commitment to the organisational vision. This kind of leadership is responsible for high levels of organisational trust, commitment and motivation, thus leading to enhanced employee performance and, in turn, organisational performance. These two examples show how different leadership paradigms lead to organisational performance (Jing & Avery, 2011). Indicators that show a link between the leadership paradigm that a leader uses and performance achieved include measures such as: decision-making capacity, power usage and power distance between employee and leader, employee commitment, employee responsibility, structure of management and leadership within the organisation, diversity and locus of control – all identifie as appropriate measures of leadership paradigms (Jing & Avery, 2011).

As leadership is difficult to define and the styles of leadership are varied, a key determinant in evaluating the link between leadership and organisational performance is the influence of context on measures of performance. Organisational performance is dependent on a range of contextual constraints that may be out of the leader's control. In such cases, the measures for leadership effectiveness may not accurately reflect leadership capacity as this is constrained by environmental forces. It is suggested that multiple performance indicators may be used to measure performance to achieve a more accurate evaluation of the leadership within a specific environment and context (de Hoogh et al., 2004).

Another key variant in measuring leadership effectiveness is the measure and the methodology used to evaluate the leadership. Performance measures have been criticised for being too subjective and too limited (de Hoogh et al., 2004). Similarly, having knowledge of a leader's prior performance can result in a bias in measurements (Binning et al., 1986) and some measures that rely on a leader's self-reporting have also been criticised for bias in measuring effectiveness that may result in a halo effect (e.g. Bass & Avolio, 1989), where the leader's performance is overly positive without identifying any weakness in their leadership. Another methodological weakness is the appropriateness of the criteria used as measures. For example, a criticism of performance methodologies is that they neglect to focus on financial performance, employee and customer satisfaction as three interrelated factors – they use either financial or non-financial measures to evaluate performance rather than define performance in both financial and non-financial terms (Jing & Avery, 2011).

A strong correlation has been identified between financial performance, customer satisfaction and employee satisfaction. Leadership effectiveness should take into account these three measures to determine the link between organisational performance and leadership (Jing & Avery, 2011).

To measure the effectiveness of a leader is challenging because effectiveness measures depend on many factors, such as who is making the judgement, levels of experience and the tasks being measured. For example, experience gained from previous roles was found in one study to have significant influence on leadership performance and effectiveness (Day et al., 2014). Others in the organisation may view the main roles associated with effective leadership differently, depending on what they expect from the leader to perform their work. For example, when asking managers, peers and subordinates about the monitoring role of leadership, peers did not rate this as an example of leadership effectiveness while managers and subordinates highly rated this skill in effective leadership (Hooijberg & Choi, 2000). Leadership effectiveness can depend on the different perspectives and expectations of leaders that are dependent on a range of people and situations that are included in leadership roles. As researchers have suggested, effectiveness may be in the eyes of the evaluator (Day et al., 2014).

Inventories for effective organisational leadership

Inventories are instruments that measure the behaviour of leaders and attempt to identify and evaluate those behaviours in terms of leadership effectiveness. The measures used in inventories are dependent on the leadership style and paradigm relevant to the leader. The most widely used leadership inventories are:

- Leadership Practices Inventory (LPI)
- Inventory of Leadership Styles (ILS)
- Multifactor Leadership Questionnaire (MLQ)
- Global Executive Leadership Inventory (GELI)
- Leadership Effectiveness and Adaptability Description (LEAD).

Leadership Practices Inventory (LPI)

Posner and Kouzes's (1988) leadership inventory identifies the key transformational leadership behaviours visionary leaders display. The five behaviours are: Challenging, Inspiring, Enabling, Modelling and Encouraging. The Leadership Practices Inventory (LPI) consists of a questionnaire of 30 items across these five dimensions and covers how the leader puts them into practice. According to research the evaluation appears to be more accurate for leaders with low to medium leadership competence as many of the items are practice-based, suggesting that the inventory can also be used for training and development purposes (Zagorsek et al., 2006). Overall, the LPI assesses the effectiveness and quality of transformational leadership (Posner & Kouzes, 1988).

Inventory of Leadership Styles (ILS)

Leadership is most effective when the style of leadership responds to a situation. The Inventory of Leadership Styles (ILS), also known as the Managerial Styles Questionnaire (MSQ), is based on the work of psychologists McClelland, Litwin and Stringer at Harvard University in the mid-1960s (see Litwin & Stringer, 1968) and was designed to measure leadership effectiveness most notably by focusing on workplace climate that either enhances or impedes performance. The ILS measures six leadership styles and how these influence organisational climate and drive team performances. The styles are:

- *directive/coercive*: this can be a threatening style aimed at gaining immediate compliance from employees
- *visionary/authoritative*: providing long-term vision and leadership by inspiring people to see the bigger picture
- *afflictive*: creating trust and harmony that has the effect of boosting morale and mitigates conflict
- *participative/democratic*: focuses on listening and being a team player; the leader values team input and seeks ways to reach group consensus and generating new ideas

- *pacesetting*: leading by example and accomplishing tasks to high standards and can rely on micromanaging to complete tasks
- *coaching*: focusing on the professional growth of employees by listening to strengths and weaknesses and how to develop employee strengths.

The ILS feedback is gathered from self-description, where the individual self-assessed their thinking, effectiveness and levels of satisfaction in their work and home life. This part identifies how the leader thinks they are behaving. The second level of data is collected from others' descriptions of the leader's behaviour. The descriptions can come from up to 12 peers, managers or subordinates where they provide feedback on the leader's effectiveness and behaviour. A comparison is then made of the surveys and shows how the leader thinks they are behaving compared to other people's assessments of their behaviour. The ILS is especially effective in assessing organisational climate because it helps show the impact of a leader's behaviour on their workplace and colleagues.

Multifactor Leadership Questionnaire (MLQ)

The Multifactor Leadership Questionnaire (MLQ) was developed by Bass and Avolio (2004) to assess a range of transactional, transformational and non-standard leadership practices. The questionnaire is based on:

- *five transformational scales*: inspirational; motivational; idealised influence (attribution and behaviour); intellectual stimulation; and individualised consideration
- *three transactional scales*: contingent reward; active management by exception; and active management by exception (or passive)
- *one laissez-faire scale*: laissez-faire
- *three outcome scales*: extra effort; effective leader's behaviour; follower satisfaction.

When these scales are assessed together, they represent a full picture of leadership practice, which is called the 'full range of leadership' (Avolio, Bass & Zhu, 2004). According to Muenjohn and Armstrong (2008), this model – which has nine correlations – could be the most appropriate and adequate way to describe the factor constructs of transformational and transactional leadership.

Global Executive Leadership Inventory (GELI)

The GELI, developed by INSEAD Professor Manfred Kets de Vries in 2005, investigates and evaluates what it means to be a world-class leader (Rook & Kessler, 2013). It is especially relevant in the current context of globalisation and mobility so that leaders need to be adaptive in different contexts. It is one of the few inventories that aim to measure global leadership by identifying and understanding leadership strengths and weaknesses and exploring how to improve leadership. The evaluation works by asking participants to answer 100 'action-and-behaviour' based questions that are designed to measure competency within 12 dimensions:

1. visioning
2. empowering
3. energising
4. designing and aligning
5. rewarding and feedback
6. team building
7. outside orientation
8. global mindset
9. tenacity
10. emotional intelligence
11. life balance
12. resilience to stress (Kets de Vries, 2005).

Participants rate their own performance and then compare their personal rating with that of their superiors, direct reports, co-workers and others, who respond to the questionnaire anonymously. The performance is measured against a norm group of senior executives worldwide (Kets de Vries et al., 2007).

Leadership Effectiveness and Adaptability Description (LEAD)

The LEAD inventory, developed by Hersey and Blanchard (1988), evaluates leaders' adaptability and leadership styles in response to different demands of a situation. It is based on the premise that flexibility of leadership styles is a necessity for effective leaders, and required of leaders, if they are to meet the organisation's goals. The LEAD instrument is a questionnaire that determines the styles of leadership that the participant uses and how followers perceive this. The questionnaire is in the form of the LEAD-Self instrument and the LEAD in which the leader self-reports on their leadership and the perception of their leadership. The LEAD-Other instrument involves staff members' assessing their leaders and results in an evaluation of the leader. The scoring of the questionnaire is based on an adaptability scale that is measured at low, moderate or high degrees of adaptability. For example, a traditional leadership style where the leader is directive and authoritarian in their style of leadership would score low on the adaptability scale. On the other hand, leadership that is more flexible and adaptive would score high on the scale. However, the scoring and assessment is dependent on the readiness and maturity of the employees and the perception of the type of leadership (Silverthorne & Wang, 2001).

TYPES OF LEADERSHIP DEVELOPMENT

Leadership development involves building interpersonal and intrapersonal capacity – this covers leader development as well as leadership development (McCauley, Moxley & Van Velsor, 1998). The development of leadership within an organisation requires that a distinction is made between leader development and leadership development. While both are necessary investments for organisations, developing the leader is an individualistic endeavour that builds the leadership capacity of the leader. Leadership development is more integrated development that involves the leader, the people and the quality of their interactions relative to the work and workplace expectations.

Leadership development is different to leader development that traditionally focuses on individual-based knowledge and skills that are associated with being in a formal leadership role. By developing the individual skills and abilities of the leader, the aim is to enable the leader to act and think in new ways that are purposeful for fulfilling their role (Coleman, 1988). Leadership development is seen as an investment in the human capital of the leader, supporting their intrapersonal and interpersonal skills.

Leadership development expands the individual and collective capacity and capability of members within organisations, to enable them to engage more effectively with the demands of leadership roles and processes. It means that the leader and group members can learn from their work rather than learning about leadership away from their workplace (Moxley & O'Connor Wilson, 1998)

The development of leadership is predicated on progressive improvement of leadership expertise through workplace learning that suggests knowledge structures and information processing necessary for progressive skill development which can be gradually learned and refined while on the job (Lord & Hall, 2005). As the leader becomes more experienced, the skill level develops from novice to intermediate and towards some expert levels. Each progressive skill level requires further development of knowledge and skills. These skills are drawn from emotional, social and work-related fields that are relevant for the particular work and organisation (Day et al., 2014).

Leadership development builds on existing levels of interpersonal competences so they become increasingly sophisticated in how information is processed and practised. Gardner (1999) describes interpersonal competence as a form of intelligence in the ability of the leader to understand and connect with people. **Interpersonal intelligence** refers to the ability to build trust, respect and commitment with followers and includes such competencies as social awareness and empathy. Interpersonal intelligence is also evident in social skills such as developing cooperation and collaboration, building bonds and managing conflict. The emphasis is on the social nature of interpersonal competence and on developing the quality of the interaction between the leader and the social and organisational environment (Fiedler, 1996). The focus on social interactions means that leadership development is not only an individual endeavour but also it becomes a shared approach.

Interpersonal intelligence – The ability to build trust, respect and commitment with followers and includes such competencies as social awareness and empathy.

When an organisation has a program of leadership development, it can, in some ways, resemble an integration strategy whereby the leader and the working group are helped to understand how to better relate and work together and build a sense of commitment to their work and to others. Most effective leadership development programs happen in the context of the workplace and are part of an ongoing strategy of personal and organisational development and learning that is tied to the strategic plans of an organisation (Day, 2001). The development of leadership in this sense extends social networks by socialising learning about self, the group and how it is organised and how it works. Some researchers have likened leadership development programs to a type of transformational strategy that involves higher levels of understanding applied to social and organisational goals and as such involves both enhanced integration and differentiation. This can be described as a form of 'organised complexity' (Gharajedaghi, 1999, pp. 92–93) where diversity is valued within more harmonious and organised working groups.

Leadership development builds the capacity of the leader and of groups of people so that they may problem solve and learn from experience to resolve issues and problems that may not have been envisaged or predicted (Day, 2001). Leadership capacity refers to enhancing cognitive and behavioural complexity. Understanding complexity and development provides a means of sense making where organisations may be having trouble when routines are no longer viable (Weick, 1993). Leadership development is oriented towards the capacity to anticipate and solve challenges across a range of situations and mitigate risks to the organisation in the face of unforeseen challenges. Organisations invest in leadership development to enhance the value of their work and workers and to protect their human capital (Lepak & Snell, 1999).

CASE STUDY 13.1

SAS – the leader in analytics

SAS – the leader in analytics – has consistently ranked among Australia's 50 best employers and has been voted one of the 'Best Places to Work in Australia'. Serving customers in 149 countries, SAS has over 14 000 employees worldwide, including 2610 in the Asia–Pacific region. The following is an outline of comments by David Bowie, Vice President of SAS Australia and New Zealand, about how SAS' focus to embed leadership into culture and every level of the business has helped create broader success.

At SAS, the business is driven by a culture of purpose, leading to employees having a high regard for the company and a strong sense of 'why I do what I do'. SAS's purpose-driven culture empowers employees to 'widen their horizons' as well as to develop leadership abilities to produce an environment that values originality and where open communication and feedback becomes automatic. This creates the climate for SAS's employees to thrive, increasing job satisfaction and producing additional value for customers.

A CEO can easily make statements about the importance of leadership but the difficult aspect is to make this happen in such a way that it becomes embedded into the company's culture and becomes everyday practice for all employees. SAS's culture gives all employees the leadership language and tools that are needed for them to be able to acquire the skills and behaviours to become leaders by having a framework that creates the conditions for success. The aim is for SAS to develop staff to their full potential. This facilitates staff understanding how they contribute to achieving SAS's goals and common purpose. Using a common language facilitates employees in being able to identify when they should lead or when they should follow. The important aspect is not about a business hierarchy but about good business behaviour and collectively 'moving in the right direction'.

Source: Adapted from Cary (2017); Donaldson (2016); and SAS (n.d.)

Critical thinking question
How does David Bowie consider a common language will facilitate his employees to develop a common sense of purpose?

THE IMPORTANCE OF FEEDBACK

Feedback is one of the methods that a manager and an employee use to share their information and evaluation about work performance. Feedback aligns workplace behaviour with the overall goals of a team or organisation. Providing feedback can be difficult, especially when delivering critical feedback may produce defensiveness and create conflict between the feedback giver and receiver. The aim is to provide actionable feedback on performance that leads to performance learning and improvement (Cannon & Witherspoon, 2005).

Feedback – A focused dialogue between a manager and an employee; a method of sharing information and perspectives about performance.

Suggestions about the delivery of feedback are that it must be consistent and credible so that the employee is able to apply the feedback to their performance. Feedback is more credible if it is written using specific and objective language (Harms & Roebuck, 2010). An example of how to deliver feedback is to first describe the behaviours, performance and the results that have been observed. Follow this with an explanation or illustration and draw on evidence to support the observations and conclusions. The feedback should include what is done well and describe what needs to be done to improve.

Feedback models
BET Model
B (*Behaviour*) is the behaviour the individual is exhibiting that is benefitting the group E (*Effect*). The effect the behaviour is having on the team's success is T (*Thank you*). This works best when delivering positive feedback.

BEAR feedback model
B (*Behaviour*) is the behaviour the individual is, or is not, exhibiting that is inhibiting the team's success E (*Effect*). The effect the behaviour is having on the team's progress is A (*Alternative*). A recommendation of the behaviour the individual could/should perform in place of the current

non-productive behaviour is *R (Result)*. This model works best when the individual needs to make change to behaviour and improve performance (Harms & Roebuck, 2010).

CORBS feedback model

Morrison (2015) has outlined the CORBS feedback model. When 'regular' is omitted, this is known as the COBS feedback model. The elements of the model are as follows:

- *Clear statement*: Give clear and concise information.
- *Owned by the person speaking*: Give your own perception, not the ultimate truth. How it made you feel. Use terms such as 'I find' or 'I felt' and not 'You are'.
- *Regular*: Give the feedback immediately or as close to the event as possible. Never delay.
- *Balanced*: Balance negative and positive feedback. Do not overload with negative feedback.
- *Specific*: Base your feedback on observable behaviour. Behaviours that the recipient can change.

The 360-degree feedback model

The introduction of 360-degree feedback has been lauded as an important management tool that most companies and organisations now use to appraise and assess their managers and leaders (Atwater & Waldman, 1998). As has been stated, 'feedback from multiple sources or "360° feedback" is a performance appraisal approach that relies on the input of an employee's superiors, colleagues, subordinates, sometimes customers, suppliers and/or spouses' (Yukl & Lepsinger, 1995, p. 45).

McCarthy and Garavan (2001) note that 360° feedback appraisal is also referred to as:

- stakeholder appraisal
- full-circle appraisal
- multi-rater feedback
- multi-source assessment
- subordinate and peer appraisal
- group performance appraisal
- multi-point assessment
- multi-perspective ratings.

360-degree appraisal – A method of systematically collecting perceptions of an individual's performance from a range of different viewpoints.

The **360-degree appraisal** refers to a method of systematically collecting perceptions of an individual's performance from a range of viewpoints. It rates performance based on information collected from different sources such as supervisors, peers, subordinates and customers. An advantage of the 360-degree model and the intense scrutiny of performance is that the feedback is more complete and provides a more accurate picture than may be gathered from relying on appraisals from a single source. The 360-degree model is an effective tool to understand the skills sets and potential of prospective leaders (Agarwal, 2009).

The growing popularity of the 360-degree feedback model illustrates the emphasis on self-understanding and self-awareness in business and leadership. It has been noted that a leader's lack of self-awareness can contribute to poor performance and have negative impact on others by increasing stress and anxiety and by negatively impacting on projects and their outcomes (Noel & Dotlich, 2008). Other reasons for the popularity of the 360-degree assessment include its relative ease to administer. It is also seen as a valuable development tool, especially as measures of organisational value come to better acknowledge the worth of human capital and resources; creating a workforce that is capable and talented, and that continually improves, is an organisational asset. The 360-degree feedback model can thus be used to assess and build competence in the form of self-knowledge and self-awareness of how managers and leaders can impact others. The nature of the relationship between leaders and followers is connected to the building of trust and commitment (Day, 2001).

By collecting and analysing information from a range of sources, the aim is to provide feedback to the recipient that would otherwise be unavailable. The rationale behind the 360-degree model is that the different perspectives of their performance offer the recipient unique and important information. The feedback process requires professional handling and sensitivity so that the trusting intentions of the appraisal are emphasised. Research (Nahapiet & Ghoshal, 1998) has established the link between 360-degree feedback and the development of trust and social capital.

If the appraisal is to be done well, it requires a careful identification of performance criteria and how these are measured. The accurate interpretation of appraisals from different sources requires a set of ratings that are fair, clear and consistent and that employees can readily understand. It requires an organisational and workplace climate in which those undergoing appraisal and those providing feedback can freely comment on one another's strengths and weaknesses without negative impact and repercussions (van der Heijden & Nijhof, 2004).

The 360-degree feedback evaluation process has several steps (Testa, 2002):

1. *Determining needs and goals*: For example, having a clear goal and purpose.
2. *Instrument selection or development*: In the context, the challenge is in determining which categories of evaluation are appropriate across multiple groups of stakeholders.
3. *Data collection decisions*: Representative sampling and confidentiality are the two main issues that drive decisions relating to data collection.
4. *Evaluating the data*: It is important to follow the traditional method for individual-based assessment such as the calculation of mean scores and the total or mean scale scores. The gaps are calculated by subtracting the focal team's score from the stakeholders' scores. For example, if the leadership team produced a mean score for 'trust' of 4.0 on a five-point Likert type scale, where 5 represents 'Strongly Agree' and the stakeholder

score was calculated as 3.0, a resulting score of −1.0 would emerge, suggesting a gap between the two groups. Aggregated measures look at 'global' congruence. The appropriate questions to ask include: Where do the greatest similarities and disparities exist within the data? To what extent do leaders' responses match those of the various groups?

5. *Taking action*: Once an evaluation is complete follow-up and implementation is required. For example, coaching combined with stakeholder follow-up can be highly successful. With this in mind, particularly as it relates to blind spots, further investigation may be necessary.

Types of feedback

Feedback information comes from intrinsic sources (internal to the individual) or external sources (referent information from outside the individual) (Greller & Herold, 1975). The different sources of feedback that come from within and from outside the organisation include:

- *The organisation*: Statistical measures, KPIs and real-time data are used to provide objective feedback to an employee.
- *Manager or supervisor*: They have experienced and have specialised knowledge of the tasks and standards of performance. They also have insight into company procedures, policy and trajectory.
- *Peers and co-workers*: Co-workers performing similar jobs understand their peer's performance and provide a different perspective for the feedback process than manager or supervisor.
- *Performance of the task*: Feedback is given relative to the success measures for the task.
- *Own performance*: Feedback comes from intrinsic sources (internal to the individual) and the individual can gauge, according to their standards, the quality of their performance. Customers can include feedback about individual, team, group and management performance though the use of surveys, customer visits, a complaint system and customer focus groups.
- *Subordinates*: 'Upward feedback' is the method of allowing subordinates to provide feedback about a manager's style and performance (Smither et al., 1995).

All sources of feedback provide a different perspective on an employee's performance. The most effective feedback should incorporate components from each appropriate source.

According to Geraghty (2013), there are four main types of constructive feedback, which may be information specific, issue-focused and based on observations. The four types of constructive feedback are as follows (Geraghty, 2013):

1. *Negative feedback*: corrective comments about past behaviour. Focuses on behaviour that wasn't successful and shouldn't be repeated.

2. *Positive feedback*: affirming comments about past behaviour. Focuses on behaviour that was successful and should be continued.

3. *Negative feedforward*: corrective comments about future performance. Focuses on behaviour that should be avoided in the future.

4. *Positive feedforward*: affirming comments about future behaviour. Focuses on behaviour that will improve performance in the future.

The four types of constructive feedback can be provided in different combinations in the form of positive, negative, direct and indirect feedback. However, for feedback to have maximum impact on an employee's performance, the amount of constructive feedback should be increased whilst decreasing criticism which is based on an opinion, judgement or negative statement about another person or their behavior. It should be noted that whilst praise, which deals with positive statements and comments, increases an employee's confidence and self-esteem, it is not an essential factor in the feedback process.

MIXED METHODS LEADERSHIP EVALUATION INSTRUMENTS

Researchers have widely studied the use of self-administered questionnaires, ranging from experiential to cross-sectional, cross-cultural and longitudinal questionnaires. The prevalence of questionnaires has led to the development of specific questionnaires that have contributed to leadership research and have become standard evaluation instruments: for example, The Ohio State LBDQ scales, Fiedler's LPC scale, and the MLQ and Team Effectiveness Questionnaire (LaFasto & Larson, 2001). The questionnaire is the instrument of choice for leadership research (Gardner et al., 2010), with 64 per cent of researchers using a questionnaire based method of data collection. As an instrument of evaluation, researchers employ the questionnaire within different theoretical framings and using a range of research designs (Bryman, 2004).

The use of qualitative methods in leadership research and evaluation can provide the depth of analysis required to investigate some of the causes behind results and findings gathered from data and quantitative analysis. Qualitative methods can add depth and provide additional explanations while quantitative methods provide instruments that can be used repetitively to provide a measure of evaluation and assessment. Both methods are complementary to leadership research (Madey, 1982).

Leadership evaluation instruments (Barge & Schlueter, 1991) include:

- *Organisational Leadership Assessment (OLA) instrument*: A reliable tool for measuring servant leadership in organisations and useful for further research as well as diagnosis in organisations (Laub, 2000).
- *Global Leadership and Organizational Behavior Effectiveness (GLOBE) Culture Scales*: Addresses cultural influences associated with leadership (Chhokar et al., 2008).

- *The Organisational Culture Inventory*: Profiles the culture of organisations and their subunits in terms of behavioural norms and expectations (Cooke & Rousseau, 1988).
- *Graen's Leader–Member Exchange measure*: Investigates the relationship between leaders and followers or members (Graen & Uhl-Bien, 1995).
- *Bass's Multifactor Leadership Questionnaire*: Evaluates transformational and transactional leadership (Avolio et al., 2004).
- *Podsakoff, Todor and Skov's Measure of Reward and Punishment*: Captures the relationships between leader reward, punishment, and subordinate performance and satisfaction punishment behaviours and subordinate performance and satisfaction (Podsakoff, Todor & Skov, 1982).
- *Kerr and Jermier's Substitutes for Leadership Scales*: Establishes certain individual, task and organisational variables that act as 'substitutes for leadership' and presents items for their measurement (Kerr & Jermier, 1978).

VIRTUAL LEADERSHIP

The increase in a globally distributed workforce has created the expansion of virtual teams and the virtual leadership of those teams. As the interaction between people and technology becomes more seamless it is increasingly important that leadership in the virtual context develops and adapts to the distributed way of working. Depending on the skills and knowledge of the employees, they can now be anywhere around the globe and be called upon to contribute and collaborate on a range of projects via telework. Virtual teams can be members of the same organisation or include members of different organisations. The teams have a flatter structure than more traditional teams and can be geographically dispersed, creating new challenges for leaders and their leadership skills. Traditional leadership skills are the foundation of effective virtual leadership; for example, leaders need to motivate employees, coordinate the work and efforts, identify and develop the potential of their employees. However, they also need specific skills and knowledge for virtual leadership (Nastase & Roja, 2013).

As virtual teams and virtual work become a more prevalent way of working, those managing and leading virtual teams require specific skills and knowledge for effective leadership. This is because despite the growth of virtual workforces, many misconceptions about leadership continue. For example, resistance to virtual work is an ongoing barrier to developing better and more effective leadership practices because the thinking continues to be that 'I can't manage what I can't see' (Snyder, 2012). Developments in virtual leadership have created a new field of leadership education and training that specifically takes in the complex and multifaceted role of leaders of virtual workforces. Virtual leadership works on three levels: communicating the vision, inspiring and motivating performance, and meeting set goals and objectives. To perform these leadership tasks, creating the optimal virtual context is foundational to ensure that the virtual team is well informed, well motivated and has the resources and capacity to achieve the objectives. A virtual leader needs to develop a sound understanding of virtual space and how it influences interactions, to underpin effective collaboration within the team and to keep the team engaged in their work (Snyder, 2012).

Effective virtual leaders can span cultural boundaries and be aware of the individual differences in their teams, which may influence communication, problem solving and ways of working (Snyder, 2012). The virtual leader needs to adapt their leadership style and methods to work with diversity. This means that the virtual leader may need to do some identity work for the team. By creating a distinct identity which reflects the diversity of the team members, the team can manage and work with cultural and or geographical differences. Group identity can be created by designing activities that focus on teamwork and that are interrelated – for example, not having individual team members working solely on a part of the project, and instead having different team members collaborate on different aspects of the project. The interdependence of activities will assist team members to become familiar with each other's skills and ways of working. In true collaboration, there is an exchange of ideas and knowledge sharing for mutual understanding, so by structuring interdependent activities for the team, the leader creates conditions of mutual trust and commitment among the team members. The virtual leader needs to have specific skills that enable team members to develop openness, communication and accept differences so trust and cohesion grow within the virtual team (Nastase & Roja, 2013).

Virtual leaders need to monitor relationships and anticipate any obstacles that may impede team cohesion and connectedness (Snyder, 2012). By being aware of cues that may indicate breakdown in team cohesion and signal potential conflicts, the virtual leader can address these early and prevent the escalation of team dysfunction.

Virtual leadership relies on technology and the personalisation of technology so that the leader is connected to the team as a priority. Staying connected to their team means that the leader is aware of technological issues early, and keeps abreast of new developments and professional training that would help the team achieve its objectives.

Virtual leaders focus on goals and meeting the objectives. This requires that the leader set achievable goals and keep employees informed about progress and any change that may be required. Having clear targets and objectives ensures that the team has a clear understanding of their roles and tasks. The virtual leader may focus on setting both individual and team goals and then finding ways to create a convergence between the two so that the individual is working cohesively with the team and is clear about their contribution and role. When virtual team members feel involved with the set goals, the foundations are set for greater commitment, cohesion and climate for collaboration (Nastase & Roja, 2013). Another important factor to ensure that goals and targets are met is the quality of feedback. Feedback is a way of leading team members to adapt their efforts and behaviour to the expected norms. The communication of feedback is a foundational skill for the virtual leader because, unlike more traditional leadership, the leader cannot rely on observation and meetings to give feedback. The virtual leader needs to ask for and provide feedback frequently and use this to collaborate and share what is going on for the team (Nastase & Roja, 2013).

The virtual leader should motivate and inspire the team to achieve their objects through effective communication and connectedness with the team (Snyder, 2012). When virtual interactions replace face-to-face communication, the challenge for leaders is how to ensure their motivational messages and communications are effective. Snyder's (2012) drivers of motivation for virtual workers include: competence – feeling valued as knowledgeable, skilled and experienced; relatedness – having the opportunity to collaborate with trusted colleagues and co-workers; and autonomy – having the freedom to manage oneself according to guidelines to achieve business goals.

Virtual leaders find it a great challenge to motivate teams through remote and virtual environments because many face-to-face communication cues are removed from the quality of the communication. The virtual leader can use different strategies to ensure that their messages are convincing and keep virtual workers on task and motivated. For example, communication of a common vision is an important tool in motivation so the virtual leader needs to ensure their message is being received in a convincing manner. Motivation is important, especially in the early part of team formation, and its success depends on how motivational messages are transmitted, and what media are used (Wright & Webb, 2011). To ensure the motivational message has the intended impact on the team, and that the vision, mission and goals that shape the team are effective, it is recommended that multiple channels of communication are used and that interaction and dialogue on the goals are encouraged (Nastase & Roja, 2013).

Research has uncovered six areas of development for virtual leaders that are necessary for managing a virtual workforce. According to Daniels (2012) these are:

1. *Reflection*: Leaders take time to examine and assess their motives, beliefs, attitudes and actions and to understand how these influence the quality of their leadership in the virtual context.

2. *Society*: Seeing the bigger picture, leaders focus on the greater good and develop greater understanding of how decisions affect the individuals, workforce, company, and more broadly, the community. This helps leaders become more attuned to the economic and environmental conditions in which the organisation operates, as well as the impact the organisation has on those conditions.

3. *Diversity*: Leaders value human differences including gender, ethnicity, age, nationality, beliefs and work styles to drive greater performance.

4. *Ingenuity*: Leaders foster an environment in which innovation can thrive, by enhancing autonomy and flexibility to promote innovation.

5. *People*: Leaders emphasise connection with others, to earn commitment, inspire effort and improve communications. Leaders strong in this area make an effort to inspire employee trust and secure employee commitment.

6. *Business*: Depending on the nature of the task and the organisation and the core business, for example, a leader's role may be to develop and execute strategies to drive profits and the bottom-line results. The role to the leaders is to enhance business goals and objectives and achieving set goals and targets.

CASE STUDY 13.2

Red Guava

Red Guava is the 'small, bootstrapped and profitable software company' behind Cliniko, a healthcare practice management system with thousands of users around the world. Based in Melbourne, Australia, Red Guava has six local staff working on site two days a week, but most of the work is done from home or wherever staff choose. The rest of the 19 team members are based in the UK, USA, Canada, Poland, Brazil, Portugal and New Zealand. Below is the response of Joel Friedlaeder, founder of Red Guava, about employing remote teams, interviewed by RemoteWorkHub (RWH, 2017).

> We work smarter, not harder. We think work/life balance is important and we work a 30 hour work week with full-time pay as standard. We have flexible work hours and location is flexible too … We would rather hire the best person available, not just the best person within a 10-kilometre radius … We have no level of management, no measurement of productivity or review. We trust when we hire someone really good that they want to do good work, and we let them do it … Technical skills can usually be learnt, so what we look for is people who are passionate about what they do. Nice people with a sense of humour. The Red Guava team relies on Slack for internal communications, GitHub for code and ZenDesk for customer support. The suite of online software allows staff on different sides of the globe to work seamlessly across time zones, providing 24–7 support and an impressive average response time of just seven minutes for Cliniko users.
>
> Repoduced with permission from Remote Work Hub

Critical thinking question

After reading the above identify the strengths and weakness of Red Guava's virtual team leadership and working culture.

SUMMARY

LEARNING OUTCOME 1: Explain the five widely used leadership inventories.

Inventories are instruments that measure the behaviour of leaders and attempt to identify and evaluate those behaviours in terms of effectiveness of leadership. The measures used in inventories are dependent on the leadership style and paradigm relevant to the leader. The Kouzes and Posner's Leadership Practices Inventory identifies the key transformational leadership behaviours that visionary leaders require. The Inventory of Leadership Styles, currently known as the MSQ, measures leadership effectiveness by focusing on workplace climate that either enhances or impedes performance. The Multifactor Leadership Questionnaire assesses a range of transactional, transformational and non-standard leadership practices. The Global Executive Leadership Inventory evaluates what it means to be a world-class leader. The Leadership Effectiveness and Adaptability Description inventory investigates leaders' adaptability and leadership styles in response to different demands of a situation.

LEARNING OUTCOME 2: Identify and describe the differences between leader
development and leadership development.

The development of leadership within an organisation requires a distinction to be made between leader development and leadership development. Leader development traditionally focuses on individual-based knowledge and skills that are associated with being in a formal leadership role, which is an individualistic endeavour to build the leadership capacity of the leader. By developing the individual skills and abilities of the leader, the aim is to enable the leader to act and think in new ways that are purposeful for fulfilling their role. Development of the leader is seen as an investment in their human capital and in their acquisition of enhanced intrapersonal and interpersonal skills.

Leadership development is more integrated development that involves the leader, the people and the quality of their interactions relative to the work and workplace expectations. It expands the individual and collective capacity and capability of members within organisations so they can engage more effectively with the demands of leadership roles and processes. Such development builds and extends the leader's existing levels of interpersonal competences, which helps them to become more adept in processing information and results in advancing their leadership practice. Further, leadership development builds the capacity of the leader and of groups of people so that they can solve problems and learn from this experience to better resolve future issues and problems, including those that are hard to predict and plan for.

LEARNING OUTCOME 3: Explain why feedback is important for evaluating leadership performance.

Feedback is a focused dialogue between a manager and an employee, a method of sharing information and perspectives about performance. Feedback aligns workplace behaviour with the overall goals of a team or an organisation. The goal of ongoing feedback is to identify where performance is effective and where it needs improvement. Giving people feedback is an act of trust and confidence. It shows that you believe in their ability to change, that you believe they will use the information to become better, and that you have faith in their potential. Furthermore, it is a sign of commitment to the team and to the organisation's larger purpose and goals.

LEARNING OUTCOME 4: Apply the key models and types of feedback, in particular the 360-degree model.

The 360-degree appraisal is also known as the multi-source assessment or the 360-degree feedback. It refers to a method of systematically collecting perceptions of an individual's performance informed from a range of various viewpoints. It provides a rating of performance based on information collected from different sources such as supervisors, peers, subordinates and customers. An advantage of the 360-degree model and the intense scrutiny of performance is that the feedback is more complete and provides a more accurate picture than may be gathered from reliance on appraisals from a single source. The rationale behind the 360-degree model is that the different perspectives of their performance offer the recipient unique and important information about their performance. Most organisations now use 360-degree feedback to appraise and assess their managers and leaders. It involves five steps: determining needs and goals; instrument selection/development; data collection decisions; evaluating the data; and taking action.

LEARNING OUTCOME 5: Understand virtual leadership.

The increase in a globally distributed workforce has created the expansion of virtual teams and the virtual leadership of virtual teams. As the interaction between people and technology becomes more seamless, there is a growing importance that leadership in the virtual context develops and adapts to the distributed way of working. Virtual leadership works on three levels: communicating the vision, inspiring and motivating performance, and meeting set goals and objectives. A virtual leader needs to develop a sound understanding of virtual space and how it influences interactions, to underpin effective team collaboration and keep the team engaged in their work. Effective virtual leaders can span cultural boundaries and be aware of the individual differences in their teams that may influence communication, problem solving and ways of working. Virtual leaders need to monitor relationships and anticipate any potential obstacles to team cohesion and connectedness, to set achievable goals and keeps employees informed about progress and any change that may be required, and to motivate and inspire the team to achieve their objects through effective communication and connectedness with the team.

REVIEW QUESTIONS

1. Suggest a few methods to evaluate leadership effectiveness.

2. Describe the differences between leader development and leadership development.

3. Explain the key features of different feedback models.

4. How can virtual teams be managed effectively? Discuss this with reference to a company that you know of that leads virtual teams.

CASE STUDY 13.3

Z Energy

This case study illustrates the key factor in Z Energy winning a 2014 Aon Hewitt Top Companies for Leaders Award. The Aon Hewitt award examines links between leadership practices and financial results across organisations in the Australasian region.

Z Energy is a New Zealand organisation that supplies fuel to retail customers and large commercial customers such as airlines, transport and logistics companies, mines and vehicle fleet operators. Among other business platforms, Z Energy operates over 200 service stations and 90 truck stops across New Zealand.

Z Energy is a 'Top Company for Leaders' because of its excellence in:

1. embedding a positive leadership culture
2. providing leadership development opportunities to all representatives of the Z brand
3. integrating leadership expectations into on-boarding and induction processes.

Embedding a positive leadership culture

Z Energy believes that extraordinary leadership is its key differentiator and is critical to delivering a world-class experience for its customers. Despite being a relatively young organisation, Z Energy has a remarkably well-established leadership framework, underpinned by two core philosophies:

- extraordinary leadership delivers extraordinary results
- you don't have to be a people leader to demonstrate leadership.

This framework is aligned with broader business strategy and forms a key part of the organisation's rhetoric. Employees are encouraged to think of themselves as Senior

Leaders, People Leaders and Self Leaders, making the emphasis on leadership universally relevant.

Z Energy links its leadership framework directly to outcomes, with key financial performance measures showing significant improvements since the rollout of development programs and customer service metrics, indicating a 22 per cent lead on competitors.

Providing leadership development opportunities to all representatives of the Z brand

A unique feature of Z Energy's leadership approach is its application beyond head office. The organisation offers all its retailers, who are not directly employed by Z, the opportunity to participate in the same 12-day leadership development program that is delivered to Senior and People Leaders from across the business. Retailers are also given access to 360-degree feedback tools and supported to embrace Z's leadership behaviours within their teams through coaching and facilitation training. Even though they are franchisees who sit outside of Z, the organisation sees retailers as key stakeholders in its success and thus critical beneficiaries of its leadership investment.

By creating a shared leadership development journey for the wider Z community, the organisation has triggered a step change in its relationship with retailers, and in turn affirmed its commitment to truly operate as 'One Team'.

> Being part of the [leadership] program has been a transfiguring experience for myself [and] the eight cluster staff who were on the program. I have witnessed … shifts in the personal lives of our people and in their … understanding of leadership for extraordinary relationships (Aon Hewitt, 2014).

Integrating leadership expectations into on-boarding and induction processes

Employees at Z Energy are expected to understand and live the behaviours of the organisation's leadership framework from day one on the job. Leadership behaviours form part of the selection criteria and hiring managers work with Z's People and Culture team to ensure new starters understand and are connected to expectations.

Prior to employment, all potential candidates receive a hard copy of 'The Z Why', a one-stop reference to Z's guiding principles. New hires are then reintroduced to leadership behaviours via RedCarpet, the organisation's pre-employment on-boarding portal, and upon commencement, receive ongoing coaching and feedback from their hiring manager.

Source: Adapted from Aon Hewitt (2014)

Critical thinking questions

1. What approaches has Z Energy taken to leadership development? Why do they work?
2. Describe, as best you can from the above, the culture of this organisation. What does this depend upon?
3. What factors contribute to the recognition of Z Energy as a 'Top Company for Leaders'?

REFERENCES

Agarwal, S. (2009). 360-degree feedback: Tool for leadership development. *Parikalpana: The KIIT Journal of Management*, 6, 80–9.

AonHewitt. (2014). Aon Hewitt Top Companies for Leaders 2014: Z Energy. Retrieved from: www.aonhewitt.com.au/Document-files/Top-Companies-for-Leaders/Case-studies/2014/2014-TCFL-case-study-Z-energy.pdf.

Atwater, L. & Waldman, D. (1998). 360-degree feedback and leadership development. *Leadership Quarterly*, 9(4), 423–6.

Avolio, B.J., Bass, B.M. & Zhu, F.W.W. (2004). *Multifactor Leadership Questionnaire: Manual and sampler set*, 3rd edn. Redwood City, CA: Mind Garden.

Barge, J.K. & Schlueter, D.W. (1991). Leadership as organizing: A critique of leadership instruments. *Management Communication Quarterly*, 4(4), 541–70.

Bass, B.M (1985). *Leadership and performance beyond expectations*. New York, NY: Free Press.

Bass, B.M. & Avolio, B.J. (1989). *Manual for the Multifactor Leadership Questionnaire*. Palo Alto, CA: Consulting Psychologists Press.

Binning, J.F., Zaba, A.J. & Whattam, J.C. (1986). Explaining the biasing effects of performance cues in terms of cognitive categorization. *Academy of Management Journal*, 29(3), 521–35.

Bryman, A. (2004). Qualitative research on leadership: A critical but appreciative review. *Leadership Quarterly*, 15(6), 729–69.

Cannon, M.D. & Witherspoon, R. (2005). Actionable feedback: Unlocking the power of learning and performance improvement. *Academy of Management Executive*, 19(2), 120–34.

Cary, N. (2017). For the 9th consecutive year – SAS earns coveted recognition – yet again placed in the top 50. Retrieved from: www.sas.com/en_us/news/press-releases/2017/august/sas-australia-best-places-to-work.html.

Chhokar, J.S., Brodbeck, F.C. & House, R. J. (2008). *Culture and leadership across the world: The GLOBE book of in-depth studies of 25 societies*. New York, NY: Lawrence Erlbaum Associates.

Coleman, J.S. (1988). Social capital in the creation of human capital. *American Journal of Sociology*, 94, 95–120.

Cooke, R.A. & Rousseau, D.M. (1988). Behavioural norms and expectations: A quantitative approach to the assessment of organizational culture. *Group and Organizational Studies*, 13(3), 245–73.

Daniels, S. (2012) The virtual leader in training. Retrieved from: http://blog.achieveglobal.com/blog/2012/07/the-virtual-leader-in-training.html.

Day, D.V. (2001). Leadership development: A review in context. *Leadership Quarterly*, 11(4), 581–613.

Day, D.V., Fleenor, J.W., Atwater, L.E., Sturm, R.E. & McKee, R.A. (2014). Advances in leader and leadership development: A review of 25 years of research and theory. *Leadership Quarterly*, 25(1), 63–82.

de Hoogh, A. et al. (2004). Charismatic leadership, environmental dynamism, and performance. *European Journal of Work and Organizational Psychology*, 13(4), 447–71.

Donaldson, C. (2016). How SAS drives success by making leaders out of everyone. *Insider HR*. Retrieved from: www.insidehr.com.au/how-sas-drives-success-by-making-leaders-out-of-everyone.

Fiedler, F.E. (1996). Research on leadership selection and training: One view of the future. *Administrative Science Quarterly*, 41(2), 241–50.

Gardner, H. (1999). *Intelligence reframed: Multiple intelligences for the 21st century*. New York, NY: Basic Books.

Gardner, W.L., Lowe, K.B., Moss, T.W., Mahoney, K.T. & Cogliser, C.C. (2010). Scholarly leadership of the study of leadership: A review of *Leadership Quarterly*'s second decade, 2000–2009. *Leadership Quarterly*, 21(6), 922–58.

Geraghty, S. (2013). Types and sources of feedback in the workplace. *Talkdesk*, 28 March. Retrieved from: www.talkdesk.com/blog/business/types-and-sources-of-feedback-in-the-workplace.

Gharajedaghi, J. (1999). *How the game is evolving systems thinking: Managing chaos and complexity – a platform for designing business architecture*, 3rd edn. Burlington, MA: Morgan Kaufmann.

Graen, G.B. & Uhl-Bien, M. (1995). Relationship-based approach to leadership: Development of leader-member exchange (LMX) theory of leadership over 25 years: Applying a multi-level multi-domain perspective. *Leadership Quarterly*, 6(2), 219–47.

Greller, M.M. & Herold, D.M. (1975). Sources of feedback: A preliminary investigation. *Organizational Behavior and Human Performance*, 13(2), 244–56.

Harms, P.L. & Roebuck, D.B. (2010). Teaching the art and craft of giving and receiving feedback. *Business Communication Quarterly*, 73(4), 413–31.

Hersey, P. & Blanchard, K. (1988). *LEAD questionnaires*, Escondido, CA: Center for Leadership Studies Press.

Hooijberg, R. & Choi, J. (2000). Which leadership roles matter to whom? An examination of rater effects on perceptions of effectiveness. *Leadership Quarterly*, 11(3), 341–64.

Jing, F.F. & Avery, G.C. (2011). Missing links in understanding the relationship between leadership and organizational performance. *International Business and Economics Research Journal*, 7(5), 107–17.

Kerr, S. & Jermier, J.M. (1978). Substitutes for leadership: Their meaning and measurement. *Organizational Behavior and Human Performance*, 22(3), 375–403.

Kets de Vries, M.F.R. (2005). *The global executive leadership inventory*. USA: Pfeiffer Publishing.

Kets de Vries, M.F.R., Vrignaud, P., Florent-Treacy, E. & Korotov, K. (2007). INSEAD Global Leadership Centre: 360-degree feedback instruments – An overview. *INSEAD Working Paper*, 2007/01/EFE.

LaFasto, F. & Larson, C. (2001).*When teams work best: 6000 team members and leaders tell what it takes to succeed*. Thousand Oaks, CA: SAGE Publications.

Laub, J.A. (2000). Development of the organizational leadership assessment (OLA) instrument. Retrieved from: www.olagroup.org/documents/development.pdf.

Lepak, D.P. & Snell, S.A. (1999). The human resource architecture: Toward a theory of human capital allocation and development. *Academy of Management Review*, 24(1), 31–48.

Litwin, G. & Stringer, R. (1968). *Motivation and organisational climate*. Boston: Harvard Business School Research Press.

Lord, R.G. & Hall, R.J. (2005). Identity, deep structure and the development of leadership skill. *Leadership Quarterly*, 16(4), 591–615.

Madey, D.L. (1982). Some benefits of integrating qualitative and quantitative methods in program evaluation, with illustrations. *Educational Evaluation and Policy Analysis*, 4(2), 223–36.

McCarthy, A.M. & Garavan, T.N. (2001). 360° feedback process: Performance, improvement and employee career development. *Journal of European Industrial Training*, 25(1), 5–32.

McCauley, C.D., Moxley, R.S. & Van Velsor, E. (1998). *Centre for Creative Leadership handbook of leadership development*. San Francisco, CA: Jossey Bass.

Morrison, M. (2015). *COBS or CORBS Feedback Model for Performance Management*. Retrieved from: https://rapidbi.com/cobs-or-corbs-feedback-model-for-performance-management.

Moxley, R.S. & O'Connor Wilson, P. (1998). A systems approach to leadership development. In C.D. McCauley, R.S. Moxley & E.V. Velsor (eds.), *The Center for Creative Leadership handbook of leadership development* (pp. 217–41). San Francisco: Jossey-Bass.

Muenjohn, N. & Armstrong, A. (2008). Evaluating the structural validity of the Multifactor Leadership Questionnaire (MLQ), capturing the leadership factors of transformational-transactional leadership. *Contemporary Management Research*, 4(1), 3–13.

Nahapiet, J. & Ghoshal, S. (1998). Social capital, intellectual capital, and the organizational advantage. *Academy of Management Review*, 23(2), 242–66.

Nastase, M. & Roja, A. (2013). Leadership in virtual organizations. Paper presented at the 7th International Management Conference, Bucharest, Romania.

Noel, J. & Dotlich, D. (2008). Action learning: Creating leaders through work. In J.L. Noel & D.L. Dotlich (eds), *The 2008 Pfeiffer Annual: Leadership development*, 2nd edn (pp. 239–47): Wiley.

Podsakoff, P.M., Todor, W.M., & Skov, R. (1982). Effects of leader contingent and noncontingent reward and punishment behaviors on subordinate performance and satisfaction. *Academy of Management Journal*, 25(4), 810–21.

Posner, B.Z. & Kouzes, J.M. (1988). Development and validation of the leadership practices inventory. *Educational and Psychological Measurement*, 48(2), 483–96.

Rook, C. & Kessler, B. (2013). *How different cultures perceive effective leadership*. Fountainebleau: INSEAD.

RWH (2017). Red Guava: Australian software company working smarter, not harder. Retrieved from: https://remoteworkhub.com/red-guava-australian-software-company-working-smarter-not-harder.

SAS (n.d.). About SAS. Retrieved from: https://www.sas.com/en_au/company-information.html.

Silverthorne, C. & Wang, T-H. (2001). Situational leadership style as a predictor of success and productivity among Taiwanese business organizations. *Journal of Psychology*, 135(4), 399–412.

Smither, J.W., London, M., Vasilopoulos, N.L., Reilly, R.R., Millsap, R.E. & Salvemini, N. (1995). An examination of the effects of an upward feedback program over time. *Personnel Psychology*, 48, 1–34.

Snyder, K. (2012). Enhancing telework: A guide to virtual leadership. *Public Manager*, 41(1), 11.

Testa, M.R. (2002). A model for organization-based 360 degree leadership assessment. *Leadership and Organization Development Journal*, 23(5), 260–8.

van der Heijden, B. & Nijhof, A.H.J. (2004). The value of subjectivity: Problems and prospects for 360-degree appraisal systems. *International Journal of Human Resource Management*, 15(3), 493–511.

Weick, K.E. (1993). Organizational redesign as improvisation. In G.P. Huber & W.H. Glick (eds), *Organizational change and redesign: Ideas and insights for improving performance* (pp. 346–79). New York, NY: Oxford University Press.

Wright, K.B. & Webb, L.M. (2011). *Computer-mediated communication in personal relationships*. New York, NY: Peter Lang.

Yukl, G.A. (2013). *Leadership in organizations*, 8th edn. New York, NY: Pearson Education.

Yukl, G.A. & Lepsinger, R. (1995). How to get the most out of 360-feedback. *Training*, 32, 45–51.

Zagorsek, H., Stough, S.J. & Jaklic, M. (2006). Analysis of the reliability of the leadership practices inventory in the item response theory framework. *International Journal of Selection and Assessment*, 14(2), 180–91.

14

CREATIVITY, INNOVATION AND LEADERSHIP

Nuttawuth Muenjohn and Adela McMurray

LEARNING OUTCOMES

After reading this chapter, you should be able to:

1. identify the determinants of organisational creativity

2. explain the process of innovation and differentiate between types of innovation

3. clarify the link between creativity, innovation and leadership

4. suggest creativity-enhancing strategies for a given organisational context

5. discuss the role of the leader in promoting organisational creativity and innovation.

INTRODUCTION

IN 2017, M&C Saatchi ranked first in Australia and New Zealand on overall innovation and product innovation, helping it to second place in the *Australian Financial Review*'s company rankings (AFR, 2017). The company's chief executive officer, Jaimes Legget, has stressed the important role creativity and innovation plays in their success:

> Creativity sits at the heart of any great innovation ... Creativity has always been our raison d'etre at M&C Saatchi and it's never been more important ... For us innovation is not an option, it's a necessity to keep ahead of a rapidly evolving marketplace and we're fortunate to have clients who share that view (M&C Saatchi, 2017).

Renowned companies globally, such as the 3M Company, Amazon, Tesla, Asian Paints and Unilever, also realise that successful innovations are a result of the effective management of organisational innovation processes. Innovation through creativity and entrepreneurial potency is the key to the sustainable economic growth of a company, nation and country:

> No matter where one looks around the world today, organisations face a common challenge: the need to improve their performance to capitalise on rapid change ... Wherever they are in the world, the most effective leaders of the 21st century will be those who can lead others in their organisations to think in innovative ways and, in fact, to drive change (Basadur, 2004, p. 104).

This chapter explains the link between creativity, innovation and leadership, starting by defining the terms *creativity* and *innovation*. Explanations of creativity and innovation processes and types of innovation follow, together with a discussion of strategies to enhance organisational creativity. Finally, the chapter explores the influence of leadership style on creativity and innovation.

CREATIVITY

Creativity is defined in various ways; according to Schilling (2005), it is the ability to produce useful and novel work. Further, it is the balanced intellectual unfolding and converging of entrepreneurial experience (Nyström, 1993). Creativity can be discussed in terms of individual creativity and organisational creativity. Individual creativity is a function of intellectual abilities, knowledge, style of thinking, personality, motivation, environment, risk taking and persistence (Schilling, 2005). In a broader explanation, extensive and seminal research works of Amabile (1996) find that individual creativity is a function of three basic components: expertise, motivation and creative thinking skills.

According to Schilling (2005), organisational creativity includes creativity of individuals within organisational social processes and circumstantial factors that influence the interaction and behaviours of individuals in the organisation. However, the contemporary view of organisational creativity focuses on the creative outcome or product: something that is novel or unique and appropriate (Amabile, 1996; Mumford & Gustafson, 1988).

> **Creativity** – The ability to produce useful and novel work.

Importance of creativity

Creativity can make organisations effective, efficient and adaptable. Efficiency enables organisations to achieve effective routines for the delivery of goods and services in higher quantities, to a higher quality, at competitive prices. Creative organisations have the capacity to react promptly to sudden changes in the market without constraining routines. In this changing world, simply maintaining organisational routines is not sufficient to ensure a company is competitive and successful. Instead, organisations need to be adaptable, so that they can master the process of changing routines purposefully. For this, organisations need to engage in continuous creative problem solving and innovation and to adopt novel technologies with first-mover advantage. However, as Amabile and Khaire (2008) point out, while creativity has been at the centre of business and essential to entrepreneurship, it has captured less attention of managers, because it is rather abstract and intangible, and so, hard to recognise. They went on to say that managers may think that focusing on enhancing operations more immediately benefits the organisation than does bringing through innovation and creativity over time. Yet essential aspects of adaptability in an organisation include external focus as well as internal focus, as new opportunities and challenges, trends, technologies, ideas and approaches become available to enhance routines. Therefore, in the contemporary world leaders are motivated to achieve efficiency and to become adaptable, so that their organisations can sustain a competitive edge.

Steps in creativity

According to Kuratko (2016), the creativity process has four steps (see Figure 14.1). It starts with knowledge accumulation. A successful creation is always supported by an adequate level of timely important information, which members of the organisation gain through reading, having conversations with others in their field, attending professional workshops, meetings and exhibitions, and so on.

Figure 14.1 Creativity process

This search helps entrepreneurial leaders to obtain a variety of perspectives on the problem in question. The second stage of the creativity process is the incubation process, a subconscious processing of the vast amount of information that has been gathered to identify a solution to the problem, often when engaged in unrelated work. The third phase of the creative process is the moment when the idea for a solution arrives, sometimes also known as the 'Eureka factor'. Sometimes this comes at an unexpected moment. To expedite the arrival of the idea, it can be helpful to daydream and fantasise about the project, work in a leisure environment, practicse the hobby, take breaks while working and make notes of ideas that arrive early in the morning and late at night. The most difficult stage is the last: evaluation and implementation. At this stage, the entrepreneurial leader must try to implement the solution, which may involve facing obstacles and accepting a risk of failure. Good practices for this stage include seeking advice from friends and professionals, becoming educated about business planning, testing the idea with knowledgeable people and noticing one's own emotions.

Creativity strategy

Robinson and Stern (1997) suggest the following ways to improve organisational creativity: alignment between employees and organisations, self-initiated activity, unofficial activity, serendipity, diverse stimuli and internal company communication. Aligning employee interests and actions with organisational goals will help the employees to recognise and respond to novel and useful ideas promptly. Allowing employees to identify an organisational problem and solve it by themselves will increase their intrinsic motivation; allowing them to work on their own projects will encourage them to think freely and confidently. The innovation company 3M has used this approach for a long time, where it is known as a 'bootlegging policy'. According to Dragon Rough (n.d.), under this policy 3M's technical employees are permitted to spend up to 15 per cent of their time developing creative ideas for the company, and these ideas are eligible to receive one of 3M's special Genesis Grants. One of the successful business ideas this funding supported is well known: the Post-it note.

Further, unofficial activity is also a way of enhancing creativity by offering a free opportunity to develop an idea. Rather than promotion within official frames, unofficial development of an idea allows the employee to make the idea as strong as possible by performing many experiments. A serendipitous discovery is finding a successful idea or reaching a result accidentally, due to employees' keen insights. Serendipity helps to bridge the distant concepts and ideas and connect and recombine them to come up with a novel, useful solution. It is essential to keep in mind that chance favours a prepared mind, and hence employees who have richer opportunities to learn and to experience a changing world may well generate more serendipitous innovations. Leaders can use various stimuli to encourage employees to think creatively, such as lectures, discussions, training and exhibitions. Finally, it is the leader's responsibility to ensure that appropriate lines of communication to support all the organisational arrangements are in place. Otherwise, miscommunications may occur and the approaches described above may be affected.

Beyond Robinson and Stern's (1997) suggestions, leaders may help employees to become creatively productive by motivating them. Employees highly value being assessed, receiving rewards and having the support of their leader. It is essential to encourage employees to engage in innovations without worrying about the risk of punishment or negativity (Amabile, 1996). The creation of such an organisational environment may help employees acquire diverse perspectives and the courage to tackle even entrenched problems in the organisation (Jung, 2001).

INNOVATION

Innovation – The introduction of a new thing or method.

Innovation is generally understood as 'the introduction of a new thing or method … the embodiment, combination, or synthesis of knowledge in original, relevant, valued new products, processes, or services' (Luecke & Katz, 2003, p. 2). Innovation has long been described as the engine of growth. Although often conflated with invention, Myers and Marquis (1969, cited in Trott, 2008) note that innovation is, in fact:

> not a single action but a total process of interrelated sub-processes. It is not just the conception of a new idea, nor the invention of a new device, nor the development of a new market. The process is all these things acting in an integrated fashion.

Invention is the conception of the idea. However, innovation is the translation of invention into a commercially viable product, service or an experience.

Figure 14.2 The stages of innovation

The conception of the idea, or theoretical conception, is the starting point of innovation but, by itself, it is neither an innovation nor an invention. The technological translation of this theoretical conception is invention. However, even if the invention seems smart, it is still not an innovation. To be considered an innovation, a business idea must be invented and must fulfil a market need so that it can be commercially exploited. In this light, innovation is revealed to be a distinctive process that needs to be managed. While inventions are the vehicle to bring innovations to the world, they only contribute to a country's economic growth if they can be successfully brought to market. A broader definition of this states that innovation is 'management of all the activities involved in the process of idea generation, technology development, manufacturing and marketing of a new (or improved) product or manufacturing process or equipment' (Trott, 2008, p. 15). The general concept of innovation can be classified into two categories: process innovation and outcome innovation (McMurray et al., 2012).

Importance of innovation

It is often argued that innovation is the engine of a nation's economic growth (e.g. Kacprzyk & Doryn, 2017). This is because innovations often help the businesses to find their own strategic and technological lever in the face of an uncertain and turbulent business environment where issues may include:

1. *Complex problems in the world*: The world is full of problems and, to address these challenges, simple and traditional mechanisms are of no use. Therefore, innovative and

disruptive approaches are essential to overcome the critical challenges faced by today's society.

2. *Entrepreneurship movement in both developed and developing countries*: Entrepreneurship is considered to be a stimulus for economic growth in many economies and, hence, many countries are now promoting entrepreneurial approaches in their societies. Innovation is an entrepreneurship enabler and a way of empowering people to reach economic prosperity. As a result, governments and organisations give a high priority to fostering innovation.

3. *Competitive advantage*: The conditions and the circumstance which make the organisation unique are generally known as **competitive advantage**. The businesses that excel in innovation can gain the benefits of competitive advantage in the face of market competition.

> **Competitive advantage** – The conditions and circumstances which make the organisation unique.

4. *The possibility of growth and enhanced profitability*: Innovative approaches will reduce manufacturing costs and enable firms to develop new platforms for growth. While reaching profit targets, with the development of novel technologies firms can improve their learning further to bring the next wave of innovation.

5. *Increasing customer expectations*: Customer lifestyles are changing and, as a result, customer expectations are also changing. In this globalised world, customer understanding and awareness are relatively higher and, hence, the demand for new and improved products with multiple benefits is expected to deliver value for money.

CASE STUDY 14.1

BOOST Juice

BOOST Juice is one of the world's most famous and loved smoothie and juice brands, founded by Australian entrepreneur Janine Allis. The following is a response from BOOST Juice's marketing director, Jody Murray-Freedman, to a question from QSR Media about BOOST's very first digital initiative, Messenger Chatbot.

> The world of digital is really changing the retail landscape and how brands communicate in this space is really beginning to set one brand apart from the other … it's just as important that brands don't innovate for the sake of innovating, rather they ensure that it adds value to the customer and overall branding strategy. For BOOST, we're often looking for initiatives that allow our brand's voice and personality to come through. We need customers to feel that it's familiar without being heavily marketed to, which we have found helps to drive engagement. Beyond just that of using digital to market to consumers, it has also helped grow our insight into our customer, who they are and what they buy. Having such insight in the QSR [quick service restaurant] industry means that we're able to communicate to our customers in spaces and times that we know get the

best cut through. It's really interesting to see where digital is taking QSR and as a brand, we are committed to always innovating and keeping with the ever-changing customer. With anything new, there are challenges and hurdles that you need to get through. The Chatbot, in particular, saw us using technology that is still very new to our customers, and hence the communication strategy around the Bot and what it does was vital to the success of the campaign. However, on the flip side the advantage of the Chatbot was that it was built on the Facebook Messenger platform, a communication platform our core customer is very familiar with. Now that we've got the bot technology available to us we're looking into how we can implement this into our other digital platforms such as the App. What the bot will allow us to do is to offer customers with more bespoke online experiences when and where they need it (QSR Media, 2017).

Reoroduced with permission from QRS Media

Critical thinking questions
1. Discuss how the benefits of BOOST Juice's digital innovation (Chatbot) would influence the company's success.
2. What challenges might BOOST Juice face in implementing this digital innovation?

Innovation process and models

Traditional discussion on innovation is built on two main schools of thought: the social deterministic school of thought and the individualistic school. According to social determinists, innovations result from combinations of external social factors such as changes in demographics, economic variables and cultural factors. They argue that innovations will occur under the right conditions. The individualistic school believes that innovations are the result of distinctive individual talents and as such innovators are born. However, presenting a comprehensive explanation, Rothwell (1994) identifies five generations of innovation process models. His five-generation innovation explanation model is a research-based clarification of how manufacturing companies structure their innovation processes over time. Accordingly, the first- and second-generation models are linear models. Rothwell found that every new generation model is a response to a substantial change in the market – for example, industrial expansion, intense competition, economic growth, inflation, stagflation, economic recovery, unemployment and resource constraints.

The first-generation model (from the 1950s to mid-1960s)

The period after the Second World War created a huge change in society with a technological and industrial presence. Industrial economic development coupled with new employment creation and changes in consumer demand paved the way for novel thinking and attitudes. The resultant scientific and technological thinking assumed that scientific approaches were a panacea. As a result, the commercialisation process of innovation was perceived as a linear model stimulated by scientific discovery and technological progression in companies. Thus, the innovation process model could be viewed as shown in Figure 14.3.

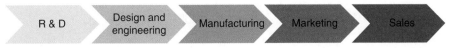

Figure 14.3 Technology push: First-generation innovation model

This model is known as the **technology push** model since it is expected that progress starts with scientists making unexpected discoveries, technologists applying them to develop product ideas, and engineers and designers turning them into prototypes for testing. The manufacturing unit produces them effectively and efficiently. Finally, marketing and sales will introduce the product to prospective consumers and encourage sales.

> **Technology push** – A model that shows innovation as being discovered by scientists, applied to make product ideas, and then made into prototypes by engineers.

The second-generation model (from the mid-1960s to early 1970s)

From the mid-1960s, competition intensified and the most efficient organisations countered it by changing the focus of their investments. Companies were in a battle for market share, and marketing was very instrumental in overcoming challenges they were encountering. As a result, the perception of the innovation process changed, and a new interpretation emerged in which demand-side factors took priority (see Figure 14.4).

Figure 14.4 Market pull: Second-generation innovation model

This model is known as the **market pull** model. However, the central focus became responding to the market's needs and it was the source of ideas driving corporate research and development.

> **Market pull** – A model in which innovation happens because of intensified competition, so that companies fight for market share and need innovative products to feed demand.

The third-generation model (1970s to mid-1980s)

With the economic downturn that occurred during the 1970s and early 1980s, companies suffered from resource constraints and they tried to reduce their rate of failure, which they considered led to waste. This led them to model the innovation process as a portfolio of wide-ranging activities. The first- and second-generation models were extremes, and a model that integrated both was proposed. Hence, a third-generation coupling model emerged.

The **interactive coupling** model improves this idea further and combines the technology-push and market-pull models (see Figure 14.5). It emphasises that innovations result from the interaction of the marketplace, the science base and the organisation's capabilities.

> **Interactive coupling** – A model that shows innovation as interaction between the marketplace, the science base and the organisation's capabilities.

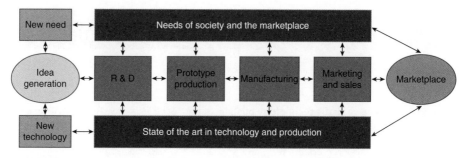

Figure 14.5 Interactive coupling model: Third-generation innovation model

The fourth-generation model (early 1980s to early 1990s)

Between the early 1980s and early 1990s, companies were focused on core business since they were at a recovery stage following the economic crunch. The importance of generic technologies with an increased strategic emphasis on technological accumulation came to prominence as a strategy and hence the notion of the global strategy emerged. Leading Japanese companies put forward the integration and parallel development of production processes and that set the background for the fourth-generation innovation model. In this model, integration and parallel development reduce a product's speed to market, as several stages of the product development process take place simultaneously. The fourth-generation model's emphasis is evident in Figure 14.6.

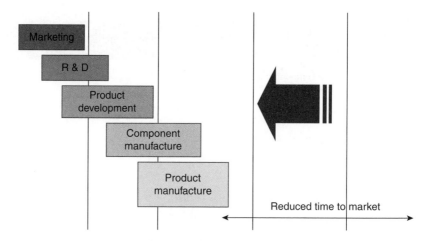

Figure 14.6 Fourth-generation innovation model
Source: Adapted from Rothwell (1994)

Based on this, contemporary innovation processes are built on principles such as technological accumulation (technology strategy); strategic networking; speedy approach to market (time-based strategy); highly integrated product and manufacturing strategies (design for manufacturability); and greater flexibility and adaptability (Rothwell, 1994). Building on these principles, innovation process in an organisation is generally organised as shown in Figure 14.7.

During the search stage, companies look for threats and opportunities for change inside and outside of the organisation. These changes may arise as either technological opportunity

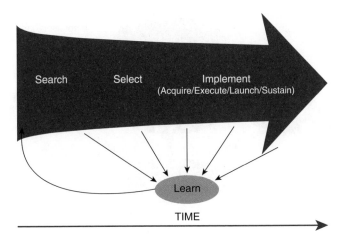

Figure 14.7 Process of innovation
Source: Tidd et al. (2005)

or changes to the requirements in the market (customer needs and wants). During the second stage, they must 'select', meaning they must decide how to respond strategically. Considering the strategic importance and level of risk attached to each opportunity, firms will decide on the opportunity to focus on. In that case, the flow of opportunities, current technological competence possessed by the firm and alignment of the opportunity with existing competence and organisational goals should be considered before deciding. Once the opportunity type is decided, implementation can begin. During this stage, four sub-activities take place: acquiring, executing, launching and sustaining. New and existing knowledge will be combined to offer a solution to the problem during acquisition. In executing, organisational knowledge will be converted into a developed innovation in preparation for the launch of a final product or service. The launch stage is when the initial adoption is managed. In the sustaining phase, plans for long-term use will be organised. Further, it is essential to note here that leaders need to consider technological achievability, market demand, competitor behaviour and regulatory and other effects during implementation. Further, the experience gained at these stages provides firms with a good learning opportunity. Therefore, they can build their knowledge base to improve the process management approaches. Finally, it is essential to note that, although this process seems to be sequentially driven, innovation can happen at any point (see Figure 14.8).

Types of innovation

Following Schilling (2005), there are four common dimensions of categorising innovations: product innovation is often accompanied by innovations in production processes; innovation is not always radical and incremental improvement can be important; innovation can enhance competence as well as destroy it; and component innovation at a modular level may achieve as much as the big-picture architectural dimension of innovation. These dimensions, which are not independent and do not offer a straightforward categorisation system that is precise and consistent, include:

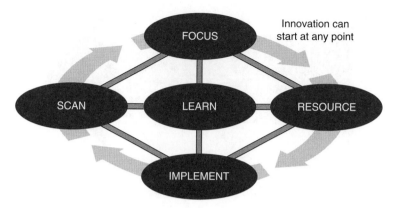

Figure 14.8 Innovation can start at any point
Source: Adapted from Holger (1998)

1. *Product and process innovations*: The most popular and common innovation types are product and process innovations. For instance, Apple iPad is a product innovation while Henry Ford's assembly-line system and strategic sourcing at GE Capital are examples of process innovation. Product innovations can lead to process innovation and vice versa. At the same time, a product innovation to one company may be a process innovation to another company.

Incremental innovation –
An innovation based on an upgraded or improved performance effect.
Radical innovation – An innovation that has an unprecedented performance effect.

2. *Radical and incremental innovations*: **Incremental innovation** enhances an existing design through improvements in the constituents and these are very common. **Radical innovation** calls for a completely new design with new components. Replacing radio's vacuum tube with the transistor was a radical innovation.

3. *Competency-enhancing and competency-destroying innovation*: When new innovations are built on the existing knowledge base, such innovation is known as competency enhancing innovation. Microsoft's Intel processors build on the 286, 386, 486, Pentium, Pentium II, Pentium III, Pentium 4, Core 2, Core i3, Core i5, Core i7 platforms and, therefore, they are competency-enhancing innovations. When the innovation is not built on the existing knowledge, it is a competency-destroying innovation – for example, the hand-held calculator's replacement of the slide rule.

4. *Component and modular innovation; architectural innovation*: When an innovation changes the existing components without a significant change to the overall configuration, it is a component innovation (e.g. wired mouse versus wireless mouse). However, when the overall system of the original product is changed and configurations are changed, that is an architectural innovation (e.g. analogue wrist watch versus digital wristwatch).

INFLUENCES ON CREATIVITY AND INNOVATION

Various factors influence creativity and innovation in organisations. Amabile (1988) identifies three categories for these factors: an organisation's motivation to innovate, its use of resources and its management practices. Organisational motivation to innovate is the basic tendency towards innovation and support for innovation in the organisational setting. An organisation may provide various forms of support such as budget, staff time or access to resources such as internal or external expertise that facilitate and promote engagement with innovation initiatives. Management practices may include the restructure of employee roles and provide freedom and autonomy at work; the provision of challenging and exciting work; the development of precise strategic goals; and the formation of work teams by drawing together individuals with diverse skills and views. Further, a study of organisational creativity has found that group characteristics and organisational characteristics also affect the creativity in the organisation (Woodman, Sawyer & Griffin, 1993). Accordingly, group characteristics include norms, group cohesiveness, size, diversity, task, roles and problem-solving approaches, while organisational characteristics refer to organisational culture, rewards, resources, strategy, structure and focus. It is essential to note that creative ideas from individuals and teams inside the organisation are a rich source of innovation.

The relationship between creativity, innovation and leadership

Creativity results from the creative thinking and know-how of an individual, based on their past experience (Amabile, 1996). On the one hand, creative thinking is visible in an individual's carefully arranged efforts to put prevailing, conventional ideas together to create novel methods to solve problems (Jung, 2001). On the other hand, creativity is built on the basic element of creative ideas, while innovation happens when an organisation successfully implements those ideas (Amabile, 1988). Yet having appropriate creative thinking skills and expertise is no use unless you have adequate motivation to mobilise or utilise them as capabilities (Jung, 2001). Therefore, leaders play a vital role in broadly defining organisational goals and facilitating the motivation process, encouraging followers to give their full support and deliver on their full potential (Bass & Stogdill, 1990). Moreover, leaders working in this way define group goals, control critical resources and provide rewards, producing a vibrant environment that enhances creativity (Jung, 2001).

Leadership styles and creativity and innovation

Leadership is not merely matching the right traits or behaviours to a given situation: it is also about how leaders motivate others to think innovatively. In this case, the leader's style has a crucial impact on the outcome of the process (Muenjohn & McMurray, 2017). For instance, transformational leadership creates a very active and emotional link between leader and follower, and the leader tries to expand their needs and aspirational horizons by transforming the follower's personal values and self-concepts (Bass & Stogdill, 1990).

This alignment between leader and follower values enhances the subordinate's intrinsic motivation much better than any other leadership style. In addition, Sosik, Kahai and Avolio (1998) have found that there is a positive relationship between group members' opinions of transformational leadership and group creativity. Muenjohn and McMurray (2017) also found that the creative discipline of design leadership has a significant effect on workplace innovation in the context of small and medium enterprises in many countries, including Vietnam, Thailand, Malaysia and Japan.

Self-efficacy – The ability to cope in a wide range of demanding or novel situations.

In addition, **self-efficacy** is believed to have a simultaneous effect on leadership effectiveness and a subordinate's creativity. The concept of self-efficacy refers to 'global confidence in one's coping ability across a wide range of demanding or novel situations' (Schwarzer & Hallum, 2008, p. 154). It is a person's confidence to succeed in specific situations (Bandura, 1997) and this personality feature may predict individual and team performance (Houghton & DiLiello, 2010). Leaders who foster confidence and autonomy among their followers increase their subordinates' self-efficacy (Okpozo et al., 2017) and promote employee creativity (Yang, Liu & Gu, 2017).

For example, Yang, Liu and Gu (2017) found in their study of Chinese bank employees that servant leadership promotes employee creative self-efficacy and team efficacy, which enables the simultaneous promotion of employee creativity and team creativity. Further, Okpozo and co-authors (2017) have shown that ethical leadership has a positive indirect effect on personal accomplishment through general self-efficacy, in a study of 203 residents in three teaching hospitals. Based on **leader–member exchange (LMX)** theory, Henson and Beehr (2017) indicated that personality characteristics such as internal locus of control and self-efficacy are the predictors of effective LMX.

Leader–member exchange (LMX) – A leadership behaviour that emphasises the relationship between leaders and followers. The relationship is based on an exchange process and usually based on positive emotional relationships.

Moreover, Redmond, Mumford and Teach (1993) have found that leader behaviour influences problem solving and feelings of self-efficacy, which in turn results in higher subordinate creativity. In addition, democratic, considerate and participative leadership styles have been found to impact positively on subordinate creativity (Hage & Dewar, 1973). As Liu and Isabelle (2017) have demonstrated, innovation climate moderates the effect of transformational leadership and transactional leadership on innovation. They have found that performance self-efficacy moderates the effects of transformational leadership and transactional leadership on innovation. The intellectual stimulation (transformational leadership) of leaders is positively related to follower innovation with high-performance self-efficacy. Contingent reward (transactional leadership) can also foster follower innovation under high-performance self-efficacy.

Moreover, transformational leaders promote innovation activities in organisations and ensure a successful life in market for the company's innovation (Mokhber, Khairuzzaman & Vakilbashi, 2017).

Characteristics of creative and innovative leadership

Several studies identify leadership style as one of the most important factors in fostering organisational innovation (Muenjohn & McMurray, 2017; Carneiro, 2008; Jung, Wu & Chow, 2003; Sidik 2012). For example, Carneiro (2008) offers a strategic leadership model, including the three pillars of knowledge, innovation challenge and the need for change. He found that strategic leadership contributes to increased innovative efforts and increased innovation positive results.

Transformational leadership, which has been applied to adaptive leadership behaviour, is considered more effective when compared with other leadership styles in enhancing organisational innovation (Gardner & Avolio, 1998; Jung, Wu & Chow, 2003; Lowe, Kroeck & Sivasubramaniam, 1996). A number of studies have identified that a CEO's transformational leadership style is positively associated with organisation-wide outcomes and innovation (Jung, Chow & Wu, 2003; Zhu, Chew & Spangler, 2005). Further, it is negatively associated with absenteeism, according to a study of senior managers in 170 firms in Singapore (Zhu et al., 2005). A CEO's transformational leadership can influence human resource management practices such as performance appraisal, training and development, and reward management systems, to enhance organisational performance (Loshali & Krishnan, 2013).

Building on the creative problem-solving literature, Rickards and Moger (2000) argue that creative performance of team members hinges on effective leadership involvements. As such, the role of the most effective leaders is not to match the right traits or behaviours to the right situations, but to help team members to coordinate and integrate their diverse styles through applied creativity processes (Basadur, 2004), such as continuously identifying, defining and solving organisational problems. Rickards and Moger (2000) recognise the creative leader's role in facilitating teams and members of the organisation. Sternberg, Kaufman and Pretz (2002) identify three leadership groups and eight ways in which creative leadership is exerted within the groups:

1. *Creative leaders who accept current paradigms and try to extend them in an innovative manner.* These leaders can be found in the organisations where there are strongly established cultures and no intention to change as they are performing well. Creative leadership styles in this context are:
   - replicators, who tend to do what others have done in the past
   - redefiners, who follow what others have done, using a new rationale
   - forward incrementers, who try to move past current paradigms by taking a few more steps
   - advance forward incrementers, who try to move past current paradigms by going still further, making substantial changes at their own risk.

2. *Creative leaders who reject current paradigms and try to replace them with a new approach*: These leaders are generally transformational and often seen as charismatic

leaders. This type of leader can be found in organisations where people believe that change is essential for survival. Creative leadership styles in this context are:

- redirectors, who try to direct an organisation in a novel direction
- reconstructive redirectors, who try to move in a new direction base on the past as a starting point
- re-initiators, who start a new approach from the scratch.

3. *Creative leaders who integrate current approaches and develop new approaches*: These leaders take the experience from analysing the past, considering their competitors and designing a new approach. The creative leadership style in this context is:

- synthesisers, who strongly believe in what they have and had the best ideas and try to put them together and synthesise a new approach.

DEVELOPING LEADERSHIP SKILLS TO ENHANCE CREATIVITY AND INNOVATION

The leadership literature discusses a diverse set of skills needed to drive creativity and innovation in an organisation. Gilley, Dixon and Gilley (2008) identify six different abilities needed to drive organisational creativity: the ability to coach, reward, communicate, motivate, involve and support others, and promote teamwork and collaboration. Among these abilities, the ability to coach is among the most important and involves questioning the status quo, approaching situations from novel points of view, and allowing organisational members to make and learn from mistakes. Coaching ensures that organisational members are inspired, optimistic and future-oriented. The ability to reward, too, enables an organisation to achieve its desired outcomes by recognising and appreciating appropriate performance. A leader who rewards can move beyond a command style of management to alert those who are at risk of stagnating that their innovation drives organisational creativity. A leader's effective motivational influence will increase employee commitment and job satisfaction. Showing confidence in employees' skills and abilities and supporting them is critical for the success of innovation. Effective management of teamwork and organising for collaboration and support are vital to ensure that organisational goals are realised.

Horth and Buchner (2009) offer an alternative perspective on the abilities that leaders need, suggesting six ways in which leaders can adopt innovative thinking:

1. *Paying attention*: This is the ability to notice things that previously went unseen. This approach does not encourage making decisions based on the first impression. Instead, a slower approach with a deep investigation into the situation and perceiving details while seeing patterns is encouraged. It is essential to look in multiple directions and listen to different views and work with different inputs.

2. *Personalising*: Looking deeply back into our own experiences introduces new and fresh perspectives on challenges and, therefore, should not be left aside. Building on your

experiences welcomes your own stock of knowledge and identifies your customer very well. Personalising requires you to work closely with your customers and thus gain an opportunity to identify their true nature.

3. *Imaging*: More than words, mental pictures of what you want and your plan to attain it are powerful tools. Ask yourself 'what if?' questions and answers, which will lead to surprising images and possibilities.

4. *Serious play*: Although business thinking is a tough process, innovation thinking requires you to bend your rules and have some fun. Try to adopt non-traditional ways of generating knowledge and awareness, which will maintain the fun aspect of your project.

5. *Collaborative inquiry*: Rather than approaching business challenges individually, collaborating with others is a sustainable and effective approach to problem solving. It is important to work with a variety of stakeholders, although it often involves a high level of complexity. This will offer you many opportunities beyond the limits of your own perspectives as an individual.

6. *Crafting*: Unlike traditional business thinking, innovative leadership requires you to craft challenges by synthesising and integrating the issues involved. Breaking down problems into small pieces and trying to see new patterns and combinations within them are encouraged under this style.

SUMMARY

LEARNING OUTCOME 1: Identify the determinants of organisational creativity.

Organisational creativity depends on the creativity of individuals working within organisational processes, and other context-specific factors that may have a bearing on the behaviours of the organisation's members. Individual creativity depends on the expertise, motivation and the creative thinking skills that organisational members tend to possess. At the same time, factors such as organisational climate, leadership style, organisational culture, resources, structure and systems all influence individual creativity. Understanding the influence of these factors helps managers to identify the potential issues involved in enhancing organisational creativity.

LEARNING OUTCOME 2: Explain the process of innovation and differentiate between types of innovation.

Noting the innovation models that have developed over recent decades, the current understanding is that innovation can occur at any stages of the general process including search, selection and implementation. At the search stage, organisations tend to conduct a situational analysis to identify threats and opportunities. Strategic responses are decided at the selection stage, while the implementation stage is concerned about operational aspects of the opportunity that have been identified. The implementation stage includes knowledge acquisition and combination, knowledge conversion to an innovation output, adaptation of the actual product and, finally, establishment of measures to ensure that the innovation is sustainable.

Product innovation and processes innovation are key types of innovation. Product innovations are uniquely output oriented and process innovations are superior methods of producing a certain output. Radical innovations are unprecedented performance-driven designs, while incremental innovations are useful improvements to the existing products. When such innovations are built on an existing knowledge base, they are known as competency-enhancing, while competency-destroying innovations call for completely new sets of knowledge and skill bases. Component innovations are changes in existing configurations, while more general change to the original configuration is known as an architectural innovation.

LEARNING OUTCOME 3: Clarify the link between creativity, innovation and leadership.

Creative ideas result from creative thinking and the skills of individuals. Innovations are built on these creative ideas, but also need technical invention, commercial application and marketability. Implementation of a creative idea into a practical outcome requires the organisation to develop an innovation-driven climate and culture. Nurturing of such a culture requires motivation through leadership. At the same time, the level and the type of creative skill and thinking needed by the organisation is something leaders need to understand. Hence, effective leadership is needed to ensure that creative resources are used to build a culture that fosters innovation.

LEARNING OUTCOME 4: Suggest creativity-enhancing strategies for a given organisational context.

Employees need an organisational environment which supports them to become free thinkers. At the same time, the organisational culture should encourage employees to take risks by working on new ideas, knowing that if they fail to realise the innovation, they will not be punished. Effective resource deployment and teamwork within the organisational processes are of paramount importance to enhance organisational creativity. Arranging the organisational culture, systems and structure to align with creativity-driven processes can help employees to improve their creative skills.

LEARNING OUTCOME 5: Discuss the role of the leader in promoting organisational creativity and innovation.

Depending on the context, a leader's choice of motivational strategies can effectively enhance creative thinking and nurture the ideas of organisational members. Engaging effectively, placing confidence in employee skills and recognising their achievements are crucial areas for a strategic leader. Raising awareness of potential risks and clearly promoting the organisation's support for employee innovation can also improve creativity.

REVIEW QUESTIONS

1. Suggest some of the methods that can improve organisational creativity.

2. Describe Rothwell's (1994) innovation process model.

3. Identify the salient characteristics of different types of innovation and provide an example for each type to justify your answer.

4. What is the role of a leader in fostering organisational innovation?

5. To what extent is organisational creativity a function of the creativity of individuals, rather than a function of organisational structure, routines, incentives and culture? Discuss this with reference to an innovative company of your choice.

Eureka! How to turn all employees into innovators

The following is an account of the creativity and innovation encouraging approaches at Planet Innovation Australia.

> The first step to sparking creativity is for the company to be vocal about its support for new ideas. Whether true or not, it's easy for employees to feel like they are discouraged from working on pet projects, and that management views them as distractions from their 'real job' … One way for organisations to show their support of entrepreneurial thinking is to introduce a program where employees are encouraged to submit ideas, at any stage of maturity, as potential projects. At Planet Innovation (PI) we did this through an initiative called the Eureka Club. With the Eureka Club, ideas are submitted by employees and displayed in the PI offices, for everyone to see and discuss …
>
> Once a mechanism for encouraging new ideas is established, the next step is to draw out the best ones from the crowd. This, however, introduces another conflict: employees with mature concepts and a high potential for profit are going to be less likely to divulge their ideas, for fear of losing equity or control over something they spent significant energy creating. Therefore, it's critical that employees are provided with incentives attractive enough to convince them to develop the project in-house, while still maximizing profitability for the company. A great example of this at PI is the product Ingeni, a device born out of the Eureka Club. Ingeni is a USB aerial with smart software that allows consumers to monitor their home's energy consumption by wirelessly connecting their PC to their smart meter. PI offered Ingeni's creator, Michael Joffe, the opportunity to run the project himself as a spin-off brand, assuring him that he would have control over the product's technical and commercial development. The product is now launched on the market at www.myingeni.com.
>
> Capturing and developing new concepts can successfully shine a light on great ideas and great thinkers, but if you really want to turbo-charge your business and turn your company into a breeding ground for innovation you must create entrepreneurs where none existed before. To incite this behaviour, PI created a competition where employees were challenged to submit their best ideas to the Eureka Club, to be voted on by their peers. The ideas that proved most popular would be developed at PI, with their creator given the opportunity to manage the project. With the Eureka Club, new product ideas were encouraged to be worked on outside normal business hours. The idea of experienced employees using their free time to work on someone else's idea may seem crazy, but it worked and with some unexpected benefits.
>
> Because the company has virtually no financial risk in the project, the volunteer team members are allowed to operate with very little oversight from management. This allows anyone interested in working on the project to do so and in virtually any capacity they want. Employees who are interested in learning more about the development process get to work on a project in a completely different role than what they typically would, expanding their skill set and obtaining greater knowledge about the many moving parts that go into commercialising a new product. Also by limiting the hours to outside 9–5, management ensures that no critical resources are being pulled off other projects and that even the busiest employees have a chance to contribute.
>
> Additionally, motivated young employees can accelerate their careers by taking the opportunity to work on a project that provides them more responsibility, influence, and exposure within the company. The result is a commercially viable project being led

by an ambitious, motivated group of employees who are quickly learning to think not just as engineers, scientists, or designers, but as entrepreneurs.

Source: Mergens (2017), reproduced with permmission from Planet Innovation

Critical thinking questions

1. What approaches has Planet Innovation Australia taken to encourage entrepreneurial activity, and why do you think they work?
2. Describe the culture of this organisation, drawing on information from the case. What factors have influenced the development of this culture?
3. What drawbacks do you see in Planet Innovation Australia's innovation process? Justify your answer.

REFERENCES

Amabile, T.M. (1988). A model of creativity and innovation in organizations. *Research in Organizational Behavior*, 10(1), 123–67.

—— (1996). *Creativity in context*. Boulder, CO: Westview Press.

—— (1998). *How to Kill Creativity*. Harvard Business Review, September–October.

Amabile, T. & Khaire, M. (2008). Creativity and the role of the leader. *Harvard Business Review*. Retrieved from: https://hbr.org/2008/10/creativity-and-the-role-of-the-leader.

Australian Financial Review (AFR) (2017). 50 most innovative companies 2017. *Australian Financial Review*. Retrieved from: www.afr.com/leadership/afr-lists/most-innovative-companies/50-most-innovative-companies-2017–20170917-gyj29i.

Bandura, A. (1997). Toward a unifying theory of behavioral change. *Psychological Review*, 84(2), 191–215.

Basadur, M. (2004). Leading others to think innovatively together: Creative leadership. *The Leadership Quarterly*, 15(1), 103–21.

Bass, B.M. & Stogdill, R.M. (1990). *Bass and Stogdill's handbook of leadership: Theory, research, and managerial applications*. New York, NY: Free Press.

Carneiro, A. (2008). When leadership means more innovation and development. *Business Strategy Series*, 9(4), 176–84.

Dragon Rough (n.d.). 3M: A culture of invention. Retrieved from: www.dragonrouge.com/businessisbeautiful/3m.

Gardner, W.L. & Avolio, B.A. (1998). The charismatic relationship: A dramaturgical perspective. *Academy of Management Review*, 23, 405–21.

Gilley, A., Dixon, P. & Gilley, J.W. (2008). Characteristics of leadership effectiveness: Implementing change and driving innovation in organizations. *Human Resource Development Quarterly*, 19(2), 153–69.

Hage, J. & Dewar, R. (1973). Elite values versus organizational structure in predicting innovation. *Administrative Science Quarterly*, 18, 279–90.

Henson, J.A. & Beehr, T. (2017). Subordinates' core self-evaluations and performance predict leader-rated LMX. *Leadership and Organization Development Journal*, 39(1), 150–68. Retrieved from: https://doi.org/10.1108.

Holger, E. (1998). *Temaguide: A guide to technology management and innovation for companies*. Madrid: Fundacion COTEC para la Innovacion Tecnologica.

Horth, D. & Buchner, D. (2009). *Innovation leadership: How to use innovation to lead effectively, work collaboratively and drive results*. Greensborough, NC: Center for Creative Leadership.

Houghton, J.D. & DiLiello, T.C. (2010) Leadership development: The key to unlocking individual creativity in organizations. *Leadership and Organization Development Journal*, 31(3), 230–45.

Jung, D., Chow, C.W. & Wu, A. (2003). The role of transformational leadership in enhancing organizational innovation: Hypotheses and some preliminary findings. *Leadership Quarterly*, (14), 525–54.

Jung, D.I. (2001). Transformational and transactional leadership and their effects on creativity in groups. *Creativity Research Journal*, 13(2), 185–95.

Kacprzyk, K. & Doryn, W. (2017). Innovation and economic growth in old and new member states of the European Union. *Economic Research–Ekonomska Istraživanja*, 30(1), 1724–42.

Kuratko, D.F. (2016). *Entrepreneurship: Theory, process, and practice*. Melbourne: Cengage Learning.

Liu, A.M.M. & Isabelle, Y.S.C. (2017). Understanding the interplay of organizational climate and leadership in construction innovation. *Journal of Management in Engineering*, 35(5), 4017–21. doi:10.1061/(ASCE)ME.1943–5479.0000521

Lowe, K.B., Kroeck, K.G. & Sivasubramaniam, N. (1996). Effectiveness correlates of transformational and transactional leadership: A meta-analytic review. *Leadership Quarterly*, 7, 385–425.

Loshali, S. & Krishnan, V.R. (2013), Strategic human resource management and firm performance: Mediating role of transformational leadership, *Journal of Strategic Human Resource Management*, 2(1), 9–19.

Luecke, R. & Katz, R. (2003). *Harvard Business essentials: Managing creativity and innovation*. Boston: Harvard Business School Press.

M&C Saatchi (2017). M&C Saatchi second most innovative company in Australia. Retrieved from: http://mcsaatchi.com.au/news/mc-saatchi-second-most-innovative-company-in-australia.

McMurray, A., Islam, M., Pirola-Merlo, A. & Sarros, J. (2012). Workplace innovation in a non-profit organization. *Journal of Nonprofit Management and Leadership*, 23(3), 367–88.

Mergens, D. (2017). Eureka! How to turn all employees into innovators. Retrieved from: https://planetinnovation.com.au/eureka-how-to-turn-all-employees-into-innovators.

Mokhber, M., Khairuzzaman, W. & Vakilbashi, A. (2017). Leadership and innovation: The moderator role of organization support for innovative behaviors. *Journal of Management and Organization*, 24(1), 108–128.

Muenjohn, N. & McMurray, A. (2017). Design leadership, work values ethic and workplace innovation: An investigation of SMEs in Thailand and Vietnam. *Asia Pacific Business Research: Special Issue: Human Capital in Asia*, 23(2), 192–204.

Mumford, M.D. & Gustafson, S.B. (1988). Creativity syndrome: Integration, application, and innovation. *Psychological Bulletin*, 103(1), 27.

Myers, S. & Marquis, D.G. (1969). *Successful industrial innovations: A study of factors underlying innovation in selected firms*. Washington, DC: National Science Foundation.

Niosia, J. (1999). Fourth-generation R&D: From linear models to flexible innovation. *Journal of Business Research*, 45(2), 111–17.

Nyström, H. (1993). Creativity and entrepreneurship. *Creativity and Innovation Management*, 2(4), 237–42.

Okpozo, A.Z., Gong, T., Ennis, M.C. & Adenuga, B. (2017). Investigating the impact of ethical leadership on aspects of burnout. *Leadership and Organization Development Journal*, 38(8), 1128–43.

QSR Media (2017). Find out how Boost Juice is ramping up its digital strategy with its first ever chatbot. Retrieved from: http://qsrmedia.com.au/technology/in-focus/find-out-whats-behind-boost-juices-digital-innovation-strategy.

Redmond, M.R., Mumford, M.D. & Teach, R. (1993). Putting creativity to work: Effects of leader behavior on subordinate creativity. *Organizational Behavior and Human Decision Processes*, 55(1), 120–51.

Rickards, T. & Moger, S. (2000). Creative leadership processes in project team development: An alternative to Tuckman's stage model. *British Journal of Management*, 11(4), 273–83.

Robinson, A. & Stern, S. (1997). *Corporate creativity: How innovation and improvement actually happen*. NSW: Berrett-Koehler Publishers, Inc.

Rothwell, R. (1994). Towards the fifth-generation innovation process. *International Marketing Review*, 11(1), 7–31.

Schilling, M.A. (2005). *Strategic management of technological innovation*. New York, NY: Tata McGraw-Hill Education.

Schwarzer, R. & Hallum, S. (2008), Perceived teacher self-efficacy as a predictor of job stress and burnout: Mediation analyses. *Applied Psychology*, 57(S1), 152–71,

Sidik, I.G. (2012). Conceptual framework of factors affecting SME development: Mediating factors on the relationship of entrepreneur traits and SME performance. *Procedia Economics and Finance*, 4(0), 373–83.

Sosik, J.J., Kahai, S.S. & Avolio, B.J. (1998). Transformational leadership and dimensions of creativity: Motivating idea generation in computer-mediated groups. *Creativity Research Journal*, 11(2), 111–21.

Sternberg, R.J., Kaufman, J.C. & Pretz, J.E. (2002). *The creativity conundrum: A propulsion model of kinds of creative contributions.* New York, NY: Psychology Press.

Tidd, J., Bessant, J. & Pavitt, K. (2005). *Managing innovation integrating technological, market and organizational change.* NJ: John Wiley & Sons.

Trott, P. (2008). *Innovation management and new product development.* Harlow, UK: Pearson Education.

Woodman, R.W., Sawyer, J.E. & Griffin, R.W. (1993). Toward a theory of organizational creativity. *Academy of Management Review*, 18(2), 293–321.

Yang, J. Liu, H. & Gu, J. (2017). A multi-level study of servant leadership on creativity: The roles of self-efficacy and power distance. *Leadership and Organization Development Journal*, 48(5), 610–29.

Zhu, W., Chew, I. & Spangler, W. (2005). CEO transformational leadership and organizational outcomes: The mediating role of human-capital-enhancing human resource management. *Leadership Quarterly*, 16, 39–52.

15

LEADERSHIP AND DECISION MAKING

Nuttawuth Muenjohn and Adela McMurray

LEARNING OUTCOMES

After reading this chapter, you should be able to:

1. describe how decision-making processes work in organisations

2. discuss how various decision-making models apply in different situations

3. identify the functions and roles of the leader in decision making

4. differentiate between leadership decision-making styles

5. explain ethical decision making and crisis leadership.

INTRODUCTION

AMAZON CEO JEFF Bezos recently told his shareholders that most of his leadership decisions are made when he has received 70 per cent of the information he ultimately expects to receive. For Bezos, the delay involved in waiting for the remaining 30 per cent is unacceptable, because making organisational course corrections promptly averts costly mistakes (Salisbury, 2017). This statement clearly implies the nature of decisions and the leadership required for today's competitive and turbulent business world. Therefore, effective leadership has become crucial for the success of organisations that struggle in the face of increased competition and a rapidly changing business environment. Decision making is part of a leader's routine duties. This makes decision making important for those who are in a leadership role.

This chapter aims to provide major theoretical explanations of the effective decision-making process. The decision-making framework, importance and difficulties of decision making, theoretical models and frameworks of decision making, different leadership requirements such as crisis leadership, and ethical leadership are discussed in detail in this chapter.

THE IMPORTANCE OF DECISION MAKING

Making good and timely leadership decisions have long been recognised as a defining characteristic of leadership (Useem, 2010). Decisions are central to success and can be perceived as difficult, confusing and anxiety-raising during critical situations. **Decision making** is a process of judging various available options to extract and crystallise the most appropriate ones. In other words, decision making is the process of making choices by identifying a decision to be made, gathering necessary information and assessing the optional resolutions available. Decision making is a crucial activity that leaders undertake, whenever they choose a course of action to deal with a problem or pursue an opportunity.

> **Decision making** – A process of making choices by identifying a decision to be made, gathering needed information and assessing the optional resolutions available.

Decision making is highly important to any organisation as it involves much of the managerial activity which directs the organisation towards a specific course of action. It entails the commitment of resources in a particular manner. It is only by making decisions and implementing them that organisational resources are mobilised and utilised to achieve objectives. It is important to remember that a leader's decisions have key implications for various aspects of the organisation. These decisions may affect people in one way or another. It is also to be noted that the decisions a leader makes reflects his/her beliefs and values. Further, leadership decisions will set an example for the followers; as followers learn about decisions a leader is making, they also realise that the leader is ready to deal with the challenge of organisational change. It is a way of showing followers that the organisation recognises any challenges, and is ready to embrace consequences of change.

THE DECISION-MAKING PROCESS

Leaders have a responsibility to make good decisions for everyone involved and, therefore, should employ a framework to facilitate the decision-making process. Leaders need to sense the changes in the business environment and recognise the need to make appropriate decisions. The success of the entire decision-making process depends on the availability of correct information at the right time. Although every leader has a unique style of leading, generally, the decision-making process involves common phases. According to Moshal (2009) and Benowitz (2001), this process comprises seven stages (see Figure 15.1 – note that different authors have given versions of this process with more or fewer stages).

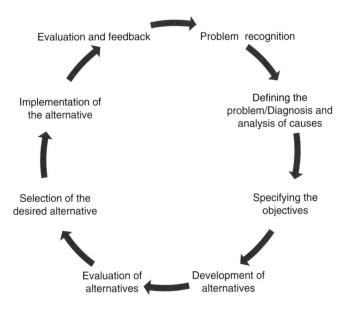

Figure 15.1 Decision-making process

Assessing all the related internal and external situations to identify the problem in detail is the problem recognition stage in the decision-making process. This approach represents the need to recognise the importance of context in decision making. While identifying the problem, it is essential to ascertain the basic nature of the problem under consideration. This will enable the leader to decide on whether the issue is tactical or functional, critical or trivial, a long-term or a short-term problem.

At the 'defining the problem' stage, the leader attempts to define the issue as clearly as possible after clarifying the problem being addressed. This stage is significant because the quality and efficiency of decision making fully depend on the clarity of the problem definition. The problem is defined and elucidated in terms of its source, scope, indications, roots, significance, seriousness, intensity and consequences. Complex and major problems are broken into simple components and studied thoroughly to create a clear big picture of the issue.

Once the problem is clearly defined, the objective specification is formulated. A set of objectives underpins decision making. The solution to a problem drives the accomplishment of the goal. Therefore, a careful and wise approach to problem solving could potentially sustain business survival or grow demand and improve market share. Decision-making objectives may either be quantitative or qualitative in nature.

Development of alternatives is crucial to the process and the results since the quality of the decisions leaders make will depend on the available options. Therefore, it is essential to ensure that the leader uncovers all the potential decision options to address a problem. However, the decision-making process is a challenging task and requires relevant and meaningful alternatives to be examined. Decision alternatives are identified, either based on a leader's experience and expertise, or through research and analysis, creative thinking (brainstorming) and innovativeness.

Previously identified decision alternatives should be evaluated based on the consequences through forecasting and other appropriate methods. Thus, the risk involved, time consumption, the efficiency of alternatives and resource position of the organisation are essential criteria in the evaluation of decision alternatives. In addition, Benowitz (2001) postulated that every decision alternative needs to be evaluated for feasibility, effectiveness and consequences. However, it should be noted that evaluating alternative courses of action, qualitative factors such as ethical and moral values, social implication, and organisational reputation should also be taken into consideration.

The final choice of decision alternatives is based on the leader's assessment, reflecting their prior experience, skills and judgement. In addition, leaders should consider other decision possibilities, appropriateness, practicality and the ease of alternative resolutions. Moreover, it is essential to consider various organisational plans, policies, rules, fundamental management philosophies, and other human-related factors with adequate attention in making the final decision.

Decision implementation involves a series of actions and utilisation of organisational resources. In addition, structural, administrative and logical organisational arrangements such as delegation of authority, resource allocation, activity assignment and establishing control mechanisms should be put in place.

Ongoing monitoring and evaluation is an essential step in this process. How well the decision is implemented, its outcome and what alternative arrangements are needed at this stage are among the concerns at this stage (Benowitz, 2001).

PROBLEMS AND CHALLENGES IN DECISION MAKING

Leaders face several problems and difficulties in making decisions. Inadequate and incomplete information creates uncertainty in decision making, and leaders often face the difficult task of assessing the problem context in order to identify potential solutions. Further, in this turbulent business environment, there are complex variables to understand, often requiring a substantial depth of information on the matter under consideration. Not only that but also the continuously evolving business environment brings many threats to organisational decision making. The external business environment is not static but continues to develop. This makes it difficult to predict the consequences of certain decisions and the influence of other variables on a leader's decision. In addition to the external business environment, threats emanating from internal business environments are also of significant importance to consider. Subordinates tend not to universally welcome new decisions that a leader makes, and hence it is likely that there will be some resistance among sections of the organisation. When a decision affects employees, they may resist implementing it, thus impeding the introduction of the desired change. Further, ineffective communication can also create considerable difficulties in the decision-making activities of leaders. When the decision and its possible consequences are not appropriately communicated to the followers, the necessary support for its implementation will be difficult to obtain.

THEORIES AND MODELS OF DECISION MAKING

In highly uncertain and turbulent business environments leaders need to understand when to make decisions themselves and when it is appropriate to delegate a solution to their management team. There are multiple theoretical decision-making models, but primarily there are two types: normative or prescriptive models, and descriptive models (Lussier & Achua, 2015). The models that aim to provide a sensible basis for decision making are 'normative' (Vroom & Yetton, 1973). The other set of models focus on the decision-making process. Models that focus on understanding rather than improvements are known as 'descriptive models'. This section focuses on these normative and descriptive decision-making models.

Normative model of leadership

It is essential that a leader knows when to take charge of decision making and when to delegate the authority to an individual or a team. In some situations, leaders should assign the decision making to subordinates or ask subordinates for relevant facts prior to making a decision. However, in an emergency or business crisis, the leader's responsibility is to make their own decisions, rather than delegate them. These different contexts and situations change the level of participation in terms of various leader-follower and situational factors. Vroom and Yetton (1973) argued that leaders can often improve group performance by using a prime level of contribution to the decision-making process and they presented the normative model of leadership decision making. Therefore, the model is directed at determining the level of input subordinates should have in the decision-making process.

Accordingly, Lussier and Achua (2015) identified five leadership styles in terms of the participation level of followers in the decision-making process. These are: they decide; consult individually; consult with a group; facilitate; and delegate.

1. *Decide*: The leader resolves the problem or makes the decision using whatever information and experience is at hand without the involvement of followers.
2. *Consult individually*: The leader may individually consult the followers by sharing the problem with them, yet does not bring them into a group and discuss the problem. Depending on the information gathered from such efforts, the leader will make the decision, and sometimes a follower's influence may be reflected in the decision.
3. *Consult group*: The leader communicates the problem to their followers in a group meeting and obtains ideas and suggestions. However, this style does not guarantee the direct influence of followers on the decision.
4. *Facilitate*: The leader communicates the problem to the followers in a group and requests them to define the problem within a given frame. The leader's role is like that of a facilitator, and does not contribute to the definition. Based on information that followers provide, the leader makes the final decision.
5. *Delegate*: The leader shares the problem among the group and collectively generates and evaluates the decision alternatives. The leader's role is to coordinate the situation, discuss the problem and make sure critical issues are adequately discussed and focused.

According to Vroom and Yetton (1973), 'decide' and 'facilitate' styles are autocratic processes while consulting 'individually' and 'group' styles are considered consultative processes. The style of delegation is known as a group process. In deciding which style is suitable for a given situation, Vroom and Yetton designed seven questions and an associated model. This model, the normative decision-making model includes:

> a time-driven and development-driven decision tree that enables the user to select one of five leadership styles (decide, consult individually, consult group, facilitate, and delegate) appropriate for the situation (comprised of seven variables or contexts) so as to maximize decisions (Lussier & Achua, 2015, p. 123).

These situations and variables are outlined below.

1. *Decision significance*: How important is the decision – high (H) or low (L) – to the success of the project or organisation? If the importance is high, then the leader must be involved.
2. *The importance of commitment*: How important is the followers' commitment – high (H) or low (L) – to implement the decision? Without commitment, no decision can be implemented in an effective or meaningful manner. Traditionally, it is advisable that the follower is involved in the decision making to increase ownership and in turn commitment to the implementation of the decision. Those decisions that enjoy a high level of follower commitment have a greater chance of successful implementation.
3. *Leader expertise*: What level of knowledge and expertise does a leader possess in this particular area? This will determine a result of high (H) or low (L): the higher the leader's expertise, the fewer followers need involvement.

4. *Likelihood of commitment*: Would the followers be committed, if the leader were to make the decision alone? If low (L), there is less need for followers' commitment if the potential decision is one follower like.

5. *Group support for objectives*: Do followers have high (H) or low (L) support for the team or organisational aims to be achieved in solving the problem? Higher levels of participation are adequate with high levels of backing.

6. *Group expertise*: What level of knowledge and expertise do individual followers have in relation to a specific decision, high (H) or low (L)? The more expertise the followers have, the greater the individual or group participation can be.

7. *Team competence*: What ability do individuals have to work together as a team to solve the problem, high (H) or low (L)? Higher team competence may achieve a high level of participation.

It is essential to note here that not all seven questions will be important in every context. Hence, the leaders need to apply them depending on the context. Based on these seven variables/questions and the five leadership styles identified previously, Vroom and Yetton (1973) have built a decision tree (see Figure 15.2).

PROBLEM STATEMENT

Decision significance	Importance of commitment	Leader expertise	Likelihood of commitment	Group support	Group expertise	Team competence	
H	H	H	H	–	–	–	Decide
			L	H	H	H	Delegate
						L	
					L	–	Consult (Group)
				L	–	–	
		L	H	H	H	H	Facilitate
						L	
					L	–	Consult (Individually)
				L	–	–	
			L	H	H	H	Facilitate
						L	
					L	–	Consult (Group)
				L	–	–	
	L	H	–	–	–	–	Decide
		L	–	H	H	H	Facilitate
						L	
					L	–	Consult (Individually)
				L	–	–	
L	H	–	H	–	–	–	Decide
			L	–	–	H	Delegate
						L	Facilitate
	L	–	–	–	–	–	Decide

Figure 15.2 Normative model for decision making

Source: Vroom & Yetton (1973), reproduced with permission of the University of Pittsburgh Press

Leader-centred decision-making model

According to this model of decision making, the leader exercises his or her power to start, direct, focus, coach and control team members. To be successful in leader-centred decision making, the leader should follow the suggestions of Lussier and Achua (2015, p. 297):

> The leader needs to concentrate on the undertaking while disregarding the emotions and personal relationships. As a leader dominating style, the leader should not give up his/her right to make the final decision although others' opinions are considered and sought for their consent. During the discussions, it is essential to have the control over the group while respectfully and decisively preventing the troublesome activities and unrelated discussion. It is advised the leaders to promote rational and logical discussions rather than emotional upsurges. It is of vital importance to leaders that they secure their authority against the group, and they may need to fight for this.

Although there are advantages to this approach, there are also possible disadvantages. Orderly conduct of meetings and decision making may lead members to become uninterested and aggrieved, resulting in a decrease in participation and a reduction in quality of decisions. Team members' acceptance of decisions may also be endangered if they feel stressed and unable to influence decision making.

Team-centred decision-making model

According to Lussier and Achua (2015, p. 287) the team-centred decision-making style is preferred when information and know-how are spread among team members; the needed commitment can only be gained by involvement; the power concentration around an individual member is a concern of others; or distasteful decisions are required to be made. This approach allows the team members to foster an energetic, creative and dedicated workforce. It ensures that employees can be relied upon to make decisions and they can be up-skilled with the necessary ability to do so. This will enhance the organisational effectiveness. The role of a leader in a team-centred model is as consultant, advisor, coach or facilitator for the team. Improved quality of group and individual decision making gives a leader the opportunity to focus more on strategic issues once freed from other activities, diffused responsibility and enhanced facilitation. Particularly when unpopular decisions and increased commitment of team members are required, this approach delivers some major advantages.

However, downsides to this approach may include: a longer cycle of decision making; the possibility of being self-serving and contrary to the best interest of the organisation if team members have different objectives to those of the organisation; the risk of achieving a poor compromise when team members cannot agree among themselves; potential confusion should the leader fear losing power; and the likely resistance to emerge from team members, who do not want to take more responsibility.

LEADERSHIP ROLES AND FUNCTIONS IN DECISION MAKING

Quinn (1988) presented the Competing Values Framework (CVF) to define eight distinctive leadership roles along two dimensions: the level of flexibility and level of focus. These two dimensions define four quadrants and eight leadership roles that address different demands in the organisational context (see Figure 15.3).

Figure 15.3 Leadership decision-making roles

The quadrant showing the producer and manager roles is known as the **'task leadership** quadrant', which is characterised by a control orientation and an external environment focused on setting and attaining goals. The leader, as producer, is expected to motivate members to enhance production and to accomplish stated goals. Leadership roles require clarifying expectations, defining issues, establishing objectives, generating rules including policies, and providing instructions.

> **Task leadership** – A leadership orientation with a higher control over organisation members and a focus on external environment in setting and attaining goals.

Quadrant two, which refers to stability leadership is concerned with monitoring and coordinating and embraces the unit's work with a control orientation including a focus on internal functions. The leadership duties require maintaining the system including the structure and flow, coordinating the scheduling of staff, and handling crises including technical and logistical issues. The leader's 'monitor' role determines whether the unit's goals are being achieved and includes maintaining awareness of the unit's status and compliance with rules including regulations and policy.

The third quadrant refers to '**people leadership**', which requires a flexible orientation with a focus on the internal unit's functioning. It emphasises subordinate mentoring and assisting group processes. While the facilitator and mentor occupy central roles here of approachable and helpful leaders must nurture the collective efforts of their subordinates including the building of teamwork and collaboration, and managing interpersonal conflict. As a

> **People leadership** – A flexible orientation and a focus on the international functioning of the organisation, emphasising mentoring of subordinates and assisting group process in the business.

mentor, the thoughtful and sensitive leader is expected to develop people through a caring and compassionate approach.

The fourth and final quadrant, concerned with 'adaptive leadership', typically has a flexible orientation and a focus on the unit's external environment. It highlights the unit's development of innovations and gaining resources. Innovators are aware of environmental changes and can identify and implement change. They take charge and meet with key external stakeholders to negotiate and gain resources for the unit.

Moreover, in leadership decision making, it is essential to understand that leadership is a process of social influence in which a person seeks the assistance of others to reach a goal. According to Chemers (2014), in a systematically structured and well-understood environment the primary responsibilities of a leader include directing and inspiring, assigning people to tasks, briefing what is expected, and assisting and encouraging goal accomplishment of the organisation. A less orderly environment calls for external adaptability, and the crucial functions include problem solving and innovation. Overall, the leader must create an atmosphere which encourages sensitivity, flexibility and creativity while the leader becomes a change agent (Chemers, 2014).

In their discussion of functional leadership, Hackman, Walton and Goodman (1986) state that monitoring and acting are two major functions of leadership in promoting an effective team. Further, to monitor the team activities, a leader needs to foresee and detect the potential problems that the team may encounter. Additionally, they should promote the actions necessary to create and maintain these performance conditions. Fleishman et al. (1991) interpreted leadership as a problem-solving behaviour, with the leader responsible for identifying the possible issues and finding solutions and implementing them. Their proposed typology of leadership functions includes information search and structure, information use in problem solving, and management of personnel and material resources.

LEADERSHIP DECISION-MAKING STYLES

There are four major leadership decision styles: directive, consultative, democratic and consensus (DuBrin, 2015). These four styles can be arranged in a continuum to reflect on the possible differences in terms of the orientation (see Figure 15.4). Accordingly, one extreme of the continuum would be the 'leader-driven decision styles' and the other 'employee/team driven decision styles'.

Directive decision making – A top-down way of making decisions, where employees have no opportunity to negotiate with leaders.

The **directive decision-making** style is a top-down approach with no negotiation opportunities given to employees. The leader takes the full controlling power of the decision making. This style is suitable for a situation where the team is comprised of junior and less experienced managers, in an emergency with time pressure, or when a business involves high risk. However, exercising such a style may cause staff disengagement and frustration.

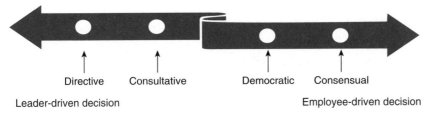

Figure 15.4 Leadership decision-making styles

On the other hand, a **consultative decision-making** style requests the team members to provide input, yet the leader holds ultimate decision-making power. This decision-making style can be adopted in situations where the manager does not possess a specific expertise required; the team is not adequately matured; and the business is a risky situation. To obtain the best results from this style, it is essential to clearly understand the expected inputs and their possible uses.

In the majority-vote-based or **democratic decision-making** style, both the leader and team members propose and vote on possible options. Such a style would be suitable for matured and very large teams. Further, this style may promote the active participation of the employees or team members. It is essential to make the rules clear and disseminated to every member of the team, and to be cautious about the influencers and followers during the voting session, to make this process successful. Team members and the leader should collectively arrive at decisions when consensus-based decision-making style is executed. This style would be ideal to further the commitment and engagement of a matured and expert team. The role of the leader would be more neutral, constructive and respective towards the members.

> **Consultative decision making** – A decision-making style that requests the team members to provide input, while keeping the ultimate decision-making power with the leader.
> **Democratic decision making** – A decision-making style in which both leader and team members propose options, followed by a voting process.

LEADERSHIP AND ETHICAL DECISION MAKING

Globalisation, taking place in an uncertain and ambiguous business environment, has made it essential that organisations focus on ethical decision-making processes. A far-sighted approach an organisation takes to meet this need results in increased consumer trust and reduced follower turnover intentions (Eisenbeiss, 2012). The seriousness of ethical decision making in business can be seen, for example, in the case of the Australian Competition and Consumer Commission (ACCC) acting in the wake of the Volkswagen diesel emission scandal. According to the ACCC Chairman, Mr Rod Sims, Volkswagen's action of using engines that appeared to have low emissions during the testing stage misled customers and was a breach of mandatory standards (Brown, 2015). The following case study considers this matter.

Volkswagen's diesel scandal – ACCC sues over dodgy emissions claims

The Australian Competition and Consumer Commission (ACCC) has started proceedings in the Federal Court against Volkswagen Audi and Audi Australia. The ACCC alleges the company used a defeat device that could detect when the car was being tested and then lower emissions during tests. It is alleged those cars would then operate differently on the road. The ACCC's Chairman, Rod Sims, stated this does not meet design standards and the company misrepresented the vehicles' environmental impact to consumers:

> [W]e are hoping to send a very strong signal to manufacturers not to seek to avoid environment and other regulations … So it has widespread implications whenever manufacturers mislead consumers as to the nature of their products. The allegations we're making here are particularly egregious (Stein, 2017).

Critical thinking questions
1. What is the lesson you learned from this case?
2. What would be the implications of this matter for Volkswagen's future in Australia, and for its consumers and competitors?

Sometimes companies earn their profits at the cost of the health and safety of the public; yet these unethical actions only lead to hard financial penalties when local, state or federal authorities come to hear about them. At the other end of the spectrum, while customers may be attracted to brands that have a strong environmental commitment, such companies often sacrifice short-term profits and focus on building towards long-term growth. The following section will locate the ethical decision-making approach in its theoretical context, with a detailed elucidation of ethical decision-making models in the leadership literature.

Models for ethical decision making

Multiple theorists have attempted to explain the ethical decision-making process of organisational leaders. The eminent work of Rest (1986) identifies four major stages in ethical decision making (Figure 15.5).

Figure 15.5 Stages in ethical decision making

These four stages are distinctive. The success in one stage does not guarantee success in the other stages (Jones, 1991). Effectively expanding on Rest's model, Trevino (1986) proposed a model where individual differences and situational considerations moderate the judgement against the ethical criteria. In addition, presenting an ethical marketing model, Hunt and Vitell

(1986) argued that prior experiences influence both a leader's recognition of the problem and their ethical judgement about what to do. Proposing a substantial change to this model, Jones (1991, p. 391) stated that 'ethical decision making is issue contingent; that is, characteristics of the moral issue itself, collectively called moral intensity, are important determinants of ethical decision making and behaviour'. Accordingly, the issue-contingent model of ethical decision making can be exhibited as shown in Figure 15.6.

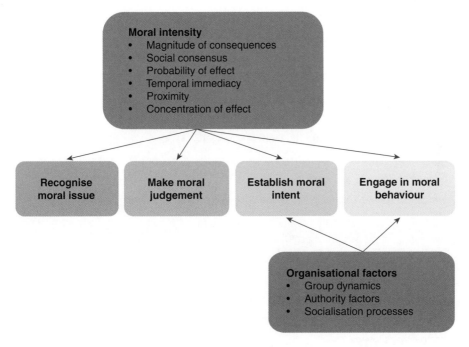

Figure 15.6 Issue-contingent model of ethical decision making

According to this model, the moral decision-making process starts by recognising the moral issue. There are two elements to consider in the recognition of a moral issue. First, a person must understand that his or her decision will affect others and care should be taken to make the best choice. Consequent to this understanding, it is to be decided what is morally correct in terms of the matter and the decision in question. This moral judgement depends on the leader's cognitive moral development. However, such a judgement will not warrant as an act of the judgement to establish moral intent. To establish moral intent, the leader needs to balance the moral factors against other factors such as self-interest. The moral intensity – that is, the extent of issue-related moral imperatives in a situation – also plays a crucial role in establishing moral intent. Once the moral intent is formed, engagement in moral behaviour will take place following the act upon the moral intention. Group dynamics, authority levels, and socialisation processes within the organisation would also significantly influence the last two stages of the model. Moral intensity is the construct that 'captures the extent of the issue-related moral imperative in a situation' (Jones, 1991, p. 372). According to Jones (1991), this moral intensity is composed of six aspects. These aspects are the magnitude of the harms or benefits of the moral act, societal agreement on the nature of an act, the likelihood that a consequential effect will take place, the time until the consequences of a moral act come into play, the nearness of a person to the consequential outcomes of an act and the number of people likely to be affected by a moral act.

CRISIS LEADERSHIP

Crisis leadership – The process of leading group members through a sudden and largely unanticipated, intensely negative and emotionally draining circumstance.

Crisis leadership is 'the process of leading group members through a sudden and largely unanticipated, intensely negative, and emotionally draining circumstance' (DuBrin, 2013, p. 3). Any emotionally charged situation that attracts negative stakeholder reaction leading to negative effects on financial well-being, reputation and survival of the organisation is considered a crisis (James, Wooten & Dushek, 2011). A tentative classification of types of organisational crisis has been proposed by DuBrin (2013), who proposes categories for several possible types of crisis:

- financial crises, such as strikes, product boycotts, law suits, bankruptcy, and major earnings reductions and stock price declines
- information-based crises such as privacy violation, loss of information and the failure of patents
- destruction of property because of events such as floods, fires and storms
- human resource issues such as the loss of key executives, high levels of illness of staff and major losses of key members of the workforce
- reputation-based crises such as those arising from negative media coverage, negative reports about the business, and rumours and negative reports about the behaviour of company employees
- violent experiences such as the kidnapping of senior executives, violent behaviour by employees towards other staff members, and violence that is perpetrated by outsiders on employees of the business.

A crisis calls for a leader who can handle it effectively. An effective crisis leader should possess characteristics such as being charismatic, inspirational and a strategic thinker willing to express compassion. Charismatic leaders support workers during a crisis and offer help to cope with stressful events. Further, during a crisis it is essential the leader is a strategic thinker. Seeing the big picture is of vital importance to fill the gap left by subordinates mired in a crisis.

Therefore, the behaviour of the crisis leader during such emotionally draining situations is crucial to overcoming the challenge. According to DuBrin (2013), one of the best accepted behavioural principles is to take decisive action to rectify the issue. It is essential to communicate the plan formulated to address the issue with the group members to assure them that something is in place to manage the situation. A leader taking highly visible actions during such a chaotic period is of considerable importance (Yukl, 2002). Therefore, the leader needs to play the spokesperson's role during a crisis. The strong presence of the leader during a crisis enhances confidence among followers and reassures customers about possible remedies to address the issues. Such a direct presence indicates that the leader acknowledges the full responsibility and expresses the accountability of the organisation. Further, this can be an effective method of communication about the issue that took place. Extensive, honest and effective communication with stakeholders will clear any doubts about the problem and set the stage to gain support from the employees, customers and other organisations. This requires the leader to be aware of information needs and communicate effectively to the related parties (DeChurch et al., 2011). Being decisive and effective in communication will bring stability to the organisation during a crisis. As DuBrin (2013) has suggested, being decisive during a crisis will circumvent the fear of failure which could constrain taking necessary action to overcome the crisis challenges.

During a crisis, the leader must deal with employees' emotional aspects as well as their own. Leaders should be able to express empathy during a crisis and display compassion to emphasise awareness of the plight of employees caught up in the negative implications of the crisis. Showing sympathy for the concerns, apprehensions and frustrations of group members is a key interpersonal skill and demonstrates emotional intelligence.

Moreover, quick adaptation to the situation and being flexible about the emerging situation is an essential behavioural requirement of a crisis leader. Optimistic thinking coupled with resilience will enable the leader to look at the situation in a resourceful manner and brings a hope for a better future. As DuBrin (2013) has found, effective behaviour during a crisis includes staying calm, planning before and during the crisis, making use of teams, re-establishing routine work immediately, exercising transformational leadership behaviour and recognition of accomplishments. The leaders' actions and behaviours following the tragic events that took place in Dreamworld, the biggest theme park in Gold Coast, Australia in October 2016, were highly criticised by the media, customers and analysts. The following case study demonstrates how this very public crisis was presented in a leading Australian newspaper, *Australian Financial Review* (Smith, 2016).

CASE STUDY 15.2

Ardent Leisure's lesson in crisis mismanagement

A company board's and management's ability to respond to a crisis reflects much of their capability and strength. The Dreamworld theme park owner, Ardent Leisure, did not respond effectively to an accident that killed four people when their raft malfunctioned on a ride at the park on the Gold Coast. In their response to the accident, the board and management including the Chairman and Chief Executive made five key mistakes in the 48 hours following the accident. The first mistake was to continue with a scheduled annual general meeting that included a proposal to pay a $860 000 bonus to the Chief Executive. The second error was to reopen the theme park three days later for a memorial day. Although the company behaved well by addressing the media on the second day after the incident, the Chief Executive was found wanting when questioned as to why the company had not contacted the families of the victims, as a reporter had been informed by one of the parents of a deceased victim. However, Ardent used the correct channels in that it reported the incident to the police rather than contacting the relatives directly, even though the media was unlikely to report that favourably. Another issue was that the Chairman carried out a plan to retire at a time when the company was encountering a crisis while intimating that he would nevertheless continue as a consultant.

Source: Adapted from Smith (2016)

Critical thinking question

To which extent do you agree or disagree with the reported reasons of the Ardent Leisure's leader and the board members' actions and behaviours during the crisis? Frame your answer based on the lessons you learned under 'Crisis leadership' above.

GENDER AND PERSONALITY DIFFERENCES IN DECISION MAKING

Writing in the *Harvard Business Review*, Benko and Pelster (2013) highlighted gender-based differences in decision making referring to a case regarding Deloitte. According to the authors, a few Deloitte staffers and seven partners gathered for a meeting to assess the suitability of a hospital consultation project in 2005. Deloitte staffers presented well, addressing all the concerns of the client in their pitch and expected to win over the partners about the project consultation. However, the Deloitte staffers felt something different to the norm since representatives were not on the same page as the Deloitte staffers were. They noted that half of the partnering team was women. In the end, Deloitte did not win the project consultation as they expected. As Gill and co-authors (1987) have argued, the environment more heavily influences women, who tend to search for more information and take more time before making a decision. Women tend to be more risk-averse and competition-averse than male decision makers. Further, social preferences seem to be more context-bound than those of men (Harris, Jenkins, & Glaser, 2006).

Among many variables which influence leadership decision making, personality is a crucial factor. Many researchers have studied the link between different aspects of personality and decision making. Personality is comprised of a person's characteristics, including a set of traits, models of thought, feelings, and behaviours (McAdams, 2009). Ferrari (2016) has found that agreeableness and conscientiousness are the most important predictors of transformational leadership style. Personality plays an important role in the decision-making process (Davis et al., 2007). Differences in decision-making approaches include personality factors such as openness, conscientiousness, extraversion, agreeableness and neuroticism (Filiz & Battaglio Jr, 2017). Filiz and Battaglio Jr (2017) have found that district governors who exhibited a higher level of extraversion are likely to be task oriented in decision making. Extraverted individuals try to collect more information in looking for prompt and pragmatic solutions (Heinström, 2003).

Further, those who exhibit a higher level of openness and conscientiousness are less likely to be task-factor-oriented and risk-averse. Further, those who are higher on openness and conscientiousness are found to be more focused on subject-related factors (Filiz & Battaglio Jr, 2017).

CULTURE AND DECISION MAKING

Studying national culture in terms of differences in decision making is an important area of study in the context of globalisation and high-growth economic interdependencies among countries. Dabić, Tipurić and Podrug (2015) have found that there are significant differences in decision-making styles in terms of national culture. Rau and Li (2011) identify that for those who are coming from individualistic nations, for instance, happiness is a socially disengaging emotion while it is a socially engaging emotion for collectivists. As a result, individualistic leaders tend to make decisions with the aim of fulfilling personal accomplishment whereas collectivist leaders expect to promote social connectedness. Further, leaders from cultures which have an interdependent social orientation (e.g. Eastern cultures) tend to believe that public good dominates individual benefits whereas those who are from independent socially oriented cultures (e.g. Western cultures) prioritise individual satisfaction and achievement. Accordingly, the leader groups from collectivist cultures tend to follow authoritative figures and guidelines while individualistic cultures tend to focus on individual needs and benefits (Savani, Morris & Naidu, 2012).

In a comparative study between Chinese and Swedish project teams, Agborsangaya and Omoregie (2016) have found that decision making is based on principles of friendship. So, in China, considerations of how to save 'face' are important, while for Swedish leaders decision making is results oriented. Therefore, Chinese meetings tend to be open-forum, analytic and logical because this supports face-saving; typically, this may take the form of a team discussion where each individual team member makes suggestions on problems or issues. By contrast, Swedish meetings are very informal and open; typically, in a team discussion every member in the team may strive to be creative in their ideas and suggestions and allow other team members to oppose their ideas, so that the best possible solution or alternative can be discovered. Further, Agborsangaya and Omoregie (2016) have found that Chinese leaders first make individual decisions and then go to the teams while Swedish leaders collectively decide on the outcomes. Understanding cultural differences in decision making will help leaders effectively decide on possible variations in their partners and competitors.

MAKING EFFECTIVE DECISIONS AS A LEADER

Virgin Group chairman Richard Branson has pointed out four major ways of making tough decisions (Feloni, 2015). These include prevention from acting on an emotional response, finding as many downsides to an idea as possible, looking at the big picture and protecting the downside. It is said that great leaders are great decision makers. Therefore, the leader should be able to make decisions with a balance between emotions and reason, as the leader's decisions affect employees, customers, stakeholders and other organisations. Leaders need to make challenging decisions and hence being 'decisive' in decision making has become a key skill needed for a great leader. Quickly arriving at the required decision and effectively communicating the decision to the rest of the group, team or the organisation are also some key abilities that a leader needs. Confident decision makers value action, speed, efficiency and consistency while they are honest, maintain clarity, loyalty and especially brevity in dealing with others (Brousseau et al., 2006). Another key defining feature and a timely important skill of great leaders is the ability to move forward quickly when there is limited information available. Understanding when to move faster and when to slow down are essential abilities of an effective leader.

Leaders must make decisions during crisis situations, sometimes in highly emotional situations. It is essential that the leader is in emotional self-control to make far-sighted decisions. Effective long-term strategic decisions can only be made when the leader is well balanced emotionally. Therefore, great leaders are aware of their emotional state and can effectively manage their emotions, which, in turn, results in smart decisions.

Another very important consideration is to trust your intuition. Leaders cannot constantly make decisions by reading textbooks or following a given theory. Sometimes you will have to make the decisions with limited information at hand and no obvious solution apparent. In such situations, it is essential to believe in your intuition and follow it to arrive at a decision. In addition, it is important to train yourself to face the risk of failures and understand this possibility.

SOCIAL MEDIA USE IN LEADERSHIP DECISION MAKING

Contemporary leadership engages in social media use purposefully to achieve organisational goals by gaining better control over the competitive and complex environment they deal with (Macnamara & Zerfass, 2012). Framing the discussion on e-leadership theory, Avolio, Kahai and Dodge (2001) emphasise that advanced information technology environments create a social effect process which empowers e-leaders to influence the attitudes, feelings, thinking, behaviour and performance of the respective followers. Accordingly, communication professionals look at this modern approach as a powerful strategic resource available for organisational goal achievement (Kahai, 2013) with the potential to improve leadership behaviours (Kiron et al., 2012). In the context of politics, social media use is a form of political participation itself (Larsson, 2013) and these novel media channels enhance the interaction and connectivity between politicians and citizens (Parmelee & Bichard, 2012).

Use of social media in organisational management brings many opportunities to the organisation. Opportunity recognition; internal and external environment-based potential threat recognition and development of relevant strategy alternatives; and integrating organisational vision with organisational core values shared among organisational members are among the key benefits of social media use in organisational contexts (Meng & Berger, 2013). The potential resolution of ethical and legal issues and conflicts, building strong links with stakeholders and effective knowledge management are further key advantages of social media use (Meng et al., 2012). According to Weisband (2008), transparency emanating from social media use often permits leaders to share ideas with stakeholders, which, in turn, results in enhanced ethical leadership.

However, growing workloads, extended working time and amplified work stress linked to increased social media use may hamper effective leadership behaviour (Jiang, Luo & Kulemeka, 2017).

SUMMARY

LEARNING OUTCOME 1: Describe how decision-making processes work in organisations.

Decision making is the process of the selection and implementation of the best alternative among many alternatives and contexts. Hence, the process includes problem recognition, problem definition, development of alternatives, evaluation of alternatives, selection of the desired alternative, implementation, and evaluation and feedback, which comprise the major phases of the decision-making process. Problem recognition is performed by assessing all the possible internal and external situations related to the problem. The second stage is problem defining which involves further clarification of the problem by focusing on source, scope, indications, significance, seriousness, intensity and consequences. Following this stage, decision making objectives are defined and alternative strategies are identified. Through forecasting decision alternatives are decided and evaluated. Final choice is made based on the assessments and prior experiences. With a series of actions and utilisation of organisational resources, the decision is implemented.

LEARNING OUTCOME 2: Discuss how various decision-making models apply in different situations.

The normative model of leadership decision making helps the leader to know when to take charge of decision making and when to delegate authority to the team. Accordingly, there are five leadership styles relative to the level of follower participation in decision making: decide, consult group, consult individually, facilitate and delegate. Further, decision significance, the importance of commitment, leader expertise, and the likelihood of commitment, group support for objectives, group expertise, and team competence determine the possible contexts applicable to these different styles. Using a combination, leaders can decide on the effective style to be applied to a given situation. In leader-centred decision-making models the leader uses his or her power to start, direct, drive, educate and control team members while team-centred decision-making model allows the team to make decisions.

LEARNING OUTCOME 3: Identify the functions and roles of the leader in decision making.

Mentor, facilitator, innovator, broker, producer, director, monitor and coordinator are eight key roles that a leader plays in decision making. Mentoring and facilitation are roles that leaders can play, generally by adopting a flexible orientation with an internal focus. This is a caring and empathetic orientation. The roles of producer and director are associated with task leadership, where the leader tends to adopt a control orientation with an external environmental focus. Goal establishment and motivating members are tasks that such leaders perform. Monitoring and coordinating roles are essentially related to control orientation and internal process focus and reflect the stability leadership approach. System structure maintenance and coordination of employee effort are major functions of this approach.

LEARNING OUTCOME 4: Differentiate between leadership decision-making styles.

There are four main leadership decision making styles. Leaders with the directive decision-making style take full controlling power of the decision making with no negotiation opportunities given to employees. The consultative decision-making style allows the team members to provide input, yet the leader holds ultimate decision-making power. Democratic decision making enables possible options from both the leader and employees to be proposed and voted on. This is also commonly known as consensus-based decision making. The first two approaches are leader-driven while the other two are more employee- or follower-driven.

LEARNING OUTCOME 5: Explain ethical decision making and crisis leadership.

Ethical leadership is built on belief in ethical values such as trust, honesty and consideration and fairness to others. Ethical leadership–based decision making tends to focus on the moral issue in the related decision-making context. Hence, moral intensity is the fundamental of this decision-making approach. Crisis leadership is the process of leading group members through a sudden and largely unanticipated, intensely negative and emotionally draining circumstance.

REVIEW QUESTIONS

1. Why is decision making important to an organisation?

2. What are the main decision-making roles and functions of a leader?

3. What is the role of a leader during a crisis?

4. Should a leader be confined to one leadership style in making decisions? What is your opinion on this?

5. How would you determine the level of participation in decision making by followers and leader?

CASE STUDY 15.3

Practical problem

Assume that you are the Human Resources and Training Manager of XYZ Food Processing firm. There are six keen and hardworking training managers under your direct supervision and they are supposed to deliver management training to 400 managers and supervisors across the country. However, one of the six training managers is a former branch manager, who is also 15 years senior to you. Despite being the highest paid team member, he is unhelpful and apparently he is not contributing equally to the team. Your company has decided to train its managers at regional offices since it is going to sell the previously used large purpose-built centre. As a result, team members will have to spend more time travelling and staying away from home although they will be compensated by extra salary. You have already designed a three-day per week course over the next year. Now it's time for you to decide whether to relocate the members to different regions to reduce the travel time and time away from home or leave the arrangements as they are. There is no significant financial difference between the alternatives. All the members live nearly 10 kilometres away from the training centre. While they are supporting you, they are not happy with the changes proposed by the company. You are going to meet your boss next week and need to make your decision by then.

Source: Adapted from Williams (2014) with permission of MTD Management Training

Critical thinking questions

1. Which style of decision making is most appropriate in this scenario?
2. What would you do to solve the problem?

REFERENCES

Agborsangaya, E.O. & Omoregie, I.F. (2016). Does culture influence decision making in project teams?: A multi case study in Sweden. *Dissertation, Masters in Industrial Engineering and Management*, University of Gävle, Sweden. Retrieved from: http://urn.kb.se/resolve?urn=urn:nbn:se:hig:diva-22971.

Avolio, B.J., Kahai, S. & Dodge, G.E. (2001). E-leadership: Implications for theory, research, and practice. *Leadership Quarterly*, 11(4), 615–68.

Benko, C. & Pelster, B. (2013). How women decide? *Harvard Business Review*.

Benowitz, E. (2001). *Cliffs quick review principles of management*. New York, NY: Hungry Minds Inc.

Brousseau, K.R., Driver, M.J., Hourihan, G. & Larsson, R. (2006). The seasoned executive's decision-making style. *Harvard Business Review*, 84(2), 110.

Brown, M. (2015). ACCC investigates Volkswagen following emissions scandal. Retrieved from: www.abc.net.au/news/2015–10-01/accc-turns-up-heat-on-volkswagen-following-emissions-scandal/6819196.

Chemers, M. (2014). *An integrative theory of leadership*: New York, NY: Psychology Press.

Dabić, M., Tipurić, D. & Podrug, N. (2015). Cultural differences affecting decision-making style: A comparative study between four countries. *Journal of Business Economics and Management*, 16(2), 275–89.

Davis, C., Patte, K., Tweed, S. & Curtis, C. (2007). Personality traits associated with decision-making deficits. *Personality and Individual Differences*, 42(2), 279–90.

DeChurch, L.A., Burke, C.S., Shuffler, M L., Lyons, R., Doty, D. & Salas, E. (2011). A historiometric analysis of leadership in mission critical multiteam environments. *Leadership Quarterly*, 22(1), 152–69.

DuBrin, A.J. (2013). Personal attributes and behaviors of effective crisis leaders. In A.J. DuBrin (ed.), *Handbook of research on crisis leadership in organizations*, vol. 1 (pp. 3–22). Cheltenham, UK: Edward Elgar Publishing.

—— (2015). *Leadership: Research findings, practice, and skills*. Boston: Cengage Learning.

Eisenbeiss, S.A. (2012). Re-thinking ethical leadership: An interdisciplinary integrative approach. *Leadership Quarterly*, 23(5), 791–808.

Feloni, R. (2015). Richard Branson explains his 8 rules for being a great leader. *Business Insider Australia*. Retrieved from: www.businessinsider.com.au/richard-branson-leadership-rules-2015–10?r=US&IR=T#/#1-follow-your-passions-but-protect-the-downside-1.

Ferrari, J.R. (2016). Called and formed: Personality dimensions and leadership styles among Catholic deacons and men in formation. *Pastoral Psychology*, 66(2), 225–37.

Filiz, E. & Battaglio, R.P., Jr. (2017). Personality and decision-making in public administration: The five-factor model in cultural perspective. *International Review of Administrative Sciences*, 83(1, supplement), 3–22.

Fleishman, E.A., Mumford, M.D., Zaccaro, S.J., Levin, K.Y., Korotkin, A.L. & Hein, M.B. (1991). Taxonomic efforts in the description of leader behavior: A synthesis and functional interpretation. *Leadership Quarterly*, 2(4), 245–87.

Gill, S., Stockard, J., Johnson, M. & Williams, S. (1987). Measuring gender differences: The expressive dimension and critique of androgyny scales. *Sex Roles*, 17(7), 375–400.

Hackman, J.R., Walton, R.E. & Goodman, P. (1986). Leading groups in organizations. In P.S. Goodman (ed.), *Designing effective work groups* (pp. 72–119). San Francisco, CA: Jossey-Bass.

Harris, C.R., Jenkins, M. & Glaser, D. (2006). Gender differences in risk assessment: Why do women take fewer risks than men? *Judgment and Decision Making*, 1(1), 48.

Heinström, J. (2003). Five personality dimensions and their influence on information behaviour. *Information Research*, 9(1).

Hunt, S.D. & Vitell, S. (1986). A general theory of marketing ethics. *Journal of Macromarketing*, 6(1), 5–16.

James, E.H., Wooten, L.P. & Dushek, K. (2011). Crisis management: Informing a new leadership research agenda. *Academy of Management Annals*, 5(1), 455–93.

Jiang, H., Luo, Y. & Kulemeka, O. (2017). Strategic social media use in public relations: Professionals' perceived social media impact, leadership behaviors, and work-life conflict. *International Journal of Strategic Communication*, 11(1), 18–41.

Jones, T.M. (1991). Ethical decision making by individuals in organizations: An issue-contingent model. *Academy of Management Review*, 16(2), 366–95.

Kahai, S.S. (2013). Leading in a digital age: What's different, issues raised, and what we know. In M.C. Bligh & R.E. Riggio (eds), *Exploring distance in leader–follower relationships: When near is far and far is near* (pp. 63–108). New York, NY: Routledge.

Kiron, D., Palmer, D., Phillips, A.N. & Kruschwitz, N. (2012). What managers really think about social business. *MIT Sloan Management Review*, 53(4), 51.

Larsson, A.O. (2013). Bringing it all back home? Social media practices by Swedish municipalities. *European Journal of Communication*, 28(6), 681–95.

Lussier, R.N. & Achua, C.F. (2015). *Leadership: Theory, application, and skill development.* Boston: Cengage Learning.

Macnamara, J. & Zerfass, A. (2012). Social media communication in organizations: The challenges of balancing openness, strategy, and management. *International Journal of Strategic Communication*, 6(4), 287–308.

McAdams, D.P. (2009). *The person: An introduction to the science of personality psychology.* New York, NY: John Wiley & Sons.

Meng, J. & Berger, B. (2013). An integrated model of excellent leadership in public relations: Dimensions, measurement, and validation. *Journal of Public Relations Research*, 25(2), 141–67.

Meng, J., Berger, B.K., Gower, K.K. & Heyman, W.C. (2012). A test of excellent leadership in public relations: Key qualities, valuable sources, and distinctive leadership perceptions. *Journal of Public Relations Research*, 24(1), 18–36.

Moshal, B. (2009). *Principles of management.* New Delhi: Ane Books.

Parmelee, J.H. & Bichard, S.L. (2012). Politics and the Twitter revolution. *How tweets influence the relationship between political leaders and the public*, Lanham, MD: Lexington Books.

Quinn, R.E. (1988). *Beyond rational management: Mastering the paradoxes and competing demands of high performance*: New Jersey: Jossey-Bass.

Rau, P-L.P. & Li, Y. (2011). Effects of group orientation and communication style on making decisions and interacting with robots. In R.W. Proctor, S.Y. Nof & Y. Yih (eds), *Cultural factors in systems design: Decision making and action* (pp. 157–72). Boca Raton, FL: CRC Press.

Rest, J.R. (1986). *Moral development: Advances in research and theory.* New York, NY: Praeger.

Salisbury, I. (2017). This Is Jeff Bezos' best advice about making big decisions. *Money*. Retrieved from: http://time.com/money/4738244/bezos-decision-making-fast.

Savani, K., Morris, M.W. & Naidu, N. (2012). Deference in Indians' decision making: Introjected goals or injunctive norms? *Journal of Personality and Social Psychology*, 102(4), 685.

Smith, M. (2016). Ardent Leisure's lesson in crisis mismanagement. *Australian Financial Review*, 27 October. Retrieved from: www.afr.com/brand/chanticleer/ardent-leisures-lesson-in-crisis-mismanagement-20161027-gscciq.

Stein, L. (2017). Volkswagen diesel scandal: ACCC sues over dodgy emissions claims. *ABC News*, 8 March. Retrieved from: www.abc.net.au/news/2017–03-08/accc-sues-volkswagen-over-diesel-emissions-scandal/8335506

Trevino, L.K. (1986). Ethical decision making in organizations: A person-situation interactionist model. *Academy of Management Review*, 11(3), 601–17.

Useem, M. (2010). Decision making as leadership foundation. In N. Nohria & R. Khurana (eds), *Handbook of leadership theory and practice: An HBS centennial colloquium on advancing leadership* (pp. 507–27). Boston: Harvard Business Press.

Vroom, V.H. & Yetton, P.W. (1973). *Leadership and decision-making* (vol. 110). Pittsburgh: University of Pittsburgh Press.

Weisband, S. (2008). Research challenges for studying leadership at a distance. In S.P. Weisband (ed.), *Leadership at a distance: Research in technologically-supported work* (pp. 3–11). Mahwah, NJ: Lawrence Erlbaum & Associates.

Williams, M. (2014). Decision making styles. *MTD Training*. Retrieved from: www.mtdtraining.com/wp-content/uploads/2014/05/Decision-Making-Styles.pdf.

Yukl, G.A. (2002). *Leadership in organizations*. Upper Saddle River, NJ: Prentice Hall.

INDEX